UN PEACEKEEPING IN TROUBLE
LEARNED FROM THE FORMER Y

UN Peacekeeping in Trouble: Lessons Learned from the Former Yugoslavia

Peacekeepers' Views on the Limits and Possibilities of the United Nations in a Civil War-like Conflict

Edited by
WOLFGANG BIERMANN and MARTIN VADSET

with a foreword by Carl Bildt and chapters contributed by Yasushi Akashi, Hans Hækkerup, Gen. Bertrand de Lapresle, Sadako Ogata, Gen. Sir Michael Rose, Lt. Gen. John M. Sanderson, Thorvald Stoltenberg, Lt. Gen. Lars-Erik Wahlgren and others

Ashgate

Aldershot • Burlington USA • Singapore • Sydney

First published in hardback 1998 by
Ashgate Publishing Limited
Gower House
Croft Road
Aldershot
Hants GU11 3HR
England

Ashgate Publishing Company
131 Main Street
Burlington,
Vermont 05401-5600
USA

Ashgate website:http://www.ashgate.com

Hardback edition reprinted 1999
Paperback edition published 1999
Paperback edition reprinted 2000

British Library Cataloguing in Publication Data
UN peacekeeping in trouble : lessons learned from the
    Former Yugoslavia
    1.United Nations – Armed Forces – Bosnia and Herzegovina
    2.Intervention (International law) 3.Security,
    International 4. Yugoslav War, 1991-
    I.Biermann, Wolfgang II. Vadset, Martin
    327.1′72′0949742′09049

Library of Congress Catalog Card Number: 98-070987

ISBN 1 84014 176 X (Hbk)
ISBN 0 7546 1026 8 (Pbk)

Printed and bound by Athenaeum Press, Ltd.,
Gateshead, Tyne & Wear.

Contents

PART THREE: MILITARY AND DIPLOMATIC VIEWS

First Section: The United Nations, the Security Council, Mandates and Means

Second Section: Concepts of Prevention and De-escalation of Conflict

Third Section: 'Learning from Doing' Peacekeeping
– Political and Practical Implications

PART FOUR: CONCLUSIONS

About the authors and editors

The editors

Wolfgang Biermann (D), PhD, has been heading the Danish-Norwegian Research Project on UN Peacekeeping (DANORP) at the Copenhagen Peace Research Institute (COPRI), Denmark, since April 1994. Since 1998 Wolfgang Biermann is adviser to the Norwegian Human Rights House Foundation, Oslo, Norway.

While currently on leave, he has since 1981 been International Security Adviser to the leadership of the Social Democratic Party of Germany (SPD).

Lt. Gen. *Martin Vadset*, retd.(N), is DANORP's Senior Project Adviser. He has served in UNIFIL (South Lebanon) as Deputy Force Commander, and from 1987 to 1990 he was the Commander of United Nations Truce Supervision Organization in the Middle East. During the latter period he led on behalf of the United Nations Secretary-General Fact Finding and Special Delegations to Cambodia, Iraq and Iran.

The authors

Yasushi Akashi (J), UN Under-Secretary General, is Head of the UN Department of Humanitarian Affairs and Emergency Relief Co-ordinator. He has served as the Head of the UN peacekeeping missions in Cambodia and in the former Yugoslavia, where he was the Special Representative of the Secretary-General. Mr Akashi has also served his government as Ambassador at the Permanent Mission of Japan to the United Nations.

Carl Bildt (S), is Chairman of the Swedish Moderate Party (Conservatives) and former Swedish Prime Minister. He served as the High Representative for Peace Implementation in Bosnia from January 1996 to June 1997 and was Co-chairman for the EU at the International Conference on the former Yugoslavia (ICFY), June to November 1995.

Col. Cees van Egmond (NL), belongs to the Royal Netherlands Marine Corps since 1969. He is both a marine and a naval aviator. He has served at the UN Department for Peacekeeping Operations (DPKO) in New York, responsible for Planning and Support (1993–97). He was battalion commander in Operation Provide Comfort in Northern Iraq after the Gulf War in 1991. On a national basis he was involved in the planning for Cambodia (UNTAC) and the former Yugoslavia.

Halvor Hartz (N), is UN Co-ordinator in the Norwegian Ministry of Justice. He served in UNPROFOR as CivPol Chief of Staff.

Hans Hækkerup (DK), is Minister of Defence, Denmark, since 25 January 1993. He graduated with a Master's degree in arts and economics from the University of Copenhagen in 1973. Hans Hækkerup was elected Member of the Danish Parliament in 1979 and held, until his appointment as Minister of Defence, several memberships in committees related to Foreign Affairs and Defence.

Søren Bo Husum (DK), is a captain in the Danish Army. He served in former Yugoslavia as UN Military Observer (UNMO).

Col. *Howard F. Kuenning* (US), is Chief of Special Programs/Policy & Plans AFSOUTH. He was Chief of Staff of the UN Preventive Peacekeeping Operation in Macedonia.

Gen. *Bertrand de Lapresle* (F), is the Governor of the Institution of Les Invalides in Paris. He was adviser to the High Representative for the Civilian Implementation of the Dayton-Paris Agreement and former Co-chairman of ICFY, with Carl Bildt, and served as Force Commander UNPROFOR from March 1994 to March 1995. Prior to that he was Commander of the French Rapid Reaction Force.

Jean-Philippe Lavoyer (CH), is Legal Adviser to the International Committee of the International Red Cross (ICRC) at its headquarters in Geneva. Between 1984 and 1994 he served in many field missions in Somalia, Afghanistan, Iraq, Kuwait and the Arabian Peninsula.

Sten Martini (DK), is Director of the Psychological Department of the Danish Armed Forces Centre for Leadership.

Lt. Col. *Jan-Dirk von Merveldt* (UK), is Chief Public Relations Officer of the British Forces in Germany; he was UN Military Press Spokesman in Sarajevo in the former Yugoslavia.

Sadako Ogata (J), is United Nations High Commissioner for Refugees since 1991. Prior to that, she held several public positions, among which Chairperson of the Executive Board of UNICEF (1976–78), Independent Expert of the United Nations Commission on Human Rights on Myanmar (1990), and Representative of Japan on the United Nations Commission on Human Rights (1982–85). Mrs Ogata also held several teaching posts among which Dean of the Faculty of Foreign Studies at Sophia University in Tokyo from 1989 until 1991.

Brigadier *Andrew Ridgway* (UK), is Director of Operational Capability at the British Ministry of Defence. He was Commander of the 7th Armoured Brigade and UNPROFOR Sector South West.

Gen. Sir *Michael Rose* (UK), former Adjutant General of the UK Army, was Commander UNPROFOR in Bosnia-Herzegovina.

Lt. Gen. *J.M. Sanderson*, AC (AUS), is Chief of the General Staff of the Australian Army and Commander Joint Forces Australia. He was Commander of the Military Component of United Nations Transitional Authority in Cambodia (UNTAC).

Max van der Stoel (NL), is OSCE High Commissioner on National Minorities.

Thorvald Stoltenberg (N), is Norwegian Ambassador to Denmark. He served as UN Mediator and Co-chairman of the International Conference on the former Yugoslavia (ICFY).

Ole Frederik Ugland (N), is a researcher at the Institute of Applied Social Sciences (FAFO) in Oslo, Norway.

Lt. Gen. *Lars-Eric Wahlgren* (S), was Force Commander UNPROFOR from February to July 1993 and served earlier as Force Commander of UNIFIL (Lebanon 1988–93) and as Contingent Commander in UNEF II (1974–75).

Prof. *Håkan Wiberg* (S), is Director of the Copenhagen Peace Research Institute (COPRI).

Boxes, figures and tables

Boxes

Figures

Tables

List of abbreviations

AFSOUTH	Allied Forces Southern Europe
AOCC	Air Operations Co-ordination Center
APC	Armoured Personnel Carrier
ARBiH	Bosnian Muslim Army
ATAF	Allied Tactical Air Force
AWACS	Airborne Warning and Control System
BH	Bosnia-Herzegovina
C & C	Command and Control
C^2	Command and Control
C^3	Command, Control and Communication
CAS	Close Air Support
CCC	Command, Control and Communication
CCTF	Commander Combined Task Force
CINCSOUTH	Commander-in-Chief Allied Forces Southern Europe
CJTF	Combined Joint Task Force
CMO	Chief Military Observer
COE	Contingent Owned Equipment
COMNAVSOUTH	Commander-in-Chief Naval Allied Forces Southern Europe
COPRI	Copenhagen Peace Research Institute
CSCE	Conference on Security and Cooperation in Europe
CTF	Combined Task Force
CTG	Combined Task Group
DANBAT	Danish Battalion
dpa	*Deutsche Presse Agentur*
EAPC	Euro-Atlantic Partnership Council
EC	European Community
EU	European Union
EUCIVPOL	European Civil Police (WEU police)
EUMM	EU Military Monitors
FAC	Forward Air Controller
FAZ	*Frankfurter Allgemeine Zeitung*
FC	Force Commander
FOD	Field Operations Division
FoM	Freedom of Movement

FRY	Federal Republic of Yugoslavia (Serbia-Montenegro)
FT	*Financial Times*
FY	Former Yugoslavia
FYROM	Former Yugoslav Republic of Macedonia (now Macedonia)
HIWG	Humanitarian Issues Working Group
HQNY	Headquarters New York (UN)
HVO	Bosnian Croat Army
ICFY	International Conference on Former Yugoslavia
ICRC	International Committee of the Red Cross
IEBL	Inter Entity Boundary Line
IFOR	Implementation Force (NATO-led)
IHT	*International Herald Tribune*
IMS	International Military Staff
IPTF	(UN) International Police Task Force
JCPC	Joint Commission Policy Committee
JNA	Yugoslav National Army
MC	Military Committee
NAC	North Atlantic Council
NACC	North Atlantic Co-operation Council
NAEWF	NATO Airborne and Early Warning Force
NATO	North Atlantic Treaty Organization
NCO	Non-commissioned Officer
NFZ	No-Fly Zone
NGO	Non-governmental Organization
NIDS	NATO Integrated Data System
ODA	British Overseas Development Administration (now Department for International Development DfiD)
OHR	Office of the High Representative
OSCE	Organization for Security and Co-operation in Europe
P5	The five permanent member states of the UNSC
PK	Peacekeeping
PKO	Peacekeeping Operation
RDMHQ	Rapid Deployable Mission Headquarters
ROE	Rules of Engagement
SA	Safe Area
SACEUR	Supreme Allied Commander Europe
SC	Security Council
SCMM	Bosnian Presidency's Standing Committee on Military Matters

SCR	Security Counsel Resolution
SDS	Serb Democratic Party
SFOR	Stabilization Force (NATO-led)
SG	Secretary-General
SHAPE	Supreme Headquarters Allied Powers Europe
SOFA	Status Of Forces Agreement
SRSG	Special Representative of the Secretary General
SRT	Bosnian Serbs Television
TOW	Tube-launched Optically-tracked Wire-guided Missile
UN	United Nations
UN CIVPOL	UN Civil Police
UN DPKO	UN Department of Peacekeeping Operations
UNDP	UN Development Programme
UNEF	UN Emergency Force
UNFICYP	UN Force in Cyprus
UNHCR	UN High Commissioner for Refugees
UNIFIL	UN Interim Force in Lebanon
UNMO	UN Military Observer
UNNY	UN New York
UNPA	UN Protected Areas
UNPF	UN Peace Force
UNPREDEP	UN Preventive Deployment Force (Macedonia)
UNPROFOR	UN Protection Force
UNSC	UN Security Council
UNSCR	UN Security Council Resolutions
UNSG	UN Secretary-General
UNTAC	UN Transitional Authority in Cambodia
UNTAES	UN Transitional Authority in Eastern Slavonia
UNTAT	UN Training Assistance Teams
WEU	Western European Union
WHO	World Health Organization
ZOS	Zone of Separation

Preface and acknowledgements

The starting point

The initial work on this book started in April 1994 at the Copenhagen Peace Research Institute (COPRI). Its Board had certified a grant to us for a project under the title: 'The Evolution of UN Peacekeeping Operations in the Post-Cold War Era – Challenge or Threat to the Authority of the UN?'.

As there were many books and projects about the evolution of UN peacekeeping, we approached the subject by utilizing our background in the political as well as military field of international peace and security. We felt that the United Nations' authority was challenged and potentially threatened by a multiplying demand for interventions in conflicts following the collapse of the Soviet empire. The research project should aggregate recommendations to improve peacekeeping. The criterion of realism and practicability hopefully would contribute to answering the question relevant for the world organization: how to manage crises and how to avoid crises overload?

In a first round of field interviews with civil and military practitioners of the UN in Croatia and Bosnia-Herzegovina, we were surprised at the wide gap between the world presented by public opinion at home and the wholly different world displayed by peacekeepers on the ground who were convinced that they had done their best to stop the killing. They referred to peacekeeping principles guiding them, principles that seemed to be unknown outside of the mission area. We came to the conclusion that the central aim of the study should be to examine the degree of applicability of 'old' peacekeeping principles to 'new' types of conflicts as experienced in the former Yugoslavia.

Aim of the book

This book is intended to fill a gap in the literature about peacekeeping in the former Yugoslavia through a combination of empirical methods. The project combines qualitative research with quantitative methods to analyse the views of the practitioners on different aspects of peacekeeping and conflict mediation.

The book has come about after several years of research, travels to Croatia, Bosnia, Macedonia and other countries, organizing UN

Commanders' Workshops, and participating in conferences with knowledgeable people working in the field, at the UN in New York, in Washington, and in capitals of Europe.

Since most of these individuals remain active in UN, military or government service, we agreed to use interviews as well as the UN Commanders' Workshops as background information without naming individuals. Interview notes, comments in questionnaires and the workshops have been recorded for confirmation and accuracy but not for attributed publication.

However, you will meet some of these people in this book, where they make us aware of the challenges and interaction of politics and practical work for peace by offering to share their personal lessons learned.

In addition, about one thousand officers from nine nations supported our research project by completing a questionnaire with more than a hundred operational and political questions and adding valuable personal recommendations.

We thank all who supported us and readily let us draw on their time and patience to answer our questions. They made it possible for us to present some of their experiences in making or keeping peace under the most appalling conditions and in an environment of hostility not limited to the warring parties. It is because of the contributions by these civilians and soldiers of peace, that our small research group, consisting of a staff of two and a few temporary assistants, could produce this book.

The supporters of DANORP

We are indebted to the Copenhagen Peace Research Institute (COPRI), in particular the director Professor Håkan Wiberg and administrative director Janne Rothberg. They gave us unbounded and encouraging support during the whole time we wrestled with the project. COPRI provided not only the main grant but also continuing support to the project, including the production of the camera-ready copy of the book, thanks to Tor Nonnegaard, who also helped with valuable comments.

We thank FAFO, Institute of Applied Social Science in Oslo, especially Dag Odnes, Kirsti Rudolfsen and Arne Grønningsæter, for assistance in establishing the Danish-Norwegian Research Project (DANORP). FAFO covered free of charge the overhead costs for the Norwegian office, gave survey support to DANORP and helped to co-ordinate with the Opinion Institute in Bergen for the quantitative part of our study. We thank Randi Jacobsen and Ole Frederik Ugland, for their research assistance provided at FAFO.

We also express our profound gratitude to the Defence Ministries of Denmark and Norway for actively supporting our research work, in particular to the respective Chiefs of Defence. In particular we acknowledge the Danish Armed Forces Institute of Leadership for its active assistance to the UNPROFOR and the IFOR survey. We thank the Ministry of Foreign Affairs of Norway and the Friedrich-Ebert Foundation in Germany for contributing additional funds to the UNPROFOR survey and the two UN Commanders' Workshops that DANORP organized in Oslo and Copenhagen.

We express our gratitude to the Norwegian Ministry of Defence for a grant provided to make this book, as well as our appreciation to NUPI, the Norwegian Institute of International Affairs in Oslo, its director Sverre Lodgaard and in particular its library and Dagfrid Hermansen, for excellent support during the writing period in 1997.

We thank the many officers from Canada, Denmark, Finland, France, the Netherlands, Norway, Sweden, Turkey and the United Kingdom who took time to answer our questionnaires and give comments. Our most sincere thanks also go to the DPKO, the UNPROFOR HQ and the Defence Staffs of countries we asked for assistance in distributing and collecting written material for our survey.

Other helping heads and hands

Beyond those contributing chapters to this book, we would like to thank Jonathan Dean (Washington, DC) and his assistant Teri Grimwood who helped us so much in editing the final manuscript. Special thanks go to the SPD, without whose generous research leave to Wolfgang Biermann, the project might never have been realized. And we want to express our thanks to the following who gave their support and inspiration to our work, among them Kurt G. Adriansen (Oslo/Bonn), John Almstrong (Ottawa), Lasse Budz (Copenhagen), Charles Dobbie (Swansea), Kai Eide (Oslo), Manfred Eisele (New York), Günther Esters (Bonn), Gerard Fischer (Zagreb), Ekkehard Griep (New York), Claire Grimes (Skopje), Ove Hoff (Vedbæk), Leonard Kapungo (New York), Hans Koschnik (Bremen), Jørgen Kosmo (Oslo), Henrik Lettius (Södertälje), Vera Mehta (Skopje), Gro Nystuen (Oslo), Herbert Okun (New York), Steven R. Rader (McLean, Virginia), Leonard Revang (Oslo), Leif Simonsen (Vedbæk), Henryk J. Sokalski (Skopje), Finn Særmark-Thomsen (Copenhagen), Peter Schmitz (Nicosia), Fridtjof Søgaard (Oslo), Uwe Stehr (Bonn), Willem Steijlen (Oirschot), Tryggve Tellefsen (Oslo), Günther Verheugen (Bonn), Heather Weeks (Ditchley), Susan Woodward (Washington, DC) and Wolfgang Zellner

(Hamburg). Many others contributed with ideas, we thank them all, unmentioned but not forgotten.

The responsibility for the content of this study, for any errors or omissions, rests solely with the authors and editors. Principally, our recommendations should not be attributed to any of these individuals or the institutions mentioned above or the contributors to the book, who may agree or disagree with our analyses or conclusions.

Last but not least we would like to thank Ingrid Norstein, Wolfgang Biermann's best friend and wife, for her wonderful patience and support during the whole time of the research project, in particular in the last phase of writing and editing the book.

The book is dedicated to our children and grandchildren in the hope that their generation can benefit from the spirit and the work of the United Nations for peace, human rights and international reconciliation.

Wolfgang Biermann and Martin Vadset
Copenhagen/Oslo
January 1998

Foreword

Whatever way you look at it, the experience of peacekeeping, peacemaking and peace enforcement in the region of former Yugoslavia is unique. Despite this, every other operation of this kind in the future will be shaped in one way or the other by the lessons learnt during the difficult years in former Yugoslavia.

None of those involved has reason to be particularly proud of their record during the years of the emerging and exploding conflicts of the area.

War could not be prevented in 1991 and 1992. The European Union had the ambition to do something in order to prevent open war from breaking out, and to manage an orderly transition from the old Yugoslavia to an order which could satisfy the different ambitions of the peoples of the area. But these ambitions were not matched by adequate abilities and instruments. The decision to start to create a Common Foreign and Security Policy had just been taken, but the instruments to co-ordinate the foreign policies of the countries of the Union were rudimentary and ineffective.

If the European Union had the will but not the ability, it was the other way around with NATO. This organization did have military instruments which could have been used to support diplomacy in cases like the shelling of Dubrovnik or the destruction of Vukovar during the second half of 1991. But there was not the will to put them to use. This fact reflected, above all, the reluctance of the United States to get involved in the conflicts of the region.

And when the inability of the European Union and the unwillingness of NATO failed to stop the slide towards war in the region, the resulting conflicts were dumped on a reluctant United Nations.

The role of the United Nations in the Yugoslav conflict has been widely criticized, not least in the United States, and the debates over this issue have contributed in no small degree to the present crisis in the world organization. But much of this criticism has been, in my view, based on misinformation and directed against the wrong targets.

The UN operation in the area that was once Yugoslavia was an operation on a vast scale: there were three separate although interrelated military operations – in Croatia, Bosnia and in the Former Yugoslav Republic of Macedonia, FYROM. The UN operation included a very large humanitarian aid effort, notably in Bosnia, the handling of the largest refugee crisis in Europe since the Second World War, and the setting up, for the first time ever since the Nuremberg Trials, of an international criminal tribunal. UN activities also included important contributions to the political search for a settlement to the conflict.

UN troops were sent to Croatia to freeze the situation in order to prevent war, to Bosnia in order to protect humanitarian relief operations, and to FYROM in order to prevent the conflict from spreading south into this area. And to a large extent UN forces succeeded with these three tasks originally assigned to them.

I remain convinced that the survival of many tens of thousands of Bosnians – primarily but not only Muslims – as well as most probably the survival of what remained of the Bosnian state would not have been possible without the presence of the UN forces during the difficult years of 1992 and 1993. If the avoidance of an even larger catastrophe can be claimed to be a success, then this was indeed a most significant success.

But quickly, the UNPROFOR mission in Bosnia became bogged down in the ongoing transatlantic controversy over the overall approach to the region. And it was these controversies which at the end of the day made the mission nearly impossible.

The UNPROFOR experience in Bosnia will forever be marked by the massive failure in Srebrenica. And there are indeed reasons to see this as a failure for the entire UN system. Yet the main failure of Srebrenica was not the failure of the troops and commanders in Srebrenica or in the theatre, but of the command authority sitting around the table of the Security Council in New York.

Indeed, the ever-widening gulf between the rhetoric in New York and the reality in Bosnia made the UNPROFOR mission increasingly impossible. In the case of Srebrenica, it was the Security Council which first took the decision to declare it a so-called Safe Area, after which the Council refused to give the commanders on the ground the resources they considered necessary in order to turn this mandate into reality. Here, the Security Council claimed it could ordain something that it in reality was not willing to carry out. Thus in practice, it left thousands of people to a fate which they thought the world had promised to protect them from.

And when the Safe Area of Srebrenica fell, after the Security Council had refused to provide either the means to defend it or to demonstrate the determination to demilitarize it, the Council climbed to even higher levels of absurdity by passing a resolution *de facto* authorising UNPROFOR to retake Srebrenica with military means. This was posturing in the absence of policy.

Clearly, the Security Council was not able to assume political responsibility for such a complex operation as UNPROFOR. The situation was certainly not made better by other well-known deficiencies of the complex and to some extent antiquated UN system. But the main failure of the UN operation in former Yugoslavia was the failure of the Security Council, and most particularly of its permanent members.

The conflict on what to do in Bosnia as well as the international diplomatic dialogue demonstrated the impotence of Europe as well as the power of the United States.

But while US power was important, it was by no means put to the constructive use it could have been. Instead, it can be argued that policy on Bosnia was to a large extent the victim of the cycles of the US political system. The 1993 inauguration of President Clinton spelt the end of the ambitious Vance–Owen peace plan (VOPP), just as the 1995 risk of disaster in the relationship with the Senate over policy on Bosnia ultimately forced the Clinton administration into a much more high-profile responsibility for the political efforts in Bosnia than it had so far been willing to contemplate.

Indeed, the move towards unilateralism in US policy proved to be one of the main problems of the period. It was clear in the administration's reluctance to support the VOPP in 1993, in the *de facto* green light to arms shipments by Iran in contravention of the Security Council arms embargo to the region, as well as in the *de facto* green light to the Croatian army attack on the UN-protected areas of Croatia in 1995. Whatever the merits in each case, these were all unilateral moves with profound consequences for the entire multilateral effort in the area.

My direct and personal role in the conflict started in the first days of June 1995 when I was appointed by the European Union as co-chairman of the International Conference on Yugoslavia. It was a difficult time. The war was accelerating and the political situation was deteriorating. We were entering the worst summer of war.

At that time, the UN operation was in deep crisis. Deployed all over the country, it had no capacity to undertake military operations, and had just gone through the ordeal of the hostage crisis. Disconnected from the political process unfolding between the Contact Group capitals, it had to reduce its own role more and more to safeguarding its own survival. There was a very evident absence of clear political guidance to the military commanders in theatre and on the ground.

Perhaps it was inevitable that things would get worse before there was a possibility to make them better. The summer and Autumn of 1995 saw a remarkable sequence of events, with the crimes and tragedies of Srebrenica as well as the Krajina in Croatia eventually forcing the international community to come together on a realistic political platform which made it possible to press the parties to the conflict into the peace agreement negotiated in Dayton and signed in Paris on December 14.

The UN operation in Bosnia was also unique in its close interaction with the different efforts of NATO. Although essential to the UN operation in a number of ways, there was an obvious tension between a NATO-centred strategy of robust intervention, preferably from the air, and a more traditional UN-oriented approach of impartial peacemaking on the ground.

By the summer of 1995, it was clear that the traditional UN operation had to come to an end. Key troop contributor countries were unlikely to support an unlimited presence in the middle of an escalating war. And NATO, including its US component, was already committed to securing the withdrawal of UNPROFOR. It was thus a matter of time and modality until NATO had to enter the scene on the ground as well as in the air.

The events at Srebrenica demonstrated, once more, that close air support in isolation was an instrument of limited tactical value. Although useful as a deterrent, its actual use tended to demonstrate its impotence more than anything else. When the F16s had returned to their base in Italy, most of them after having failed even to see a target, Mladic's soldiers just marched into Srebrenica.

The threat to use air power was then turned into a threat of wide-ranging air strikes, necessary not least in order to protect the air units from the supposed strength of Bosnian Serb air defence assets. And when this threat, together with the action of the artillery of the Rapid Reaction Force on Mount Igman, was unleashed on 30 August as a reaction to the shelling of Sarajevo, it by necessity spelt the end of the UN mission in Bosnia as the mission had been conceived up till then.

The expanded NATO air campaign turned the military tide in preparing the way for the collapse of the Bosnian Serb army before the advancing units of the regular Croat army in western Bosnia, thus bringing the division of territory very close to the desired end-state of 49% versus 51%. But it was not the air campaign alone that made the political difference that paved the way for the peace agreement.

In Geneva in early September, the entire international community, as well as the government in Sarajevo, accepted the continued existence of Republika Srpska, while the Serb representatives accepted the continued existence of an independent state of Bosnia and Herzegovina. The Dayton negotiations sorted out the details – in which the devil often hides! – of the agreement in principle that had been reached in Geneva.

The peace-implementation operation conducted by the NATO-led Implementation Force (IFOR) is beyond the scope of this study. But it is worth remembering that, while the UN force in the middle of the war had limited resources and an increasingly broad mandate, the NATO-led force after the cease-fire had very strong capabilities and a very narrowly defined mandate. Success and failure are relative concepts.

Much can and must be learnt from all the experiences – political, humanitarian, military – gained during the difficult years in Yugoslavia. This volume is an important contribution of that debate. Wherever the international community will try in the future to prevent war, contain a conflict or preserve a peace, the experience of the years in former Yugoslavia will shape those efforts.

Carl Bildt
Stockholm
3 April 1998

Maps

Map 1   Yugoslavia 1990

Map 2   Croatia. UN Protected Areas according to the Vance–Owen Plan

Map 3   Bosnia-Herzegovina. The Vance–Owen Plan, January 1993

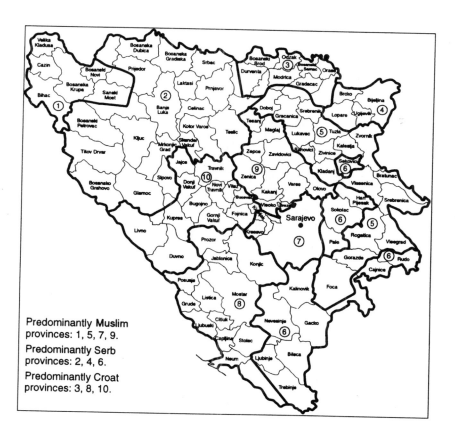

Predominantly **Muslim**
provinces: 1, 5, 7, 9.

Predominantly **Serb**
provinces: 2, 4, 6.

Predominantly **Croat**
provinces: 3, 8, 10.

Map 4 Bosnia-Herzegovina. The Union of Three Republics (Owen–Stoltenberg Plan), August 1993

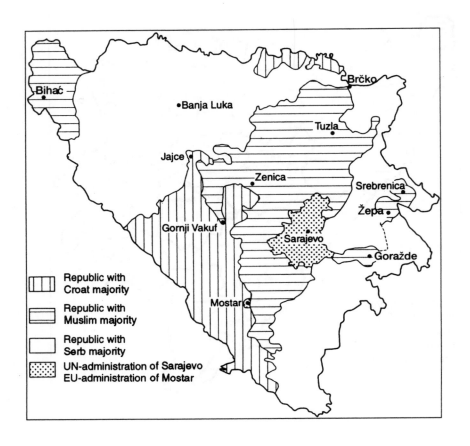

Map 5   Bosnia-Herzegovina. The Dayton Agreement, December 1995

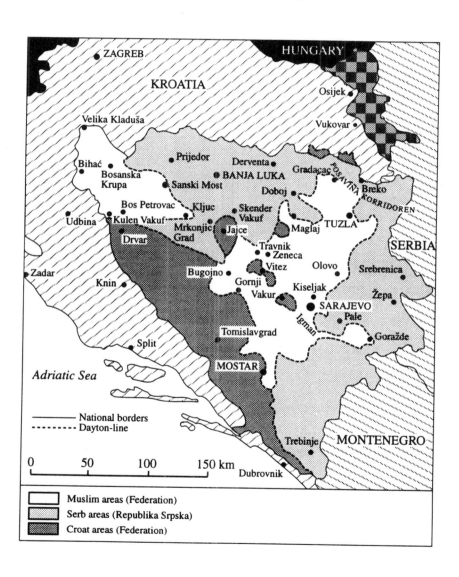

Part One

INTRODUCTION

1 About this Book

HÅKAN WIBERG[*]

The editors of the present book, Dr Wolfgang Biermann and Lt. Gen. (retd.) Martin Vadset, first met in Bonn in Spring 1993 at an international hearing on the former Yugoslavia.[1] The discussion there on use of force by NATO and the UN revealed a wide gap between the 'cautious' approach common to military officers and the interventionist arguments of several politicians and academics. To put it baldly, the traditional justification for political control over the military was put into question by the heated debate, where 'calm generals' tried to tame 'wild politicians', rather than the other way around. Part of the background for this debate was the vast increase of UN operations after the end of the Cold War – often accompanied by unrealistically high expectations.

Both Biermann and Vadset have a professional background in issues of peace and conflict resolution – the former as an international security adviser to the SPD, the Social Democrat Party of Germany, and the latter as a Norwegian general in several UN peacekeeping operations. This common interest led them to conceive a research project on a key issue concerning UN operations: the applicability and possible modifications of peacekeeping principles, procedures and mediation techniques in the 'new' type of conflicts – civil wars, and especially those with ethnic aspects. In 1994, they received a two-year research grant from COPRI for this project, now named the Danish-Norwegian Research Project (DANORP).

The present book is the main result of this project, studying what peacekeepers perceive as the lessons learned from their experience. While the wars in the former Yugoslavia have served as the main 'area of reference', the book also covers some aspects of peacekeeping in Somalia, Cambodia and the Middle East. It combines different methods of research by collecting and analysing data, including:

- Open-ended interviews with top-level civilian and military practitioners (Chapters 2 and 3)

- Two international workshops, held in Oslo in 1995 and in Copenhagen in 1996, where lessons learned were discussed by UNPROFOR commanders (Chapters 4 and 5)

---

[*] Prof. Håkan Wiberg is Director of the Copenhagen Peace Research Institute (COPRI).

- A questionnaire survey covering several hundreds of UNPROFOR officers from several countries (Chapter 6).

In addition to the analysis carried out by the two main researchers, a major part of the book (Part Three) provides a forum where prominent military and civilian staff sum up specific lessons learned from the operations in the former Yugoslavia. Their experiences provide a major input into the conceptual discussion of future UN peacekeeping.

This accords with the practical aims of the book. By giving voice to the experiences of leading practitioners, it attempts to bridge a deep gap between abstract models and political ambitions on the one side, and empirical realities on the other. The book is not intended to compete with the mushrooming literature on the former Yugoslavia, which ranges between superb scholarship and partisan calls-to-arms. By focusing on the application of peacekeeping principles in conflicts with elements of civil wars, it aims at supplementing that literature – and having a broader scope than it.

The conceptual point of departure of the book is the evolution of UN Peacekeeping Operations (PKO), as portrayed in *An Agenda for Peace* of the UN Secretary-General of June 1992 and in his *Supplement to An Agenda for Peace* of January 1995.[2] In the latter work, the Secretary-General re-emphasizes respect for traditional peacekeeping principles as a major key to success in a UN PKO: consent of the parties to the operation, impartiality of the peacekeepers *vis-à-vis* the parties and the use of force by peacekeepers in self-defence only. These principles are likewise reflected in the NATO doctrine for operations to support the UN, named 'Peace Support Operations'.[3]

Experience has shown that, to the extent the more 'robust' NATO-led Peace Implementation Force (IFOR)/Stabilization Force (SFOR) has been able to implement its mandate, it has been by behaving much like a traditional PKO, depending on the consent and willingness of the parties to co-operate and comply.

Bluntly put, the policy choices that actors in the international community may wish for political or moral reasons to have when intervening in conflicts with elements of civil war is one thing, but real, feasible options in these situations tend to be far more limited. Identifying criteria of practicability and feasibility for UN mandates is a challenging task, not only for academic research, but also for political and military decision makers who wish to avoid counterproductive actions.

To do precisely this has been the major challenge of the present book: finding ways to utilize and to systematize the accumulated knowledge of UN personnel in order to identify political and operational 'secrets of success' and 'reasons for failure'. The book's combination of quantitative and qualitative methods makes it unique in offering a comprehensive picture, based on solid practical experience, of the challenges peacekeepers face when operating in civil wars and similar conflicts. It provides rich insights in defining 'practicability tests' that should be applied in future both to public demands and proposed mandates for peacekeeping operations.

Notes

1 Biermann, Wolfgang (ed.), *Internationale Anhörung zur Praxis der UN-Blauhelme*, von der Projektgruppe 'Internationale Politik' des SPD-Parteivorstandes am 25. März 1993 in *Bonn, Frieden und Abrüstung*, Nr. 2/1993 (Juni).
2 Boutros-Ghali, Boutros, 'Supplement to an Agenda for Peace, Position Paper of the Secretary-General on the occasion of the Fiftieth Anniversary of the United Nations, A/50/60-S/1995/1, 3 January 1996', in: *An Agenda for Peace*, 2nd edition, United Nations: New York, 1995, p. 5ff.
3 *Bi-MNC Directive for NATO Doctrine for Peace Support Operations*, 11 December 1995, PfP unclassified, p. 12ff.

2 From Stoltenberg–Owen to Dayton

INTERVIEW WITH THORVALD STOLTENBERG ABOUT
PEACEKEEPING PRINCIPLES, POLITICS AND DIPLOMACY[*]

WB: Ambassador Stoltenberg, our research project is investigating the viability of UN peacekeeping as a means for the United Nations to intervene in conflicts, demanding co-operation and co-responsibility by the parties involved to solve the conflict. We see peacekeeping as distinct from enforcement. The latter normally requires the intervening force to occupy an area against the will of at least one party and take over full responsibility for imposing a solution on them.

We would like to discuss with you one of the central questions raised in this book: are the three UN principles of peacekeeping – consent of the parties, impartiality and non-use of force by the peacekeepers other than in self-defence – realistic guidelines for today's peacekeeping operations also under civil war circumstances like those you experienced in the former Yugoslavia? What do these principles mean for a UN mediator? How far were these principles violated? Did they make your work more complicated?

TS: My answer is simple. These key principles were the basis for the UN peacekeeping operation in the former Yugoslavia. The problem was that, more and more, public reaction, public relations, media, and then politicians around the world, pressed for actions by the UN peacekeeping force which were not in accordance with these peacekeeping principles. One of many problems during the whole operation was that the United Nations were constantly criticized for not undertaking offensive military action which the UN did not have a mandate for. The UN peacekeepers, young people, were not sent to Yugoslavia by their families, by their parliaments as combat forces.

I learned when I was young that war is too dangerous to leave to the generals. I tried to live according to that rule when I was Defence Minister. But I must admit I learned in the former Yugoslavia those who really

---

[*] Thorvald Stoltenberg was interviewed by Wolfgang Biermann in Copenhagen, Denmark, 16 October 1997.

adhered to these principles were not so much the politicians, but definitely the generals. Thanks to the generals, the UN peacekeeping forces lived up to the UN principles.

WB: There were in fact a number of Security Council resolutions with reference to Chapter VII, which you can interpret as not being in accordance with these principles.

TS: This situation shows that the politicians did not take this mandate and its principles the same way the generals on the ground did. And one more 'lesson learned': the fewer people governments had on the ground, the more courageous statements they gave, demanding that 'you must undertake military action'. American and German politicians were in the forefront of demanding more military actions while they had not a single young woman or man as a UN soldier on the ground. The French and the British were called cowards. But they had thousands of their own people there. That's why I hope that, in the future, members of the Security Council will be obliged to provide personnel for UN peacekeeping operations. When you do have personnel on the ground, your statements as a politician are much more balanced and responsible than when you do not have your own people on the ground and can afford 'courage' on behalf of other people, other nations' young people.

WB: What does this mean in the face of the atrocities which took place? The demand to 'do something' – to undertake an offensive enforcement operation – is based on the assumption that you can do something to stop the war, to stop the atrocities. The question is whether this argument is valid, or illusionary?

TS: No, I don't think it's illusionary. But I also don't think it's realistic. Both Lord Owen and myself contacted several governments, and as far as I recall, only the Turks and the Iranians were ready to send combat forces. No other governments were ready to do that, because I think the decision to risk lives is left to national governments – to the nation state – rather than to moral attitudes. We may not like it, but that's the fact.

And then, there is another angle. You can discuss the shift to bombing that eventually came in Autumn 1994. Did it really promote peace? I think that it turned out the wrong way. One consequence was the hostage taking of UN personnel, with another bombing in May 1995 and subsequent hostage taking.

Then, the second step: the next day, representatives of those governments and organizations that had hostages being taken – as far as I

recall, 370 hostages – were at the door of President Milosevic, and asked
him to help them to get these hostages well-returned. He said he would do
his best, but he could not promise success. He managed to get those
hostages back. But who was the real winner? Milosevic. He strengthened
his position more than ever. And later he was the key player in all
subsequent negotiations. But that was not the intent of the bombing.

On the other hand, there is no doubt the Croatian attack on the Serbs in
Croatia in Sector West, Krajina, facilitated the negotiations that led up to
the Dayton Agreement. The result was a weaker Serb party. That made it
easier to get an agreement. Now, you may ask: is this the right way to get
peace? And is it right to accept a war to get this peace? This can be
discussed as a moral issue, but there is no doubt this made the eventual
Dayton Agreement easier to achieve.

Then the third point: what is impartiality? It is not impartiality to
massacre, to rape, to take hostages; but it is impartiality aimed at the final
peace agreement, because a peace imposed on one of the parties could not
be a solid agreement for a lasting peace.

WB: I would agree that peace against one party is not sustainable. But
doesn't this contradict what you said earlier about (in my words) the 'peace
benefits' of the Croat attack because it helped Dayton. The September '95
bombing of Serb positions is also often argued to be a military contribution
to peace. One can also hear the view that, with the Holbrooke Plan, the
Serbs had already in August '95 been promised what they wanted: the *de
facto* recognition of Srpska, a Serb war aim that was never before accepted
by the West – but it seemed necessary to convince the Muslims to accept
this compromise giving the Serbs their own republic in Bosnia...

Was the key to Dayton more a political than a military one – the fact
that the international community was united behind the efforts to make
peace by compromise between the three parties? This united support for
'peace through compromise' was not forthcoming in 1993 and 1994 as
regards the agreements negotiated by you and Lord Owen, was it?

And the second question concerns the Krajina operation: was 'Operation
Storm' the consequence of a deliberate blind eye against the Croats?

TS: There's no doubt that it was all that...

WB: ...But this was one of the most 'efficient' operations of ethnic
cleansing. Through it, Croatia not only changed the military balance
facilitating Dayton, but also created a serious problem for implementing
Dayton: if you want to bring refugees back to their hometowns, as intended
in Dayton, an important return road has been closed – the road to Croatia.

Many thousands of Serb refugees from Krajina are now in Srpska, living in Croat or Muslim houses. And if you don't settle the Krajina problem, enabling the Serbs to return, you're back again to a major problem in implementing Dayton with respect to the return of the other refugees. Isn't there a problem here with impartiality?

TS: Your question is based on a false assumption – namely, that the international community was impartial. That's not the case. They were partial, in supporting the Muslims or Bosniaks. They turned a blind eye to the Croats and were against the Serbs. You may discuss whether this was justified or not, but it was a fact; there's no doubt about it. You mentioned Krajina. We can discuss whether one should be partial or should be against the Serbs, for the Muslims, and should turn a blind eye to the Croats. But we can't hide from the fact that this was the case. This was how it operated the whole time. There was not really impartiality – at least not in 1994 and 1995.

WB: This leads me to two further questions. The first question refers to the early stage of conflict, when discussion about diplomatic recognition started. Was the lack of impartiality by major international players, who indicated sympathy and eventual recognition for the republics seceding from Yugoslavia, a political signal fuelling the conflict? If the international community had been united in saying: 'We do not take sides, no recognition before you have agreed on some solution among yourselves' – could such a political signal have had the effect of calming down the dynamic of violence in the very early stage?

Secondly: then, once the dynamic had started, there is the question of military intervention in an early stage to stop the killing. Some people argue that if the world community had acted with a military intervention in Vukovar in 1991, then the whole process may have been stopped. Do you agree?

TS: Let me take the last question first. I think it is a very interesting issue whether a military intervention at the time of Vukovar would have stopped the war. But even more interesting is the fact that this question was at that stage purely theoretical. No parliaments or governments were ready to send their young people as battle forces to Croatia. That's for sure. Still, I think the issue should be discussed, as a sort of psychological preparation for the future. At another time maybe one should send in battle forces. But then you are back to the feelings of the people. People are normally not ready to leave their motherland, their nation state, to die in another country. We have not come that far in international thinking. We like to speak as though we are at that stage, but that's not the case. So, I think it's an interesting theoretical discussion, but it was impossible in practical terms.

Then comes the other question: recognition. You know, of course, that there were preconditions for recognition, for instance the catalogue of preconditions written by the Badinter Commission, supported by the European Community. These were specific points that must be met. And the EU decided that these points had been met by the declarations of the three republics concerned. Now, you can discuss whether these declarations on their own were enough evidence.

Recognition was definitely not the way to prevent the war; that's for sure. Lord Carrington was right; there's no doubt about that today. But that is an afterthought.

For a time, as Foreign Minister of Norway, I was in doubt. I was in close contact with Hans Dietrich Genscher, the German Foreign Minister, on this issue, and I called him the night before the final decision in the EU was taken and I questioned the policy of recognition. I am in no doubt that Genscher's intention was to find a solution. It was not, as claimed by some, part of old German policies of 1940 towards Croatia. I know him very well, his intentions were the best.

WB: Germany had at that time just been unified, had itself just fulfilled the 'right of self-determination'. However, German unification – negotiated in consent between the two German states and with consent of their neighbours and the big powers – was often equated with Yugoslav separation in conditions of disagreement among each other. In other words, there was a mix-up over self-determination in the 'regulated marriage' of the two Germanies and in the 'wild divorce' of the Yugoslav republics. It was nearly forgotten, that a 'wild marriage' of the Germans during the Cold War would have led to a hot war.

By the end of 1991, there were reports from Bosnian peace organizations that arms were distributed all over Bosnia and that they expected a war after the March 1992 referendum on independence. In early January 1992 there was a discussion with Willy Brandt about a possible initiative of Nobel Peace Laureates to appeal for a postponement of the referendum and to ask the three groups – Bosnian Muslims, Croats and Serbs – first to negotiate their agreement on the constitutional rights. After Willy Brandt had talked to some of his colleagues, however, he said there was no possibility of delay: 'The package is all tied together, the political machine is running like a steam roller.'

I recall one of the statements you made some time ago: what happened in Yugoslavia can also happen again somewhere else because of a wrong political course. Was Yugoslavia exploding because there were no political leaders ready for compromise? Should a 'lesson learned' from the former Yugoslavia be a strong call for a political culture of compromise as the ruling norm in international as well as internal affairs?

TS: The Danes are one of the most peaceful people in the world. Denmark is one of the few nations where the word 'compromise' is a word of honour. In Denmark, compromise does not mean to lose honour. In most other countries you stand on your principles. And if you eventually have to compromise, you consider it some sort of a loss. Here in Denmark, it is a gain, and I think that if this 'culture of compromise' were contagious, it would be good for peace in the world...

WB: Was the missing 'culture of compromise' the reason why in 1993 your plan with Owen did not really come about, although it was very similar to Dayton...

TS: We had negotiated this agreement. All parties agreed, including President Izetbegovic and Prime Minister Silajdzic, on the implementation of the agreement. But suddenly the Bosniak parliament decided against it. I was told that the Americans had also advised against it, because they felt the agreement was not *morally* acceptable. There were three objections: One, the agreement carves up Bosnia. And it did. Two, it accepted land acquired by force. And it did. And, third, it did not give the Muslims enough land; it gave 33.3%, but that was exactly what they had demanded.

So the war went on for another two years. And we got Dayton. Dayton divides Bosnia – not in three, but in two-and-a-half, in the sense that there are two parts, but one is almost divided in two again. And the federation is not functioning. Dayton accepts land acquired by force, and it has given the Muslims *less* territory than the Muslims controlled even in 1993 – namely, somewhere between 28 and 30%.

I asked my American friends why was this all right in '95, but not in '93? The real difference between the two agreements, you can find in the churchyards in Bosnia. Thousands and thousands of people killed, and 250,000 more refugees. The answer in '95 was, 'when we finally came to the negotiating table, we recognized that, *morally*, the most important thing was to stop the killing.' I agree; I agreed fully. I agree both with the moral acceptance of what was most important, and I support Dayton wholeheartedly. I only regret that the war had to go two more years. In my opinion, this was the most expensive adult education ever.

WB: Again, was the missing 'culture of compromise' the reason why in 1993 peace failed?

TS: The parties to the conflict were ready for peace in 1993 – but not the international community. The international community demanded the ideal peace, which became less and less attainable with each additional month that the war was allowed to continue.

There was a gap here between attitudes, opinions and decisions and the reality – you might say, between resolutions and reality. People were against the Serbs because of Serbian atrocities. But the UN Security Council was also not willing to follow up its resolutions with action in reality. Let me take one well-known example: the decision by the Security Council to establish Safe Areas was a good one. The UN military leaders then asked for 34,000 more soldiers to implement this resolution. They got 4,700. And that gap between the good resolution and the reality on the ground resulted in the situation in Srebrenica, to take one of the worst consequences.

I'd like to add something. There has been a lot of criticism of UN operations in the former Yugoslavia. And that's fair enough. When you go into a peacekeeping operation in a difficult crisis, there will always be criticism, and I don't react against that.

But I do want to remind the critics of who it was who lost their young people in order to create peace in the former Yugoslavia. Who was there during the war to reduce violence and help hundreds of thousands to survive? It was the United Nations and the European Union. It was young people from Britain, France, Spain, The Netherlands, the Nordic countries, Russia, Ukraine, Malaysia, Kenya, Canada, Pakistan and many other countries. These UN and EU forces lost more than 300 young people. More than 4,000 were wounded among the 23,000 UN soldiers in Bosnia, inadequately equipped for actual war.

Then peace came. And then NATO came in, in the beginning with 120,000 troops – 60,000 in Bosnia, 60,000 around the area. I fully hope NATO will stay. And I support the fact that they came in with 120,000 well-equipped soldiers, and in peacetime.

But I do not see the criticism of the UN and EU as fair. The UN and the EU were there during war. NATO is there with much larger and better equipped forces during peacetime.

WB: Do you think in the future it could be realistic that NATO would send a force under a UN mandate to stop the killing in an ongoing civil war without taking sides, and afterwards, when peace is agreed, comes the UN force – this would be logical, but would it be realistic?

TS: First, I hope we could have not another 'Yugoslavia'. That's my hope. But we must be prepared for situations like that. And I think there is a whole new system we're coming to now where the UN takes decisions and delegates their implementation to regional organizations – NATO, EU or OSCE in Europe, in other parts of the world, other regional organizations – and that on the basis of the UN mandate, regional organizations will operate. That is a possible architecture for the future. And that could certainly bring a situation where you first have NATO in assisting to end a war, and then you have the UN to keep the peace rather than the other way around.

WB: I would ask you to give a summary of your three major lessons for the future.

TS: You have to decide at the very beginning. If you want to have peacekeeping with the consent of all parties concerned, you cannot expect that the young people in those peacekeeping forces suddenly be turned into combat forces. That is the first lesson.

The second lesson is that the overriding moral basis for this work is the rule: 'Don't kill!' Every day that war goes on, there will be more massacres, more hatred, more ethnic cleansing. Priority number one must be 'stop the killing!' And when the killing has stopped, you can start looking for a better way for people to live together.

And the third lesson should be, give more information to the public. To world opinion and to the national audience. I think point three is the most difficult one, and the media must take a greater responsibility.

WB: But this means that the UN must have the media on the spot and inform the people?

TS: Yes, on all spots. And on the ground, and not in one place, in different places to inform from all angles.

WB: Let's imagine, because military intervention forces are scarce, that there is need for diplomatic intervention forces. To my view, it seems sometimes difficult for diplomats or politicians to understand how to handle conflicts. I refer to your initial statement from which I conclude that the generals were often more helpful in handling the conflict than politicians. Do you have an idea of what you would recommend to governments, what to write into a 'cookbook for peacemakers', so that they can really help to de-escalate conflict?

TS: I don't agree with your assumption. If it is not politicians and diplomats who are used to conflicts and to making compromises – and you started the whole interview by saying the most important thing is compromise – who else is going to make these compromises? The politicians and diplomats are the right people to handle crises. A cookbook? Yes, but it must be a very general cookbook, because rules and advice could make it easy to believe that the same sort of crisis reoccurs and reoccurs. I have been close to crises and wars in Hungary in '56, Chile, Nigeria and Biafra at the beginning of the '60s, Vietnam at the end of the '60s, Chile '73, Central America in the beginning of the '80s, and then Yugoslavia. I've been on the spot in all these places. None of them is alike. Perhaps there is one very simple, basic piece of advice, but be careful to avoid giving an impression that all crises are much the same.

WB: Was there one situation where you were in conflict between your impartial approach as a mediator and the mandate you had? Was there any situation where you would say, I should have given a stronger signal, threatened to resign, is there any place where you were at such a critical point?

TS: I never, in my three years in Yugoslavia, considered resigning. I could be exhausted, I could be frustrated, I could be unhappy; but to resign, no. I think to resign would have been to give up, and that is not my inclination. I disagree with people who resigned. I think it is an extremely important work, and it would not help to resign. It's a very unpleasant job. There is constant physical and psychological bombardment. I didn't want the job, but I accepted it, and I never thought of resigning.

WB: ...Even if you were in conflict between the mandate and your approach, you did not want to give up because you could at least reduce violence?

TS: Yes – and I was privileged to appear monthly in the Security Council, to give my reports and to answer questions, and sometimes got my views accepted, other times not. But should I resign because the Security Council did not agree with me? No, I felt that I should continue to contribute to save lives and promote peace.

WB: Thank you, Ambassador Stoltenberg.

3 Setting the Scene

The Challenge to the United Nations: Peacekeeping in a Civil War

WOLFGANG BIERMANN and MARTIN VADSET

Peacekeeping principles – ruling guideline or misguiding rules for UNPROFOR?

Introduction

Our intention in this book is to document lessons learned from the former Yugoslavia which may be useful for the international handling of future *civil war-like conflicts*. We use this term as a brief characterization of the traditional definition of 'intra-state conflict either with or without external involvement'.[1] We consider that civil war-like conflicts require a type of treatment by the international community that is distinctly different from classic war between states.

The purpose of the book is limited. The main question addressed is whether 'traditional peacekeeping principles' are still a viable basis for intervention by the United Nations in intra-state conflicts. In addition, recent experience raises the question of whether these or similar principles also apply to an operation mandated by the UN Security Council, but executed under the command of NATO. We limit our analysis to basic military-political conditions rather than the full complexity of civil-military and humanitarian aspects in multifunctional 'second-generation peacekeeping'.

As mentioned in Håkan Wiberg's introduction to the book, we do not intend to present here a new in-depth analysis of the history of the Yugoslav conflict. However, authentic analyses of practical experiences are given in Part Three of this book, with unique contributions by military and civilian leaders of the UNPROFOR operation, among them the Special Representative of the UN Secretary-General, UNPROFOR Force Commanders as well as other key persons. They provide first-hand information of most important political, military and humanitarian aspects of the United Nations commitment to the former Yugoslavia.

In Part Two of the book, lessons learned from two UN Commanders' Workshops and from a survey of about one thousand military officers involved in peacekeeping are documented.

In this chapter, we want to describe some political and operational scenarios which can exemplify the conditions under which the United Nations had to operate in the former Yugoslavia. We recall some events, facts and conditions which may have been forgotten, but which are important to understand the setting of the scene to which other parts of the book refer.

'Traditional' peacekeeping

General. Over the decades since the United Nations first deployed military units in a peacekeeping mission – UNEF in 1956 – the lessons learned have been distilled into three basic principles for UN peacekeeping:

- Consent by participants in the conflict

- Impartiality by peacekeepers

- Use of force by peacekeepers in self-defence only.

These traditional peacekeeping principles have been complementary to each other and have had crucial conceptual implications. Without impartiality of the troops there is no consent. To be perceived as impartial requires that the peacekeepers limit the use of force to self-defence only.

Despite a widespread perception, intervention by the UN into civil war types of conflict is not new. 'Traditional' peacekeeping has not always been a simple operation of monitoring a 'desert buffer zone'. For example, UN forces in Congo/Zaire (ONUC) 1960–1964 sent to end a civil war after secession of the Katanga province, had a large humanitarian component in addition to the military and police component, and were in many aspects similar to the UNPROFOR operation.[2] ONUC was highly controversial in the UN, where many perceived the operation as 'the UN's Vietnam'.[3]

After the end of the Cold War, however, it was not expected that a brutal civil war could also start in the middle of the reunited Europe, nor, if it happened, that the international community could barely cope with it. New in this situation was obviously the widely shared overestimation of the 'ability of the UN to intervene effectively in internal conflicts'.[4]

The *Peacekeeper's Handbook* compiled by the International Peace Academy commends UN peacekeeping particularly as a tool to handle 'intrastate and community level conflict'. In its 1984 edition, the *Handbook* lists six of thirteen current UN Peacekeeping Operations (PKO) as conflicts of intra-state character.[5] Although the UN has never adopted an official definition for peacekeeping, the definition proposed by the *Handbook* has been used by the UN for many years. It has defined peacekeeping as the

> ...prevention, containment, moderation, and termination of hostilities between or *within* states, through the medium of a peaceful third party intervention organized and directed internationally, using multi-national forces of soldiers, police and civilians to restore and maintain peace.[6]

Characteristics. Peacekeepers have a role that is quite distinct from that of combat soldiers. They are guests, not occupiers. Their activities are open, not hidden. Their rules of engagement (ROE) are transparent, not secret. They show where they are deployed and do not seek to conceal their positions. In conflict situations, their role is de-escalating rather than escalating to solve military conflict. Their approach is co-operation rather than confrontation. They treat the conflicting parties to a conflict as partners, rather than enemies. Peacekeepers have no right to 'kill and destroy' unless it is in self-defence.

Operational restraint. Acting within these rules obviously limits the range of possible military action. Traditionally, UN Peacekeeping Forces act under various restraints, as the *Peacekeeper's Handbook* explains: their mandates tend to vague terms and ambiguity in order to meet the requirements of all members of the UN Security Council. As a result, this 'often handicaps UN Peacekeeping Forces in achieving total effectiveness'.[7] Finally, the principle of consent of the host country also has meant that the use of covert intelligence systems is not acceptable. In 'intrastate conflicts, it can damage relations and diminish trust and confidence'. The UN had 'therefore resolutely refused to countenance intelligence as part of its peacekeeping operations'. In the spirit of traditional peacekeeping, these restraints, though militarily inhibiting, made 'third party peacekeeping more credible and viable...'.[8]

Internal pacification. In intrastate conflict 'with or without external involvement, the role performed by the UN Force or Mission would be aimed at bringing about an end to violence by peaceful means and thereafter preventing a renewal of fighting; achieving thereby a de-escalation of tension, the reestablishment of social and military stability, and the creation of conditions in which a mediated settlement might be more readily agreed to by the parties to the dispute'.[9]

Buffer force. In the process of internal pacification, one of the key operational measures aimed at de-escalation is the establishment of a *buffer zone* between the territories controlled by the belligerent parties. A buffer force is also a 'means of keeping two military forces apart *within* a state, while negotiations *are in progress*'. The role in this case is 'insuring that the buffer zone is in no way infiltrated by either side',[10] to assist the implementation of arms control agreements on the territories of the belligerents and to create stability in the area. Accompanied by energetic mediation efforts, the buffer zone is a starting point of change until a political settlement is agreed upon.

Box 3.1 UN Charter and UN Convention about safety of UN personnel

Art. 105 of the UN Charter

1. The Organization shall enjoy in the territory of each of its Members such privileges and immunities as are necessary for the fulfilment of its purposes.
2. Representatives of the Members of the United Nations and officials of the Organization shall similarly enjoy such privileges and immunities as are necessary for the independent exercise of their functions in connection with the Organization. (...)

Convention on the Safety of United Nations and Associated Personnel of 9 December 1994

The General Assembly
(...) urges States to take all appropriate measures to ensure the safety and security of United Nations and associated personnel within their territory (...)

Article 2
Scope of application
(...)
2. This Convention shall not apply to a United Nations operation authorized by the Security Council as an enforcement action under Chapter VII of the Charter of the United Nations in which any of the personnel are engaged as combatants against organized armed forces and to which the law of international armed conflict applies.

Legal status. More crucial, even if not in the centre of public discussion, is the effect of the legal status of peacekeepers on the safety of peacekeeping troops: peacekeepers operating under Chapter VI of the UN Charter (Peaceful Settlement of Disputes) are normally protected by Article 104 and 105 of the UN Charter, giving them a status comparable with the diplomatic immunity of United Nations officials. This legal status is normally established in concrete terms through a Status of Forces Agreements (SOFA).[11] In December 1994 the UN General Assembly passed the 'Convention on the Safety of United Nations and Associated Personnel' in order to strengthen the position of UN peacekeepers. However, the convention shall not apply to UN troops operating as combatants in an 'enforcement action under Chapter VII' of the UN Charter.[12]

For example, capturing or detaining UN peacekeepers is illegal, a criminal act. Once UN forces act in a combat mission, however, they have the status of combatants, submitted to international humanitarian law. Capturing combatants, is then taking 'prisoners of war' rather than a criminal act, provided they are treated according to the rules of the Geneva Conventions.[13] In acting under restraints, UN peacekeepers share the privilege of being protected by a legal status of immunity, along with civilian employees of the United Nations.

The new agenda

Since the end of the Cold War, Peacekeeping Operations (PKOs) have been extended tremendously and have been affected by exaggerated and often unfulfilled expectations. Faced by ethnic or civil conflicts escalating into most brutal wars, parts of the public press for restraint in becoming militarily involved. The other side of the debate has been dominated by demands that the UN should, unlike in traditional peacekeeping operations, act more effectively by becoming

- Less reliant on the consent of the parties to a conflict
- Less impartial
- More forceful and coercive.

It is a commonly accepted 'conclusion' that following the end of the Cold War, the UNSC is able to act against violators of international law and agreements without the risk of a veto from one of the five Permanent Members ('P5'). In the minds of many, this new 'freedom of action' by the Security Council was confirmed by the fact that no veto blocked the mandate for the US-led coalition to repel Iraq's aggression against Kuwait in 1991.

Although the Security Council has, explicitly or implicitly, authorized most peacekeeping operations under Chapter VI of the UN Charter, 'Pacific Settlement of Disputes', UNSC resolutions frequently mandated UN peacekeeping operations in Somalia and in the former Yugoslavia with explicit reference to Chapter VII of the UN Charter, 'Threats to International Peace and Security'.[14] Politicians, peace researchers and sometimes even former pacifists introduced new terminologies to illustrate a new readiness to use force for the good cause of peace: Some used the term 'peacemaking', traditionally used for diplomatic mediation, instead of enforcement, or 'robust peacekeeping'[15] to indicate decisive action by peacekeepers, others praised air power for its capability to transition from peacekeeping to coercion[16] or rediscovered the medieval philosophy of 'justified war' for humanitarian intervention.[17]

Parallel to this new belief in enforcement, there was widespread criticism of the UN, the UNSC and in particular of the peacekeepers on the ground, for being too weak, reluctant and ready to capitulate in the face of criminal warlords. In the face of this trend, the UN Secretary General expressed embarrassment at the world community for being co-responsible for the massacres in Rwanda. Because of failure of governments to provide troops and equipment to help the survivors, 'our readiness and capacity for action has been inadequate at best, and deplorable at worst'.[18]

UNSC: Tough resolutions without resources

Despite general demands to 'show muscle', most nations, including the P5 and the powerful NATO alliance, are in fact quite reluctant to intervene with their ground forces in military conflicts. Many nations have declared readiness to designate forces for the United Nations, but only a few have actually formalized their Article 43 commitment to do so. Of 66 countries who notified capabilities to the UN Stand-by system which was introduced in 1992, only eight have formalized their commitment in a Memorandum of Understanding.[19]

Somalia was deserted by the major powers after 'showing muscle' led to casualties. At the height of the massacres in Rwanda, UN peacekeepers were withdrawn. While the UNSC declared Safe Areas (SAs) in Yugoslavia without providing the ground troops to protect them, troop contributors repeatedly speculated about UN withdrawal from Bosnia. Russian hopes for Western peacekeepers to engage in settling ethnic conflicts in the CIS area ultimately had to be cut back to some 150 military observers in Tajikistan and Georgia, mandated by the UNSC.[20]

There was an obvious contradiction between resolutions by the UNSC, reacting to public demands to 'do something' on the one hand – and the reluctance of governments to provide troops for UN missions on the other hand. It seems that the new situation after removal of Cold War restrictions gave the UNSC a new freedom to pass resolutions rather than a new freedom to act.

In particular, UNPROFOR was agonized by tough-sounding resolutions followed-up with inadequate human, material and financial resources. These resources were often too little or came too late to implement resolutions, but they were enough to put the blame for failures on those in the UN bureaucracy or the peacekeepers in the field who had to execute a very challenging task without the support they needed.

Peacekeeping principles and the limits set by reality

Criticism of unrealistic demands to intervene, however, requires a proper answer to the question of 'realism': what is practicable and feasible in peacekeeping in the world as it is? What is a 'realistic' answer to the challenges the UN and the international community have been facing in the former Yugoslavia – not to mention the hardship inflicted on the local population?

Are traditional peacekeeping principles a realistic operational guideline for UN troops in missions to an ongoing civil war-like conflict, where consent is fragile, impartiality challenged and the use of force frequently provoked by the conflicting parties? Should diplomacy and political actors of the international community act in accordance with these principles? If not, why are these principles, applied by 'Blue Helmets' over many years, not followed by political actors? Or did UN Force Commanders in UNPROFOR, by insisting on these principles, show that they did not understand that times had changed?

In his report of 3 January 1995 to the Security Council, the UN Secretary-General found it necessary to reduce expectations raised by his 1992 *Agenda for Peace*[21] and to re-emphasize the unique value of peacekeeping. He stated that, according to his analysis, successful peacekeeping operations were those that respected the 'principles' of peacekeeping, whereas in 'most of the unsuccessful operations, one or other of these principles' were violated or not adhered to.[22] Some commentators had interpreted enforcement proposals in the UNSG's *Agenda* of 1992 as 'an increased willingness to run risks' and had expressed concerns 'about the lack of practicability of the proposals'.[23] Therefore, the UNSG's arguments in the 'Supplement to An Agenda for

Peace' could be interpreted as a return to the principles, to less ambitious and more realistic UN operations.

Political reality vs. operational reality – the political feasibility gap

Two major aspects of realism are often confused with one another or their interdependency is not adequately recognized: operational and political realism. This book deals mainly with operational aspects of peacekeeping in the former Yugoslavia. However, UNPROFOR force commanders felt that political decision making often ignored operational realities and requirements as the latter were repeatedly articulated by force commanders and the UNSG.[24]

The reasons for this shortcoming may be the peculiar distinctive rules of international political decision making: 'political realism' – applied in the political reality of bodies like the UNSC – is often dictated by requirements such as concealing political differences among key players, reacting to the media and public expectations, and eventually finding a compromise to pass a resolution with the highest feasible level of consensus among the participants. In the case of the Yugoslav crisis, this 'political realism' in New York or in various governmental conferences was often in contradiction to the 'operational realism' the UN military commanders considered necessary to meet operational requirements in the field. In other words, the mission suffered from the wide gap between political wishes and operational reality. In this book, we call this shortfall a feasibility gap[25] in political decisions.

More enforcement, less support, more chaos – the dilemma of UN peacekeeping in a civil war-like conflict

National interests and risks. The feasibility gap between political expectations and the practical possibilities of UN peacekeepers is not only a result of political decision making remote from operational reality. Limits on UN peacekeeping operations are also set by a further factor which is likewise political in nature: reluctance to accept the risk of casualties.

National interests limit the willingness of governments to participate in a UN mission when there is a risk of sacrificing lives of their national citizens. National governments are normally willing to take the very difficult decision to sacrifice civilian and military lives only in cases where vital national interests are being challenged, for example, in the case of defence of national territory. This attitude may contradict the public's expectation that governments will act tough, but the public's mood can shift immediately in favour of withdrawal if something goes wrong the day after. Public expectations are inconsistent and sometimes contradictory. They narrow the political basis for the use of force in a UN peacekeeping operation.

Vicious circle. Moreover, the events in Mogadishu highlighted not only practical and operational requirements[26] but also the dilemmas that can arise in a transition from peacekeeping to enforcement. The far-reaching political consequences of the operational chaos that sometimes follows enforcement actions are often interpreted as an inability of peacekeepers to fulfil their mandate,[27] although, in reality, the reasons can be found in the gap between political wishes and the operational reality on the one hand and, on the other hand, the gap between the scope of national interests involved and the threshold of tolerance to national casualties. In the case of Somalia, these gaps finally led to the abrupt end of the mission.

In Yugoslavia, General Sir Michael Rose repeatedly warned against 'crossing the Mogadishu Line'. In the case of Bosnia and Croatia, 'crossing the Mogadishu Line' had repeatedly disastrous consequences for the dispersed peacekeepers, who were 'neither mandated, deployed nor equipped for peace enforcement or to fight a war'.[28]

The negative interaction between operational and political implications of enforcement elements in UN peacekeeping operations can be summarized as follows:

1. The introduction of enforcement elements into UN peacekeeping operations requires larger and well-trained units, better Command and Control facilities, including highly qualified specialists, etc. Only a few nations are able and willing to provide such capabilities. This increases the dependency of the UN on a few nations

2. The greater risks of such operations increase *national interference* in UN missions by governments which have a legitimate responsibility for their nationals. This process reduces the military efficiency of the force and can thus even increase the risks of the operation[29]

3. Finally, greater risks increase *national reluctance* to contribute troops, which *per se* adds to the risks and inefficiency of UN missions.

In other words; a mandate to use force does not prevent a UN intervention from facing a vicious circle: more enforcement – less support – more chaos in UN operations.[30]

In the following section, we address a few examples of the vicious circle of enforcement-chaos which UNPROFOR had to experience due to the feasibility gap between political decisions and the reality on the ground.

The pressure on UNPROFOR to use force

A number of UN Security Council resolutions mandated UNPROFOR to act under Chapter VII of the UN Charter. Understandably, public opinion expected UNPROFOR to be an 'enforcement operation' and its troops to act forcefully. Many politicians followed this interpretation. Labelling UNPROFOR as a 'Chapter VII operation', however, again reflected a 'political reality' in conflict with operational reality.

First, a reference to Chapter VII in a Security Council resolution does not necessarily imply the use of military force in the traditional sense of war-fighting. Many of the measures mentioned in Article 41 of the UN Charter are not of a militarily robust character. However, the fact that the Security Council had in the context of the Gulf War referred to Chapter VII and had used the formula 'with all necessary means', contributed in Bosnia to an ultimate public expectation of offensive military action.

Second, in practice, UN commanders were able to utilize the 'Chapter VII aspects' of the mandate only in support of a 'Chapter VI mission', that is, of a UN peacekeeping mission equipped and organized to be impartial, to seek consent of the parties and to use force only in self-defence. The fact that UNPROFOR commanders repeatedly presented their operation as 'Chapter VI' missions had nothing to do with 'disobeying' or 'ignoring' a Security Council 'Chapter VII' mandate or even being 'cowards toward the Serbs', as some media tried to suggest. Their insistence on carrying out a 'Chapter VI' mission reflected the limits set by the operational reality in the field. It would be irresponsible if commanders had given enforcement orders to troops, which were sent, trained, equipped and deployed as peacekeepers.

Many contributions in this book written by force commanders illustrate the dilemma of using force and risking 'mission creep'. The main reasons for these pressures can be summarized as follows:[31]

> *Experimental reaction to hostile environment.* Pressure to use force was a reaction to the unexpected deterioration of the situation. International differences about the best way to react to the conflict led to various provocations and attacks against the peacekeeping troops to which the UN had to react.

Lack of peacekeeping training. The size of the UNPROFOR operation exceeded by far earlier PKOs. The UN was not able to recruit enough troops with officers trained and experienced in peacekeeping also under hostile conditions, as e.g. in UNIFIL/UNTAC. Instead, the UN often had to rely on troops well-trained for combat rather than peacekeeping.[32]

Divergent philosophies of NATO and the UN. NATO as a supporter of UNPROFOR had traditionally a quite different philosophy than UNPROFOR itself.[33] Moreover, the political leadership of NATO did not feel the same commitment as UN officials and commanders to be impartial towards the parties.

Political contradictions among Western governments. Partisan side-taking by major members of the alliance contributed to the erosion of the parties' consent to the UN mission. NATO as well as the UN became a hostage of the conflicting parties: they were testing out 'which side are you on' and demanded or provoked 'Chapter VII-reactions' in a typical action-reaction process.[34]

UNPROFOR was under continued pressure to be 'credible' *vis-à-vis* the international community through using coercive force against the party identified as the most guilty one. This 'enforcement' setting of the 'peacekeeping scene' was a conceptual burden on the peacekeepers: at the least, it hampered mediation efforts by the force commanders and at its worst, it put the whole peacekeeping mission at risk by an enforcement-chaos circle that came close to crossing the Mogadishu line.

The enforcement–chaos vicious circle I: Effective use of force with counter-effective consequences

One example of the vicious circle of 'enforcement-chaos' is the events during intensive fighting around the Bihac 'safe' area in November 1994:[35]

After a decision taken by the NATO Council on 19 November 1994, NATO received authorization to bomb Bosnian Serb positions. On 21 November, as a reaction to a violation of the no-fly zone, NATO bombed the origin of the violation, a Krajina-Serb airfield in Udbina (Croatia). This did not lead to major reactions from the Serb side. However, by targeting air defence radars against NATO aircraft, the Serbs provoked an escalation by NATO aircraft, which destroyed Bosnian Serb air defence radars around Bihac two days later.[36]

At the outset, the air strikes were euphorically welcomed by the media: 'The time of empty threats is over!'[37] But the Serb reaction was disastrous for both NATO and the UN, and the press speculated about the end of UNPROFOR – 'UN out of Bosnia?'.[38]

Bosnian Serb counter-measures – provocations like blocking UNPROFOR freedom of movement, taking hostages, activating Sam-2/ Sam-6 anti-aircraft missiles – made it practically impossible even to continue routine NATO air surveillance or humanitarian flights. Later, NATO itself was in trouble: NATO's ambassadors failed to reach agreement on a US plan for demilitarizing the Bihac area, not least because NATO governments refused to provide enough ground troops to implement such a plan.

Addressing demands for 'tough action', Boutros-Ghali expressed reservations, because of 'the danger that peacekeeping in former Yugoslavia will end in the same humiliating way as the UN mission to Somalia'.[39]

Again, in May/June 1995, the UN ran through a phase of humiliation through hostage-taking following the NATO airstrikes. On 25 May 1995, NATO bombed strategic targets – Bosnian Serb ammunition depots near Pale. NATO had proposed these strategic targets already during the events mentioned above in Autumn 1994, but at the time the UN rejected NATO's proposal. UNPROFOR wanted to maintain the principle of appropriate use of force in self-defence only against the origin of a violation and not to relinquish impartiality by hitting strategic targets.[40]

This time, the UNPROFOR commander in Sarajevo asked for NATO airstrikes against targets near Pale, after a first ultimatum against Bosnian Serbs to return heavy weapons they had removed from UN collection sites ran out by noon on 25 May 1995. Another ultimatum was given for noon on 26 May 1995. According to news reports from Sarajevo, the air attack took place about two hours before the deadline of the second ultimatum to return the weapons had expired.[41] However, NATO and the UNPROFOR HQ in Sarajevo explained that the second attack was 'a reaction to the shelling of Tuzla', rather than a premature strike due to the ultimatum.[42] We mention these details to exemplify the sensitive dynamic of the enforcement-chaos vicious circle, rather than to establish whether the second air strike was premature or not. In any case, the Bosnian Serbs, presented themselves – with public support from the Pope of the Serbian Orthodox Church – as victims of an unjust attack, declared UNPROFOR an 'enemy' and took some 370 UNPROFOR soldiers as hostages.

The enforcement-chaos vicious circle II: Ineffective threat of using force with counter-productive consequences

Another example is the case of the 'Safe Areas'. Their background is outlined thoroughly in other chapters by Lt. Gen. Wahlgren and other prominent co-authors.[43] Here we mention only some characteristics of the Safe Area orders. The UNSC declared Safe Areas without providing UNPROFOR with the 34,000[44] troops which the UNFC had required to establish defensible SAs through an agreed demilitarization, with a buffer zone between the parties controlled and defended by the UN. This UNPROFOR proposal, which had already been implemented in Srebrenica in April 1994, was rejected by the Security Council in Summer 1994. Instead, the Council decided for a 'light option' with about 7,600 troops,[45] of those, less than 5,000 arrived within a year's time.[46]

Instead of providing sufficient peacekeepers to separate the warring parties, action by Bosnian government troops inside the SAs and NATO airstrikes were supposed to 'protect' the Safe Areas, which were monitored by a few UN Military Observers. The horrible outcome of this procedure in Srebrenica is well known. Part of the tragedy is the fact that UN commanders were not taken seriously when they predicted that the Security Council's concept would be a danger rather than a protection for the Muslim population in the Safe Areas.[47]

Avoiding the enforcement-chaos vicious circle I: Use of force in self-defence

The Tuzla battle. There are examples of the robust use of military force, applied according to peacekeeping rules. By the end of April 1994, Danish tanks were involved in a fierce fight with a Bosnian Serb artillery unit which, after attacking Muslim positions, suddenly launched a massive attack on a UN post (NORBAT). The incident is worth studying carefully under the aspect of the type of forces and in particular the type of training required for self-defence in a violent environment according to PKO ROE:

> *Use of force in self-defence only.* The Danes acted as they had been trained for PKO tasks. The Danish unit gave from the very beginning of the attack clear warnings to the Serbs, also by demonstratively illuminating their own white-painted Leopard tanks. Only after the Serb position continued firing against NORBAT positions, the Danish unit fired several dozen shells precisely on the attacking Serbian position. In order to act with transparency and restraint, the

Danish unit neither asked for close air support nor did it react in revenge.

Impartiality. Prior to the 'battle' the Danes had proven their impartiality, by providing humanitarian help and protection to Muslims in Tuzla and to the Serbs by protecting Serbian school children with armoured transportation and by building a road out of reach of snipers.

Consent. After the shoot-out, the Danish commander immediately communicated with the Serb side to clarify that the Serb unit had broken its commitment not to attack UNPROFOR. The Serb commander accepted this, and although the massive Danish reaction led reportedly to many Serb casualties, the battle did not escalate further, nor did the Serbs seek revenge.[48]

According to *Newsweek*, this massive Danish reaction to Serb attack was criticized by UN officials. UNPROFOR Commander Michael Rose, however, endorsed the Danish action a few days later at a meeting with Nordic Defence Ministers in Korsør, 2 May 1994 as being in full compliance with the UN principles of impartiality and minimal use of force in selfdefence, and an example to learn from.

Avoiding the enforcement-chaos vicious circle II: 'Impartial' show of force

The Sarajevo Agreement of February 1994. NATO's 'Sarajevo Ultimatum' of 9 February 1994, after a UN request to establish a Total Exclusion Zone, was more balanced and impartial than the public perceived it to be. In addition, it was followed up by the mediation efforts of the UN Force Commander in Bosnia which gave Sarajevo months of relief.

While the NATO ultimatum demanded 'all' sides to withdraw their heavy weapons 20 kilometres from Sarajevo, the Bosnian-Serb capital Pale, only three kilometres away, was explicitly excluded; Pale could keep its heavy tanks. One Serb worry, shared in NATO and in UNPROFOR, was to avoid Muslim infantry infiltrating and capturing areas held and populated by Serbs, and thus provoking a continuation of the fighting in and around Sarajevo.

The ultimatum would not have worked without both the strict impartiality of General Sir Michael Rose and the reassurance to the Serbs by 'partial' Russian peacekeepers who denied the Bosnian Muslim infantry opportunity to move into Serb positions where heavy weapons were to be removed. Eventually, this procedure led to the implementation of an UNPROFOR-brokered agreement of 9 February 1994 between the Bosnian

Muslim and Bosnian Serb army. The agreement included not only the removal of heavy weapons from the Sarajevo area but also resupply with water and energy, leading to months of relief for the suffering city. Sir Michael Rose gives more information about this phase of relative peace around Sarajevo in his chapter.[49]

Unfortunately, the successful peacemaking effort of the UN Force Commander was not accompanied by a political follow-up by the international community to bring the conflicting parties to a political compromise.[50] Consequently, though the peacekeeping force was able to gain time to conclude political agreement it could not compensate for the failure to do so.

Summary of lessons learned

These examples concerning the 'enforcement-chaos vicious circle' illustrate the difficult balance between self-defence or the 'impartial' show of force to back up peacekeeping on the one hand, and putting the entire peacekeeping mission under risk by using force deliberately to penalize particular parties to the conflict on the other.[51]

The enforcement-chaos vicious circle was entered whenever the 'Mogadishu line' was crossed – by air attacks on 'strategic' targets like air defence radars or ammunition depots. These were perceived by the Bosnian Serbs as 'unjust', because similar non-compliance by the other parties to the conflict were not punished by NATO airstrikes. Regularly, the consequences were reprisal, hostage-taking, and a process of deterioration.

The use of force in self-defence, even if carried out decisively, did not harm the peacekeeping operation, provided the general attitude of the troops was in accordance with the principles of peacekeeping.

Under hostile circumstances, a peacekeeping force can also play an active and successful role of mediation in the mission area, if there are defined areas controlled by the parties. This allows demilitarized buffer zones controlled by the peacekeeping force. The same applies to the Safe Area concept – as initially mediated in Srebrenica by the UNPROFOR Force Commander Wahlgren – designed in a similar pattern of defined territories and buffer zones.

Impartial peacemaking activities by the UN force can only succeed if political actors in the international community are also joining together in bringing about political agreements. Impartial peacemaking fails if major external actors can be played on by the parties to the conflict or even side politically or militarily with one of the parties.

UNPROFOR's situation did not favour peacemaking through mediation. UNPROFOR was under frequent pressure to relinquish impartiality by using force to coerce. And in those cases where UNPROFOR succeeded in brokering agreements, they were not followed by joint efforts to bring about a comprehensive settlement. The same happened to most agreements which had been brokered by the international mediators.

In our comments above, we have analysed the enforcement setting of the peacekeeping scene as one conceptual obstacle for UNPROFOR. In the following section, we analyse another conceptual obstacle which hobbled UNPROFOR from the very beginning: the decision by the EC in Summer 1991 never to accept any 'new borders' even if they were agreed upon by the parties.

This position reduced the room to manoeuvre of any mediator and broker to find a compromise between parties, and made agreements creating traditional peacekeeping 'buffer zones' nearly impossible, as described in the beginning of this chapter.

However, there are exceptions, cases where UNPROFOR peacemaking efforts were in harmony with parallel joint diplomatic endeavours of the international community. Examples are the cease-fire at the beginning of the Croat-Muslim Federation in Spring 1994, and the cease-fire of October 1995, setting the scene for the Dayton Agreement.

The impact of recognition on peacemaking and peacekeeping

Recognition and internationalization of conflict

Initially, the European discussion of possible recognition of former Yugoslav republics had a strong link to current German history. Recognition was understood as an acknowledgement of the right of 'self-determination' which the Germans would carry out in 1990 through the unification of the two German states. German opinion equated the term 'self-determination' with two wholly dissimilar situations – German unification, which was negotiated by agreement between the two German states, their neighbours and the big powers – and the dissolution of Yugoslavia in disagreement among the component republics. Few Germans were aware of the basic differences between the Yugoslav separation and German unification.

Later, the discussion was influenced by the heavy force the Yugoslav army used to prevent secession from Yugoslavia. The separatist governments were recognized, although they neither had full control over the claimed territory [52] nor acceptance by relevant ethnic minorities on their territory. This contradicted established international practice.

In practical terms, the EC decision of 16 December 1991 to recognize the independence of former Yugoslav republics applying for it, 'created new international law', and the international community eventually accepted it.[53] This does not mean the existence of an internationally accepted right of secession, which must be accorded by the state from which a seceder would like to separate.[54] Lord Owen argued that democracies too would defend their integrity against secession, but democratic leadership would probably weigh carefully between compromise and fighting.[55]

Recognition made the emerging states and their borders a subject of legal protection by the international community. Thus the violent internal conflict between the Yugoslav republics and the Yugoslav Federal Republic became an 'international' rather than intra-state war.

In contrast to this, the 'internationalization policy' was not pursued in the case of the follow-up conflicts between sovereignty claims of the now former Yugoslav republics and similar claims of minority nations inside their new borders. Neither the Serbs in Croatia, the Croats and Serbs in Bosnia-Herzegovina, nor the Albanians in Serbia received the same reward from the international community for their claim of self-determination as did Slovenia, Croatia, Bosnia and Macedonia. Consequently, the original conflict about the borders of the Yugoslav Federation was transformed into a similar conflict about the borders of the newly independent successor states.

In a memorandum of 13 July 1991 to the European Community (EC) governments, the Dutch EC presidency proposed overcoming this dilemma by proposing a mandate to mediate compromises about peaceful changes of the internal Yugoslav borders prior to their eventual international recognition as part of a regulated divorce between the Yugoslav nations. The EC presidency stated in the paper that the right of self-determination should not be applied selectively to the existing Yugoslav republics without applying it to the national minorities inside these republics.[56] Germany and the other EC governments rejected the Dutch proposal because it would 'open a Pandora's box', and because borders following ethnic settlements were outdated.[57]

Lord Owen commented that the refusal of the EC to negotiate agreements about the internal borders of the Yugoslav republics was one of the worst possible mistakes in the process of 'premature recognition'. He argued that the refusal impaired EC crisis management in Summer 1991 and affected adversely all further peace negotiations after September 1991.[58]

In early December 1991, two weeks before the EU decision to grant recognition to the former Yugoslav republics, UN Secretary-General Pérez de Cuéllar and the EU mediator, Lord Carrington, warned that premature recognition would contribute to the escalation of violence. Lord Carrington feared in particular that recognition of Bosnia-Herzegovina would eventually contribute to 'set Bosnia-Herzegovina alight'. In addition, the United Nations would have to consider 'responsibility for indefinite peacekeeping' (see Box 3.2).

Box 3.2 Lord Carrington's letter of 2 December 1991 to Dutch Foreign Minister, Hans van den Broek

> 8 KING STREET
> ST. JAMES'S
> LONDON SW1Y 6QT
>
> 2 December 1991
>
> Dear Hans:
>
> ...I think it right to put my views on paper and hope perhaps that you will find it possible to circulate them to your EC colleagues.
>
> On 4th October we agreed with the three Yugoslav principals that recognition would be granted within the framework of an overall settlement of the Yugoslav problem – a position subsequently endorsed by the EC...
>
> An early recognition of Croatia would undoubtedly mean a break-up of the conference, as I cannot see that the Serbs would be prepared in those circumstances to continue, nor would the Croats and Slovenes be much interested in its continuance.
>
> There is also a real danger, perhaps even a probability, that Bosnia-Herzegovina would also ask for independence and recognition, which would be wholly unacceptable for the Serbs in that republic, in which there are something like 100,000 JNA troops, some of whom have withdrawn there from Croatia. Milosevic has hinted that military action would take place there if Croatia and Slovenia were recognized. This might well be the spark that sets Bosnia-Herzegovina alight.
>
> Recognition would also call into question the role of the peacekeeping force which would be deployed in the context of a continuing peace conference. Ministers would no doubt like to consider how the UN would view the situation in which there was no political machinery to achieve a settlement whilst they had the responsibility for indefinite peacekeeping.
>
> Yours
>
> Peter (Carrington)

Operational implications of 'premature recognition'

Our mention here of these early warnings by Lord Carrington, as well as the warning by former UN Secretary-General Pérez de Cuéllar in an exchange of letters with the EC (see Box 3.3) against 'premature recognition' is not intended to weigh the rights or wrongs of recognition. This task can be left to the historians.

In the context of this book, however, we analyse recognition of the seceding Yugoslav republics with respect to the operational implications of recognition for UN peacekeeping operations.

Recognition undermined the principle of impartiality of UN troops and limited their capability to negotiate agreements like cease-fires and buffer zone agreements between normally equally accepted parties to a conflict controlling their respective territories or areas. Lord Owen's comment concerning the change of borders according to ethnic settlements should be seen in this context.

The July 1991 decision of the EC not to mediate peaceful changes of the then internal borders of Yugoslavia before recognition was granted was highly relevant from a peacekeeping point of view. This was indicated by Lord Carrington with his warning against 'indefinite peacekeeping'.

The principle not to negotiate borders made mediation of a compromise between nations fighting for 'self-determination' extremely difficult, in particular when they fought in behalf of living together in coherent geographical territories 'suddenly' separated by international borders along formerly irrelevant internal borders. Shifting from a majority or equal status into a minority status under a now 'foreign' government made the situation even worse where nationalist leaders united 'their' ethnic group by a simple message to the other: 'Why should I be a minority in your state when you can be a minority in mine?'[59]

As a matter of fact, only when the 'no change' principle was violated in the later stage of the war, did peace agreements become possible.

Box 3.3 Exchange of letters between the UN Secretary-General and the EU Presidency, December 1991

Letter of 10 December 1991 by UN Secretary-General, Pérez de Cuéllar to Dutch Foreign Minister, Hans van den Broek, President of the EC Council of Ministers

The Secretary-General

10 December 1991

His Excellency

Mr H. van den Broek
Minister for Foreign Affairs of the
Kingdom of the Netherlands

Dear Foreign Minister,
I wish to share with you concerns which I have in regard to the situation in
Yugoslavia.
These concerns have been deepened by the report that I have just received from
my Personal Envoy, Mr Cyrus R. Vance who returned last evening from a
fourth mission to Yugoslavia. They have also been deepened by the outcome of
yesterday's informal meeting of the Presidents of the six Yugoslav republics,
which Lord Carrington convened in The Hague in his capacity as Chairman of
the Conference on Yugoslavia.
I shall shortly be reporting to the Security Council on the outcome of Mr
Vance's mission. As far as the United Nations peacekeeping operation in
Yugoslavia is concerned, difficulties persist – owing to the fact that the Geneva
agreement of 23 November is not being fully implemented. A paper
comprising a concept and operational plan of a potential peacekeeping
operation has, however, been left with the principal parties by Mr Vance. It has
met with a wide measure of agreement from them.[60]
In his report to me yesterday, Mr Vance has described widely expressed
apprehensions about the possibility of premature recognition of the
independence of some of the Yugoslav republics and the effect that such a
move might have on the remaining republics. Leaders of Bosnia-Herzegovina
and Macedonia were among the many political and military figures who last
week underscored to Mr Vance their strong fears in this regard. More than one
of his high-level interlocutors described the possibly explosive consequences
of such a development as being a 'potential time bomb'.
Given these anxieties, I believe that the Twelve were correct when they
reiterated, at their special EPC Ministerial meeting held in Rome on 8
November, that the prospect of recognition of the independence of those
republics wishing it, 'can only be envisaged in the framework of an overall
settlement...'. As we know, that overall settlement is being pursued by the
Conference on Yugoslavia under the Chairmanship of Lord Carrington.
Let me be clear: I am not in any way calling into question the principle of self-
determination which is enshrined in the Charter of the United Nations.
However, I am deeply worried that any early, selective recognition could
widen the present conflict and fuel an explosive situation especially in Bosnia-
Herzegovina and also in Macedonia; indeed, serious consequences could ensue
for the entire Balkan region. I believe, therefore, that uncoordinated actions
should be avoided.
I should be grateful if you could bring my concerns to the attention of your
partners among the Twelve, given the particular responsibility of the United
Nations for the maintenance of international peace and security.
Please accept, dear Foreign Minister, the assurances of my highest
considerations.

(signed) Javier Pérez de Cuéllar

Answering letter of 13 December by Hans-Dietrich Genscher, Foreign Minister of Germany, to the UNSG Pérez de Cuéllar (unofficial translation)[61]

Dear Secretary-General,

Foreign Minister van den Broek has brought your letter to my attention and that of the other Foreign Ministers' of the European Community. I would like to express my deepest concern that the formulations used in the letter and its publication in the interim are likely to encourage those forces in Yugoslavia who until now have strongly resisted a successful conclusion of the peace process. According to the assessment of the European Community and the Monitors, the Serbian leadership and the Yugoslav Peoples Army share the main responsibility for non-compliance with the cease-fires and for the stagnation of the Yugoslavia Conference in The Hague for several weeks.

To refuse the recognition of those republics who wish independence would necessarily lead to further escalation of violence by the Peoples Army because it would feel confirmed in its policy of conquest. I want to emphasize that in Europe, according to the Final Helsinki Act and the Charter of Paris, borders are inviolable and must not be changed by the use of force. The EC has therefore demanded that the internal and international borders of Yugoslavia be respected.

Let me express my confidence that the joint efforts of the United Nations, the CSCE and the European Community will finally bring peace to the peoples of Yugoslavia and provide them a prosperous future.

Yours sincerely
(signed) Hans-Dietrich Genscher

Answering letter of 14 December 1991 by UNSG Pérez de Cuéllar to Foreign Minister Hans-Dietrich Genscher

The Secretary-General

14 December 1991

His Excellency
Mr Hans-Dietrich Genscher
Vice-Chancellor and Minister for Foreign Affairs
of the Federal Republic of Germany, Bonn

Dear Mr Minister,

I have received your letter of 13 December in which you refer to mine of the 10th to Minister van den Broek, current President of the EC Council of Ministers.

I agree with you that public statements can exacerbate the tensions in Yugoslavia. That is why mine have been few and carefully considered.

Let me recall that at no point did my letter state that recognition of the independence of particular Yugoslav Republics should be denied, or withheld indefinitely. Rather, I observe that the principle of self-determination is enshrined in the United Nations Charter itself. The concern that I continue to have relates to the prospect of early, selective and uncoordinated recognition. In this connection, I cannot but note the omission from your letter of any reference to the common position adopted by you and your colleagues of the Twelve at the Special Ministerial EPC Meeting held at Rome on 8 November 1991. You will recall that the Declaration issued by the Twelve on that occasion stated that 'the prospect of recognition of the independence of those Republics wishing it, can only be envisaged in the framework of an overall settlement'.

Furthermore, you will no doubt be aware of the contents of the letter sent by Lord Carrington, Chairman of the Conference on Yugoslavia, on 2 December to Minister van den Broek in which Lord Carrington stated that early and selective recognition 'would undoubtedly lead to the break-up of the Conference'.

I trust also that you will have learned of the deep concern that has been expressed by the Presidents of Bosnia-Herzegovina and Macedonia, as well as by many others, that early selective recognition could result in a widening of the present conflict to those sensitive areas. Such a development could have grave consequences for the Balkan region as a whole, and it would seriously undermine my own efforts and those of my Personal Envoy to secure conditions necessary for the deployment of a peacekeeping operation in Yugoslavia.

I am confident that you will understand that in view of my responsibilities under the Charter, I am duty bound to express such concerns when they are also my own.

Needless to say, I am entirely in agreement with you in supporting the principle set out in the Helsinki Final Act and the Charter of Paris that rules out changes of borders by force. That principle also flows from the provisions of the United Nations Charter.

Please accept, Mr Minister, the assurances of my highest consideration.

(signed) Javier Pérez de Cuéllar

Successful agreements contrary to the EU premises but compatible with traditional peacekeeping

All successfully negotiated agreements in former Yugoslavia included in one way or another a compromise over 'new borders' according to ethnic settlements or military lines of confrontation, at least in preliminary form. Consequently, they were implementable by traditional peacekeeping methods as quoted from the *Peacekeeper's Handbook* in the beginning of this chapter. Typical elements of implementation were buffer zones and demilitarization of the zones of separation.

These operational concepts of peacekeeping were essential for successful activities of UNPROFOR as well as IFOR/SFOR. Referring to the Second UN Commanders' Workshop of April 1996, the Danish Defence Minister, Hans Hækkerup concluded:

> ...classic peacekeeping tasks and techniques, as separation of forces and interposition, appears to remain indispensable prerequisites even for the new 'second generation peacekeeping', if peacekeeping is used as an active instrument bringing about the basis for control and resolution of conflicts. ...The conclusion of the Washington framework agreement of 1 March 1994 and the later establishment of the Muslim–Croat Federation is described as setting the scene for a classic peacekeeping operation in which forces can be separated and fighting brought to a conclusion, and the October 1995 cease-fire, the Dayton Agreement and the subsequent deployment of the NATO-led Implementation Force made this come true.[62]

From Washington to Dayton

Successful agreements – full support. The two most important agreements in Bosnia are also in accordance with the 'buffer zone' concept of traditional peacekeeping:

> *The Washington Framework Agreement* of Spring 1994 and the later establishment of the Muslim-Croat Federation set the scene 'for a classical peacekeeping operation in which forces can be separated'. [63] Albeit fragile, the Federation continued to exist and became part of the Dayton Agreement.

> *The Dayton Agreement* of 1995 establishes a zone of separation – the Inter Entity Boundary Line (IEBL) – based on a cease-fire agreed upon by the parties with UNPROFOR in October 1995. It separates the military forces on the basis of clearly defined territories.

In case of the Washington Agreement, UNPROFOR could successfully end the Croat-Muslim war in Bosnia by separating the military forces of both sides and implementing the other provisions of the cease-fire. In case of the October 1995 cease-fire, UNPROFOR could successfully separate the military forces of the Federation and the Bosnian Serbs; by this UNPROFOR prepared an important condition for the Dayton Agreement of

November and the subsequent deployment of the NATO-led Implementation Force (IFOR) in December 1995.

Successful implementation of both the Spring 1994 and Autumn 1995 cease-fires by UNPROFOR was based on a traditional 'buffer zone' concept and *unity of policy* – the unanimous political support from the international community, in particular from the United States.

Successful agreements – failed support. The following agreements were mediated by UNPROFOR or by the international mediators with the same patterns of ethnic territories and borders:

> *The Stoltenberg–Owen Plan* of 21 September 1993 was a negotiated compromise accepted by the leaders of all three parties. It included a variety of provisions on the Bosnian constitution, human rights, the legal system and territorial agreements on zones of separation.[64] In its provisions it was very similar to the Dayton Agreement.[65] However, the Stoltenberg–Owen Plan was heavily criticised by friends of the Bosnian government as 'rewarding Serb aggression and ethnic cleansing'.[66] That agreement failed in the face of American reservations and subsequent resistance of the Bosnian Muslim parliament.[67] Consequently, the war and further ethnic cleansing continued until the Dayton Agreement [68] stopped the fighting.
>
> The first *Safe Area* in April 1994 was successfully agreed and initially implemented in Srebrenica, including a classic borderline with a zone of separation, demilitarization and a UN buffer force. Three months later, in June 1994, the UNSC dismissed the concept and decided to accept deployment only of Government troops inside the Area.[69] Thereafter, Srebrenica was the object of heavy fighting, and was later stormed by Bosnian Serbs, killing or ethnically cleansing the Muslim population.

These agreements, although agreed upon by the parties and implementable with the traditional buffer force concept, finally 'failed' after they were rejected by the major powers. The result of this discord was in each case a consequent disaster for the people concerned, and left UNPROFOR as a peacekeeping force without an appropriate mandate, looking impotent against the escalation of war and ethnic cleansing.

By not permitting compromise agreements on the borders of areas that were controlled by the conflicting parties, the international community prohibited a situation necessary for successful peacekeeping. A peacekeeping force was logically not appropriate for establishing borders of territories that were recognized by the international community, but not accepted by the parties controlling large parts of them. At the end, the parties created their territories by war.

Paradoxically, this provided the international community with a favourable basis for traditional peacekeeping – buffer zones controlled by the UN peacekeeping force, separating the parties each controlling 'their' territory – at the time when NATO took over the command from the UN. That created a new challenge: NATO had to adapt its doctrine to the new tasks.

Traditional peacekeeping and military doctrine developments

Contrary to the debate in the public and in the political establishment, military doctrines concerning peacekeeping in civil war-like conflicts tend to a 'more cautious and restrictive practice' and the 'avoidance of an unintended mixture of peacekeeping and peace enforcement operations'.[70] The Somalia experience was a turning point in this regard. In addition, the UNPROFOR experience with the above-mentioned events in Bosnia after NATO airstrikes in November 1994 led also to further reconsideration of peacekeeping principles, as a comment by the NATO Secretary-General of November 1994 shows:

> I do not believe (...) that we can pursue decisive peace enforcement from the air while the UN is led, deployed and equipped for peacekeeping on the ground. If we have learned anything from this conflict, it is that we cannot mix these two missions...[71]

These conclusions correspond with the traditional UN view, reconfirmed by the UN Secretary-General's 'Supplement to An Agenda for Peace' (January 1995), stating that it is 'important to avoid mandating enforcement tasks to a peacekeeping mission'.[72] This trend is also reflected in doctrinal developments in the US and the UK. Traditionally, the US doctrine focused 'on war-fighting as the primary role of armies, in distinction to British and Canadian concepts',[73] and on resort 'to the overwhelming use of military force as a solution'.[74] The earlier US Army doctrine advocated peacekeeping as only one element in the full spectrum of escalation.

This attitude changed, however, after the lessons learned in Somalia.[75]

Meanwhile, impartiality and consent [76] – which by nature limit the use of force – have become central principles for successful peacekeeping also in the latest American doctrine adopted after 1994.

The British doctrine of 'Wider Peacekeeping' is based on the evaluation of a wide range of British experience in violent environments, including operations like UNPROFOR. It gives concrete operational examples for the application of consent (as a guiding principle), impartiality and (deviating to some extent from the UN principle 'use of force in self-defence only') for the 'minimal use of force' on the tactical and operational level in a mission: An example concerning the 'impartial' use of force on the tactical level is the following:

> The principle of impartiality will also offer guidance on whether and how force might be employed. Force may be used impartially in large measure to protect a humanitarian convoy. However, the bombing or arming of particular factions would clearly abandon impartiality, since it would deliberately penalize or favour particular parties to the conflict.[77]

The British doctrine states a clear dividing line between peacekeeping and enforcement, but goes beyond the stricter application by the UN of the principle of using force in self-defence only.

According to UK precepts, enforcement, however, would 'require substantial force restructuring and redeployment, evacuation of unarmed monitors and civilian workers, and the termination of humanitarian operations'.[78] This scenario, written in early 1994, corresponds precisely to the situation of UNPROFOR during the above-mentioned rounds of air strikes and hostage-taking in May/June 1995. It took two years of bitter experience before the above doctrinal lessons were applied in Summer 1995. After these events of hostage-taking, UN Military Observers were withdrawn, and the rapid reaction force was deployed under the British UN commander in Sarajevo. This phase of enforcement was possible after peacekeeping activity was ended through the withdrawal of the peacekeepers from Bosnian Serb areas.

The US Army doctrine emphasizes the psychological and potentially disastrous political implications of crossing the dividing line between peacekeeping and enforcement. The US Field Manual warns against the confusion that can arise when it 'is often incorrectly assumed that they (peacekeeping and peace enforcement) are part of a continuum.[79] There is a broad demarcation between these operations'. The commanders are reminded that the 'goal is to produce conditions which are conducive to peace and not to destroy an enemy'.

In general, British, American and NATO manuals on peacekeeping look more like modifications of peacekeeping procedures and mediation techniques in order to cope with civil war-like conflicts, rather than advocacy of war-fighting concepts.

With respect to operations in civil war-like conflicts, this doctrinal-conceptual development applies also to the WEU since its 'Petersberg Declaration'. Former WEU Secretary-General Willem van Eekelen describes appropriate peacekeeping as 'a moderate policing concept rather than a war-fighting concept'.[80] The WEU found a niche and developed competence by participating in police-type operations like embargo control on the Danube river and in the Adriatic Sea, organizing the WEU police under the EU administration for Mostar 1994/1995, and the OSCE-mandated operation 'ALBA' in Albania from April to August 1997 to protect humanitarian supply and provide security during the elections in July 1997.

NATO too worked on developing appropriate doctrine. There have been joint efforts in NACC which established a clearing-house to support professionalization of military, political and humanitarian peacekeepers, including international standardization of training, equipment and operations.[81] The January 1994 Brussels summit confirmed NATO's determination to take on new missions and decided to establish a new military mechanism, Combined Joint Task Forces (CJTFs), to carry out such missions. CJTFs were conceived as mobile headquarters that could be detached from their normal roles within the integrated military structure.

This does not mean that these structures are only planned for missions similar to United Nations peacekeeping. Obviously NATO wants to keep the option for all kinds of out-of-area operations. NATO's military doctrine for 'Peace Support Operations', however, has not changed since December 1995 and is clearly in broad conformity with UN peacekeeping principles.[82] Far from changing it, according to NATO's evaluation of lessons learned from the IFOR/SFOR experience, these lessons confirmed NATO's peacekeeping doctrine. A revival of key peacekeeping principles seems to be evident, despite the short period of offensive NATO operations, that is deliberate force, in Autumn 1995.

Support for peacekeeping is also a question of resources. While the overall costs for UNPROFOR, including civilian and police personnel, amounted to 1.124 billion US dollars in 1993 and 1.900 billion in 1994,[83] the costs for the NATO-led force amounted to about 5.0 billion US dollars in 1996 and 4.0 billion US dollars in 1997.[84] These high costs could explain the revival of peacekeeping in general and possibly of peacekeeping under UN command again in the future. In the US Defense Department too, peacekeeping is perceived as a comparatively cheap and efficient investment: 'The more effective an international peacekeeping capability becomes, the more conflicts can be prevented or contained, and the fewer reasons there will be for Americans to fight abroad.'[85]

In Part Two of this book, we give a summary of the discussion of lessons learned by military commanders during two UN Commanders' Workshops, the research project organized in Spring 1995 and 1996. These reports are followed by the results of a survey among some one thousand officers, presenting a summary of their views on possibilities and limits of peacekeepers under conditions of one of the most difficult UN operations ever organized.

Part Three of the book presents accounts by people who had the burden of responsibility for the UN operation in various leading positions during the United Nations peacekeeping operation in the former Yugoslavia.

Notes

1 International Peace Academy, *Peacekeeper's Handbook*, Pergamon Press: New York, 1984, p. 31.
2 Common characteristics of UNPROFOR and ONUC are a/o that they were operations to an intra-state conflict (secession of Katanga), extensive humanitarian tasks for the UN and e.g. Safe Areas for refugees during an ongoing war; different is the fact that in the case of the Congo the UN took sides against the secessionist state (Katanga) while in the case of Yugoslavia the UN had to respect that the secessionist states (Croatia, Bosnia and Macedonia) were recognized and had become members of the United Nations.
3 Durch, William (ed.), *The Evolution of UN Peacekeeping, Case Studies and Comparative Analyses*, St. Martin's Press: New York, 1993, p. 8; for details see in: W. Durch, 'The UN Operation in the Congo 1960–1964', in ibid., p. 315 ff.
4 Berdal, Mats R., *Fateful Encounter: The US and UN Peacekeeping*, Survival Vol. 36, no. 1/1994, p. 30.
5 Up to 1984, the *Peacekeeper's Handbook* lists the following UN Peacekeeping Operations, authorized by the UNSC or the UN General Assembly, as missions to conflicts with intra-state characteristics: ONUC (Congo, 1960–1964), UNFICYP (Cyprus 1964–), UNIFIL (Lebanon, 1978–), UNOGIL (Lebanon, 1958), UNYOM (Yemen, 1963–1964), DOMREP (Dominican Republic 1965–1966); ibid., p. 41ff.
6 *Peacekeeper's Handbook*, ibid., p. 22 (emphasis by the authors). The same definition was used in documents of the NAA, in *Peacekeeping & International Relations*, March/April 1994, p. 17, in: *Rose-Roth Seminar on The Theory and Practice of 'Peacekeeping'*, Background Document, North Atlantic Assembly: London, 21–23 February 1994.
7 *Peacekeeper's Handbook*, ibid., p. 39.
8 Ibid., p. 35.
9 Ibid., pp. 23 and 31.
10 Ibid., p. 31 (emphasis by the authors).
11 Ibid., p. 32ff and p. 361ff.
12 UN Document GA/Res/49/59 84th Plenary Meeting 9 December 1994, Article 2 (2).
13 See Lavoyer, Chapter 16 in this book.
14 See e.g. UN Resolutions No. 713, 724, 757, 770, 781, etc.
15 Kühne, Winrich (ed.), *Blauhelme in einer turbulenten Welt*, Nomos: Baden-Baden, 1993, p. 51ff.

16 Solli, Per Erik, in *UN and NATO air power in the former Yugoslavia*, NUPI Report No. 209, October 1996, p. 19.
17 Syse, Henrik, "'Rettferdig krig' – moralske refleksjoner", *Aftenposten*, 23 March 1997.
18 'UN Report', Friday 3 June, *Wireless File*, US Information Service Press Section: No 104, June 3, 1994; see also Boutros-Ghali interview in *Der Spiegel*, 6 June 1994.
19 IISS, *The Military Balance 1997/98*, Oxford University Press: London, 1997, p. 275. Concerning Danish initiatives to strengthen the UN Stand-by regime, see Hækkerup, Chapter 18 in this book. Nordic nations were among the first to increase the contribution to the UN Stand-by Force, see *Beredskap for fred: Om Norges framtidige militære FN-engagement*, St. meld. nr. 14 (1992–93).
20 United Nations Observer Missions in Georgia (UNOMIG) and in Tajikistan (UNMOT), see: *The Military Balance 1997/98*, ibid., p. 281ff.
At a peacekeeping conference in Moscow, Russian defence ministry officials expressed their wish to have Canadian and Austrian battalions deployed in the CIS and to be represented in Command positions (Moscow Conference, *Partnership for Peacekeeping*, June 22, 1994).
21 Boutros-Ghali, Boutros, *An Agenda for Peace, Preventive Diplomacy, Peacemaking and Peacekeeping*, United Nations: New York, 1992.
22 Boutros-Ghali, Boutros, 'Supplement to an Agenda for Peace', *An Agenda for Peace, 2nd edition*, United Nations: New York, 1995, p. 14.
23 Weiss, Thomas G., 'Problems for Future U.N. Military Operations in An Agenda for Peace', in Kühne, Winrich (ed.), *Blauhelme in einer turbulenten Welt*, Nomos Verlag, Baden-Baden, 1993, p. 177ff.
24 See UN Commanders' Workshops, summarized in Chapters 4 and 5 in this book.
25 The term *feasibility gap* plays a prominent role in our analysis of the UNPROFOR survey in Chapter 6 of this book.
26 See 'UN Peacekeeping: Lessons Learned in Managing Recent Missions'; *Report to Congressional Requesters*, US General Accounting Office: Washington DC, December 1993.
27 See e.g. Berdal, *Whither UN Peacekeeping*, Adelphi Paper 281, October 1993, p. 26 ff.
28 See Rose, Chapter 9 in this book.
29 According to John Mackinlay, even under the aspect of protecting own soldiers only, national interference may be counterproductive because it *'reduces effectiveness by national interests'* ('Successful Intervention' in *International Spectator*, Vol. 47, November 1993, No. 11, p. 659).
30 See e.g. 'Chaos in Somalia Overwhelms Efforts to Build a Nation-State', *International Herald Tribune*, 6 September 1994.
31 Mentioned in interviews with UNPROFOR personnel and discussed at UN Commanders' Workshops, summarized in Chapters 4 and 5 in this book.
32 See in particular Wahlgren and Egmond, Chapters 10 and 17 in this book.
33 See Chapters 4, 8 and 10 in this book.
34 See Chapters 7 to 10, and the interview with Stoltenberg (Chapter 2).
35 Sources: 'UN And NATO In Struggle Over Bosnia', *Financial Times*, 26/27 November 1994; 'No Extra Troops For UN Force', *The Independent*, 21 December 1994; Volker Rühe, 'Zu den Beratungen der NATO-Verteidigungsminister über das weitere Vorgehen in Bosnien', Interview in *ARD Morgenmagazin*, 14 December 1994; 'Generalstabschefs schließen weitere Truppenentsendung aus', *FAZ*, 21 October 1994; 'UN Commanders Agree on Sharpening Troops' Effectiveness', *IHT*, 21 December 1994; 'Cease-Fire Or Not, Outlook For Bosnia Bleaker Than Ever', *IHT*, 23 December 1994; 'Croatia Raises Fears Of New War', *FT*, 13 January 1995.

36 *NATO's role in peacekeeping in the former Yugoslavia*, NATO Fact Sheet No. 4, March 1997.
37 'Überfälliges Signal', *Die Welt*, 22 November 1994; 'Die Zeit der leeren Drohungen ist vorbei', *Frankfurter Neue Presse*, 22 November 1994.
38 'FN ut av Bosnia?', *Arbeiderbladet* (Norway), 26 January 1995.
39 'No extra troops for UN force', *The Independent*, 21 December 1994.
40 Interviews at UNPF HQ in Zagreb, November 1995.
41 *dpa*, No. 0175, 0188, 26 May 1995.
42 *dpa*, No. 109, 30 August 1995; Interviews in UNPROFOR HQ, November 1995.
43 Detailed description of legal as well as operational implications of the Safe Areas are given by Lavoyer, Wahlgren, Chapters 10 and 16; concerning the political implications, see Akashi, Chapter 7 and other contributions by force commanders in Part Three of this book.
44 *Report of the Secretary-General 14 June 1993*, UN Document S/25939.
45 UN Document UNSC Resolution 844 (1993); further see *The UN and the Situation in Former Yugoslavia*, Reference Paper, 23 January 1995, UN Document UN DPI/1312/ Rev.2 and Add. 1 -January 1995- 3M, p. 15 ff.
46 See interview with Thorvald Stoltenberg in this book.
47 See 1st UN Commanders' Conference, Chapter 4 in this book.
48 Interviews with a high-ranking official from the Danish Ministry of Defence and with Danish and Norwegian officers during May 1994.
49 See Rose, Chapter 9 in this book.
50 See the criticism of the Contact Group at the 1st UN Commanders' Workshop in May 1995, Chapter 4 in this book.
51 The problem of weighing the use of force in peacekeeping is also addressed in the British Doctrine, see Army Field Manual, *Wider Peacekeeping*, Fourth Draft, Ministry of Defence: London 1994, pp. 2–12.
52 Hampson, Françoise J., 'Staatsbürgerschaft, Ethnizität, Nationalität: Haben Nationen ein Recht auf Staatenbildung' in Hans-Joachim Heintze (ed.), *Selbstbestimmungsrecht der Völker – Herausforderung der Staatenwelt*, Dietz Verlag: Bonn 1997, p. 60ff.
53 Zayas, Alfred de, 'Selbstbestimmungsrecht und Vereinte Nationen' in Heintze, ibid., p. 163.
54 Hampson, Françoise J., ibid., p. 64.
55 Owen, David, *Balkan Odyssee* (German edition), Carl Hanser Verlag, München/Wien: 1996, p. 54.
56 Owen, David, ibid., p. 47ff.
57 Owen, David, ibid.
58 Owen, David, ibid., p. 48ff.
59 The Yugoslav author Vladimir Gligorov, quoted in the preface of Susan Woodward, *Balkan Tragedy, Chaos and Dissolution after the Cold War*, The Brookings Institution: Washington DC, 1995.
60 The Secretary-General is referring to the *Vance Plan* for Croatia.
61 The unofficial English translation was prepared by the editors. The German original is in the UN archives.
62 Hans Hækkerup, Danish Defence Minister, in a letter to DANORP, 11 March 1997.
63 Hans Hækkerup, ibid., Brigadier Ridgway describes details of the successful implementation of the Washington Agreement in Chapter 13 in this book.
64 'Agreement relating to Bosnia and Herzegovina, 20 September 1993'. The agreement included a/o an Appendix I, *Constitutional Agreement* including various amendments, Appendix II, including an *Agreed Arrangements* concerning the name of the republics, UN administration for Sarajevo, EU administration for Mostar, protection of human

rights and reversal of ethnic cleansing and an Appendix III with *Military Agreements*, time tables, procedures for Joint Commissions, etc.

65 Gro Nystuen, 'The Constitution of Bosnia and Herzegovina – State versus Entities' in *Revue des Affaires Européennes*, no. 4/97 (special edition on Bosnia).

66 Statement by Vera Wollenberger, Protokoll des Deutschen Bundestages, 23 September 1993.

Similar reproaches against the Stoltenberg–Owen agreement were formulated by the Legal Adviser to President Izetbegovic, Professor Francis Boyle: 'When I was instructed by the Bosnian President Alija Izetbegovic to sue Britain in November 1993, I put out a statement at the UN announcing that the Owen-Stoltenberg Plan violated the Genocide, Racial Discrimination, and Apartheid Conventions – it clearly did.', in *Bosnia Info pages* (http://www.cco.caltech.edu/ ~bosnia/ status/status.html).

67 See interview with Thorvald Stoltenberg in the beginning of this book.

68 Also the Dayton Agreement was criticised by Francis A. Boyle: 'I am fully prepared to return to the World Court immediately for the purpose of obtaining an official order against this carve-up of the Republic of Bosnia and Herzegovina' in *Subject: The Dayton Agreement. Memorandum To the People and Parliament of the Republic of Bosnia and Herzegovina*, November 30, 1995   (http://www.xs4all.nl/~frankti/Boyle_articles/dayton.html).

69 For details see in Lt. Gen. Wahlgren's chapter.

70 Hoffman, Hansrudolf, 'Keine Alternative zur Friedenssicherung der UNO', *Neue Zürcher Zeitung*, 19 May 1994.

71 NATO Secr.-Gen. Claes, *Statement to the NAA*, 18 November 1994 in Washington DC; emphasis marked by the authors.

72 Boutros-Ghali, Boutros, *Position Paper, Supplement to An Agenda for Peace*, Executive Summary, 5 January 1995, UN Information Center for the Nordic Countries, Copenhagen.

73 Last, Major David M., 'Report on a Peace Operations Workshop held at the University of Maryland, 15–17 February 1994' in *Peacekeeping & International Relations*, March/April 1994, p. 17, in *Rose-Roth Seminar on The Theory and Practice of 'Peacekeeping'*, North Atlantic Assembly: London, 21–23 February 1994, Background Document, Annex paper.

74 John MacKinley at the London NAA Conference, 21–23 February 1994, in a statement about *Development of International Peace Forces*.

75 See *International Peacekeeping and Enforcement*, Hearing, US Congress, Senate Committee on Armed Services, Subcommittee on Coalition, Defence and Reinforcing Forces: July 14, 1993.

76 The British PKO doctrine sets consent as the central category of PKO and subordinates impartiality; The British Army interprets consent in the sense that peacekeepers have to strive for it, but not as a given fact. The principle of consent could include e.g. that a peacekeeper insists on agreed rules and that he is allowed to use moderate force if he is hindered from fulfilling the mandate agreed on by the parties, see (UK) Army Field Manual, *Wider Peacekeeping*, Fourth Draft, 1994, pp. 2–10.

77 *Wider Peacekeeping*, ibid., pp. 2–12. See also the 'Tuzla Battle' described in this chapter.

78 *Wider Peacekeeping*, ibid., pp. 2–15.

79 *FM 100-23 Peace Operations*, Version 6, 19 January 1994, HQ Dept. of the Army, W.D.C., pp. 1–3.

80 The Secretary General of WEU, Willem van Eekelen, interview with the authors in Brussels, 16 March 1994.

81 NACC appointed Denmark to establish a 'clearing-house' to co-ordinate efforts in this field.
82 The official NATO doctrine is documented in *Bi-MNC Directive for NATO Doctrine for Peace Support Operations*, PfP unclassified, 11 December 1995.
83 IISS, *The Military Balance 1994/1995*, Brassey's: London, 1994, p. 275.
84 IISS, *The Military Balance 1997/1998*, Oxford University Press: London, 1997, p. 284.
85 *International Peacekeeping and Enforcement*, Statement by US Undersecretary of Defense, G. Frank Wiesner, Hearing before the Subcommittee on Coalition Defense and Reinforcing Forces, Committee of Armed Services, US Senate: July 14, 1993, p. 17.

Part Two

FIELD EXPERIENCES, PERCEPTIONS, RECOMMENDATIONS

4 From UNPROFOR to UNPF
Peacekeeping with Peace Support but without Peace

WOLFGANG BIERMANN and MARTIN VADSET

Force Commanders' discussion, May 1995

Introduction

In May 1995, DANORP invited key UNPROFOR personnel to a first UN Commanders' Workshop in Oslo to discuss the possibilities and limits of peacekeeping in the former Yugoslavia.

The workshop took place at a critical phase of the UNPROFOR mission. However, there were some grounds for optimism. Shortly before the conference started, CNN reported that President Milosevic had agreed in informal peace talks with US mediators on the outline of a peace plan – the later Holbrooke Plan – including a draft map, the recognition of Bosnia and a certain degree of autonomy for the Republika Srpska. But a few days after the workshop, the war escalated, and the Bosnian Serbs provoked NATO airstrikes on 25 and 26 May 1995. Several hundred UN Observers were taken hostage. These events finally led to the end of the UNPROFOR mission.

This chapter describes discussion by leaders and key personnel of a UN peacekeeping force about their efforts to improve conditions for peace in an ongoing war, efforts 'guided' by a divided international community. Surprisingly, our small research project was among the first to organize an international forum where UNPROFOR Force Commanders exchanged their experiences and views. We believe the UN and key political decision makers could have avoided wrong assessments and decisions about the UNPROFOR operation if they had at an earlier stage shared collective experiences and advice from the responsible military and civilian leaders in the field.[1]

As in all interviews and surveys of the project, participants were granted non-attributed quotes. This guaranteed confidentiality and an atmosphere of openness. Participants agreed however, to publish a non-attributed report containing the main elements of discussion. The full record of the First and Second UN Commanders' Workshops (Copenhagen, April 1996) have been published as Working Papers.[2] This and the following chapter give an account of highlights with original quotes, followed by a summary of the course of discussion at each of these conferences.

Highlights from the discussion: Comments by Commanders

Political nature of the conflict

The conflict arose from the imposition of international borders which were contested. It was not so much a civil war as a fight among three factions for the right to national self-determination. Each faction was fighting for what it perceived as the survival of its own nation. Paradoxically, the government that would have had to consent to self-determination of two of the factions was itself one of the three factions...The UN (especially at Security Council level) could not decide whether it was protecting the sovereignty of a member state or the principle of self-determination. Some thought that the UN was there to protect the Bosnians; others regarded the UN as upholding the principle of sovereignty. From whom in this situation should we obtain consent to the peacekeeping operation? The goal of imposing international norms of sovereignty threatened impartiality of the peacekeepers. Each faction aimed to get political recognition for their own nation and to gain control of more territory.

Military characteristics of the conflict

The war in former Yugoslavia (FY) was fundamentally a civil war, mostly urban, and its participants employed large combined operational actions to terrorize the population. The terrain was difficult and mountainous and the weather was often very bad. The warring factions were trained for guerrilla warfare, using facilities both dispersed and underground. They were therefore not really vulnerable to air strike. The large number of warring parties (at least five in the Bihac pocket) included a banditry element.

This is fundamentally a civil, and mostly urban war, using terrorist methods: artillery guns are shelling the towns, tanks are standing very close to a school or a hospital. This practice was used more with an aim to terrorize the population, not unlike terrorist bombings, than to achieve any specific military objectives, carried out by conducting large combined operational actions.

Peacekeeping principles

The classic peacekeeping principles of consent, impartiality and use of force in self-defence remain fundamental to success.

But nations need to know how to interpret 'self-defence'. The amount of force that is used in the first weeks of a UN peacekeeping operation is key. Should it be moderate or robust? Negotiations need to be conducted consistently and the UN must be ready to use force in self-defence against all parties. Factions will tolerate the use of force in self-defence if they can see it is being done in an even-handed fashion – in an impartial way.

The diplomatic process frequently violated peacekeeping's basic principles. Political direction and diplomacy in FY was often partisan, inconsistent, inflexible and inappropriate.

Enforcement elements in the mandate

The introduction of enforcement elements into the mandate was not only a risk for the UN mission. It also influences the parties to the conflict and raised expectations of a direct military undertaking by the international community.

Use of force and force protection

The established peacekeeping process called for the separation of combatants and the establishment of defined 'blue lines' between them. The deployment of UN troops along such 'borders' was the next necessary step in order to initiate negotiations, but also to deter attack. Troop positions should be fortified in order to protect UN troops and avoid casualties. This precaution had not been taken in Croatia, which meant that UN troops were forced to withdraw when their positions had been assaulted by Croatians. A mobile reserve also needs to be established.

Protected areas in Croatia and Safe Areas in Bosnia

No UN forces were provided to implement the establishment of UN Protected Areas/Safe Areas (PAs/SAs). Given the requirement for them, the UNPAs/SAs should have been demilitarized, with a buffer zone controlled and defended by sufficient UN troops.

Instead, the UN Security Council decided that Bosnian government troops should be allowed into the Safe Areas. This led to the abuse of Safe Areas because the Bosnians used them to regroup and employed them as bases from which to attack the Bosnian Serbs.

Sanctions

Sanctions...should not simply be regarded as a means of inflicting punishment, but also be used as incentive and encouragement. Sanctions have to be applied with greater flexibility, to maintain overall consistency with UNPROFOR's operations.

Diplomacy

The Contact Group's actions were slow and cumbersome because detailed aspects of all proposals had to be agreed between the major powers first – an activity that paralyzed the diplomatic process. The approach had not proved effective, taking four or five months to come up with a proposal ...The 16-months break in active negotiations since January 1994 encouraged the Bosnian Serbs to adopt a more radical approach. The attitude of the Serbs reflected conflict between the extremists led by Karadzic and the moderates encouraged by Milosevic...Who would gain the upper hand in the Serb camp – Karadzic...or Milosevic and the moderates – remained to be seen. Diplomatic dialogue should be stimulating, inclusive and seek to integrate, not marginalize, parties to the conflict.

International diplomats pursued national interests, which made it difficult for the political head of the Mission, Mr Akashi, who was never able to predict how the international community would respond. He could have taken a much firmer line if he had known that he was going to be supported.

Military Observers (UNMOs)

UNMOs' co-operation with NGOs and UNHCR was vital...Ideally, UNMO teams were unarmed intermediaries of multi-national composition who did not represent any particular nation or interest...UNMOs enjoyed relative freedom and ease of access to warring parties...The credibility of UNMOs, however, rested only on their impartiality and neutrality.

UNMOs are accurate, cost-efficient and effective...But you cannot use UNMOs as reconnaissance troops since it will compromise their impartial status.

NATO

NATO's best contribution was its troops' common doctrine and training.

UNPROFOR's relations with NATO have been excellent...Nevertheless, co-operation between these two organizations is rendered delicate by the different, if not opposite nature of their respective cultures.

In order to act, NATO's military assets must aim at achieving a military effect...its military leader applies the principles of warfare, favours surprise and military efficiency, and thinks in terms of war. In peacekeeping missions, the military commander applies opposite principles, imposed on him by his mission, his assets and the safety of his troops.

Course of discussion – main lessons learned

In this section, we summarize from Commanders' statements the main lessons they considered they had learned from their experiences in former Yugoslavia.

Characteristics of the UNPROFOR mission

The first objective: to provide assistance in the delivery of humanitarian aid by UNHCR. This was the first reason of UNPROFOR deployment in Bosnia.

The second objective: to establish conditions permitting the resumption of negotiations between the parties. This relies essentially at least on sufficient calm on the battlefield, and, at best, on the cessation of all military hostilities on the ground. We reached this point simultaneously in Bosnia, in Croatia and in FYROM (Macedonia) at the eve of last year (1994).

The third objective: to monitor the various cease-fire agreements signed by the parties, for example the Washington agreement signed on 18 March 1994 by the Bosnian Croats and the Bosnian government forces, the cease-fire agreement between Croats and Krajina Serbs, signed on 29 March 1994; and the agreement of cessation of hostilities in Bosnia and Herzegovina, signed on 31 December 1994.

Strategic direction

The strategic direction of peacekeeping operations in former Yugoslavia (FY) devolved largely from directives issued by the UN Secretary General. These directives reflected influences of many different political authorities with diverse and not necessarily converging agendas. Prior decisions by the major powers also exerted an effect, building many contradictions into the situation in FY and prejudicing the peacekeeping mission's potential for success. In addition, constraints imposed by troop-contributing nations on the employment of their national contingents, and by NATO, the EU and the OSCE on forces and personnel under their control, had further significant influence on the strategic direction of peacekeeping in FY.

Diplomatic recognition of new states

Participants agreed that an important political lesson was learned: that the full implications of emergent states receiving a separate international identity must be considered before political recognition was granted. Premature identification of borders through recognition restricted room for manoeuvre for a political settlement. This also created later problems, such as providing an incentive for civil war about territorial control by opposing national groups, in particular in the case of secession from a multi-national state, where borders claimed by the seceder are not based on a consensus of the population in the territory. Historical background, ethnic mix and regional stability should determine both the desirability of a state's political recognition and its timing.

Diplomacy

It was the task of the political policymakers, not the military peacekeepers, to find a solution to the conflict that was acceptable to all parties. The diplomatic process in FY often fell well short of meeting the basic principles of peacekeeping. Political direction and diplomacy in FY were often partisan, inconsistent, inflexible and inappropriate. Too often, the negotiation process marginalized parties to the conflict and was slow, insensitive, ineffective and divorced from current realities.

Contact Group negotiations in Bosnia, requiring that detailed aspects of all proposals be agreed in advance, had proved slow, cumbersome and unrealistic, paralyzing the diplomatic process. Contact Group members had not always backed up their agreed diplomatic proposals. The resultant delays had proved lengthy, greatly exacerbating suffering in Bosnia.

The deliberate diplomatic isolation of the Bosnian Serbs had caused them to radicalize and harden their position.

Diplomatic dialogue should be stimulating, inclusive and seek to integrate, not marginalize, parties to the conflict. Imposed diplomatic solutions in a peacekeeping situation were likely to fail, as events in Bosnia had shown.

Mandates

The degree of importance, difficulty and complexity of a UN peacekeeping mission had to be matched by a similar degree of effort in providing assets and men. By virtue of their intimate understanding of the situation on the ground, the Head of Mission and the Force Commander needed to be consulted when new Security Council resolutions were written. Setting fresh objectives for the force had to be complemented by decisions to provide the extra materiel, technical and tactical means of achieving those objectives. Failure to do this would discredit the mission. Mandates needed to be defined in detail and be commensurate with the characteristics and principles of peacekeeping.

Introduction of enforcement elements into the peacekeeping mandate is not only a risk for a UN mission. It also influences the parties to the conflict and raises expectations of a direct military undertaking by the international community.

For the commander of the UN peacekeeping force, the clarification of the mandate was a basic necessity as it represented the foundation on which he would accept risks and set tasks.

Relations with NATO

Co-operation between UNPROFOR and NATO was excellent, but sometimes delicate because of their different, if not opposite, cultures. NATO's military assets sought to achieve a military effect which normally entailed the destruction of a target. NATO's military commanders therefore tended to apply the principles of warfare, favouring surprise, offensive action and military efficiency. Peacekeeping commanders, however, applied opposite principles dictated by the mission, assets available and a paramount concern for the safety of troops. In future, the directives given to UN troops and to supporting regional organizations should be developed together, following parallel evaluation appropriate to the situation on the ground. In particular, it is paramount that regional defence organizations, such as NATO in their UN supporting role, plan and organize their efforts in accordance with the principles of peacekeeping.

Peacekeeping missions in Europe should also seek to develop closer co-operation with the Organization for Security and Co-operation in Europe (OSCE).

Training

In a peacekeeping mission, the retraining of a combat soldier to a peacekeeping role is vital. Training of the mind is as important as physical training. Soldiers must be able to understand the culture and attitude of the local population and to de-escalate critical situations. Before commitment, military units had to be told of the political goals to be reached, their precise missions, logistic conditions, the length of commitment and rules of behaviour and engagement. Especially in a civil war-like conflict, sustained, effective training of UN soldiers is vital to the success of a peacekeeping operation.

UNPROFOR's operational environment and concept

The operational environment in FY had a number of characteristics that made peacekeeping there very different from conventional military operations as well as from traditional PKOs. There were no enemies to be fought, but rather partners with divergent interests with whom peacekeepers were obliged to maintain absolute impartiality and objectivity in their dealings. Distinction between civilians and combatants was difficult because of the civil-war nature of the situation. Furthermore, the mission could only succeed if all parties could be convinced to accept and to consent to the continuing presence of United Nations forces. Dialogue was the basis of peacekeeping actions and had to be maintained at all costs. There was no viable military solution to the situation, nor was there a victory of a conflicting party to be won. A solution could only be found between the warring parties under the aegis of the international community and by the political arm of the mission.

Peacekeeping force characteristics

Peacekeeping forces are by their very nature and composition necessarily heterogeneous – a characteristic that imposed many constraints. Peacekeeping forces also lack vital logistic assets, and service support staff normally given to conventional military units.

It is important that political decision makers keep these characteristics in mind. If the UNSC or national decision makers wish to undertake enforcement operations they must be aware that a peacekeeping force is inappropriate for war-fighting.

Credibility

Credibility in peacekeeping requires characteristics such as impartiality, coherence and consistency. It is important that this is understood by *all* UN troops. Local confidence often depended on the effective performance of the UN. Negotiations should be conducted in such a way as to preclude parties appropriating the benefits of agreements and walking out on their obligations. Negotiations needed to be conducted consistently and, if possible, factions had to be held to their agreements.

Coherence

Political consistency has to precede military consistency. The peacekeeping force could function only if backed by the politicians. Unity of effort is vital to both the political and military elements of a mission and between the UN and regional organizations. Diplomacy, economic development, humanitarian support and military operations have to be blended into a coherent strategy and implemented as a consistent and joint activity.

Regular meetings between the mission and most of the NGOs are necessary to ensure practical co-operation in the field. By sharing information, a better analysis of the overall situation was facilitated.

Military officers need to be trained to understand the political process. At the same time political leaders must understand the potential as well as the limitations of a peacekeeping force.

Transparency

Transparency is an important requirement of the UN so that factions would know what would be tolerated and how UN troops could be expected to react. Warring factions needed to be told of the UN mission and what actions the UN force was going to take.

Principles of peacekeeping

Incompatibility of peacekeeping and peace enforcement

A clear distinction must be made between peacekeeping, in which impartiality is fundamental, and peace enforcement, where one of the parties involved inevitably becomes designated as the enemy. Political decision makers must be aware of this fact. Peacekeeping and peace enforcement cannot be mixed.

Given the vulnerability necessarily imposed on peacekeeping forces by their task, participants agreed that the classic peacekeeping principles of consent, impartiality and use of force in self-defence also remained fundamental to the success of peacekeeping operations in civil war-type situations such as that in FY.

Consent

The success of a peacekeeping mission depended upon the acceptance of that mission and its mandate by the local public.

Firmness and impartiality were necessary to promote public confidence. Peacekeeping should also involve participation in local events – the hosting of visits and provision of humanitarian aid would assist in this process. The UN were guests and not occupiers and were obliged to respect culture and religious traditions. Objectivity was essential – especially when dealing with different ethnic groups.

In the case of a preventive mission like that in Macedonia, the peaceful environment granted greater freedom of movement, made it easier to establish working relations with the local population and thus avoided UN soldiers becoming a separate caste in the local society.

Impartiality

Impartiality was an overall necessity – but was often absent from the diplomatic process. Diplomats did not seem always to understand the prevailing sensitivities in the area confronting those who had to conduct operations on the ground.

The multi-national composition of UN forces was an important contribution to projection of an impartial image. The strength of UN Military Observer (UNMO) teams, for example, derived from their status as unarmed intermediaries of multi-national composition who did not represent any particular nation or interest. Impartiality did not mean lacking opinions and failing to react to wrong-doing – but maintaining it was very difficult in managing misbehaviour by the parties to the conflict.

Use of force in self-defence only

The ways in which force was applied by UNPROFOR varied between battalions on the ground. Clear guidelines on the use of force should be developed in conjunction with New York and agreed with troop-contributing nations. Nations needed to know how to interpret 'self-defence'. The amount of force that was used in the first weeks of a UN peacekeeping operation was key. Factions would tolerate the use of force in *self-defence* if they could see it being done in an even-handed fashion.

The implications of using force by UNPROFOR

Application of force

The mission must remain within the limits of peacekeeping and not evolve towards peace enforcement. Its role in FY was to support the political-diplomatic peacemaking process. 'Political' resolutions passed by the Security Council were often contradictory and not in accordance with the principles of peacekeeping. Sometimes firmness was required, sometimes not. Standard guidelines could not always be set. The use of force could only be determined by assessing the situation and the immediate consequences of using force. Such judgements had to be made by local commanders. UNPROFOR had been applying force daily in this way in a constrained and legitimate fashion. It was unrealistic to suggest, for example, that air support could enable a peacekeeping force to transit effectively to peace enforcement. Such a change in posture required additional assets, a complete reorganization, a new mandate and the agreement of all the troop-contributing nations.

Tanks in a PKO

On the one hand, main battle tanks can be very useful to enhance the robustness of our self-defence reactions. This was demonstrated by the efficient reaction of the Danish tank crew which legitimately returned fire at Bosnian Serb positions near Tuzla.[3]

On the other hand, in a civil war-like conflict, the warring factions could deliberately use this reinforcement of UN firepower as pretext to initiate a provocation-reaction-retaliation spiral and so put the UN mission at risk. Therefore, in case of heavy weapons being part of a UN peacekeeping force, transparent information to the local population about the mandate and the purely defensive role of the PK force becomes most important.

Close air support and air power in a PKO

It is important not to confuse the close air support of peacekeepers with deliberate offensive interdiction missions. Close air support might prove effective in the early stages as a demonstration of will. But militia-based civil war-type conflicts often rendered close air support of doubtful practicality. Terrain and weather were often unsuitable, as was the nature and disposition of warring factions who sometimes used facilities both dispersed and underground and therefore not vulnerable to air strikes. The use of air power in peacekeeping missions must observe the principles of minimum force and should take place *transparently* and *impartially* against any party violating the rules.[4]

Defence of safe areas

The greatest difficulties facing the mission in BH (Bosnia-Herzegovina) arose from the mandate of deterring attacks against six designated Safe Areas and of maintaining the regime of total exclusion zones around Sarajevo and Gorazde. UNPROFOR was neither provided with a precise mandate nor with the necessary personnel of its own to demilitarize the Safe Areas and establish buffer zones which the UN controlled and protected. Instead, the purely declamatory Safe Areas were places of tensions where the parties could threaten each other. Merely to 'declare' Safe Areas was a mistake, and it is questionable if a peacekeeping force is suited to defend them without establishing a zone of separation and without the personnel required. In any case a Safe Area must be demilitarized and agreed upon by the parties involved.[5]

Public information

Significance of public information

In FY, the media were a lead actor in events and in setting the international agenda. In addition to formulating crucial international perceptions, the media also influenced the unity and credibility of the UN and NATO and shaped the decision-making process in New York, Brussels and other world capitals. Military effort required active information support capable of disseminating timely, relevant information in appropriate language. A fundamental requirement was therefore providing a co-ordinated, unbiased information service for the international and local media, and in particular the local population, to counter propaganda put out by the factions – if possible speaking directly to leaders and people above the heads of faction leaders. Correct handling of the media therefore constituted a vital ingredient of peacekeeping and an effective public information capability represented a major tool of the peacekeeping operation. This capability was vital in FY, but it was not provided.

Public information requirement

The presence of hundreds of journalists in FY created high media pressure. The UN management of the media was very poor. There is an urgent need for the UN radically to alter its approach to public information. The UN needs resources, manpower, international and local media monitoring, a media strategy and, above all, direction and co-ordination.

UN public information officers at all levels in UNPROFOR area were required to answer questions on developments and on major political, military and policy issues – something that was not co-ordinated. Preparation, training and guidance were not made available for UNPROFOR. The UN needs updated technological media resources with output facilities for radio, TV and print. All forms of available media need to be exploited. The public pronouncements of UN spokespersons also have to be co-ordinated. The competing concerns of accuracy of information and speed of reaction had to be balanced. Members of the international community also needed information relating to their own contingents and issues of national interest which media policy needed to cover.

Command and control

Command in the field

It is unrealistic for nations contributing to peacekeeping operations to expect a comprehensive degree of command and control. Based on the mandate and principles of peacekeeping, UN commanders need to be given the freedom to develop their own plans and not be subject to detailed supervision.

At the highest level in the theatre of operations, the permanent presence of a political official on the ground is essential. Such an official has to have the appropriate margin of initiative – especially to assess the political pertinence of certain applications of force. The teamwork of General de Lapresle and Mr Akashi allowed the formulation of common political and military positions on all the problems that were faced in FY. Close co-operation was vital between all the components of a UN mission, including the head of civil affairs.

A strong think-tank at Special Representative to the Secretary-General (SRSG) level is also important to analyse political, sociological and psychological factors in order to understand and anticipate the actions of the main parties to the conflict. It is important too for the force commander and SRSG to meet the UN Secretary-General and Under Secretary-General for Peacekeeping every two or three months. This keeps everyone in touch, encouraged commonality and strengthened the authority of the SRSG in local negotiations.

Unity of policy

Unity of command is useless without unity of policy. Closer political-military co-operation is essential to improve unity of policy. If 'too many pilots are flying the UNPROFOR plane' (Force Commander de Lapresle), warring parties may play to different actors in the peacemaking process and could set at risk the success of the mission. Therefore, consultation of the force commander and the SRSG in the decision-making process of the Security Council, ICFY and Contact Group should be improved.

Notes

1   The Lessons Learned Unit of the DPKO organized a Lessons Learned Conference with key actors in Somalia, however, it refrained from doing so with respect to UNPROFOR, reportedly because of political controversies in the UNSC.

2 Biermann, W. and Vadset, M., *UN Commanders' Workshop May 1995: Lessons Learned from the Former Yugoslavia*, COPRI Working Papers 5/1996; Biermann, W. and Vadset, M., *2nd UN Commanders' Workshop April 1996, Windows of Opportunity and Realistic Options in the former Yugoslavia 1991 – 1993 – 1995*, COPRI Working Papers 15/1996; jointly published with the Norwegian Institute of International Affairs (NUPI) (NUPI Working Paper No. 563), and as Columbia International Affairs Online (CIAO) Working Paper, Columbia University, USA.

3 See reference to the 'Tuzla Battle', Chapter 3 in this book.

4 For more details see in Chapter 8 in this book.

5 We want to emphasize that this assessment was given in May 1995, before the tragic end of Srebrenica and other Safe Areas. This only underlines the crucial lesson that UNSC decisions should be made in consultation with the Force Commanders rather than illusionary political expectations.

5 From UNPF to IFOR

Windows of Opportunity 1991 to 1996

WOLFGANG BIERMANN and MARTIN VADSET

Force Commanders' discussion, April 1996

Introduction

In April 1996, a few months after the deployment of IFOR, the project invited military and civilian leaders from twelve nations to the Second UN Commanders' Workshop in Copenhagen.

At this point, the international presence in Bosnia had been transformed from the UN-led United Nations Protection Force (UNPROFOR) to the UN-mandated and NATO-led Implementations Force (IFOR). The command authority was transferred from the UN HQ to the NATO HQ.

The Commanders' Workshop was designed to review existing and missed opportunities from the beginning of UNPROFOR up to the deployment of IFOR, including the challenges facing the UN in Eastern Slavonia and in Macedonia.

This chapter gives therefore a summary of peace plans and events, seen from the point of view of the key practitioners who were directly involved.

As in the previous chapter, we document an account of highlights with original quotes, followed by a summary of the course of discussion. The complete record has been published as a joint Working Paper by COPRI (Copenhagen) and NUPI (Oslo).[1]

Highlights from the discussion: Comments by Commanders

Similarity of peace plans and the price for peace

> The proposed peace settlements, from Carrington's in 1991 onwards, were amazingly similar. It is a matter of regret that the Spring 1993 (Vance–Owen Plan) and the Autumn 1993 agreements (Stoltenberg–Owen Plan) were ultimately not accepted. The Dayton Agreement is similar to these agreements...It was argued that the Bosnian Muslims should get more land area. The 1993 agreement gave them 33%. The Dayton Agreement dropped it to 28%.

...It was also argued that, in principle, it was unacceptable to recognize land taken by force,...that it was wrong to carve up Bosnia and that it was instead necessary to establish a multi-cultural society. But...violation of these principles was unavoidable, in Dayton as well as in earlier peace agreements...High moral goals were paid for with the lives of Bosnian people. The price of a perfect peace was a long war. That should be remembered in future negotiations.

Experimentalism

If there is any meaning to the term 'mission creep' in this context, it is that we crept up the scale of commitment, as one expedient after another failed to work...Political realities impair the ability of diplomats and military planners to design the 'right-size' solution and level of commitments at the outset of PKOs. For peace operations where classic peacekeeping is not feasible, and where no single national interest is at stake, we may be constrained to take a 'trial and error' approach...We have to go through the learning process on what works and what does not. The press will certainly enjoy criticising us during the process...

...It is fair to say that the former Yugoslavia is the most complex peace challenge to date in the post-Cold War world, with well-equipped warring factions, with leaderships sophisticated in negotiating with neighbouring patron states, but without major strategic consequences for any major Western power. In this situation, perhaps it was inevitable that we engaged in an experiment.

Over-expectations

...There was a consistent tendency for political and military authorities to overstate the efficacy and inventiveness of military forces that were given set limits within which they had to operate. There were over-expectations on what the military would be able to achieve with various versions of peacekeeping, and combinations of peacekeeping and the threats to use force...

For IFOR, I would say that over-expectation is also a problem – though not with the same impact as the earlier cases. IFOR's latitude to use force is a fact. But this does not mean that IFOR is the right tool for facilitating civil reconstruction, or introducing nation-wide law and order into B-H.

The way to IFOR

I want to distinguish between peace enforcement and peace implementation, with the key difference that in the latter, we put the burden of responsibility on the former warring factions, not the peace force...Prior to Dayton, it is debatable whether there was a peace to keep, much less one to enforce. For Dayton, it was important that the Parties freely engaged in the terms and in the territorial settlement of the Peace Agreement.

There was a sense in which the environment was ripe for a peace agreement – not only for the international community but for the Parties. The Parties had to see themselves as gaining from the Agreement.

The difference between UNPROFOR and IFOR

...IFOR is implementing their Peace Agreement, not enforcing an imposed solution. This distinction underpins the whole NATO involvement and the IFOR mission, including the one-year duration and, of course, it makes NATO's job much simpler than UNPROFOR's ever was. UNPROFOR never had the benefit of such a solid agreement...

You will recall the sloping shoulder syndrome, the constant turning to UNPROFOR when too difficult a situation had to be faced up to, the desire to turn the UN into the scapegoat for their own failures. Now they are learning that they must solve problems themselves and we see each success as yet more evidence that each achievement makes it that bit harder for them to go back to war. For the first time recently, I have detected a genuine desire to reap the benefits of...peace. It is very encouraging.

Why Dayton can work

The Dayton plan will work for two reasons. First it will be difficult for those who want to fight within the former Yugoslavia to mobilize people. Any such move would be extremely unpopular. All the leaders have lost part of their authority. An international presence will discourage a resumption of hostilities. Second, as long as the US is actively involved, it will work because of the unique authority of the US to make it work.

Responsibilities

What did we learn in terms of general principles? If I had to point to one thing, I would say we learned something about putting the responsibility for peace on the former warring factions. Given a peace agreement, the military forces implementing the peace need to be aggressive and consistent in refusing to take responsibility for the factions' behaviour.

Impartiality

It was not possible to gain a lasting peace without the agreement of each of the parties...Logically speaking there could be no peace agreement without impartiality. The Dayton Peace Agreement could not have been agreed upon without impartiality.

Peacekeeping and the use of force

There was an increasing pressure on the UN to use force. Close air support to defend the peacekeepers was used and worked well. Then there was pressure for major air strikes...Those pressing for the use of force were often not themselves involved...UN troops were peacekeepers. General Michael Rose was strong enough to resist pressure because of the risk to the lives of his own troops...The hostage-taking of thinly spread peacekeepers (on one occasion 240) following air attacks proved the point.

Preventive deployment in Macedonia

The UN and the US struggle with the same problems: how to select among competing crises, less willingness to deploy fewer forces, and budget shortfalls, In this environment, preventive concepts hold a weak hand. Major powers tend to deploy soldiers only where they have important or vital interests, yet UNPREDEP shows that pre-crisis diplomacy and preventive deployment are cost-effective and practical in nature.

On one particular occasion, the Macedonian government complained that 'their' UN commander should not contact the potential enemy, highlighting a problem of host-nation 'ownership' of a preventive force. None the less, the commander in March 1994 began meeting with the military command in Belgrade.

Many US representatives admit today that they have learned a lot, and that they have a better understanding of traditional peacekeeping after serving a couple of years with 'Nordics' in Macedonia. Today the co-operation between the US and Nordic Battalions can only be described as excellent. Very useful exchange of soldiers' programmes and joint exercises have taken place.

Eastern Slavonia

UNTAES could make its programme work. It all depends on the sincerity of Tudjman and Milosevic, however, since any success would have to include both presidents' willingness to support the UN's efforts. It would also depend upon the preparedness of the parties to co-operate. There are certain concerns what might happen after UNTAES.

I am concerned that Eastern Slavonia could be forgotten. It deserves focus. There are 200,000 people there. Another raid into Eastern Slavonia is possible unless an international focus is put there. Such an attack would again complicate matters in the region.

EU foreign policy

We must remember that the EU represents 15 foreign policies and not one (like the US). Russia, Japan and China were not interested. US power and authority is unique. If the US and Europe ever disagree seriously that will have dramatic impact on European security.

Window of opportunity 1991/92 – the Vance Plan for Croatia

The Vance Plan

On 27 November 1991, UN Security Council Resolution 721 (1991) endorsed efforts for the deployment of a UN peacekeeping operation in Croatia/Yugoslavia. 1992 heralded the Vance Plan. An Implementing Accord was signed in Sarajevo on 2 January 1992. The UN was represented on this occasion by a military liaison officer and a team of civilians who were present at the signing. The UN Secretary General sent military liaison officers with the task of promoting maintenance of the cease-fire. Six weeks later, on 15 February 1992, the UN Security Council confirmed the acceptance of the Cyrus Vance Plan by all parties and agreed to establish UNPROFOR, mandated to be deployed on Croatian territory, with a headquarter in Sarajevo, the capital of the, at that time, 'peaceful' Yugoslav republic of Bosnia-Herzegovina. On 21 February UN Security Council Resolution 743 approved financial support of UNPROFOR for one year.

The Vance Plan was a result of a six-month negotiation process. There was never any question of European capitals providing combat troops for the plan. No enforcement, only peacekeeping, was an available option. Planning with the UN and EU had to proceed on that basis. The plan's aims were summarized as follows:

-   The cessation of hostilities
-   The withdrawal of the Yugoslav National Army (JNA) from Croatia (to prevent the partition of Croatia)
-   The demilitarization of UN Protected Areas (UNPAs)[2]
-   The restoration of Croatian authority in the UNPAs
-   To facilitate the return of displaced families to the UNPAs.

It was significant that the measures detailed above were agreed upon only by Croatia and Serbia, while the Krajina Serbs objected strongly. The UNPROFOR mandate in Croatia did not have their consent.

UNPROFOR in Croatia

Deployment. At the beginning of UNPROFOR in Croatia, UN military assets amounted to four battalions from Canada, Nepal, Argentina and Denmark plus 100 UN civil police (UNCIVPOL) and civilian staff. Deployment followed the arrival of the advance party on 5/6 March 1992.

UNPROFOR with its military and civilian components was deployed in areas containing significant Serb minorities where inter-communal tension had led to armed conflict.

Civil Affairs work in Sector West (Croatia) focused on dealing with local authorities and the people of the region and implementing a series of confidence-building measures – all of which sought to establish normality in daily life.

Major tasks of the initial UNPROFOR mandate in Croatia included carrying out or supporting demilitarization, monitoring and overseeing the work of the local police forces, and facilitating the return of all displaced persons (for whom the lead agency was the UNHCR). The daily work of Civil Affairs in the early period tried to disseminate correct information. This involved explaining the mandate and the concept of implementation, emphasizing that UNPROFOR was not an occupation force but a neutral peacekeeping force. Still, in both the Croat as well as Serb entities, the UN was perceived as biased.

UNPROFOR activities in Croatia included the following:

The introduction of low-level confidence-building measures. This involved assisting in arranging contacts between the authorities and non-governmental organizations, community and town hall meetings, and radio programmes including 'call-in shows'.

Periodic meetings at the Demarcation Line (Zones of Separation). This included the reunion of family members.

Village visitation programme. Displaced persons were allowed to visit the villages (deserted or destroyed) of their origin located in other parts of the Sector. These displaced people also undertook damage assessments and often cleared up their property. Agricultural activities also took place in the areas controlled by the opposing faction. Visitation was an important element of the normalization process.

Economic rehabilitation and reconstruction. Small-scale, quick-impact projects were set up through the UN. Bilateral and multilateral financial arrangements were made.

Humanitarian assistance. This included the delivery of food packages and medical care. Forty per cent of families were mixed Serb/Croatian.

Human rights. Monitoring human rights included reviewing such things as alleged harassment, employment opportunities and access to schools. The UN Civil Affairs office intervened with local and, if necessary, with central authorities.

Repair of physical infrastructure. For instance, through direct contacts between the parties, water was provided in Serb areas and electricity in Croat regions.

Obstacles to implementation of the Vance Plan

A variety of obstacles to the implementation of the Vance Plan were caused by UN procedures:

Slow deployment. Deployment was slow, lasting from the first UN observers (UNMOs) in January 1992 to 14,000 men in February 1993. There were also significant resource constraints (including vehicles and interpreters).

Unclear mission objective. The mission objective was unclear. This was reflected in an inconsistent long-term strategy. There was also weak linkage between policy and implementation, with no discernible connection between political negotiators and those implementing the agreement on the ground.

Inconsistent UN Security Council resolutions. Some resolutions were not consistent with one another. For example, the definition of 'substantial minorities' was unclear. In addition, the basis on which the UN Protected Areas in Croatia were formed according to the Vance Plan, was changed. While UN Security Council Resolutions 740 and 743, both adopted during February 1992, stated that the implementation of the peacekeeping plan was in 'no way intended to prejudge the terms of a political settlement', resolutions adopted later in principle confirmed Croatia's sovereignty over the UNPA's and gave the Krajina Serbs less reason to be co-operative with UNPROFOR. There were also problems with the concept of 'Pink Zones'.[3]

Weak co-ordination and co-operation. UNPROFOR's various components (military, Civil Affairs, UNCIVPOL and UNMOs) were not well co-ordinated.

Lack of dynamism. Owing to lack of regular contact with the UNPROFOR HQ in Sarajevo there were no guidelines for periods of seven to eight weeks for the civilian element deployed in Croatia. As a result the tendency was to focus on day-to-day problems. And that meant a lack of vision for the future and a non-dynamic approach. The mandate was viewed as a ceiling, not a floor. As a result, the spirit of the mandate was not fulfilled.

Lack of community development. There was no concept for post-conflict community development. Dealings were mainly made with the authorities in a top-down approach rather than working upwards through the communities. More people should have been co-opted into joint activities. With assistance of the UN, the communities in war-torn societies needed to experience more relatively simple but noticeable improvements.

Poor UN media. With the exception of a few minutes of air-time per day, UN media was practically non-existent. The regional media of the parties was able to disseminate biased information and manipulate the public perception of the mandate and associated operations.

Insufficient involvement of local communities in the peace process. There were too few innovative ideas to tie people into the peace process.

Lack of consistency. There was a lack of consistency in applying pressure to the parties concerned.

Mismatch of troop commitments to requirements. A continued deficiency in UNPROFOR was that in Croatia (as well as later in Bosnia) there was a significant shortfall between the estimated requirements of troop levels and the numbers that the UN Security Council actually authorized. The gap between requirement and provision was huge: the Vance Plan was estimated to require 40,000 troops to secure the Protected Areas in Croatia. The UN Security Council authorized 13,000.

The extension of UNPROFOR mission to Bosnia and Macedonia in 1992 [4]

After the referendum on independence from Yugoslavia and subsequent recognition, the civil war in Bosnia escalated. UNPROFOR's mandate was extended to Bosnia and – as preventive deployment – to the former Yugoslav Republic of Macedonia (FYROM). In addition, UNPROFOR had an operational mandate in Serbia and Montenegro and a liaison presence in Slovenia.

The extended mandate of UNPROFOR had a threefold purpose:

First of all, it sought to alleviate the humanitarian consequences of the war, notably through helping in the provision of humanitarian aid.

Second, after it was extended to Bosnia-Herzegovina, it sought to contain the conflict and mitigate its consequences by imposing constraints on the belligerents through the establishment of such arrangements as a 'No-Fly Zone', Safe Areas (SAs) and exclusion zones like the Total Exclusion Zone (TEZ) of February 1994 in Sarajevo and April 1994 in Gorazde.

Third, UNPROFOR sought to promote the prospects for peace by negotiating local cease-fires and other arrangements, maintaining these where possible and providing support for measures aimed at an overall political settlement.

On 31 March 1995, the UN Security Council decided to restructure and rename UNPROFOR, replacing it by three Peacekeeping Operations: UN Confidence Restoration Operation in Croatia (UNCRO), UNPROFOR (Bosnia); and UN Preventive Deployment Force (UNPREDEP) (Macedonia); interlinked by the UN Peace Force Headquarters (UNPF-HQ) in Zagreb. The UNPF-HQ was also responsible for liaison with the governments in the Federal Republic of Yugoslavia and other concerned governments as well as with NATO.

Window of opportunity 1993/94 – The Vance–Owen and Stoltenberg–Owen Plans for Bosnia-Herzegovina

General course of events [5]

In January 1993, the chairmen of ICFY, Cyrus Vance and Lord Owen presented a draft agreement (Vance–Owen Plan) on cessation of hostilities, a constitution and a map dividing BH into ten provinces. It was signed by the leaders of the Bosnian Muslims and Croats in March 1993. Under high international pressure, Karadzic signed the plan on 2 May 1993 in Athens; afterwards, the Bosnian Serbs who then controlled 70% of Bosnia, rejected it in a referendum. The Bosnian Serbs had at that time no motivation to accept an agreement based on the Vance–Owen Plan.[6]

On 21 September 1993, a new peace agreement (the Stoltenberg–Owen Plan) was accepted by the leaders of each of the three Bosnian parties, but was a few days later rejected by the Bosnian Muslim parliament.[7]

At the end of 1993, Croatia was stable. The Christmas truce in Croatia in 1993 lasted into 1994, and also took effect in parts of Bosnia. Cease-fire lines were more or less stable. All over the mission area there were UN-controlled weapon storage sites, signs of demilitarization, and military police replacing combat units.

After the Stoltenberg – Owen Plan failed, the situation in Bosnia deteriorated. In February 1994, after a NATO ultimatum, the Total Exclusion Zone (TEZ) was established around Sarajevo; another one followed in Gorazde in April 1994.

Flash points were Sarajevo and the exclusion zone, Gorni Vakuf, the Vares pocket, the Brcko corridor, Bihac and Gorazde. Events in Gorazde in April 1994 represented a dress rehearsal for 1995.[8] There was a cease-fire in Sarajevo monitored by UNPROFOR, but no-man's land was dominated by Bosnian government forces within two days of the cease-fire being announced.

Missed opportunities

According to some participants, the Vance–Owen Plan set permanent borders that were non-negotiable. The Vance–Owen Plan was thus inflexible and presented itself as a 'take-it-or-leave-it' option. This was one of many missed opportunities.

Another window of opportunity had 'opened' a few months later with the achievement of bringing, after substantial Croat and Serb concessions, the three parties in Bosnia to accept the Owen–Stoltenberg Plan in September 1993. 1994 was also reckoned to be a window of opportunity for a peace agreement between Croatia and the Krajina Serbs.

The failure of the peace agreements could be attributed to lack of joint political back-up by major powers – something that Dayton did not lack. In distinction to Autumn 1995, the negotiation process was at that time (in 1993) overshadowed by deep disagreements in the EU and between Europe and the United States. With international support for UNPROFOR absent in 1993, it should have been evident that a UN Peacekeeping Operation could not perform the role of backing up the peace process. It was generally recognized that the important shift that led to Dayton was created by the political movement of the US in 1995.[9]

Seized opportunity 1994: The Croat/Muslim Coalition

The Washington Framework Agreement of 8 March 1994 between Bosnian Croats and Muslims represented a breakthrough which created the Muslim–Croat Federation. This set the scene for a classic peacekeeping operation in which forces were to be separated and intense fighting brought to a conclusion. The Croat–Muslim Federation changed the balance of forces and stopped the fighting between these two factions. But the federation agreement was a meeting of minds at the top – with differing views at ground level. The prime task was to carry forward the fragile coalition.

Safe Areas

In April 1993, UN Security Council Resolution 824 established the new concept of Safe Areas. The objective of setting up Safe Areas at Sarajevo, Bihac, Tuzla, Srebrenica, Zepa and Gorazde was to protect civilians, not the opposing forces deployed in the areas. In Srebrenica, the Commander of UNPROFOR, General Wahlgren, negotiated an agreement to demilitarize the Safe Areas and informed HQ New York. The Agreement for the Demilitarization of Srebrenica signed in Sarajevo on 17 April 1993 specifically excluded the presence of armed persons or units other than UNPROFOR within and around Srebrenica. Canadian troops were deployed to control and protect the area.

However, on 3 June 1993, a new UN Security Council Resolution (836) gave specific permission to Bosnian government military and paramilitary units to remain within the Safe Areas. This was a violation of impartiality and also of the safe havens principle under international humanitarian law.[10]

After many incidents the UNSG again suggested full demilitarization by both sides within and around the Safe Areas.[11] The parties involved lacked confidence in the UN – a vital requirement if areas were to be handed over to UN control – since no government was willing to commit the troop levels that Safe Areas demanded.

Window of opportunity 1995/96 – Dayton and the transition to IFOR

The Holbrooke Plan. Dayton was a window of opportunity that had been seized based on the long previous experiment. The Holbrooke Plan was a bargained compromise and reflected all the expected contradictions. It included provisions that the US Congress required to approve the deployment. Some workshop participants felt that this opportunity could have been seized earlier.

Holbrooke Plan Concept. A main precondition of NATO involvement had been a peace agreement. The parties had to see themselves as gaining from the Agreement. This was a critical part of Mr Holbrooke's and the Contact Group's concept to bring the parties to agree on a reasonable compromise of their interests, including the fact of separate political entities inside Bosnia, the Muslim-Croat Federation and the Republika Srpska. Based largely on the engagement and power of the US, the parties did sign.

IFOR was implementing *their* Peace Agreement, not enforcing an imposed solution on the parties. This distinction underpinned the IFOR mission and made NATO's job much simpler than UNPROFOR's ever was. IFOR had the unchallenged political support from all members of the UN Security Council, the European Union and NATO. Only during a very short period – during the transition from UNPROFOR to IFOR – could the UN Force benefit from such unity of support, enabling UNPROFOR to implement the cease-fire agreed upon by the parties in September 1995 and to prepare the transfer of the command authority from the UN to NATO. Last but not least, deployment of an overwhelmingly NATO-led force on the ground provided a credible deterrent against anyone who might contemplate violating the cease-fire.

The situation four months after IFOR deployment

There were solid achievements in inducing patterns of co-operation. The Joint Military Commission[12] mechanism was working. On the civil side, slowly, at the working level, parties were learning to co-operate on some of the technical aspects of reconstruction. Formerly there had been constant desire to turn the UN into a scapegoat for the parties' own failures. Now the parties were learning to solve problems themselves. Each achievement made it harder for them to go back to war.

Transition from UNPROFOR to IFOR. June 1995 saw the beginning of a process of change for UNPROFOR and NATO as a team. Military measures, such as the introduction of the Rapid Reaction Force gave indirectly more authority to the Force Commander UNPROFOR.

With respect to the transition from UNPROFOR to IFOR, NATO's consensus-building and consultation/decision-making processes had worked well, especially considering its lack of experience with peacekeeping operations. By the time of the Workshop, 45% of the International Police Task Force (IPTF) had been inducted. The combination of IPTF activity and IFOR's zone of security seemed to prove effective.

Challenges to IFOR

Compliance. Lack of compliance was a cause for concern, especially as IFOR was beginning to accept Balkan intransigence and delay as a matter of course. IFOR's military tasks were far from over.

Post-IFOR planning. IFOR should shift its position in order to support the civil side. An *ad hoc* co-ordination group would be put together to improve work with other elements of the operation. IFOR's biggest difficulty was convincing the local people that stability would continue *next* year. Reconstruction demanded long-term stability. Participants agreed that post-IFOR planning needed to be conveyed to the people now – otherwise IFOR might be perceived as a band-aid with no long-term end-state in view. A comprehensive package ought to be presented to the Bosnian peoples as a target and incentive for peaceful co-operation.

Negative signals. There were also negative signals. The Federation was causing major concern for the future perspectives of the Dayton Agreement – as was the distance and self-isolation of the Republika Srpska. It was still not clear that the patterns of co-operation intended by the Peace Agreement would take root.

Return of Refugees. IFOR worked closely with UNHCR. A particular concern was the return of refugees and displaced persons. However, the possibility of returning to 1991 positions had become something of a dream.

Conclusion

UNPROFOR and NATO had been able to contribute to the political momentum for the current settlement and peace implementation operation. Ideally, one general conclusion might have been that NATO peace implementation should have preceded UN peacekeeping. But such a conclusion was felt to be somewhat naïve in the light of actual political circumstances. The international community tried to apply the tools it had available during 1991 to 1995, based on what it considered to be politically reasonable levels of commitment at the time. Various tools and levels of commitment failed and the experiment continued.

Yet this experimentation turned out to be costly in human terms. The situation reached the point where the credibility of international institutions and specific nations began to be as much at stake as the actual peace itself.

Media coverage of bloody events had affected the integrity of NATO and leading nations. Peace in Bosnia took on dimensions larger than the local achievement of peace. This raising of the stakes and learning from successive experimentation resulted in IFOR.

There were significant parallels between IFOR and UNPROFOR. IFOR, a combat force ready and willing to use overwhelming force, was conducting a peacekeeping mission. The main difference was the consent of the parties to give IFOR the right, ability and legalization by mandate to implement the Peace Agreement ending a war, while UNPROFOR peacekeepers, by far not a combat force, were sent into an ongoing war in order to gain time for a peace process.

It would be fair to say that former Yugoslavia constituted the most complex peace challenge to date in the post-Cold War world, with well-equipped warring factions, leaderships skilled in conducting sophisticated negotiations with neighbouring patron states, but without major strategic consequences for any major Western power. In this situation, experimentation was perhaps inevitable. As a patient, FY was in 1996 no longer in intensive care and could manage to undertake daily tasks. However, it required long-term therapy.

UN Transitional Authority in Eastern Slovenia (UNTAES)

Course of military events. The Croatian army started 'Operation FLASH' on 1 May 1995 to forcefully reintegrate Western Slavonia (UNPA of Sector West). The operation could have been finished in four hours, but UNPROFOR succeeded in gaining time to allow the Serbs living in the area to leave. Later, UNPROFOR had the obligation to protect the Serbs who could not escape.

The Krajina Serbs would not use the word 'reintegration'. An estimated 200,000 Krajina Serbs fled, and the UNSC received reports about grave violations of human rights and looting of Serbian property in the 'newly liberated' areas. [13] On 9 August UNPROFOR managed to conclude a truce which enabled the Serbs to escape.

The present plan agreed, on 12 November 1995, sought to reintegrate Eastern Slovenia into the Republic of Croatia. This had been generally agreed. The Serbs were not really in the mood to fight and realized that there was no other way but to accept and implement this plan. This laid the ground work for the deployment of the UN peacekeeping force in Eastern Slavonia, UNTAES. [14]

UNTAES – concept. The purpose of UNTAES was to achieve a peaceful reintegration of mostly Serb-populated Eastern Slovenia into the Croatian legal and constitutional system. UN Security Council Resolution 1037 authorized the commitment of a force of up to 5,000 UN troops (Belgian, Russian, Pakistani, Jordanian, Ukrainian and Argentinian) plus civilian police with a Czech hospital and Slovak engineers. The force included 464 UNCIVPOL and 220 civilians including border monitors. The military task was to supervise and facilitate the demilitarization (expected to be voluntary) and to monitor the safe return of displaced persons and refugees to their places of origin. There were approximately 80,000 displaced Croats and 80–100,000 displaced Serbs.

The task of the civilian component was to establish a Temporary Police Force, define its structure and size and develop a training programme. The civil component would undertake tasks relating to civil administration and public services in addition to facilitating the return of displaced persons and refugees and co-ordinating plans for the development of economic reconstruction of the region. The first group of 20 Serb and 20 Croat policemen would be trained in Budapest the following week (after 15 April 1996). Neutral uniforms would be used.

IFOR would provide a back-up capability, including close air support for the purpose of self-defence of the UN peacekeepers in Eastern Slavonia. The Transitional Administrator was basically responsible for governing the region. The Transitional Authority worked through a Transitional Council, including a representative of the Government of Croatia, the local Serbs, the local Croats and other minorities.

The Transitional Council was advisory in nature. Its chairman, the Transitional Administrator, had sole executive power. The Transitional Administrator ran a succession of implementation committees to facilitate reintegration and make sure that all plans were in line with Croatia's overall plan for redevelopment and reconstruction. The most important implementation committee was the one on police.

The committees sought to make the Serbs aware of possibilities to improve their situation through co-operation. Other implementation committees included Civil Administration, Public Services, Education and Culture, Return of Refugees and Displaced Persons, Human Rights, and Elections.

Prospects. Workshop participants believed that UNTAES could work. The future prospects depend heavily on the sincerity of Croatia and Serbia, however, since any success would have to include both presidents' willingness to support the UN's efforts. It would also decisively depend upon the preparedness of the parties in Eastern Slavonia to co-operate. There are certain concerns what might happen after UNTAES. Some participants advocated a continued UN presence.

The Macedonian experience [15]

Factors for success. Although UNPREDEP was deployed on unilateral request and consent of the host country only, it could be described as traditional by means and methods. Peacekeeping techniques learned in earlier missions were valid. Significant amongst the factors contributing to success has been correct timing, a clear and feasible mandate and the consent of the host nation.

Operational elements of success in this kind of environment included:

- A UN presence that showed the UN flag as much as possible (on the border and also within communities)

- Good personal relations with all parties and at all levels

- Immediate reaction to incidents at a local level before the situation escalated

- And a readiness to raise issues at a higher level if necessary

- Troop readiness, reserves, good discipline and politeness, special peacekeeping training in addition to basic military training, also selecting people with the right attitude and screening out the 'Rambos', and strict impartiality.

However, other, mainly political factors also contributed to the absence of conflict in Macedonia including:

- US diplomacy and policy in the Southern Balkans, including deterrence through the presence of American military forces

- International sanctions against Serbia

- The work of international agencies (such as the OSCE, ICFY, UNHCR and others)

- Relatively moderate behaviour by Macedonia's neighbours (who were not helping – but also not threatening military action)

- Finally, Macedonia's attempts to maintain and encourage a viable multi-ethnic society.

Stability was enhanced, however, by the unanimous UN commitment, i.e. the undisputed support by major nations. It focused international and regional attention on Macedonia, thus moderating internal and international political friction. Presence alone was a powerful element of prevention. Although the media took little interest in 'calm and quiet' situations, the UN commitment served to focus international attention on Macedonia.

Notes

1 Biermann, W. and Vadset, M., *2nd UN Commanders' Workshop April 1996, Windows of Opportunity and Realistic Options in the former Yugoslavia 1991 – 1993 – 1995*, COPRI Working Papers 15/1996; jointly published with the Norwegian Institute of International Affairs (NUPI) (NUPI Working Paper No. 563), and as Columbia International Affairs Online (CIAO) Working Paper, Columbia University, USA.

2 United Nations Protected Areas (UNPAs) were established in the mainly Serb-populated areas of Croatia like Krajina, Eastern and Western Slavonia.

3 Pink Zones = 'certain areas of Croatia controlled by the JNA and populated by then largely by Serbs, but which were outside the agreed UNPA boundaries. It also recommended the establishment of a Joint Commission chaired by UNPROFOR and consisting of representatives of the Government of Croatia and of the local authorities in the region, with the participation of the European Community Monitoring Mission (ECMM), to oversee and monitor the restoration of authority by the Croatian Government in the pink zones', *The UN in former Yugoslavia*, Ref. Paper Revision 4, UN Department of Public Information: New York, 30 April 1995.

4 For details about the history of UNPROFOR see in *The United Nations in former Yugoslavia*, Ref. Paper Revision 4, ibid., p. 4 ff.; see also 'Annexes, Historical

Supplement, UNPROFOR', The Army Field Manual, Vol. 5, *Wider Peacekeeping:* London, 1995.

5 For further details, see *The UN in former Yugoslavia*, ... ibid., p. 11 ff.

6 Early January 1993, at a Geneva summit of the leaders of the three conflicting Bosnian parties (Mate Boban, Alija Izetbegovic and Radovan Karadzic) and the presidents of FR Yugoslavia (Dobrica Josic) and Croatia (Franjo Tudjman), the chairmen of ICFY, Cyrus Vance and Lord Owen presented a draft agreement (Vance–Owen Plan) on cessation of hostilities, constitution and a map dividing BH into ten provinces, reflecting a geographic and ethnic mix of population.

On 25 March 1993, the plan was signed by Boban and Izetbegovic, while Karadzic refused to sign. Under high Serbian, Russian and other international pressure also Karadzic signed the Vance–Owen Plan at the Athens conference on 2 May 1993. On 5 May 1993, the Bosnian Serb parliament rejected the plan.

7 After several separate meetings with the mediators Lord Owen and Thorvald Stoltenberg in Geneva, an agreement was reached on a peace agreement, including constitutional principles and territorial questions. At a meeting on the British aircraft carrier *HMS Invincible* on 20/21 September 1993, President Izetbegovic accepted the draft after several concessions from the Bosnian Serbs and Croats. The Bosnian (Muslim) parliament, however, rejected the plan at its meeting on 27 September 1993.

8 The Workshop discussion referred to the hostage-taking of UNPROFOR personnel after air attacks.

9 On 18 May 1995 the American negotiator Robert Frasure announced that he had agreed with President Milosevic in principle on a peace settlement. Details of the agreement were then reported by CNN: The Frasure-Milosevic plan included a separate Bosnian entity Republika Srpska with the right of 'special relations' to Serbia (similar to the Bosnian Croats' ties with Croatia), the 51:49 territorial distribution according to the Contact Group Plan, mutual recognition of Yugoslavia and Bosnia and the conditional lifting of sanctions.

The *de facto* acceptance of Serb autonomy in Republika Srpska was a fundamental shift from the earlier US position. A few days later, the Administration, pressured by the US Congress, renounced its promise to lift the UN embargo against Yugoslavia by the UNSC. The blueprint of the Dayton Agreement, the Holbrooke Plan, however, included the same principle of compromise – acceptance of Srpska vs. recognition of Bosnia (see: Honig, Both, *Srebrenica*, ibid., p. 160 ff. and Owen, *Balkan Odyssee*, ibid., pp. 357ff and 429).

In one of our interviews in Sarajevo, November 1995, an UNPROFOR officer answered to the question whether in September 1995 'Were the Serbs bombed to the negotiation table?': 'The Bosnian Serbs had already been promised what they were fighting for: Srpska. But the US Congress and the Sarajevo Government were opposed to a Serb Republic in Bosnia. Probably, they had to be impressed by the bombing to accept that deal.'

10 With respect to international law, the UNSG emphasized 'the need to demilitarize the Safe Areas and thus establish a regime that would be in line with the Geneva Conventions of 12 August 1949 and the Additional Protocols thereto of 1977, which have gained general acceptance in the international community' (UN Document S/1994/1389). See also contributions by Lavoyer, Ogata and Wahlgren, Chapters 10, 11 and 16 in this book.

11 In his 9 May 1994 report to the UN Security Council, the UNSG suggested that a Safe Area concept could only succeed under the conditions

'a) That intention of SAs was to protect people, and that UNPROFOR's protection was not intended to make it party to the conflict;

b) that the execution of the task should not detract but rather enhance UNPROFOR's mandate to supply aid and to contribute to the implementation of cease-fires and local disengagement...the Secretary-General, on 1 December 1994, submitted to the Security Council a report containing his further proposals on the implementation of the concept of Safe Areas...he said that in order to achieve the overriding objective of...protection of the civilian population and delivery of humanitarian assistance, the existing regime needed to be modified. The Safe Areas should be clearly delineated and completely demilitarized. Demilitarization should be accompanied by the cessation of hostilities and of provocative actions in and around the Safe Areas.

The ability of one party to retain troops, weapons and military installations within a Safe Area, the Secretary-General continued, created an unstable situation and drew attacks from the opposing party. The use of force by UNPROFOR to repel such attacks in defence of the Safe Area was inevitably construed as 'taking sides' in the conflict and could have a destabilizing effect throughout Bosnia and Herzegovina. Moreover, UNPROFOR was not equipped to repel such attacks, and air power was frequently an inappropriate means of doing so.' (*The UN in the former Yugoslavia*,...ibid., p. 37.)

A few weeks before Srebrenica and Zepa were taken by Bosnian Serb forces, in his report to the UNSC of 30 May 1995, the UNSG openly criticized the consequences of the Council's earlier decision to permit deployment of governmental troops in the SAs and warned that 'the only effective way to make Safe Areas...truly safe...is to define a regime acceptable to both parties'. (Report of the Secretary-General, S/1995/444, 30 May 1995, p. 12.)

Concerning the grave violations of human rights after the fall of Srebrenica see: UN General Assembly, Human Rights Situation and Reports of Special Rapporteurs and Representatives, 3 November 1995, p. 21 ff.

12 Joint Commissions were one of the lessons learned by IFOR from UNPROFOR; see Ridgway, Chapter 13 in this book.

13 *Human Rights Situation and Reports of Special Rapporteurs and Representatives*, Statements, 3 October 1995 by the President of the UNSC, the UN High Commissioner on Human Rights, Ayala Lasso, and SRSG Akashi, UN General Assembly, 3 November 1995, pp. 4–18.

14 UNTAES = United Nations Transitional Authority in Eastern Slavonia.

15 For details about UNPREDEP, see Kuenning, Chapter 14 in this book.

6 Lessons Learned in the Field

A Survey of UNPROFOR Officers

WOLFGANG BIERMANN and OLE FREDERIK UGLAND*

Introduction

This chapter describes lessons learned by the peacekeepers in the field, from their service in former Yugoslavia. Since these military officers were deployed in one of the most difficult peacekeeping operations thus far, evaluation of their experiences may also be relevant for less complicated future operations. The analysis is based mainly on questionnaire interviews of officers who served in UNPROFOR. A limited survey of IFOR personnel was added later.

The challenges

The challenges faced by UNPROFOR officers in former Yugoslavia were manifold. As analysed in previous chapters, their situation was characterized by:

- UN mandates with a wide spectrum of humanitarian, civilian and military tasks

- Continued hostilities and an environment in the mission area often hostile to the UN presence

- Contradictory Security Council resolutions and opposing policies of major nations

- Mandates that included military tasks inconsistent with UN peacekeeping principles and impossible to realize with the resources provided

---

* The authors would like to express their gratitude to Prof. Håkan Wiberg and Lt. Gen. Martin Vadset for their valuable comments in the process of writing this chapter.

- National interference in operational decisions of the UN commanders

- Continuous criticism of the peacekeepers for not doing 'enough'

- And last, but not least, frequent humiliation by the conflicting parties.

Although this list is necessarily incomplete, it illustrates the complexity of the challenges to the peacekeepers. The central problem raised in this chapter is simple: how can peacekeepers work under such conditions? To better understand how peacekeeping principles can be applied in the field, three main themes are addressed:

- To what extent are normal peacekeeping principles a usable guideline for carrying out peacekeeping in the Yugoslav area of operation?

- How are these principles interrelated to each other in the everyday experience of the peacekeepers?

- What can UN peacekeeping realistically achieve in the difficult reality of an ongoing civil war?

Our initial thesis is that, despite some references in various UNSC Resolutions to Chapter VII enforcement, the military personnel of UNPROFOR understood their role primarily as that of soldiers in a mission for peace, rather than as a combatant with the mission of defeating an enemy. The difference between the status of a 'peacekeeper' and of a 'combatant' has vital consequences for the troops involved.

The survey

Principles and doctrines are often developed remote from the field where they are supposed to work, even if they are a result of proper analysis of lessons learned, and intended to reflect the requirements of reality. The people actually implementing a UN mandate – the peacekeepers themselves – thus represent a focal point for an assessment of the practicability of doctrinal principles and methods. Our research project approached the problem from two angles.

UNPROFOR survey. Initially, after evaluation of literature, documentation and media reports, background interviews were carried out during 1994/1995 with key personnel at NATO, the WEU and UN headquarters, and with UNPROFOR officers of all ranks in the field in Croatia and Bosnia. These interviews provided first-hand information relating to implementation of the UN peacekeeping principles and a wide range of information about other operational and political aspects of UNPROFOR.

Next, the interviews were complemented by a survey to cover a broader set of officers and to compare the possible spread of diverging opinions according to nationality, military rank and peacekeeping experience in a systematic way. DANORP designed, in co-operation with the Danish Armed Forces Centre of Leadership, a questionnaire on the basis of statements and opinions quoted from interviews, media and doctrinal papers and the first UN Commanders' Workshop in May 1995. Respondents were invited to mark their degree of agreement or disagreement with listed 'statements'.[1] A second UN Commanders' Workshop was held in Copenhagen in April 1997 and provided important input for the evaluation of the results.

It was evident from the outset that it would be difficult to achieve an entirely representative survey of UN peacekeepers. First, financial resources were limited. Second, the background information needed to select military respondents is restricted or classified, and also difficult to obtain when personnel are spread across several countries. Third, follow-up of non-responding officers was difficult once they had left the mission area or their units. However, through detailed procedures for questionnaire distribution and collection, the project attempted to ensure a sample with fairly high degree of representativity.[2] A total of 1,200 questionnaires were distributed. Of these, 916 were completely filled in and returned. This high rate of response was possible through the indispensable assistance from Defence Ministries, Chief of Defence Staffs and in the UN DPKO.

As a consequence of the design of the survey, the figures presented below should be read as an *impressionistic picture* where general trends are more important than the exact percentages.[3] Rather than emphasising that 85% or 76% of the officers agree to a certain statement, the main finding is that about eight in ten share the view expressed. When the officers are divided further into subgroups of rank, nationality, etc., the precision of the statistical representativity of percentage figures decreases due to smaller numbers of respondents.

IFOR survey. During the Spring of 1997, DANORP followed a recommendation of the second UN Commanders' Workshop to carry out a survey to compare attitudes of IFOR officers with those of UNPROFOR. Resources and time did not allow for a fully representative survey for the NATO-led force. Nevertheless, with assistance from the Danish Armed Forces Centre for Leadership and the Chief of Defence Staff in Norway, we succeeded in interviewing a limited group of about 60 Danish and 40 Norwegian officers. Results from this survey will be used for purpose of illustration in the following sections.

Chapter outline

The following discussion is centred around the three main questions listed above, addressed by distinguishing between challenges facing UN peacekeeping from 'inside' and from the 'outside' respectively. Internal challenges refer to the applicability of peacekeeping principles by the UN troops with respect to the operational conditions in the field. External challenges focus for instance on media influences and interference by other international actors in the area of operation. Finally, we asked the officers to suggest improvements to UN peacekeeping operations and to assess the realism of what can in fact be achieved.

The conflict as seen from the peacekeepers' point of view

The many challenges listed in the beginning of this chapter illustrate the complex reality that confronts the officers on arrival in the area of operation. They face diverging views on the conflict as well as actions taken by the various parties being in war against each other. During individual interviews in the field, we often heard criticism of a 'blind eye of the international community' towards Croatian warfare like the destruction of East Mostar, the killing of Muslims there, and of Serb civilians in the Medak pocket.[4] These events were mentioned as being 'not appropriately reported'. As a point of departure, and to establish some background for the following analysis, let us see how UNPROFOR officers perceive the political conflict in their mission area (Figure 6.1).

The internationally predominant view of the war was that the Bosnian Serbs and Serbia were the most guilty parties in the war. The brutal shelling of Vukovar by the Yugoslav Army in 1991, and later the frequent shelling of Sarajevo by Bosnian Serbs, as well as reports about the Omarska concentration camp, are well-known examples of atrocities committed by Serbs. There is, however, no unanimous perception of the conflict on the part of the peacekeepers. This does not imply that they have not made up their minds, as nine in ten actually take a stand on the various issues.

A clear majority of six in ten officers agree, two in ten 'strongly', that the conflict was mainly a result of Serb aggression to create 'Greater Serbia'. But even more accepted – eight in ten agree on this – is the more 'equalizing' notion that the conflict is mainly a civil war among different ethnic or religious groups.

Figure 6.1 UNPROFOR officers' attitudes to the conflict in the former Yugoslavia[5]

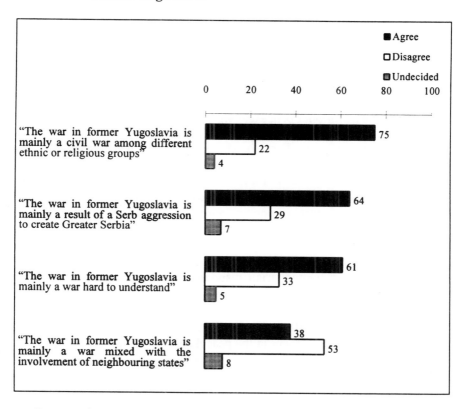

Conversely, there is much less agreement that the war is mainly a conflict mixed with the involvement of neighbouring states. Only four in ten agree with this. Adherence to this latter statement would be the logical answer in case of systematic support to the notion of an aggression by Serbia to create 'Greater Serbia'. Obviously, these views conflict with the typically expressed public opinion in the officers' home countries.

This interpretation should however be seen in the light of the fact that half of the officers claim the conflict to be 'hard to understand'. This notion is illustrated by a variety of comments added by the respondents to their questionnaires. A Norwegian officer commented on this 'hard to understand' statement as 'the only question I could answer without hesitation'. A high-ranking Turkish officer noted: 'It is really very difficult to understand this war.' The strong opinions many people may have due to cultural affinity to a group or under impression of media reports are weakened by the immediate experience of a more complex reality of war.

The challenge from 'within'

Most organizations face internal challenges related to their general organizational goals as well as to the means required to reach them. In this section, we look into the central challenges related to the adequacy and applicability of general UN peacekeeping principles, as well as the education and training of officers sent to the field to implement them.

The role of the traditional peacekeeping principles

A major question to the officers is whether in a civil war-like conflict, the traditional peacekeeping principles – consent of the parties, impartiality by the peacekeepers, non-use of force other than in self-defence – are still valid as guidelines for UN soldiers. Is it possible to maintain the traditional distinction between peacekeeping and enforcement?

We confronted the officers with a variety of statements in order to have their opinion on the three principles as such. We asked how far should or could these principles be applied by UN peacekeepers, in particular if they have to carry out a humanitarian mandate? Are traditional peacekeeping principles a hindrance for a humanitarian operation?[6] Or is 'sticking to the principles' a precondition for the success of a UN operation?

Let us see how the officers in the field perceive the principles and the possibilities for applying them in the peacekeepers' day-to-day reality.

The principle of consent

There is no doubt that in a civil war, consent of all parties to assistance by the UN in conflict settlement is fragile. We consequently address the issue of obtaining and maintaining consent of the parties to the UN, rather than claiming that consent exists *a priori*. The officers are also asked whether and how consent could be established with local war-lords? And, if consent of the parties is fragile or deteriorating, what are the means available or required for its re-establishment? What levels of consent are seen by peacekeepers as paramount requirements for the ability to carry out their mandate? Is it sufficient to have consent at the top level of national leaders, or is consent also required at the grass roots? (See Figure 6.2.)

Figure 6.2 UNPROFOR officers' attitudes to the principle of 'consent' in a hostile environment

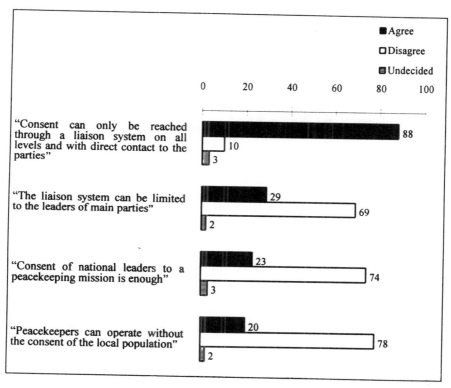

The various statements represent four different types and levels of consent, ranging from the top leaders to the local population. One statement claims that consent of national or other main leaders of the warring parties is sufficient for peacekeeping in a civil war-like environment. It was rejected by seven in ten officers. The claim that the liaison system could be limited only to the leaders of the main parties is also widely rejected. Furthermore, nine out of ten officers see the need to go beyond linking the liaison system to the leaders of the main parties. Nine in ten agree that a comprehensive liaison system with direct contacts to all levels, including the local level, is required to (re-)create consent.

In other words, the idea that top-level consent is sufficient as a basis for peacekeeping is widely rejected among the officers. There is widespread support for continued local contacts at the tactical level, which is seen as essential for the implementation of the mandate. The best chance for creating and maintaining consent is to bring the management of the conflict beneath the level of top leaders.

The argument that top-level consent is not enough to sustain peacekeeping under civil war conditions is based on practical experience rather than on theoretical considerations, as comments by many officers show. A French officer commented on the humanitarian effects of broad consent for humanitarian efforts:

> By personal contacts (or low-level meetings) with warring military local commanders, it's possible to get a local and temporary cease-fire in order to repair energy and water networks. (We succeeded on it in Sarajevo.)

A Finnish officer explained the interaction of consent and impartiality and on the implications of using force:

> The UN is not a invasion force, gentlemen! OK, the NATO air attacks in Bosnia did the job but I still think that the UN must not become a warring party or take sides.

A Canadian officer explained the impact of local consent to the moral of the troops:

> Dialogue and patience are essential in peacekeeping. It is good to have consent of the local population – makes your job easier. Better for the moral of the soldiers.

Three important empirical lessons can be learned from these views. First, the principle of consent is a valid and necessary operational basis for peacekeeping in a civil war-like conflict. Second, consent is not a given condition. In particular under civil war-like situations, it has to be strived for on a daily basis, and at all levels. Third, decentralisation of the mechanisms to create consent is required. Decentralisation can in fact be both realistic and efficient, as demonstrated by the experience with Joint Commissions in Central Bosnia.[7]

Turning briefly to the survey on IFOR experiences, similar opinions on the requirements of consent apply to the NATO-led force. About nine in ten Danish and Norwegian IFOR officers agree that 'consent can only be reached through a liaison system at all levels and with direct contacts to the parties'. Furthermore, eight to nine in ten reject the notion that the liaison systems can be limited only to the leaders of the main parties. Finally eight in ten agree that the Joint Military Commissions are an excellent tool to create and keep consent.

The reactions from both UNPROFOR and IFOR officers confirm experiences of traditional UN peacekeeping missions like UNIFIL, that the key to stopping the shooting and gradually building confidence between the UN and the parties to conflict is the development of relations at the local level in the area of operation. In political terms, this also signals the opinion that the power of a strong defence alliance is not enough to impose agreements made at the top level. It requires the application of the 'old' peacekeeping principle of creating consent at each level.

The principle of impartiality

Figure 6.3 UNPROFOR officers' attitudes to the principle of 'impartiality' in civil war situations

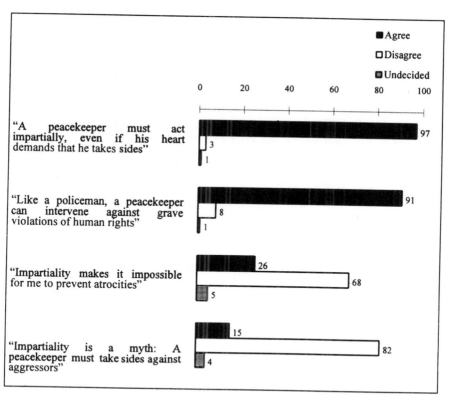

The principle of impartiality is based on the necessity that international troops avoid involvement on the side of one of the conflicting parties against the other, and operate strictly without taking sides. However, what does impartiality mean to the peacekeepers when the principle is severely challenged, as for example in situations of grave violations of human rights? (See Figure 6.3.)

The figure presents four different statements. The first two are quoted from interviews with officers in the field. The latter two reflect arguments taken from parliamentarians interviewed in Germany and Norway.

Again, the principle is easily adopted in the field. The normative claim that impartiality is a 'must' with which the officer must comply even when his heart tells him otherwise receives strong support and is approved by an almost unanimous officers' corps. Going to the opposite position that impartiality is a myth or prevents action against atrocities, we encounter similarly strong rejection from the officers.

The statements that impartiality is 'a myth in the light of atrocities' or 'makes it possible to prevent atrocities' reflect expressions made by parliamentarians in the open interviews and are formulated with strong rhetoric plausibility. It takes a certain act of will by the respondent to say 'no' rather than 'yes'. Consequently the widespread 'no' responses to these opinions are noticeable, and indicates a strong signal against frequent criticism of UNPROFOR's impartiality as being 'neutral' and 'doing nothing' towards atrocities in Bosnia-Herzegovina.

In other words, the officers strongly disagree with the common interpretation of impartiality as an attitude of neutrality towards horrible crimes. On the contrary, most UNPROFOR peacekeepers say that they want to and can intervene against grave violations of human rights, and see the possibility of preventing atrocities. Many officers commented on this view along the following lines:

> Impartial UN peacekeepers should – in deed must – act to prevent atrocities.[8]

> The presence of UN forces assures atrocities are not committed, as none wants war crimes to be witnessed.[9]

> To act impartially is a basic principle. It is really important to be perceived as being impartial if we want to be respected when intervening against atrocities.[10]

> Since the presence of UNPROFOR, the death toll has decreased by more than 90%, camps were dissolved and our presence has stopped many atrocities. The media are looking at the 10% dead and forget the 90% of lives saved.[11]

In other words, the principle of impartiality is still vivid among the peacekeepers. It is perceived as a precondition rather than a hindrance to act against violators of human rights. Although the opinions presented focus on impartiality only in humanitarian situations, impartiality as a general principle seemingly has a strong foothold and includes the will to act if possible. Even-handed intervention against grave misbehaviour by parties to the conflict is not necessarily interpreted as taking sides in the conflict.

The principle of using force in self-defence only

The traditional principle of 'using force in self-defence only' implies that a peacekeeper must utilize force only when the life of a peacekeeper or his unit is at stake. Figure 6.4 displays the UNPROFOR officers' views on the issue.

Figure 6.4   UNPROFOR officers' attitudes to the principle of 'use of force in self-defence only'

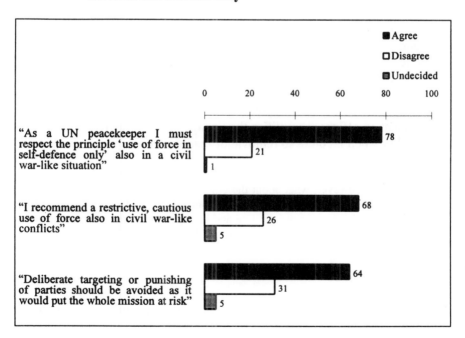

Again there is widespread support for the 'old' principles. Eight in ten officers agree that the use of force should be restricted to self-defence, also in civil war-like situations. The idea is taken even further. Seven in ten officers hold the view that also targeting or punishing of the parties should be avoided. Again, this does not imply a truly pacifist attitude. There is prevalent recommendation to the use of 'restrictive and cautious' rather than offensive force in such conflicts.

The practical interpretation of these opinions is further illustrated by operational statements (figures not shown) relating for example to the question of *using force to protect humanitarian convoys,* which was a central issue in the humanitarian tasks of UNPROFOR. Also on this issue, the use of force is seen as legitimate only as long as it is moderate. Only four in ten officers, and only two to three in ten officers of higher ranks, agree that the use of weapons could be recommendable in order to get through a humanitarian convoy when blocked by stone-throwing or violent civilians. Several comments to this question indicate that the officers prefer the use of 'non-lethal force', with police-like tactics and warning shots, etc.

Following up on the convoy protection issue, seven in ten officers hold the view that moderate use of force is practicable only to protect humanitarian convoys against armed attacks. Eight in ten agree that more force is acceptable against any party that denies the freedom of movement for UN troops, although only 'if applied impartially' against all parties. In other words, the strong support for the principle of non-use of force does not contradict willingness – under certain conditions – to engage in robust self-defence. At the same time there is a clear limit. The majority of officers reject the idea of using force beyond self-defence for deliberate punishing of attackers or aggressors. This means that reprisal tactics used in combat operations are not accepted.

A Canadian officer exemplifies the linkage between the use of force and impartiality when it comes to removal of roadblocks:

> If you decide to shoot your way through a roadblock today, you may succeed. However, what about the other 25 roadblocks on your way to the delivery site? When you come back tomorrow, the tactical situation will be different. Once you cross the line and become one of the warring factions, do you honestly believe you can go back to the status of being impartial?[12]

'Hawks' and 'doves'

We have so far registered widespread support for general peacekeeping principles among the officers. At the same time, opinions are not unanimous. The question arises as to what degree the same people defend all the principles at the same time, or whether a 'dove' position on one issue is compensated by a 'hawk' position on others.

Let us make an experiment, by looking further into the interrelationships between the attitudes. In his reactions to the various statements concerning consent, impartiality and the non-use of force other than in self-defence, each officer is given a low score if he strongly adheres to the UN principles (dove) and a high score if he does not (hawk). Summarizing across the scores, the final distribution gives us a total score range from low scoring 'doves' to high scoring 'hawks' (see Figure 6.5).[13]

Figure 6.5 UNPROFOR officers by score on an attitudinal index reflecting support to the UN peacekeeping principles

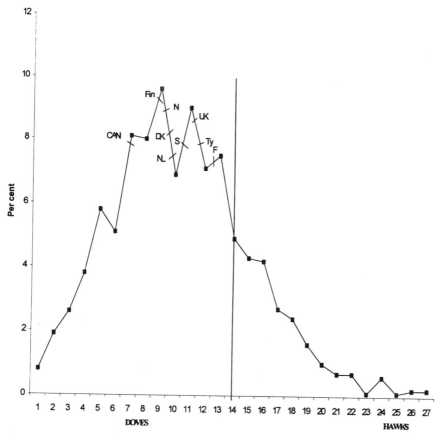

Figure 6.5 displays a 'bell-shaped' curve. Most officers tend to hold the same consistent trend of opinions on all issues. They are largely found to the left of the middle dividing line between 'doves' and 'hawks', which implies a significant 'bias' in favour of the UN principles in general. The

proportion of 'hawks' is only two in ten officers, and even these have a position close to the dividing line.

The fact that there is more or less unanimous support for the peacekeeping principles among the officers implies that background factors such as age or military rank, previous mission experiences, etc., are less important than would otherwise have been imaginable. The only factor which distinguishes 'doves' from 'hawks' in our questionnaires is nationality. We have marked the position of each nation along the curve in Figure 6.5.[14]

Roughly speaking, Canadians and Finns turn out to be the 'strongest' adherents to the UN principles, and French, Turkish and British officers the 'weakest'. Closest to the Canadians and Finns we find the Norwegians, then the Danes, the Dutch, and finally the Swedes. By and large, these are small differences in a picture of great similarity.

The fact that nationality is the most significant background characteristic in this respect, can be explained by different traditions and experiences in peacekeeping. As will be seen below, some differences in peacekeeping attitudes between Nordic/Canadian officers and European nations are visible.

Training requirements

In addition to the general peacekeeping principles and their workability in the field, an important question is to what degree the officers are being sufficiently prepared for their mission. In order to gain from the insight of the officers' practical experiences with their own preparatory training, we asked them about training requirements and about individual skills which they see as vital in order to do peacekeeping (see Figure 6.6).

The table shows nearly unanimous acceptance of the distinctive training requirements of peacekeeping. Nine in ten officers reject the statement that military training 'alone' is sufficient to fulfil the role of a UN officer. The idea that soldiers can be ordered on peacekeeping missions while only officers need training for this, is rejected by seven in ten officers. There is also widespread recognition that the training received prior to deployment is inadequate, as supported by seven in ten officers. The lack of training before going to the field may be balanced by additional training in the mission area. Half of the officers (not shown) disagree, however, with the idea that they could catch up by training in the mission area upon arrival.

Figure 6.6 UNPROFOR officers' attitudes to training requirements for peacekeeping

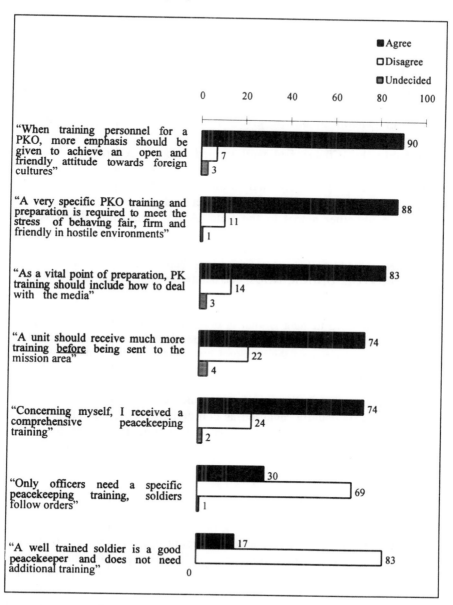

The main training shortages, identified by nine in ten officers, are inappropriate introduction to local culture, poor training in how to stay friendly in a hostile environment, and the lack of training in handling media. The preparedness in these areas is obviously not appropriate, although it is crucial for troops operating in a foreign country and most decisive for being accepted by the local population. Comparison with our survey of IFOR officers reveals that they too do not feel well enough prepared for these tasks.

Finally, shifting from the issue of unit training to personal experiences, most UNPROFOR officers claim to have received a comprehensive peacekeeping training. This view seemingly runs counter to the view that officers in general should be given more specific training to meet the challenges in the field.

Probably the officers feel well trained both in general (professional training) and specifically for their UN service, but they are not satisfied with unit training. The individual soldier should therefore be given more training both as an individual peacekeeper and as part of a unit, in co-operation with other actors in the field. A few comments illustrate this interpretation:

> There should be a 'meeting of the minds' between military units, UNMOs, UNCIVPOL, UNHCR, NGOs, etc. before the deployment. The command elements should be educated together.[15]

> Scenario-based training is vital in order to expose soldiers to the myriad possibilities of problems that one will potentially face. Also it is imperative that all ranks receive this, because the majority of the contacts with the locals and belligerents is carried out by NCOs, without officers around.[16]

Summarizing the findings, we may conclude that traditional training, even though it is usually regarded as comprehensive, is not sufficient for the peacekeepers to carry out their tasks. The conclusion goes for IFOR officers as well, who show views nearly unanimously in accordance with the UNPROFOR opinion.

The challenge from 'outside'

While understanding of peacekeeping principles and adequate training are central to the manageability of a peacekeeping operation under conditions of civil war, there are several external challenges to the mission. Peacekeepers face the impact of news media and other actors in the field. They may have to meet demands from other large international organizations operating in the same area. In addition, governments and politicians tend to interfere. Let us take a closer look first at the non-military influences, then the role of NATO and finally the issue of backing UN forces by air power.

The role of media and politicians

Some of our respondents point out that the behaviour of the conflicting parties to the troops often reflects 'like a seismograph'[17] media reporting in troop-contributing countries. When discussing the present survey in national headquarters, some were even afraid that publication of results by officers of individual nations could negatively affect reactions by the warring parties against the UN troops on the ground. Moreover, UNPROFOR was exposed to a variety of pressures to move in the direction of enforcement.

What is the impact of external events and actors on the conditions and options on the ground, as seen by the peacekeepers? Figure 6.7 displays the officer's views on some of these possible influences.

Live media reports bring the conflict to the international community as well as to the parties of the conflict. Seven in ten officers agree that the *international* media have a significant effect on conditions in the mission area, and claim that the media encourage one side in the conflict while provoking the other. Six in ten officers hold the *local* media of the conflicting parties as most responsible for the escalation of violence. The fact that handling of media was so poor in UNPROFOR[18] is to our opinion puzzling, due to the lessons learned from the Cambodian experience where the UN – after initial resistance in the UNHQ in New York – used its media offensively to contribute to the success of the UNTAC operation.[19] It is not possible from our survey to evaluate whether internal UN problems or external political actors prevented the possibility of the UN to 'go on the air'. But it is remarkable that such a high number of officers rate the international media as being responsible for fuelling the conflict between the parties by either encouraging or provoking more aggressive behaviour. Many officers also gave personal written comments in the questionnaire on this issue. To quote a typical one:

> UN missions need a very strong and capable 'media machine' to 'compete' with the locals and the international media.[20]

Other factors of irritation for the peacekeepers are contradictory politics of the international community and interference by individual nations. Nearly eight in ten officers support the view that contradictory mandates decided by the UN Security Council make the peacekeeping job difficult. Six in ten support the notion that troop-contributing countries are interfering in operational matters. This becomes all the more serious as eight in ten claim that interference by individual countries in operational matters can put the work of peacekeepers unnecessarily at risk.

Figure 6.7   UNPROFOR officers' attitudes to the impact of external actors on the mission

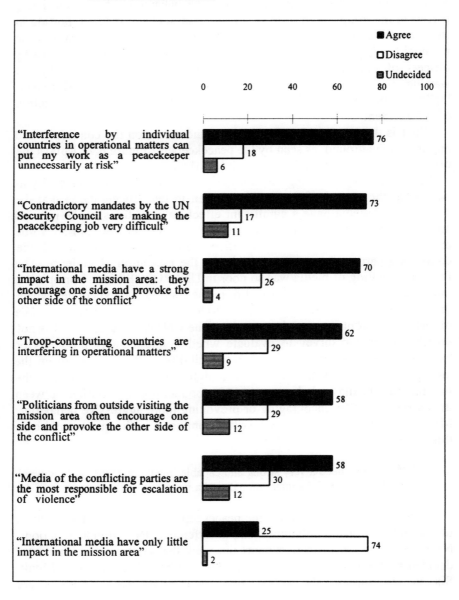

The latter result shows that many UNPROFOR officers share the criticism by the SRSG and force commanders against contradictory policies or interference of major nations during the UNPROFOR operation. The wide support of the argument that the interference could put the work of peacekeepers 'at risk' can be interpreted as an alarming signal of divergence between the remote 'political reality' in the capitals and the 'operational reality' in the field.

In distinction to UNPROFOR, the NATO-led IFOR and, later, SFOR operation has had better conditions with respect to the 'challenge from outside'. Similar to Thorvald Stoltenberg's argument in the beginning of this book, the joint participation of all major nations on the ground is crucial for a successful peacekeeping because it has a moderating effect. Eight in ten IFOR officers support the notion that 'IFOR/SFOR runs well because all major NATO nations have ground troops involved', and even slightly more state that 'participation of ground troops of all major NATO countries is vital to avoid that the parties try to play them against each other' (figures not shown).

In addition, participation of e.g. US troops has a positive effect on the application of peacekeeping principles in the operation itself, as a Norwegian IFOR officer noted from his experience:

> Impartiality is the most crucial aspect of peacekeeping. A good example of how this works is the US. They were strongly biased during the UNPROFOR operation. But they were able to operate with a great deal of impartiality and respect from the Serbian side during IFOR.

On the other hand, some comments indicate also a possible risk to IFOR through violation of impartiality by major nations by giving one-sided support, e.g. the 'train and equip' programme or by channelling international aid primarily to the federation. Also NATO's own lessons learned evaluation sees a certain challenge to impartiality of the IFOR operation through national political climates and agendas. In addition, while the NATO-led Implementation Force, unlike UNPROFOR, has had no command and control problems on the 'strategic level', on the 'operational level' IFOR in some cases faces the problem of interference by national governments wishing to retain ultimate control through parallel national chains of command.[21]

In this regard, the opinion of six in ten IFOR officers 'that troop-contributing countries should not interfere in operational matters' (figure not shown), shows that also a NATO-led and not only a UN operation is exposed to 'challenges from the outside'.

The role of NATO

There has been a continuous debate on the specific characteristics of NATO and UNPROFOR concerning their lack of a common philosophy, while at the same time they have required mutual support. The most obvious expression of the different conceptual approaches [22] between NATO and UNPROFOR was the conflict over the 'dual key' procedures with respect to NATO air power in support of UNPROFOR.

To what degree are these differences in general objectives relevant for successful peacekeeping? We confronted the officers with a set of statements concerning co-operation of NATO and UNPROFOR, as displayed in Figure 6.8.

Figure 6.8   UNPROFOR officers' attitudes to the relationship between NATO and UNPROFOR

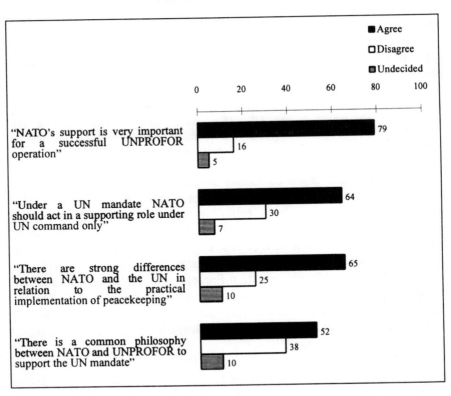

We notice that one in ten officers did not take a stand on these issues. As with other questions in this survey, the numbers of 'don't knows' may represent both lack of information as well as situations where military officers possess information but are hesitant to give a qualified assessment. This interpretation is supported by the fact that the proportion of 'undecided' votes is higher in the case of political than for most of the operational issues.

The general statement that there is a common philosophy between NATO and UNPROFOR to support the UN mandate, is agreed by a good half of the officers. However only one in ten agrees strongly. Concerning the practical implementation of peacekeeping, the common ground between NATO and the UN is weaker. Nearly two-thirds agree that there are strong differences between NATO and the UN in the practical implementation of peacekeeping. Two in ten strongly support this view, as compared to the marginal number that strongly disagrees.

Although the two organizations in the view of the officers do not share a common philosophy, operational support by NATO is frequently welcomed. The fact that NATO's support is perceived as vital, may indicate that officers feel the need to compensate for military weakness of the UN by referring to NATO's military strength. In other words, NATO may, again according to the officers, fill a military capability deficit of the UN.

We will look more thoroughly into the issue of 'capability gaps' below. Suffice it here to say that the great majority of officers give a clear priority in favour of the United Nations. Nearly two-thirds strongly support the notion that under a UN mandate, NATO should act in a supporting role under UN command only. Only one in ten 'strongly' rejects this notion. The UN support is striking as most of the officers interviewed are in fact part of NATO armies.

Air power

With UNPROFOR, the use of NATO-backed air power was introduced as a new element in UN peacekeeping. Air power included support to the peacekeepers in self-defence in the form of Close Air Support (CAS), enforcement of No-Fly Zones (NFZ) and protection of so-called Safe Areas (SAs). From the open interviews, we became aware of a widespread scepticism as regards the practicability of offensive air strikes in a peacekeeping operation, while the possibility of requesting air power to defend the troops on the ground was basically accepted. Pressures from the public to 'bomb the Serbs', the American debate about 'Lift and Strike'[23] and disputes between NATO and the UN about dual-key procedures are covered in other parts of this book.

The main issue at stake here is the officers' opinion on the applicability of air power in peacekeeping operations. As expected, this issue turned out to be more controversial than on any of the other items (see Figure 6.9).

Figure 6.9   UNPROFOR officers' attitudes to air power backing

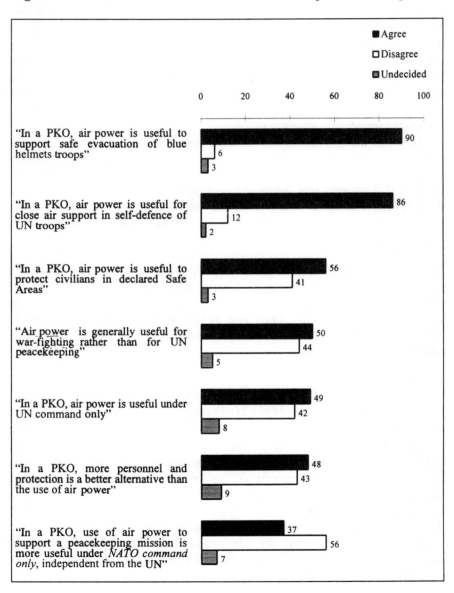

First, the use of air power to defend Safe Areas is controversial among UNPROFOR officers. The controversy is most clearly revealed in the disputed concept of Safe Areas, as recapitulated in chapters by Lt. Gen. Wahlgren and other authors.[24] This background, and the tragic end of the Safe Areas, help to explain the relatively large divergence of attitudes on this topic.

Second, attitudes on use of combat aircraft are quite different in the context of self-defence. As long as air power is intended to protect or defend the peacekeepers and to improve conditions for peacekeeping rather than taking sides in a conflict, its use is not regarded as controversial. Nine in ten officers welcome Close Air Support in self-defence of UN troops, and the use of air power in case of emergency evacuation.

The related enforcement of no-fly zones is also generally accepted by nine in ten officers (figure not shown). The prohibition of military flights was aimed at reducing military activities by all parties, and was therefore in principle considered 'impartial' even if one party has fewer aircraft available. The Bosnian Serbs eventually accepted downing of aircraft violating the NFZ. Instead of reacting with reprisals, their commander claimed to be 'not responsible' for aircraft having been shot down by NATO.[25]

Third, aside from these specific cases, the general value of air power in support of peacekeeping is questioned by many officers. Half of them see air power as a tool of war-fighting rather than peacekeeping, and believe that having more personnel and improved protection is a 'better alternative' to air power. In particular, the higher military ranks (not shown) have more doubts about use of air power. Officers coming from 'traditional' peacekeeping nations and those with previous peacekeeping experiences in other UN operations, are less prone to support the use of air power than the 'new' ones. On the other hand, the above mentioned widespread acceptance of air power in support of self-defence, no-fly zones and safe evacuation, is independent of rank or nation.

Reservations over the use of air power can also be seen in connection with a general impression among the officers that the UN Security Council reached its decisions without regard for the views of Force Commanders (several statements, table not shown). This opinion is shared by nine in ten of the officers. However, only half of them find it *realistic* to expect improvement in communication between the political leadership in New York and the leadership in the field.

Finally, the mixed feelings about the use of combat aircraft in peacekeeping operations are also reflected in answers to the question about who should be in charge of air power supporting the mission. Officers are split in two equal halves as to whether air operations should be under 'UN command only'. The statement that NATO should have the command over air operations, independent from the UN, is rejected by nearly six in ten.

It may be worth mentioning that the survey indicates some national divergencies on the question of command in case of the use of air power (table not shown). While more than six in ten Dutch, Norwegian, Finnish and Swedish officers are *against* 'NATO command only', more than half of the Danish, British and Turkish officers *favour* it.

Recommendations by the officers

Following the examination of challenges facing UN peacekeeping, it is time for us to review possible recommendations based on experiences in the field. Here we examine further the workability of the UN practices themselves, as well as the relationship between the UN and 'outside' organizations. Finally, we evaluate recommendations against the reality of field conditions.

Recommendations to improve peacekeeping

The survey shows an overwhelming identification of UNPROFOR officers with the use of the established peacekeeping principles as a guideline and with the United Nations as the mandating as well as leading agency, also with regard to NATO. We then asked for concrete recommendations to improve peacekeeping operations, and asked the respondents to differentiate between what they personally desire, and what they consider realistic from a professional point of view (see Figure 6.10).[26]

The table confronts the officers with three different possible recommendations to improve peacekeeping. The suggestion of closer cooperation between NGOs, relief organizations and the military component in preparing for a PKO, receives almost unanimous support. On the other hand, only six in ten officers regard this suggestion as having realistic chances of being implemented. This picture corresponds well with the statements about training requirements displayed above, and points at an important area for improvement.

Another major problem illustrated below, is the *unity of command*. More than seven in ten officers agree that 'too many pilots are flying the UNPROFOR plane'. The preference for UN command is obvious. Nine in ten prefer, five in ten even 'strongly' demand, that the Special Representative of the UN Secretary-General and the UN Force Commander should be responsible for all aspects of the mission. However, only six in ten officers regard this as a realistic option, obviously reflecting the difficulties UNPROFOR faced with respect to contradictory mandates and pressures from various sides.[27] On the other hand, it may be a concession to NATO's well-organized military power that every other UNPROFOR officer welcomes the proposal to give NATO 'full responsibility' for the military part of the mission. Obviously, NATO is seen as capable of handling this issue, reflected by the fact that nearly all of those in favour also find it realistic to give NATO responsibility for the military tasks. In other words, even though the IFOR model was not discussed at all at the time when the UNPROFOR survey was conducted, the idea of giving full responsibility for military tasks to NATO was probably breeding in the minds of the UNPROFOR officers.

Figure 6.10   UNPROFOR officers' recommendations to improve UN peacekeeping

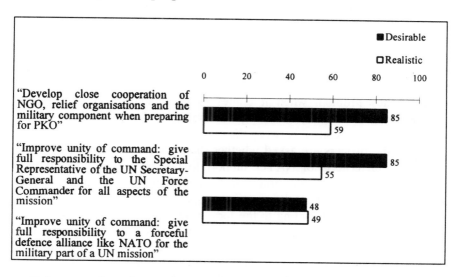

Taken together, the preferences expressed in favour of the UN as the agency leading the mission are strong. Even if some five in ten officers agree in general, only two in ten 'strongly agree' to handing over responsibility for the mission to NATO. At the same time nearly nine in ten generally agree, and more than five in ten 'strongly agree' to giving the UN full responsibility for 'all aspects of the mission'.

On the other hand, the officers indicate essentially no divergence between desirability and realistic prospects when supporting the delegation of military responsibility to NATO. We may conclude pragmatically that NATO simply is seen as having sufficient capability in handling clearly military tasks, as opposed to the UN. In addition, a NATO command may be expected to improve the unity of the military command, a quality which was frequently absent in UNPROFOR. This, and the experience of a poorly supported, under-equipped UN force, is widely analysed by the contributions of key actors in Part Three.

Finally, the vital role of the media in bringing the conflict to the attention of the outside world as well as to the conflicting parties, is reflected in wide support for the proposal that the UN should establish its own TV and broadcast facilities. But again, only half of the officers find the idea realistic.

Improving UN-NATO relations

The limitation of NATO to a military role that is desired by most officers is significant. Although a greater military role for NATO is welcomed, a large majority of UNPROFOR officers advocate the primacy of the United Nations as the lead agency. They believe NATO should have a supporting role only. One could perhaps say that the officers support a stronger military responsibility for NATO as long as the United Nations is not sufficiently militarily equipped, and has a shortfall in military 'capability'. Conversely, NATO is perceived as having a legitimacy problem as well as a proficiency problem when it comes to the management of complex peacekeeping operations, including civilian tasks. Let us look at officer views on how the relation between the two organizations can be improved.

When the officers are asked whether there should be joint UN-NATO agreement on criteria of NATO support to UN peacekeeping activities, there is a close to uniform opinion in favour of such joint standards. This strong notion could reflect the experience that NATO and the UN were not always in accord when acting in the former Yugoslavia. It is also reflected in the statement as to whether NATO should refrain from taking sides in a conflict. Eight in ten officers support this recommendation, which clearly favours the UN approach. The same attitude, although with slightly less intensity, is also expressed by the idea that NATO members should support a permanent UN peacekeeping force, for rapid deployment under the command of the UN Secretary-General. Seven in ten officers agree here, while the proportion 'strongly' agreeing declines. The demand that NATO countries should contribute troops to a UN Stand-by Force, receives slightly higher support, and is welcomed by eight in ten UNPROFOR officers.

Figure 6.11 UNPROFOR officers' recommendations to improve UN–NATO relations

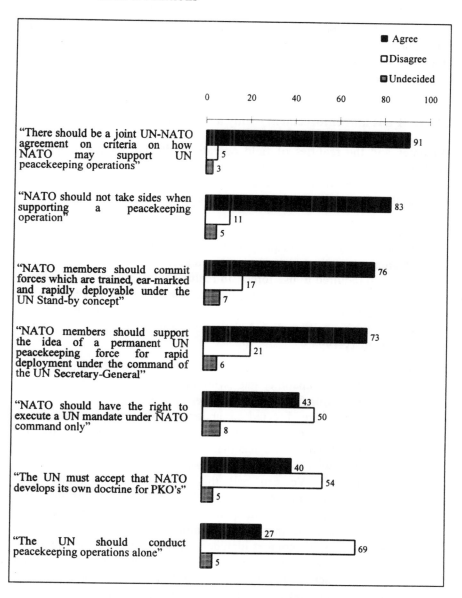

In sum, the support by officers with peacekeeping experience in Bosnia and Croatia for a standing UN force is remarkable, especially when taking into account the controversial nature of this idea in the international community, and the fact that it is not at all a common position within the UN or in NATO. More controversial for peacekeepers are the demands that the UN should accept that NATO develops its own doctrine for PKOs, and that NATO should have the right to execute a UN mandate under NATO command only. Here the officers are split in two. A slight majority disagrees, but four in ten would still accept a more active role for NATO in the field of peacekeeping.

UNPROFOR and enforcement – only a 'capability gap'?

Mandates and the realities of field operations do not always match one another. There is often a gap between intentions and reality, either because the capabilities are missing or because intended actions are not feasible. Let us illustrate a few such 'gaps':

> *Capability gap.* A mandate can include more missions than the troops are trained and equipped for. This was the case in Somalia and Bosnia, where the troops were given additional, unrealistic mandates and also required to use force. 'In reality, nothing is more dangerous for a peacekeeping operation than to ask it to use force when its existing composition, armament, logistic support and deployment deny it the capacity to do so', the UNSG warned in his position paper of 3 January 1995.[28]
>
> *Feasibility gap.* The question may rise whether the UN mandate only suffered from a capability gap (which might be closed by additional troops and armaments), or whether some of the missions the peacekeepers were directed to undertake were not feasible for a peacekeeping force. The latter conclusion is underscored by the UNSG himself when he states that the dynamics of enforcement 'are incompatible with the political process that peacekeeping is intended to facilitate?'[29] We can call this shortfall a 'feasibility gap' complementary to the common term 'capability gap'. With this term we seek to conceptualize the qualitative dimension of a mission that normally cannot be met even by more potent military forces. [30] 'Feasibility' in this context includes a whole set of requirements for bringing a peacekeeping operation to success, such as abilities of the troops to de-escalate tense situations, political and diplomatic ability to handle crises, and the requirements of civil emergencies or other non-military capabilities.

Mission creep. Often, external political ambitions add to the 'feasibility gaps', which the troops have to tackle. They result in 'mission creep', feared by many commanders and difficult to handle. Examples are a) tasks which come up as 'spontaneous' reactions to political pressures or humanitarian emergency situations, beyond or even in conflict with the mandate (*spontaneous mission creep*), b) tasks which are unsuitable even if there is no capability gap (*unsuitable tasks*), c) tasks which cannot be fulfilled within the time frame (*inappropriate timing*), and finally d) tasks where the mission is gradually dragged deeper into additional mandates.

The unwillingness of NATO's military leadership to be given too many additional tasks is well documented. Former SACEUR Gen. Joulwan has adamantly opposed the idea of peacekeepers trying to arrest war criminals.[31] Western support of Mrs Plavsic in the internal Bosnian Serb struggle led the American SFOR commander Gen. David L. Grange to warn that SFOR should not take sides in the struggle: 'If we don't maintain an even hand, I would not be able to accomplish the mission.' [32] NATO undertakes many efforts to close these 'feasibility gaps' by supporting a variety of civil-military and political activities.[33]

With respect to peacekeeping and enforcement, officers may advocate reluctance towards enforcement actions because they simply do not have the operational means to use military force, e.g. to impose compliance. In such a case, preference for a 'moderate peacekeeping approach' instead of robust enforcement, could be the result of tactical *military* considerations.

Reluctance to undertake enforcement could also result from a *political* consideration of the type of 'even if I could, I should not do it'. For example, the use of force could have a counter-productive effect on the aims of the mandate. In such a case, officers may express reluctance to undertake enforcement action because there is a *feasibility gap*.

To explore such 'gap-situations', we will look further into the tasks which the officers believe should be executed by UNPROFOR peacekeepers, and the extent to which these tasks are deemed professionally 'realistic'. Figures for IFOR are included for illustration (see Table 6.1).[34]

The table presents issues related to three different areas of peacekeeping. Starting with tasks associated with traditional peacekeeping, it then deals with humanitarian tasks and finally looks at enforcement-like tasks. Let us deal with each item in turn with respect to UNPROFOR, while we will make the comparison with IFOR below.

Table 6.1   Feasibility gaps: UNPROFOR and IFOR officers' attitudes to desirable tasks and the realism of fulfilling them

Possible Tasks for Peacekeepers UNPROFOR and *IFOR (italicised)* *	desirable	realistic
'TRADITIONAL PEACEKEEPING' TASKS:		
Mediation between hostile groups/	92	80
in case of conflict, mediate between hostile groups	88	81
Strengthen cease-fires/	93	71
secure the cease-fire line (Zone of Separation)	94	91
Create better conditions for political settlement/	86	58
create conditions for permanent political settlement in Bosnia	83	45
Avoid being perceived as an occupant/	87	62
avoid being perceived as an occupant	92	63
Convince parties to talk to each other/	93	66
convince parties to seriously talk to each other	91	65
Get local support to the UN mission/	88	67
get local support to the IFOR/SFOR mission	81	69
HUMANITARIAN TASKS:		
Reduce violence and atrocities against civilians/	97	70
reduce violence against civilians	95	64
Facilitate return of refugees/	79	46
assist refugees and displaced persons to return to their homes	68	47
Open access of Red Cross and other agencies to detention	87	60
camps/ *open access of Red Cross or other agencies to prisoners or detained persons*	85	62
ENFORCEMENT-LIKE TASKS:		
Reduce military fighting/	92	48
hinder the parties to resume military fighting	97	93
Create conditions to enforce law and order/	86	41
enforce law and order	74	52
Punish attackers and aggressors/	56	19
punish violators of the Peace Agreement	74	49
Eliminate snipers/	83	41
prevent terror against ethnic minorities	91	60

* Italic statements were presented in April 1997 to Danish and Norwegian officers having served under the NATO-led force. We refer to 'IFOR' because most of the officers served before it was renamed 'SFOR' in December 1996. The formulations of tasks are partly modified to meet the same sense under different conditions and mandates: UNPROFOR carrying out peacekeeping in an ongoing war, IFOR/SFOR in peace, after a peace agreement was signed by all parties.

UNPROFOR

Traditional peacekeeping. The figures reveal a more or less unanimous pattern. Nine in ten officers support all the tasks of mediation between hostile groups, strengthening of cease-fires, creation of better conditions for political conflict settlement, fulfilment of UN Security Council mandates, avoidance of being perceived as an occupying power, convincing parties to talk to each other and gaining local support for the UN mission. Similarly, on most issues, seven in ten officers also find the task realistic. The gap between desirability and realism is the smallest for the two tasks of mediation between hostile groups and strengthening of cease-fires while the gap is the largest in the issue of improving conditions for a political settlement. Nevertheless, six in ten UNPROFOR officers see the latter as a realistic task. Given the fact that they operated under war conditions, this realism assessment is peculiarly high.

Humanitarian tasks. Here again, there is widespread approval among the UNPROFOR officers for including humanitarian tasks in their mission. This includes unanimous support for tasks like reduction of violence and atrocities against civilians, facilitating the return of refugees and opening of access for Red Cross and other agencies to detention camps. Again the expected realism is fairly high. The exception is perhaps facilitation of the return of refugees, deemed realistic by only five in ten. The fact that seven in ten rate the reduction of violence and atrocities as realistic, is remarkable, taking into account that UNPROFOR worked with few resources under the conditions of an ongoing war. The generally high realism of the humanitarian tasks corresponds with the above notion that maintaining a reputation for impartiality is not an obstacle to action against atrocities by an individual peacekeeper.

Enforcement-like tasks. Finally, we asked the officers to assess the desirability and the realism of enforcement-like tasks. One should remember that the SRSG and UNPROFOR force commanders were repeatedly blamed for being hesitant to act. Reluctance to act can, however, generally be based on sound reasoning. As indicated above, there may be a *capability gap* within the UN, implying insufficient capability to act. In such a case it is relatively easy to say 'no'. Or there may exist a *feasibility gap,* a feasible reason not to act because the effect of the move would not serve its intended purpose or because, ultimately, the action could put the whole mission at risk. In such cases it is wise not to act, even if the capability to do so is available. Several examples in this book describe situations where NATO was ready to provide the capability for forceful action, but where the action was not 'feasible' and as a result had counterproductive effects.[35]

The issues addressed under enforcement are reduction in military fighting, creation of conditions to enforce law and order, and elimination of snipers. All these tasks are widely perceived as desirable and are supported by eight in ten officers. But here the feasibility gap becomes much more prominent than for the issues of traditional peacekeeping and humanitarian tasks. Only half of the officers see these tasks as realistic for a UN mission.

Among the enforcement issues, one of the most emotional and, in the light of the brutality of war, the most difficult one is 'punishment of attackers and aggressors'. This is also for the UN peacekeeping a highly atypical approach, reflected by the fact that only half of the officers see punishment as desirable (three in ten say 'strongly desirable'). The widespread agreement that punishment is not a realistic option for peacekeepers is a strong message. It may reflect the earlier mentioned negative experiences after air attacks in Bosnia. At the same time it also confirms UN policy and lessons learnt from the disastrous outcome of incidents where punishment or revenge has played a role, as in Somalia 1993 and Beirut 1983. Among the two in ten who actually find it realistic, only less than one in ten rate this task as 'very realistic'.

Looking further into the background of the officers, it is revealed that higher and lower ranking officers do not take very different stands on the three types of tasks, although there is a general shared trend among higher officers to be more cautious about the question of using force. Four in ten rate it 'very unrealistic'. However, looking closer at their national background, we observe a striking difference concerning the desirability of punishment. On the one end of the spectrum we find that six to seven in ten of Finnish and Norwegian officers reject the notion of punishment. At the other extreme, seven in ten Turkish and French officers see punishment as desirable. The differentiation is even more striking when looking closer into the degrees of support for the respective positions. Punishment is rated as strongly desirable by four in ten Turkish and French officers, while the same goes for only one in ten Norwegian and Finnish ones.

In sum, the gap between desirability and realism widens as one moves from traditional peacekeeping and humanitarian tasks, to enforcement-like tasks. In particular, the question of the extreme version of enforcement – forceful military sanction – shows a deep gap between desirability and ability. While about half of the officers would like to punish aggressors, most officers agree that this mission is unrealistic for UN troops. The differences in national response, however, indicate a quite different philosophy in this question between peacekeeping nations of different backgrounds in military history and in peacekeeping operations.

IFOR compared to UNPROFOR[36]

There is no doubt that the character of the IFOR mandate is quite different from UNPROFOR. Ironically, the former is implementing a mandate that looks much more like a peacekeeping mandate – UNPROFOR's mandate.[37] Thus UNPROFOR represents somehow a peacekeeping force in an 'enforcement' mission, while IFOR represents a war-fighting troop in a 'peacekeeping' mission.

While not necessarily representative of all officers with service in IFOR, the opinions expressed may give some indicative ideas on tasks which are seen as best handled by IFOR, and tasks which are seen as better handled by 'Blue Helmets'. And, there may of course be areas where it does not make much of a difference whether a UN or NATO-led force is doing the job.

Comparing UNPROFOR officers with IFOR officers, our thesis is that possible deficits in the future success of tasks given to IFOR will not flow from lack of 'military capability'. In contrast to UNPROFOR, those tasks eventually rated as less realistic by IFOR would indicate 'feasibility gaps' because these problems will be encountered by an international military force operating under optimal conditions of peace and with nearly unlimited military resources.

We expected that IFOR, given its overwhelming military authority, was unlikely to have any relevant 'deficit' in relation to a) purely military tasks, and b) tasks we categorized as 'enforcement-like' tasks. This seemed to be confirmed by the fact that more than nine in ten officers rated IFOR as being 'more accepted by the parties than UNPROFOR' because of its robust military power (figures not shown in table).

None the less, turning back to Table 6.1, we see that the actual picture is much more differentiated. It is in the field of mainly military tasks, for instance in securing the cease-fire line – a classical peacekeeping task – and in military 'enforcement-like' tasks, where IFOR enjoys rates of realism much higher than in UNPROFOR. While for example five in ten UNPROFOR officers find it realistic that they can reduce or hinder fighting, the comparable rate within IFOR is nine in ten. In the light of the fact that UNPROFOR worked in the middle of a war, whereas IFOR worked on the basis of a peace agreement, the most significant aspect in this single finding is that every second UNPROFOR officer is optimistic that the UN forces could carry out such a task.

The opinions expressed by the IFOR officers may also reflect less hesitancy and a feeling of greater capability to use force in order to successfully compel the parties to comply with the mandate, and to 'punish' forcefully violators of the peace agreement. Concerning military 'punishment' there is a tremendous difference between answers given by UNPROFOR and IFOR officers to similar tasks. About seven in ten find it 'desirable' 'to punish violators of the Peace Agreement', while at the same time five in ten IFOR, but only two in ten UNPROFOR officers, see 'punishment' as a realistic task to bring the parties to compliance.

In other words, there seems to be no military capability gap for NATO in implementing the military parts and punishing violators of the Dayton agreement. But only half of the IFOR officers find the latter task realistic. If so, their opinion indicates that even an overwhelming military capability power has its limits in enforcing an agreement.

The picture concerning other *enforcement-like* task looks quite different, however, when the officers are confronted with more politically relevant tasks like 'enforcement of law and order'. Here seven in ten IFOR officers find the task desirable, while only half of them find it realistic. Prevention of terror against ethnic minorities is rated as a realistic task only by six in ten officers – although the prevention of 'deliberate violence to life and person' of refugees and displaced persons belongs to the IFOR tasks according to the Dayton Agreement.[38]

Concerning other traditional *peacekeeping tasks*, the results are also remarkable. Gaining local support for IFOR is rated as desirable by eight in ten IFOR officers, but only four to five regard it as realistic. The feasibility gap is considerable, and IFOR officers feel a slightly bigger gap between desirability and attainability of local support for the mission than UNPROFOR. IFOR and UNPROFOR officers see a similar problem in avoiding being perceived as an 'occupant', or in convincing the parties to talk to one another, rated in both cases as desirable by nine in ten, and realistic by six in ten. Both, UNPROFOR as well as IFOR officers, feel to the same extent – eight in ten – able to mediate in the case of hostilities. Concerning the creation of conditions for a political settlement, desired by most, IFOR officers (five in ten) are less optimistic than those in UNPROFOR (six in ten).

These figures may be interpreted in several ways. IFOR may demonstrate the absence of a feasibility gap for enforcement tasks as long they are predominantly military. Military tasks are feasible for a defence organization, and NATO's competence and strength provides confidence that there is no capability gap. UNPROFOR, characterised by under-equipped resources, had to face the capability deficit repeatedly.[39]

But that does not necessarily reflect an attitude among the officers that IFOR is the better and therefore the future alternative to UN peacekeeping. On the NATO side, the survey has revealed a considerable feasibility gap. This may reflect the fact that the ability to restore law and order is perceived as having less potential to be successful in post-Dayton peacetime, as compared to the traditional UN blue helmet. Figure 6.12 shows some of the feasibility assessments by IFOR officers concerning the implementation of the Dayton Agreement.

Figure 6.12 IFOR officers' attitudes to the feasibility of tasks expected from the Dayton Agreement

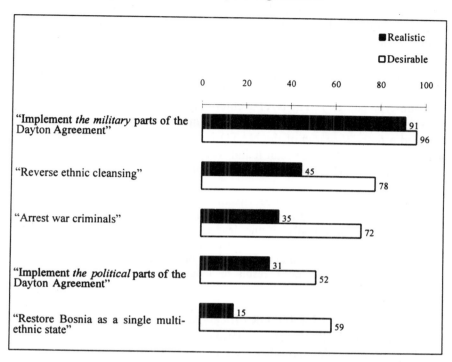

More than nine in ten IFOR officers find it desirable as well as realistic to implement the military parts of Dayton. Concerning the implementation of the political parts of the Dayton Agreement, however, IFOR officers are less optimistic that they can succeed. Only three in ten believe that success is realistic. The low 'success rate' is complemented in other important, specific political issues. Less than half believe that with the IFOR operation, there is a real chance of reversing ethnic cleansing. Six in ten IFOR officers believe it desirable that Bosnia be restored as a single multi-ethnic state, while fewer than two in ten see a realistic chance that this mission can succeed. About one-third believe in the arrest of indicted war criminals although seven in ten would like to see this happen.

The limited possibility for success through military intervention seen by peacekeeping officers represents a very strong message when seen in the light of opinions articulated by IFOR officers concerning the importance of NATO influence, power and authority for the success of the operation (not shown). Nine in ten agree that the mission is accepted by the parties because IFOR has the full backing of NATO and can use robust force to implement the mandate. However, military power is not enough, and as shown earlier, most IFOR officers do not consider themselves well prepared for non-military challenges of their mission, in particular with respect to understanding of the local culture and acting in a friendly manner in hostile situations.

At a press conference in Sarajevo 12 September 1997, SACEUR General Clark emphasized that SFOR was 'not trained in riot control, in the finer arts of crowd control' and would rather use lethal force against 'intifada-type tactics'.[40] The NATO chief may have had a deterring *political* message to the extremists in Bosnia in mind. But he could also have revealed a *feasibility gap* of the NATO-led force in handling public unrest or provocations with other than lethal weapons which could contribute to a scenario that NATO's peace support doctrine has warned against:

> The unnecessary use of force will adversely affect the perceived impartiality and credibility affect to the organization, leading potentially to the loss of consent...Additionally, it may lead to an overall increase in the level of violence throughout the mission area...Any recourse to force should be aimed at resolving and defusing a situation, not escalating it. A short term tactical success...could result in long term damage to the strategic mission.[41]

The views of the UNPROFOR officers, as well as comments by Danish and Norwegian IFOR officers, underline the feasibility gap of NATO in handling law and order and other civilian tasks. As an example for many of his compatriots, a Danish officer noted:

> It is necessary to concentrate more efforts on the civilian part of the Dayton Agreement. Otherwise, the military force will be expected to do tasks it is not trained for, e.g. police work, civilian aid and political negotiation.[42]

One of his Norwegian comrades noted in the same spirit:

> IFOR/SFOR should concentrate on what it can best, which is the military part of Dayton. IFOR/SFOR should play a lesser role in the civilian part of it, and this role should be clearly defined before deployment.[43]

This confirms some of NATO's own lessons learned, as Secretary-General Solana pointed out: 'Experience in Bosnia revealed a gap between the ability of SFOR to provide for a secure environment, and the problems of domestic police force in guaranteeing law and order locally under democratic control.'[44]

Conclusion

The starting point of our analysis was the widespread notion that UN operations in new civil war-like conflicts have challenged the 'old' peacekeeping approach of the United Nations, based on the principles of consent, impartiality, and the non-use of force other than in self-defence. The major problem raised is how the old principles work in the field under the 'new' circumstances.

Our initial thesis was that the military personnel in UNPROFOR understand their role primarily as soldiers in a mission for peace rather than as combatants to defeat an enemy. To better understand how peacekeepers can work under the new conditions, we have interviewed a selection of UNPROFOR (and IFOR) officers using a standard questionnaire. The problem has further been treated as a challenge to the UN peacekeeping force from the 'inside' as well as from the 'outside' from the viewpoint of their direction by the Security Council or by national decision makers. It is dealt with under three general headings, which can now be reviewed based on the main findings.

The first question addressed is to what degree traditional peacekeeping principles are still seen as usable guidelines for peacekeeping in the area of operation. The survey indicates overwhelming support for a common 'peacekeeping approach'. Most officers still adhere to the traditional peacekeeping principles. On the other hand, while the officers according to their own view are well trained, traditional training is seen as insufficient with relation to handling of media and understanding of the local culture in the mission area. At the same time, these issues are regarded as vital to peacekeepers operating in a civil war. Attitudes are, however, somewhat different between 'traditional' and 'new' contributors to UN peacekeeping operations; the newcomers tend to take more 'combative' stands than those with a longer history in the field.

The second question raised is how the principles are interrelated with each other in the everyday experience of the peacekeepers. In general, we can say that UNPROFOR officers still perceive their role as one of a traditional peacekeeper, as reflected also in their positive opinions towards the traditional peacekeeping principles. Comparing the officers' attitudes toward various questions reveal that most of them take the same positive stand on each. The overwhelming majority appear as 'doves' in this respect, while only a few take a general 'hawk' position.

While peacekeepers differ in their opinion on the desirability of active use of military force in a PKO in general, disagreement may be less visible when it comes to its usefulness in practice. The opinions expressed show that the reality of a UN mission makes most of the officers agree that certain enforcement tasks are simply not achievable. Their conclusion, that they should behave like peacekeepers and not like enforcers, is contrary to expectations of the public in respective nations, and to media reports or political statements that peacekeepers should 'act tough'.

It is also evident that external factors such as troop-contributing governments, international media, politicians and local organizations, have considerable influence on the capability of peacekeeping officers to fulfil their mission. Many officers go as far as to say that interference in operational matters can put their work as peacekeepers unnecessary at risk.

Concerning UNPROFOR's relationship with NATO, the strength of NATO is primarily seen as its indispensable military professionalism even though the alliance made an enormous effort to integrate and practise UN principles in the former Yugoslavia. In the reality of complex political and humanitarian operations, however, the officers see the UN and its Blue Helmets, in some cases as equally and in other cases even more, appropriate to apply the 'soft' tools of peacekeeping, required for de-escalation and settling of conflicts than a heavily armed NATO force. Partly, but importantly, the reason for this also is most probably embodied in a recognition of the UN as the less controversial actor when introduced to assist in solving international crises.

Finally we raised the question of what can be considered a realistic achievement for UN peacekeeping in the difficult reality of an ongoing civil war-like conflict. Traditional *peacekeeping* tasks receive a high degree of support among the peacekeepers, but there is also a high rate of expectation as to what can in fact be realistically achieved. *Humanitarian tasks* also receive a high degree of support, although expectations as to what is a realistic achievement in this field are significantly smaller. Military *enforcement* and law and order enforcement tasks receive relatively low support among the UNPROFOR officers. Expectations as to what is realistically achieved are consequently also pretty modest.

Looking at the three overall questions in combination, we observe what may be defined as a sound scepticism among officers as to what can possibly be achieved by an international force. Where the UN has a military capability gap, they support stronger military responsibility from NATO. Where NATO has a feasibility gap in relation to the complexity of peacekeeping, the officers prefer the UN as the leading agency.

Notes

1 We used the answering scheme 'strongly agree – agree more than disagree – disagree more than agree – strongly disagree', and temptation to choose a 'neutral' position was reduced by offering a separate category 'undecided', etc.

2 To maximize control, the following procedure was applied:

The survey population was concentrated on officers serving with UNPROFOR; a major group, in particular from Nordic countries, had in addition experiences from other UN PKO like UNIFIL, etc.

Questionnaires were delivered to contact partners in Defence Commands or in the area of operation, who were asked to return – if possible some 150–200 questionnaires of each troop-contributing country represented.

Within each nation, officers were divided into three groups according to high-, middle- and lower military ranks.

Questionnaires were in most cases randomly distributed among the officers through Defence Ministries or Defence Commands. Two exceptions were made in this case. The Norwegian officers were offered questionnaires following their de-briefing meetings after home rotations and filled them in on a voluntary basis. Turkish questionnaires were randomly distributed in their area of operation in Bosnia-Herzegovina.

With the exception of about 40 Swedish questionnaires distributed during May 1995, all questionnaires were filled in between September and December 1995. This means for interpretation of survey results: all officers were aware of the escalation of war since the end of May 1995, of 'hostage-taking', the final brutal acts of ethnic cleansing by Bosnian Serbs conquering Srebrenica and Zepa, and by Croatia's 'reintegration' and ethnic cleansing of Krajina. Participants were also aware of the NATO operation 'Deliberate Force' during September 1995 which was presented in the media as a great success, in contrast to the UNPROFOR operation that was generally perceived by the public opinion as a failure or even disaster.

3 An important implication for the survey representativity is the sample size. Covering more than 900 officers it is fairly large, given the financial resources available. Still, like any survey, it faces statistical error, in particular when the sample is disaggregated to subcategories (for example distinguishing between different nationalities). As a rough rule of thumb, the statistical margin of error increases the closer the response pattern approaches a 50/50 distribution, and the smaller the sample size. For example, if 50% of all the officers surveyed agree to a statement, the 'true' proportion among the officers in the field will be in the range of 43–57% (given simple random selection and over 95% confidence that the true value lies between that range). If 10% of the officers agree, the 'true' value will be around 7–13%. When broken down further according to background characteristics, the number of respondents for each subgroup will be smaller, and statistical margins of errors can increase further.

4 Interviews with WEU police officers in Mostar, November 1994; see also Husum's chapter in this book.

5 The total sum of results in per cent can deviate by plus/minus one per cent point due to round-up procedures.

6 See e.g., Chopra, Jarat and Mackinley, John, 'Second Generation Multinational Operations', in: *The Washington Quarterly*, Vol. 15, No. 3, Summer 1992, p. 113 ff; Weiss, Thomas G., 'Problems for Future UN Military Operations in "An Agenda for Peace"', in: Kühne, Winrich (ed.), *Blauhelme in einer turbulenten Welt*, ibid., p. 183; Lewis, Samuel W. and Sisk, Tom, 'Enhancing Stability: Peacemaking and Peacekeeping', in: Graham, James R. (ed.), *Non-Combat roles for the US Military in the*

Post-Cold War Era, National Defence University Press: Washington DC, 1993, pp. 29–63.

7   See Ridgway, Chapter 13 in this book.

8   Questionnaire remarks by a British Lt. Col.

9   Questionnaire remarks by a British Captain with experiences from Cyprus and Bosnia.

10 Questionnaire remarks by a French Major with experiences from Cambodia and Bosnia.

11 Questionnaire remarks by a British Lt. Col. interviewed November 1994.

12 Questionnaire remarks by a Canadian Lt. Col.

13 The officer is given the score of 1 if he strongly favours the UN principle and the score of 5 if he is against the principle. The two intermediate positions of partly supporting and partly opposing it are given the scores of 2 and 4 respectively, while those undecided are given the intermediate value of 3. The total score thus ranges from 9 for the most pro-UN principle adherents to 45 for the most anti-UN principle opponents.

14 The position along the continuum is represented by the mean attitude index score for each nation.

15 Questionnaire remarks by a Canadian officer.

16 Questionnaire remarks by a Canadian Captain.

17 A high-ranking Danish officer expressed concern about possible negative reactions in the field if survey results were published by single nations about their attitudes to the parties.

18 See Merveldt, Chapter 15 in this book.

19 See Sanderson, Chapter 12 in this book; also: Findlay, Trevor, *Cambodia, the Legacy and Lessons of UNTAC*, SIPRI Research Report No. 9, Oxford University Press: London 1995, p. 152.

20 Questionnaire remarks by a Norwegian UNMO deployed in Mostar.

21 IFOR Lessons Learned Seminar October 1996, NATO School (SHAPE) in Oberammmergau, Germany.

22 See in particular Lapresle, Chapter 8 in this book.

23 'Lift and Strike' stands for 'lift the embargo' and 'strike the Serbs'.

24 See Wahlgren, Chapter 10 and the First UN Commanders' Workshop, Chapter 4. Thorvald Stoltenberg concludes in his book *'tusen dagene'* as one of his lessons learned for the future that the gap between word and action, power and responsibility should be avoided. He refers to the Safe Areas having showed the deadly consequences of promising more than one is able or willing to fulfil. Permanent members of the UNSC should therefore not only have the right to take decisions on the use of military forces but also the obligation to participate with their own troops to share the risks of their decisions. (Stoltenberg, Thorvald and Eide, Kai: *De tusen dagene, fredsmeklere på Balkan*, Gyldendal Norsk Forlag: Oslo 1996, p. 404ff.)

25 Interviews by the editors at UNPROFOR HQ Zagreb, October 1994 and briefings in UNPF HQ, November 1995.

26 The survey method to couple the categories 'desirable/realistic' is as a result of careful discussion during the pilot tests of the questionnaires. The opinions about what is 'desirable' primarily express individual normative attitudes, even if they are to some extent the 'limits of reality' moderating a personal 'wish'. The category 'realistic' is given by the respondents as a matter of professional assessment as a practitioner in the field.

        This interpretation has been confirmed by feedback interviews made with participants after the survey was finalized.

27 A variety of examples are given in Akashi, Chapter 7 in this book.

28 *Supplement to An Agenda for Peace*, p. 15.

29 Ibid.

30 A most striking example of 'capability gaps' on the one hand and 'feasibility gaps' on the other are the contradictory Safe Areas concepts discussed at several places in this book and in detail described in Lavoyer's and Wahlgren's chapters:

    a) A demilitarized Safe Area, as negotiated in Srebrenica in March 1993 and mandated by UNSC Resolution 819, with a zone of separation controlled by UNPROFOR. This concept was feasible but was denied the necessary military capability...the task suffered from a capability gap.

    b) Later, with UNSC Resolution 836, SAs were, backed by NATO air power, imposed on the Serbs without demilitarization, zones of separation, etc. This concept was not at all feasible for a UN force, based on an illusion of 'enforcement' (or it would have required a major occupation force). The task suffered from a feasibility gap.

31 'Raid in Bosnia. A Turning Point For Peacekeepers', *IHT*, 12/13 July 1997.

32 *SHAPE & SFOR News*, 20 October 1997.

33 See e.g. the list of progress presented by the NATO Secretary-General at the *European Forum Berlin, Panel on Pan-European Peacekeeping*, 8 November 1997; SHAPE, PfP/IFOR unclassified, Lessons Learned Seminar January 1997 (NIDS).

34 As the mandate and conditions of the UNPROFOR and the NATO-led operation are different, wording of statements were slightly different. Moreover, as mentioned introductorily, the IFOR survey is not covering all participating nations, and is limited to Danish and Norwegian officers. Hence direct statistical comparison is questionable. However, a statistical check-up of separate Danish and Norwegian UNPROFOR officers with the rest of the UNPROFOR officers along these issues demonstrates *no* significant differences in attitudes expressed.

    Therefore, the experiment of comparing opinion trends of UNPROFOR and IFOR on potential gaps between desired tasks and estimated realism could be worth doing to compare possibilities and limits of peacekeepers under different operational conditions.

35 See various references to Safe Areas. For other events we refer to the chapters by major actors in Part Three as well as to Chapter 3, 'Setting the Scene', about the 'vicious enforcement-chaos circle'.

36 To avoid accidental nation-related deviations from the complete UNPROFOR survey, we have also compared the Danish and Norwegian IFOR figures with only Danish and Norwegian UNPROFOR officers. The Danes and Norwegians demonstrate no deviances from the total UNPROFOR officers corpse.

37 See a/o contributions by Akashi and de Lapresle, Chapters 7, 8 and the Second UN Commanders' Workshop, Chapter 5 in this book.

38 'Article VI, Deployment of the Implementation Force', Annex 1-A, *Agreement on the Military Aspects of the Peace Settlement*, General Framework Agreement, ibid., p. 1229ff.

39 See Akashi, de Lapresle, Rose and Wahlgren, Chapters 7–10 in this book.

40 'I told President Milosevic last week when I saw him that these intifada-type tactics must be stopped. They will not succeed against SFOR. SFOR, you see, is not a police force. It's not trained in riot control, it's not trained in the finer arts of crowd control. It's a military force. It's given a mission; it accomplishes that mission. It has the authority and the capability to use lethal force should it be so threatened. It will use that force. Should it use lethal force, I want to underscore that the responsibility for the casualties that might result rest with the perpetrators of the actions against SFOR.' (General Clark, in *Transcript: Joint Press Conference*, 12 September 1997, 1415 Hours, Coalition Press Information Centre Holiday Inn, Sarajevo.)

41 PfP Unclassified Bi-MNC, *Directive for NATO Doctrine for Peace Support Operations*, 11 December 1995, p. 14.

42 Questionnaire remarks by a Danish SFOR officer.

43 Questionnaire remarks by a Norwegian SFOR officer.
44 'Panel on Pan-European Peacekeeping', *European Forum Berlin*, 8 November 1997 (NIDS).

Part Three

MILITARY AND DIPLOMATIC VIEWS

First Section

The United Nations, the Security Council, Mandates and Means

Part Three

MILITARY AND DIPLOMATIC VIEWS

7 Managing United Nations Peacekeeping

The Role of the Security Council vs. the Role of the Secretary-General

YASUSHI AKASHI[*]

The successful management of any complex endeavour requires a well-understood delineation of responsibilities amongst those participating in the endeavour, as well as a clearly defined objective. Success also requires that each participant competently fulfil the tasks assigned to them, and avoid trampling upon the areas of responsibility of other participants. The players and management on a baseball team all know their respective responsibilities, as do the members and producers of an orchestra. Just as no General Manager of a baseball team would rightly consider making a decision on whether a runner should try to steal a base, no flutist would dream of playing the part of a trombone. These rather elemental and self-evident rules of management also apply to United Nations peacekeeping. In fact, it is even more crucial to respect these rules when managing a peacekeeping operation than most other endeavours, given the highly charged political context, the military stakes and the oftentimes strategic interests of major world powers involved. When these rules are followed, the chances for success of a peacekeeping operation are at their best. When these basic rules are ignored, or respected in the breach, as was the case in the former Yugoslavia, the likelihood of success drops precipitously.

In this chapter, I examine the respective roles of the United Nations Secretary-General and of the Security Council in managing the exceedingly complex operations of peacekeeping. Drawing on my experiences in Cambodia and in the former Yugoslavia, I highlight instances when sound management practices were followed, and others when they were not, and point out the differences in results. While I use the term Secretary-General throughout the chapter, I am also referring to his Special Representative in

---

[*] Yasushi Akashi (J) is UN Under-Secretary-General for Humanitarian Affairs and Emergency Relief Co-ordinator. He served as the Special Representative of the UN Secretary-General (SRSG) in the former Yugoslavia.

the field, and to the senior decision makers on peacekeeping in the Secretariat, in particular the Under-Secretary-General for Peacekeeping Operations.

Although managing peacekeeping operations is highly complex, the role of the Security Council is in essence policy setting, and the role of the Secretary-General is policy implementation. In Cambodia, the Council established the objectives for the peacekeeping operation in advance of its deployment, as stipulated in the Paris Peace Agreements, and then left it to the Secretary-General to implement. In times of difficulty, the Council lent its political weight and influence in support of the Secretary-General. The result of this approach was largely successful. In contrast, in the former Yugoslavia, the Council repeatedly involved itself in policy implementation; at times it appeared almost as if the Council wanted to run the day-to-day operations of the United Nations Protection Force. Also, largely due to the somewhat incoherent policy approach of the Council to the conflict, the Secretary-General at times became involved in policy setting. The assumption of certain responsibilities by both the Security Council and the Secretary-General that rightly belonged to the other resulted in confusion and, in the end, poor management of the peacekeeping operation in the former Yugoslavia.

In addition to being competent at fulfilling these respective roles, it is crucial that both the Security Council and the Secretary-General are credible, and seen to be so, by the parties on the receiving end of a peacekeeping operation (PKO). So much of peacekeeping has to do with image, perception and strength of will. A Security Council or Secretary-General that is not considered credible by one or more parties to a conflict will soon be subject to exploitation and opportunism by that party or parties. The need to maintain credibility, in addition to competence, must be borne in mind when examining the performance of the Council and of the Secretary-General in managing peacekeeping operations.

The fundamental role of the Security Council in managing United Nations peacekeeping operations is policy setting. A policy, if it is to make any sense at all, must have an objective. Thus, once a decision in principle has been taken by the Council to dispatch a peacekeeping operation, but prior to actually authorizing one, the Council must decide on the objectives it intends to achieve through the operation. The objectives should be clear, readily understood and achievable. Depending on an analysis of the political-military context in which the peacekeeping operation is to be deployed, and the objectives established, the Council must then decide whether to authorize a 'traditional' peacekeeping operation under Chapter VI of the UN Charter, or an enforcement operation under Chapter VII.[1] This decision will largely determine the resources required for attainment of the established objectives. The Security Council must then authorize a force with all the requisite resources to achieve the stated goals. It is imperative that the Council not shrink from authorizing and when necessary from advocating to have the resources required for the mission it has established. Once the Council has taken these steps, its primary responsibilities have been fulfilled, and it should then defer to the Secretary-General to implement the policy it has established.

During the life of a peacekeeping operation, the Council of course should remain well informed of progress in achieving its established goals. If the Council determines that the eventual success of the operation is at risk, or that fundamental provisions of the peace agreement that initially called for the dispatch of a peacekeeping operation are being violated, or that there are unacceptable obstacles being placed in the way of the operation, then it should take appropriate action following close consultations with the Secretary-General. Such action could be in the form of the Council's President calling in the Ambassador from the offending country, for the President to make comments to the press or an official Presidential Statement, or the Council could pass a Resolution. In certain cases, the dispatch of a Security Council mission to the operational theatre may be appropriate. It is crucial, however, that when considering an effective response to a given situation, the Council pay due regard to the issue of credibility. If Presidential Statements, for instance, have been made on several previous occasions in the same conflict with no apparent ameliorating effect on the party concerned, the Council may be doing itself a disservice by issuing yet another Presidential Statement that is likely to be ignored, and hence to call into question the Council's credibility.

Normally, the two essential conditions for international conflict resolution are the will of the parties to find a solution, and an international consensus on the general framework for a solution. Prior to the dispatch of a classical, Chapter VI peacekeeping operation, the Council must first determine if the former condition is present, and at the same time produce and maintain the latter. While this rule should generally be followed, exceptions may be required in the case of humanitarian emergencies. However, in such cases, the objectives of the mission must be tailored accordingly, and must be effectively communicated by the United Nations to the general public and to the parties in conflict.

To succeed at maintaining consensus in support of a peacekeeping operation, the Security Council should remain focused on the mission objectives that it originally established, and avoid getting distracted by or drawn into the tactical or operational issues with which the Secretary-General will routinely be confronted. The Council as a whole, and its individual members, ought to support the Secretary-General as he carries out his assigned tasks and defer to him on questions of implementation. There of course would rightly be exceptions to this practice in particularly serious matters, such as the ultimate success of the mission, fundamental principles of law or morality, or the safety of UN troops.

The role of the Secretary-General in managing peacekeeping operations is, in its most general sense, implementation of the policy established by the Security Council. This role, however, involves a plethora of responsibilities, and in certain areas stretches beyond just implementation. One of the most crucial roles of the Secretary-General that will have a substantial impact on policy setting is the provision of information and analysis to the Security Council. In most cases, the Council establishes a peacekeeping operation following the submission of a report by the Secretary-General to the Council. The report normally describes consultations that the Secretary-General or an envoy has had with the parties in conflict, an analysis of the political-military situation, recommendations for the dispatch of a peacekeeping operation, what its mandate should be and what resources would be required to fulfil the mandate.

Thus, although the Council itself is fully charged with making policy decisions, its decisions are heavily influenced by the analysis and recommendations of the Secretary-General, whose views are particularly important on the issues of mandate, including mission objectives, and resources. The Secretary-General tends to be more realistic about what is achievable by a UN force than the Security Council, which at times has demonstrated a tendency to engage in wishful thinking in response to political pressures or mass media reporting. The role of the Secretary-General is a heavy responsibility for both the SG and the SG's staff. It requires them to be competent both in obtaining the necessary information, and in carrying out sound analysis of that information prior to making a recommendation on the dispatch of a peacekeeping operation.

Once the Security Council has passed a Resolution authorizing a peacekeeping operation, which is in effect a policy-setting document, the Secretary-General's primary role becomes the implementation of the established policy. The Secretary-General should be given wide latitude in determining how best to implement the policy, but does not have leeway in deciding to implement the policy or not, or which parts of the policy should be implemented. If the Secretary-General has a fundamental disagreement on a policy matter with the Council, or believes that the situation on the ground has changed to such an extent that the original premises upon which the Council's policy were based have changed, then the Secretary-General has the right and the obligation to inform the Council of his views and/or of the changed circumstances. However, unless and until the Council has acted on the Secretary-General's information, he remains obligated to pursue the policy established by the Council.

In addition to reporting on fundamental changes to the mission environment, the Secretary-General has a routine reporting responsibility to the Council. Such routine reports come in the form of verbal briefings to the Council, or periodic reports as requested by the Council, and are designed to keep the Council fully informed of the mission's progress. The Secretary-General must alert the Council to difficulties he may be having with implementation, and inform it of measures he intends to take to address those difficulties. If he is unable to resolve a problem on his own, the Secretary-General may request the Council's support. Reversion to this option should, however, be used with relative infrequency in order not to diminish the currency of the Council's intervention.

In managing a peacekeeping operation, the Secretary-General must also be the lead Manager. United Nations' missions are by their nature multinational; diverse cultures and approaches to conflict are found in the military chain of command. There are usually differences in perspective between the military and the civilian elements of a peacekeeping operation as well. Normally, a UN peacekeeping operation has a civilian leader, the Special Representative of the Secretary-General (SRSG), and several civilian components, for instance civil affairs, civilian police, maybe a human rights component, and/or an electoral component. The military component is generally the largest, by far, in terms of both personnel and resources. Each component will have its own interests and priorities. Sometimes, contrary to established principle, certain national military contingents may be pressured by their home governments to be responsive to national imperatives in addition to their responsibilities to the United Nations. The competing interests of different components, the cultural differences both between national contingents and between the civilians and the military, and the occasional pursuit of national interests through troops assigned to a UN operation, can all be sources of divisiveness in a peacekeeping operation. The Secretary-General has a crucial role to play in creating and maintaining a team spirit in a PKO, a united approach, and a unity of purpose in pursuit of the mandate established by the Security Council. This role falls largely on the Special Representative of the Secretary-General in the field.

The SRSG also has an important responsibility to ensure that the personnel working in a PKO are held to the highest standards of professional and ethical behaviour, and that they respect local laws, customs and culture. It is imperative that personnel, civilian or military, who represent the United Nations and wear the UN insignia, respect the values and the human rights principles which the UN itself has promulgated and for which it stands.

If both the Security Council and the Secretary-General fulfil their respective roles, then the United Nations will have done what it could to design, deploy and manage a successful PKO. Of course, except in enforcement operations, final success also depends in part on the willingness of the parties to work with the UN and to make the PKO a success. In Cambodia and in the former Yugoslavia, the UN was confronted with wildly different environments. In Cambodia, the external conditions for success were present, and the PKO was well managed by both the Security Council and the Secretary-General. In the former Yugoslavia, the external conditions were hostile and worked against the UN, and sound peacekeeping management practices were not consistently followed.

After years of being caught in the strategic tussle between the superpowers over influence in Southeast Asia, Cambodia was one of the first countries to benefit from the *rapprochement* between the Soviet Union and the United States that preceded the end of the Cold War. The fruitless negotiations on the Cambodian conflict of the 1980s were transformed into the comprehensive and productive negotiations of the early 1990s that resulted in the Paris Peace Agreements of October 1991. The Agreements, signed by 19 countries including the five permanent members of the Security Council, were an expression of the strong international consensus in support of both the resolution of the Cambodian conflict and the modalities by which this would be achieved. This consensus remained in place throughout the duration of the United Nations Transitional Authority in Cambodia (UNTAC), the peacekeeping operation that was deployed to Cambodia.

The four major Cambodian parties also demonstrated a willingness to abandon their military conflict and achieve a peaceful settlement of their dispute.[2] In the case of the Khmer Rouge, and to a lesser extent the State of Cambodia, their commitment to the Peace Agreements later came into question due to their unwillingness to respect some of the Agreements' key provisions. Ultimately, and despite some disagreements, there remained sufficient commitment to the Agreements by the three parties other than the Khmer Rouge to keep the peace process on track and to hold elections in June 1993.

The Paris Peace Agreements, negotiated with the extensive involvement of the permanent members of the Security Council, became in essence the UNTAC mandate. The Agreements set a clear objective for the peacekeeping operation, democratic elections, and described a strategy that would achieve the objective. Mandates were spelled out in the areas of military, police, civil administration, human rights, rehabilitation and of course elections. Thus, when UNTAC arrived, a solid framework was in place, and UNTAC knew what it was supposed to accomplish, but not always how it was supposed to accomplish it. With clearly defined tasks, it was relatively easy to decide upon the resources required, which were then provided without too much difficulty.

Not surprisingly in such a complex operation, problems arose in implementation. The Khmer Rouge refused to disarm until UNTAC had done more in the field of civil administration. The Khmer Rouge's refusal prompted the State of Cambodia also to refuse to disarm. The Khmer Rouge intermittently threatened to, and finally did pull out of the process. Yet, when confronted with these challenges to the peace process, both the Security Council and the Secretary-General stood their ground and maintained their focus on established and agreed-upon objectives. The Secretary-General kept the Council informed of developments on the ground, and the Council supported the Secretary-General in his efforts to implement the Paris Agreements. The Council avoided the temptation to react to every setback with a new resolution. From 16 October 1991, when it created UNTAC's advance mission, UNAMIC, until 27 August 1993 when it ordered the withdrawal of UNTAC, the Council passed only 12 Resolutions and issued only eight Presidential Statements related to the peacekeeping operation. None of the actions by the Council changed the strategy or the ultimate objective of UNTAC.

UNTAC's mission in Cambodia benefited from an international consensus in support of peace not only amongst major international powers but also key regional powers including the ASEAN countries, Japan and Australia, a well-crafted peace agreement, a commitment by the parties to peace, a clear mandate, a clearly defined objective, and from the provision of the resources required to achieve that objective. The Security Council did its part by establishing the mandate, asking the General Assembly to provide the resources, then turning the job over to the Secretary-General, while offering political support when necessary. The Secretary-General did his part by implementing the mandate, reporting on developments on the ground, seeking political support when required, and remaining focused on the objective of the operation. As a result, successful elections were held, post-electoral turmoils were resolved, and UNTAC was able to leave the country having achieved its primary objective.

The conditions so crucial to success in Cambodia were unfortunately lacking in the former Yugoslavia. The involvement of the international community in the conflict in the former Yugoslavia, and in particular Bosnia-Herzegovina, was fraught with problems and misjudgements throughout. The United Nations Protection Force (UNPROFOR), later

renamed United Nations Peace Forces (UNPF), was required to operate in a
hostile political and military environment from the time of its creation in
1991, until an improved political situation developed and the war in Bosnia
ended in late 1995, at which time UNPROFOR was replaced by the
NATO-led Implementation Force (IFOR).³ Although UNPROFOR never
met all the expectations placed on it, one should keep in mind that the
fighting in Bosnia finally ended during UNPROFOR's mandate and that,
by the time IFOR arrived in December 1995, the war was over and a peace
had been agreed to by all sides. Throughout its existence, UNPROFOR
pursued its mandate in the midst of a brutal war fought by three parties.
While each party repeatedly asserted its interest in peace, what they were
really interested in was peace on their own terms. There was never a time
when all three parties simultaneously showed a willingness to make the
necessary sacrifices to achieve overall peace, until they were brought to
Dayton, Ohio in November of 1995. The raging war, and the determination
of the parties to pursue the war option, created an exceedingly hostile
environment for UNPROFOR.

UNPROFOR also suffered from a hostile external political environment.
The different views amongst the permanent members of the Security
Council on the origins and nature of the war in Bosnia, and what should be
the response of the international community, was, in the end, responsible
for many of UNPROFOR's shortcomings. Council members, and
particularly the permanent members, were wildly divided on what the
United Nations should do, and hence on what UNPROFOR's objectives
should be. This division resulted in an ambiguous mandate, which was
frequently altered by subsequent Resolutions that made the mandate even
more unclear. The need to achieve unanimity amongst the permanent
members often produced language in a Resolution that was vague and
subject to varying interpretations, or contradictory. The lack of unity of
outlook by Council members, and the resultant ambiguities in the
UNPROFOR mandate, forced UNPROFOR to operate under the guidance
of the Secretary-General only, in an area where major powers' strategic
interests were at stake. In such a situation, it was inevitable that
UNPROFOR would be criticized not only by the parties on the ground, but
also by Council members, some of whom thought UNPROFOR was doing
much too much, and some others who were convinced UNPROFOR was
not doing nearly enough.

UNPROFOR was placed in the middle of a war between the Bosnian
parties, and in the middle of a strategic struggle between major powers.
Thousands, and later tens of thousands of Blue Helmets were sent to
Bosnia and told not to intervene in the fighting; their job was to protect the
delivery of humanitarian assistance. Yet the war in Bosnia inflicted terrible

cruelties upon civilian populations, with the Bosnian Serbs and Bosnian Croats mainly responsible for the worst war crimes in Europe since the end of the Second World War. For the UN soldiers, armed, flying the UN flag and familiar with the ideals of the Organization, yet told not to intervene to stop the atrocities being committed around them, their anomalous situation often resulted in confusion, morale problems and bitterness. The press who reported on the war, often themselves besieged in Sarajevo, habitually depicted UNPROFOR as complacent and ineffective at putting a stop to the atrocities occurring around it. Yet these news reports were rarely accompanied or supplemented by an objective analysis of UNPROFOR's mandate and the political and military constraints under which it operated. The unending criticisms and demands to do more that daily appeared in newspapers and on television screens added to both the confusion and the sense of frustration felt by some UNPROFOR personnel.

Due in large measure to the press reports coming out of Bosnia, the general public in the West, and in particular in the United States, demanded that the United Nations do more to stop the atrocities and to help the war's victims, generally considered to be the Bosnian Muslims. The United States government, which had allied itself with the Muslim-dominated government in Sarajevo, sought to expand UNPROFOR's mandate in pursuit of these objectives. It was not prepared, however, to send American ground troops to UNPROFOR. Over the course of the war, and as a result of insistent US diplomacy, the Security Council gave UNPROFOR a variety of additional responsibilities. In some cases the Council authorized UNPROFOR, under Chapter VII of the UN Charter, to use 'all means necessary' to achieve the new goals. UNPROFOR was transformed by increment but not by design from a Chapter VI operation to a mixture of a Chapter VI and a Chapter VII operation, authorized to use force under certain conditions, and in pursuit of certain goals. UNPROFOR was told to be an impartial peacekeeper operating under traditional peacekeeping rules of engagement, including the resort to force only in self-defence, in some cases and in some places, but also to use its enforcement powers to achieve its goals in other cases and other places.

This paradox was exacerbated by the different and at times contradictory language that accompanied the authorization to use force. The most blatant example of this is the well-known Resolution 836 that expanded UNPROFOR's responsibility towards the Safe Areas, and authorized UNPROFOR 'in carrying out the mandate...acting in self-defence, to take the necessary measures, including the use of force, in reply to bombardments against the Safe Areas...'. An argument can be made that UNPROFOR should, or should never have been given the responsibility to 'deter' attacks against Safe Areas. Yet it defies logic and basic military common sense to authorize UNPROFOR to use force to do so, but to limit that use of force to cases of self-defence. If the Council's objective was to deter attacks against the Safe Area, as seems to have been the case, no self-defence provision should have been included. This is a clear example of the Council reacting to political expediencies at the expense of the UNPROFOR mission, and in defiance of operational realities and requirements.

The competing interests of the Council's permanent members, and the resultant inability of the Council to develop an overarching strategy toward Bosnia, resulted in the Council responding to tactical developments, issuing mid-course changes, and passing Resolutions that often reflected the domestic political needs of the members rather than the operational and strategic requirements of UNPROFOR. This practice, strategically unwise under any circumstances, was particularly alarming and dangerous because of the peacekeepers' presence in the midst of a raging war.

Differences of opinion between Council members on the appropriate role for the UN in Bosnia were reflected in the ambiguous language used in Council Resolutions on UNPROFOR. The UNPROFOR Headquarters saw a stream of ministers, ambassadors and generals pass through urging the UNPROFOR leadership to act one way or another, depending on the perspective of the government that sent them. These mixed political signals emanating from the Council chamber and from government representatives in Zagreb placed UNPROFOR in a difficult position, and made it the subject of an unending barrage of criticism. With a consensus absent in the Council, lacking a strategy, and burdened by an unclear mandate, UNPROFOR was forced to chart its own course. There was only limited support for a 'robust' enforcement policy by UNPROFOR. UNPROFOR thus chose to pursue a policy of relatively passive enforcement, the lowest common denominator on which all Council members more or less agreed.

The proliferation of Security Council Resolutions and Presidential Statements tended to diminish the credibility of the Council. Gripped by the perceived need to 'do something' in response to the carnage routinely shown on television screens, the Council passed one Resolution after another, and issued Presidential Statement after Presidential Statement. Over three-and-a-half years, the Council regularly demanded an end to hostilities, respect for civilian life, freedom of movement for UNPROFOR, etc. Between 21 February 1992, when UNPROFOR was first deployed, to December 1995, when UNPROFOR was instructed to withdraw, the Security Council issued 81 Resolutions and 85 Presidential Statements related to the conflict in the former Yugoslavia. It was evident almost from the beginning that the parties routinely ignored them. The willingness of the Council to continue to issue Resolutions and Presidential Statements that were going to be simply ignored became, in a certain sense, a vicious circle: the more the Council said, the less it was listened to by the parties on the ground. This of course made the job of UNPROFOR much more difficult. In high-level political negotiations, or discussions between military commanders on the ground, the usefulness of referring to Security Council documents and insisting that they be respected progressively lessened.

Another effect of the proliferation of Council documents, and their frequent disconnection from realities on the ground, was a loss of respect for and confidence in the documents by UNPROFOR military officers. It was reported that one very senior UNPROFOR military commander about half-way through his one-year tour, when offered the latest Council Resolution, declined to read it, explaining that, because the Council paid no attention to what was happening on the ground, he no longer paid any attention to what it produced. Some commanders, lacking faith in the Council's ability to guide the mission, thus started acting based on their own judgement, and doing what they thought was best for their troops or for the mission, rather than what the Council instructed.

This unfortunate situation reached its peak with Security Council Resolution 1004, passed unanimously 12 July 1995, two days after the Bosnian Serb takeover of the Safe Area of Srebrenica. The Council, acting under Chapter VII, demanded that the Bosnian Serbs 'respect fully the status of the Safe Area', 'withdraw from the Safe Area', ensure the complete freedom of movement of UNPROFOR, and requested 'the Secretary-General to use all resources available to him to restore the status...of the Safe Area...and calls on the parties to cooperate'. This Resolution was passed after several days of concerted military attacks by the Bosnian Serbs against Srebrenica, after all UN personnel in the Safe Area had been militarily neutralized, and after many had been taken hostage by the Bosnian Serbs. The Serbs had clearly demonstrated their intentions. It was, at that time, militarily impossible for UNPROFOR to take Srebrenica back by force; to do so would have required a major infusion of new and different troops and equipment sufficient to give UNPROFOR an all-arms war-fighting capacity. The Council's decision, on 12 July, to demand that the Serbs respect the status of the Safe Area, and to request the Secretary-General to use all resources available to restore the status of the Safe Area, was a demonstration of its divorce from the realities on the ground.

Surely UNPROFOR could have done some things differently and, in some cases, better. Managing a large, complex peacekeeping operation will never be easy or flawless. UNPROFOR's managerial faults, perceived and real, must however be considered in the context of UNPROFOR's mission environment, which has been described above.

I believe that the Secretary-General and the Security Council have learned much from the bitter experience of UNPROFOR. Fundamental mistakes made in the management of UNPROFOR are not likely to be repeated. Peacekeeping as a whole has developed in such a rapid and dramatic fashion from the period of UNTAC to UNPROFOR and beyond. While mistakes were made, much that is positive was accomplished, and many lessons learned about how to and how not to manage a PKO. The Security Council must design a strategy and define a set of goals for a peacekeeping intervention, and provide the resources and the political support necessary to pursue the strategy and achieve the goals. The Secretary-General must provide accurate information, sound analysis and practical recommendations to the Council on peacekeeping operations. Once a force has been authorized by the Council, the Secretary-General must faithfully and competently implement the mandate decided upon by the Council, while keeping the Council informed of developments on the ground.

These common sense rules are not necessarily enough to ensure success; they are, however, indispensable to success. If they are not respected, unsatisfactory, and perhaps tragic consequences may result. If they are followed, and if the Council bases its decisions on common sense and the principles of the Organization, then the future of peacekeeping can be a bright one indeed.

Notes

1   In this chapter, I am using the term 'peacekeeping' in its generic sense, to refer to activities authorized by the Security Council under both Chapter VI and Chapter VII of the United Nations Charter, unless otherwise indicated.

2   The four parties were the State of Cambodia, controlled by the Vietnamese and Soviet-supported Hun Sen; the Khmer Rouge, backed by China; FUNCINPEC, the Royalist party; and the Khmer People's National Liberation Front (KPNLF); the latter two were supported mainly by Western countries. The Khmer Rouge, FUNCINPEC, and the KPNLF comprised the Coalition Government of Democratic Kampuchea, recognized by most countries and the United Nations as the official government of Cambodia until the Peace Accords.

3   For the sake of simplicity, I will use the term UNPROFOR, even when referring to UNPF.

8 Principles to be Observed

for the Use of Military Forces Aimed at De-escalation and Resolution of Conflict

BERTRAND DE LAPRESLE[*]

The mission

First of all, I will recall the UNPROFOR military objectives in this peacekeeping mission because these goals guided our actions, from myself, as Force Commander, down to the level of the soldiers in the field.

This was a multi-faceted mission which was constantly changing and evolving. I shall limit myself to recalling three main mission components:

The first component of UNPROFOR's mission was to provide assistance in the delivery of humanitarian aid by UNHCR; this was, as everyone knows, the first reason for deployment of UN forces in Bosnia.

The second component of the mission was to establish conditions permitting the resumption of negotiations between the parties. Such conditions are essentially at least a sufficient level of silencing weapons on the battlefield, and, at best, the cessation of all military hostilities on the ground. We had reached this point simultaneously in Bosnia and in Croatia, and of course in Macedonia at the eve of 1994.

The third component of the mission was to monitor the various cease-fire agreements signed by the parties, for example the Washington agreement signed on 18 March 1994 by the Bosnian Croats and the Bosnian government forces, the cease-fire agreement between Croats and Krajina Serbs, signed on 29 March 1994 and the agreement on cessation of hostilities in Bosnia and Herzegovina, signed on 31 December 1994.

Reading through these three mission components calls for one important remark: the very wording of these missions shows the main difficulty for the military commander on the ground, which is to translate into military terms a mandate written in diplomatic language which is in fact a political –

---

[*] Gen. Bertrand de Lapresle (F) was Force Commander UNPROFOR from March 1994 to March 1995 and Military Adviser to the High Representative of the International Community in former Yugoslavia, Carl Bildt, from June 1995 to December 1996.

and sometimes ambiguous – compromise, reached within the Security Council.

The context

These three mission components had to be carried out in an environment for which few NATO and Western countries' officers are trained. Let me mention as examples a few features which were characteristic of UNPROFOR's operating environment and which made that environment so different from that of a conventional military operation.

First, in a peacekeeping mission, there are no enemies to be fought. Instead, there are partners who themselves have diverging, if not outright conflicting, interests and with whom UNPROFOR had to maintain absolute impartiality and objectivity in its dealings. Furthermore, this was a peacekeeping mission which could be successfully implemented only if all parties accepted the presence of United Nations forces, not only theoretically, but really and daily. IFOR has experienced how difficult this reality can be, even when 'Status of Force Agreements' have been agreed and signed, which is a very important prerequisite to any peacekeeping mission.

Dialogue at each level had to be the basis of UNPROFOR's action. Every break of this dialogue would lead the negotiations to a stalemate, the situation on the ground to confusions and misunderstandings, and eventually to tragedy and failure. So this dialogue had to be maintained at all cost, and that was the first guidance I gave to my subordinates.

There was no viable military solution to the problem UNPROFOR was faced with, nor was there any victory to be won by the military. This, of course, does not change the fact that the soldier's role was essential, in particular to establish the security environment necessary to allow the action of political authorities and civilian agencies. But this fact must lead us to think about the evolution of the function of the military in the settlement of this new type of conflict, and about the position of the military in the chain of command of the overall operation. The only victory that UN personnel could hope to achieve would have been a solution found between the warring parties under the aegis of the international community and by the political arm of the mission.

UNPROFOR characteristics

As a military tool, UNPROFOR was not able to win a victory. Notwithstanding its title, UNPROFOR was not really a force: it had neither the means, nor the organization, the training, or the command and control system to be an operational military force:

1. The troops were supplied by 37 contributing nations, hence the heterogeneous character of the Force, which entailed many constraints on our professionalism and our action.

2. We had neither fixed communications nor logistical assets at our disposal, the control of which was almost exclusively vested in UN civilian staff, nor could we count on the standard support or service support normally given to a military force in the field.

3. The mix of troops was established on the basis of the very specific requirements of a peacekeeping mission, with an overwhelming proportion of infantry and too little support, especially in terms of engineers, operational logistics, and observation and utility helicopter assets.

The staff was made up of officers with vastly different military cultures: NATO member states and former Warsaw Pact countries, as well as countries with long traditions in peacekeeping missions.

At theatre level, political direction, which is a particularly prominent feature of such an operation, was provided by the Special Representative of the Secretary-General, Mr Akashi. And I would like to take this opportunity to pay tribute once again to him for the excellent job he was doing under very high pressure. The Special Representative acts according to directives issued by the Secretary-General, who in turn implements Security Council Resolutions. Yet the Security Council is itself the reflection of political authorities with extremely diverse and not necessarily converging agendas.

More than once we were in difficult situations during 1994: while negotiating with the parties, we had to take into account other diplomatic initiatives which we were not well aware of, and which, in the worst case, proved themselves totally counterproductive when related to SRSG's objectives.

In the same spirit, another feature of such an environment is the existence of national constraints imposed on their contingents by some contributing nations reflecting their own interests.

Last but not least was the presence throughout the theatre of operations of hundreds of journalists, leading to very high media pressure, especially in Sarajevo.

A unique operation in former Yugoslavia

In addition to the overall background characteristics of any peacekeeping operation, the unique context in which the UN operation in former Yugoslavia took place must be kept in mind. Numerous interdependent parameters must be recalled.

This was fundamentally a civil and mostly urban war, using terrorist methods of action: artillery guns were shelling towns, tanks were deliberately posted very close to schools or hospitals. This technique was used more with the aim of terrorising the population, not unlike terrorist bombings, than of achieving specific military objectives carried out in the framework of large combined operational actions. Add to this:

-   A very difficult and mountainous terrain
-   Weather conditions that are most of the time very bad
-   Warring factions trained for guerrilla warfare, using facilities both dispersed and underground – and so not very vulnerable to air power
-   The number of warring factions (at least five within the Bihac pocket in 1994/1995), with their own psychological, sociological, historical and cultural sensitivities, which had to be known and taken into account by UNPROFOR, as it has to be by anyone who wants to help these countries solve their problems
-   Lastly, I must underline alcohol, smuggling, black market, and many illicit and Mafia activities which changed a local soldier, be it Serb, Croat, or Muslim, into a bandit.

Another main concern was the crucial and vital problem of continuous provocations by the parties deliberately aimed at eliciting a vigorous reaction from the international community in their favour. If this reaction was unjustified, it would be dramatically misinterpreted by the victims, who would seek immediate retaliation.

Peacekeeping and not enforcement: the use of force by UNPROFOR

UNPROFOR had to remain within the limits of peacekeeping and not evolve toward peace enforcement.

That did not mean that we could not use force, but this force had to be used in accordance with the principles of peacekeeping and not because of external pressures or interests not directly connected with our mission in former Yugoslavia.

These rules for the use of force must be well established and clear, and, moreover, well understood by those against which the force is finally used. In peacekeeping, only a minimum of force can be used to achieve a specific aim; it is more a political signal than an effort to achieve a military objective.

Warnings must be given before the use of force, collateral damage must be avoied, and the use of force must always be relevant, timely and proportionate to the violation.

Immediate self-defence reactions come under this definition, as does close air support. And I would like to take this opportunity to pay tribute to NATO and its pilots, the help of whom was crucial and indispensable to the continued exercise of our mandate. Strictly following these rules, UNPROFOR did use force in a constrained legitimate way, and it did use it more than any previous peacekeeping mission. UNPROFOR was, as a matter of fact, the first force ever to use NATO's air support, as has been the case, for instance, during the Gorazde crisis in April 1994, or against Udbina airfield in November 1994.

Despite this, the equation 'Blue Berets plus air support equals peace enforcer' is always absurd. For UNPROFOR, it was especially absurd because of the terrain, because of the nature of the troops on the ground, and because of the mandate.

It is also absurd to believe that with some additional equipment, a peacekeeping force can be changed into a peace-enforcing force, and can cross the threshold which separates a non-combatant force from a combatant force. Such a change in posture requires not only some additional assets but also a complete reorganization, a new mandate and the agreement of all the troop-contributing countries (TCNs), if not the consent of the parties.

Use of minimum force

The major problem for the use of force by UNPROFOR derived from the fact that a much higher level of military enforcement had been required under Chapter VII of the UN Charter in this mission than had traditionally been the case in previous peacekeeping missions. On this issue, I would like to enlarge upon two specific topics : the usefulness of tanks and the use of air power.

Tanks. Should UNPROFOR improve its safety and security by deploying more main battle tanks?

On the one hand, main battle tanks are very useful to enhance the robustness of our self-defence reactions. This was demonstrated in May 1994 by the efficient reaction of the Danish tank crew who quite legitimately returned indirect fire at Bosnian Serb positions near Tuzla.

But on the other hand, the use of such heavy weapons could be a further step towards an escalation of violence where the parties could go much further than we could, and might encourage the warring factions to use force beyond the actual capability of any UN peacekeeping force.

Moreover, in this context of civil war-like conflict, the warring factions could deliberately use this reinforcement of UN firepower to initiate a provocation-reaction-retaliation spiral and so put the UN mission at risk.

These were basically the reasons why I preferred not to request more main battle tanks.

Air power. The greatest difficulties facing the mission in Bosnia resulted from the use of force by UNPROFOR beyond the legitimate frame of self-defence. This use of force came about through the need to deter attacks against the six designated Safe Areas and the need to maintain the regime of the total exclusion zones for heavy weapons around Sarajevo and Gorazde.

Without the support of NATO, it was quite clear to me and to General Sir Michael Rose that the UN mission in Bosnia would have failed immediately. As General Rose said, 'The presence of NATO airplanes in the skies gave me the confidence to deploy peacekeepers in dispersed and remote places, and of course it was NATO that preserved the total exclusion zone regimes'.

I firmly believe that, acting in self-defence, the use of close air support was indispensable and SRSG and myself used it without any hesitation every time the security and safety of our soldiers were at stake. On a few occasions, there was clearly been no alternative for the UN than to request air power for self-defence.

After the deployment in the second half of 1994 of sophisticated ground-to-air defence systems by the Bosnian Serbs, which threatened NATO aircraft, the situation became more difficult. At that period of UNPROFOR's history, close air support action could have led to an escalation of the war because NATO would have required suppression of the enemy air defences prior to the engagement of its aircraft. Bosnian Serbs could in turn have provoked this type of action in order to rally Serb public opinion more widely to their cause.

I would like to underline a few points about the use of air power in support of UNPROFOR-type missions. The use of air power must abide by the principles of the minimum use of force in peacekeeping missions. As a result, prior to deciding any air action, the decision maker must answer the four following questions:

- What are the political goals for such destructive strikes?

- What would be the appropriate targets for air attack which could enable us to achieve these goals? Do they exist in sufficient numbers?

- What next? What might be the military and political consequences of such an action? And what could or should be the next steps? Would they be consistent with the answers to question 1?

- What preventive actions and measures must be planned to anticipate the consequences and to ensure the safety and security of the force? Are they implementable prior to the use of air power?

Improvements and efficiency

Observations drawn from my recent experience help me in identifying some actions and principles which are important to improve the operational effectiveness of this kind of UN peacekeeping operation.

This effectiveness rests, first of all, on the clarity of the political goal, and of the subsequent military instructions for the application of the mandate given to the Force. It also rests on the quality of training, the general organization and the deployment mode of the Force.

For a military decision maker, the definition of a mandate as clearly as possible is a basic necessity as it is the foundation on which he will accept risks for his soldiers and set unambiguous tasks for his military commanders.

This means, for instance, that a Security Council Resolution has to be written with the help of military advisers, or that it will have to be translated into military language with the approval of the political authorities involved.

This mandate must be fully supported by the Parties themselves. There cannot be any peacekeeping mission without the explicit consent of the parties, and also without an adequate structure of the peacekeeping force.

The will to clarify objectives and subsequent missions should be concretely expressed in the previous planning work done in New York. This work should result in an operational concept backed by an in-depth military audit and supported, if possible, by the conclusions of a fact-finding mission, as called for by the 'Agenda for Peace'.

A number of actions could improve the initial planning of operations:

- Reinforcing the UN secretariat with trained staff provided by contributing nations as soon as the principle of deployment is agreed

- Careful updating of data on force components on standby by the multi-national management team (an innovation which should be fully exploited)

- Fully using the experience and know-how of the existing planning cells in multi-national political and military organizations such as NATO or the Western European Union when deploying troops in zones where these organizations are especially involved.

The quality of training

The training of personnel requires special attention. It is quite obvious that combat training must be the major part of the overall training for troops involved in UN operations, especially for land forces in direct contact with belligerents. But all our officers must be trained in skills specific to operations under UN supervision. Positive steps in that direction are for example the various booklets and documents written and published by some Nordic countries, as Norway, and by the Canadians.

Organization and the chain of command

As regards the organization of the command structure at the highest level in the theatre of operations, the permanent presence of a political official on the ground is a must. I particularly appreciated that a permanent representative of the Secretary General was designated shortly before my own arrival.

This official must have the appropriate margin of initiative, especially to decide whether the use of force of a certain magnitude is politically pertinent. For a year, Mr Akashi and myself worked as a team, which allowed us to adopt common political and military positions on the problems we were faced with. To this team, we must add the Head of Civil Affairs (HCA), whose importance is crucial. Close co-operation and teamwork between all the components of any UN mission are among the key factors for the success of the mission.

Problems are often more complex than initially thought, and a magnitude of various parameters, political as well as military, must be analysed. I therefore believe there is a necessity to have a strong think-tank at the SRSG's level, as was the case in Zagreb with the Analysis and Assessment Unit under the leadership of Dr Woodward. Political, sociological and psychological analysis are really paramount to identify problems during the decision-making process and to understand and anticipate possible adequate future moves.

The description of the organization of the chain of command would not be complete without mentioning UNPROFOR's relations with New York and NATO.

Relations with New York were excellent and very reliable, and they needed to be so. I would only like to mention the very useful possibility we had to meet the Secretary General and the Under-Secretary-General for peacekeeping operations every two or three months.

I firmly believe in the fruitfulness of such meetings to explain the current situation on the ground to the New York headquarters and discuss problems and solutions. They strengthened the authority of the SRSG, especially when some new and separate diplomatic initiatives could lead people to believe that there were 'too many pilots in the plane'.

Generally speaking, UNPROFOR's relations with NATO have been excellent, despite occasional difficulties. Nevertheless, co-operation between UN and NATO is rendered delicate by the different, if not opposite nature of their respective military cultures.

In order to act, NATO's military assets must aim at achieving a military effect, and must therefore have a target, the destruction of which will stand as concrete proof of the mission's success and enhance NATO's credibility. Consequently, every NATO's military leader, because of his culture, is motivated to apply the principles of warfare, favours surprise and military efficiency, and thinks in terms of war. In peacekeeping missions, on the contrary, military commanders very often have to apply opposite principles, imposed on them by their mission, their assets and the importance given to the safety of their troops.

In this spirit, it seems essential that, in the context of a given mandate, the directives given to the UN troops and to the supporting multi-national organization should be developed in parallel, coherent with that of the situation on the ground.

The commitment of military units

Before any commitment, units must be informed as clearly as possible about the political goals to be reached, the precise missions to perform, the logistical conditions of the operation if possible, how long the commitment will last and what the rules regarding behaviour and engagement will be.

To reduce the risks brought upon the forces, they must have at their disposal effective defensive weapons.

Finally, the smooth working of logistical support is a guarantee of efficiency on the ground. It is necessary to have a good knowledge of the requirements and of the available resources. In this respect any Force Commander should – in my view, and contrary to what was the case for UNPROFOR – be given increased responsibility and freedom of action in the field of logistics.

Interaction between UNSC and the operation in the field

I firmly believe that the Head of Mission and the Force Commander should be consulted when new Security Council Resolutions are written, as they are the most knowledgeable in terms of the situation on the ground.

Setting new objectives without providing the Force with the material, technical and tactical means required can only end up discrediting the Force, both in the eyes of the warring parties and of the international community.

It is also important that any new task given to a UN peacekeeping mission clearly accord with the basic principles for peacekeeping operations. Switching to peace enforcement would necessarily require a complete reorganization of the force, most specifically as regards the command structure and the assets already deployed.

Conclusion: some lessons learned with UNPROFOR

I would like to emphasize four points:

1. It is most important that any mandate be defined with all the specificity required, and be fully commensurate with the assets available and with its real purpose. This will avoid raising false hopes and eventually blaming the Force deployed for not having done what was expected.

2. The more important, difficult and complex a UN mission is, the more efforts must be made to provide assets and troops adapted to an ever-

evolving situation in the field. As has just been underlined, setting new objectives, without providing the Force, in a timely manner, with the new human, technical and tactical means required, can only end up discrediting the Force, both in the eyes of the warring parties, and in those of the international community.

3. It is not the military peacekeepers, but the political peacemakers who should find a solution politically acceptable to all parties, and then, it is up to the parties themselves to be committed in the full implementation of the agreed solution.

4. A clear distinction must be made between peacekeeping, in which impartiality is fundamental, and enforcement, where one of the parties involved will inevitably be designated as the 'bad guys'. In that spirit, peacekeeping and the use of force other than in self-defence should only be seen as alternative techniques, rather than as concurrent and compatible options.

These are some of the lessons learned that I want to underline in the hope of improving the effectiveness of future UN military commitment. With better preparation and improved modes of action, these principles should increase the chances of success and the security of personnel devoted to the cause of peace, and therefore the credibility of the United Nations.

Some observations after UNPROFOR

I would like to add a few observations and suggestions relevant to the period following the Dayton Agreement and the subsequent deployment of a NATO force in Bosnia-Herzegovina (IFOR and presently SFOR).

Military lessons

The nature of the force. Any NATO-led military force like IFOR/SFOR is expected to be different from a UN PKO; for example, it should be able to control the situation, to keep the guns silent and to compel the parties to comply with the military aspects of any cease-fire or peace agreement.

This force must be large, and robust enough to be credible. It must have the right ratio of engineers, logistics, air mobility and so on, and not only a lot of infantry, as was the case for UNPROFOR.

It must be tailored, and equipped, in order to have constant strategic and tactical superiority over any party. To achieve that, this Force must apply all the usual NATO basic warfare principles.

It must also have efficient staff officers, designated for their professionalism, and not for their nationality only.

Intelligence. We must also underline the need for a good and effective intelligence system, which is all the more difficult in a multi-national force, when the natural tendency of contributing nations is not always to share sensitive military information.

Public information. We must also have a very professional public information system, able to provide reliable and accurate information, not only to the different contingents, but mainly to the Parties, in their own language, and to the international media.

Military observers and civilian police. Another vital point not always stressed enough is the key role played by well-trained military observers, monitors, and, last but not least, by civilian police personnel, which are essential for the success of such a post-civil war operation as this one in former Yugoslavia.

The limits of IFOR/SFOR. The Parties very quickly appreciate the gap between what over-equipped international soldiers are able to control and perform, and what unarmed civilian police are able to impose. Currently, for instance, neither IPTF nor SFOR have the means and ability to deal with massive movement of civilian population. They are able to remove physical obstacles to freedom of movement. But the psychological barriers are much more difficult to deal with.

On the one hand, SFOR has the military strength to provide the overall security environment; but could never provide main battle tanks to accompany any resettled population as requested by the Bosnian government, because these tanks could have to stay for years. On the other hand, IPTF has a mandate which is to monitor and to train the local police and not to perform a local policing mission or to re-establish order by force.

The factions exploit this gap in a very clever way, as we can see in Mostar, in the Zone Of Separation, for civilian freedom of movement, or for war criminals, only to take a few sensitive examples. This is of course very detrimental to the image of international Forces, as the war is in fact going on with unchanged goals through other means.

International support. Lastly I want to underline the necessity in order to do a proper job of consistent support by the international community.

The tragedy of Srebrenica during the UN period illustrates this point. The main dramas come from unbearable discrepancies between missions assigned to the military and the means granted to the military commander.

Actually, the responsibility for Srebrenica falls neither on the Netherlands contingent, nor on General Janvier. The responsibility lies in the Security Council's decision not to accept the military evaluation which stated that some 35,000 soldiers would be needed to implement the new mission to establish Safe Areas. The difference between the 35,000 soldiers requested first by General Wahlgren, and then by General Cot, and the very few thousands the international community eventually provided led inevitably to disasters.

Consistent international support is as important for a UN PKO as it is for a NATO-led operation. But a strong regional defence organization like NATO may be more vulnerable to humiliations than the UN, the global collective security organization. The UN is often blamed for the failures of its key member states. The UN can politically survive this role of scapegoat without lethal damage – NATO would probably not.

Political military lessons

The chain of command. Whatever the clarity of the mandate and the strength and quality of the Force, nothing can be achieved without a clear, well-cut and unified organization of the chain of command, which must integrate all the military and civilian components.

I am well aware of the sensitive problems linked with any multi-national operation. But I remain convinced that, as in our respective national organizations, if we want to succeed, the military and the civilian components of any operation, be it a multi-national operation, must be under the same single political leadership, whatever this might be, either the Security Council, or any regional organization, or international body.

Close co-operation and teamwork between all the components of any peacekeeping mission are among the key factors, for the success of the mission. And therefore everything must be organized, so that this teamwork is structurally made easy, and does not rely on the goodwill of authorities mandated by parallel chains of command.

Civil-military co-ordination. With that in mind, I am not sure that the current system used between SFOR and the civilian leaders of the Peace Agreement in former Yugoslavia, is, in its underlying principle, a sound concept, as opposed to the 'dual key' system, despised as it was, which I personally appreciated, when UNPROFOR was clearly 'in charge', with AFSOUTH 'in support'.

While there is a very complex interrelation between the civilian and the military aspects of the Dayton Peace Agreement, the two parallel and separate chains of command – military (SFOR) and civilian (the High Representative) – following their legitimate own agendas, could create discrepancies between all the different international actors, which could be very damaging for the success of the mission as a whole.

Currently, the process of frequent meetings of the 'Principals', as they call themselves, in charge of the military and the different civilian aspects of the Dayton Agreement, does work, but it implies a very goodwill of all partners, which cannot reasonably permanently be taken for granted.

'One mission, one success, one team' is SACEUR's motto – I personally think we should add 'one single leader'.

The system set up for the United Nations operation in Eastern Slavonia, UNTAES, under the unique leadership of Ambassador-General Jacques Klein, seems to me far more appropriate for that kind of operation than the Dayton Agreement system.

The transitional period between UNPROFOR and IFOR

I would like to underline a very important point which, so far, I think, has not been stressed enough by the international community, and should not be forgotten by NATO, when learning lessons from IFOR. This is the key role played by the 18,000 UNPROFOR troops deployed on the ground during the transitional period, between the initialing of the Agreement in Dayton on 21 November 1995, and the transfer of authority to IFOR, on 20 December.

The UNPROFOR Nordic troops in Sector North, the UNPROFOR British troops in Sector South West and the UNPROFOR French troops in Sarajevo clearly created the best conditions, not only to ensure a perfect arrival and deployment of the additional NATO troops, especially the US, but moreover in leading the Parties to comply with the first very early and ambitious deadlines set up in Annex IA of the Peace Agreement.

Knowing the terrain and the leaders, having to change only their beret to become IFOR soldiers within a second, their performance has been outstanding, and created a vital springboard for the IFOR mission to rapidly and successfully get under way to respect these most demanding deadlines.

IFOR and its enforcement capability

It is of critical importance to have a precise idea of what is militarily enforceable and what is not, so as to impose deadlines only on what is really enforceable, or linked with a credible threat.

From a military point of view, the implementation of the Dayton Paris Peace Agreement has gone very well up to D + 120 (120 days after initial deployment). The mandate was clear cut, the tasks were workable and precisely defined, the strength and the equipment of the Force were appropriate, and above all, the main military provisions of the agreement were enforceable.

It is quite obvious that the provision of Annex IA, which matches the interest of the Bosnian Serb Army, namely the separation of forces, explains the very co-operative behaviour of Bosnia Serb military.

Later on, the problems faced by IFOR became more difficult, because IFOR was not able to enforce compliance with the civilian FOM, the return of refugees, or the arrest of war criminals. For obvious reasons, you can force an army to demobilise before an agreed deadline, but you can hardly enforce a way of avoiding the transformation of this army of soldiers into an army of unemployed, many of them becoming easily involved with criminal activities and breaches of law and civilian order. And you cannot enforce a lasting settlement of refugees in an area where, as a minority, they are rejected by the majority population.

In short, genuine reconciliation is not enforceable through military incentives.

We also have to admit that the one-year deadline set for IFOR, and the late decision concerning the follow-on forces, has obviously had very counterproductive results for financial institutions and businesses looking for long-term security in Bosnia-Herzegovina, before investing there.

Conclusion

I would like to emphasize the following points:

1. It is most important that any mandate for a peace force be defined with all the specificity required, and that it be fully commensurate with the assets available, and with its real political purpose. This will avoid raising false expectations, and eventually blaming the Force deployed for not having done what was expected.

2. Unity of command for both the military and the civilian components, as well as the full support of the international community, are paramount for the success of any operation, both in terms of consistency and efficiency.

3. The more important, difficult and complex a peacekeeping mission is, the more effort must be made to provide fully adequate troops and assets, adapted to an ever-evolving situation in the field. Setting new objectives without providing the Force in a timely manner, with the new human, technical and tactical means required, can only end in discrediting the Force, both in the eyes of the warring parties, and in those of the international community.

4.   It is not the military peacekeepers, but the political peacemakers, who should find a solution politically acceptable to all parties, and then, it is up to the Parties themselves, to be committed in the full implementation of the agreed solution.

5.   Finally, anybody involved in a peacekeeping mission needs the support of the contributing nations, as well as the backing of international public opinion. Together with the compliance and commitment of the Parties, it is the united effort of the international community and its willingness to support the peace process and the actors in the field that are essential to achieve a lasting peace.

9 Military Aspects of Peacekeeping

Lessons Learned from Bosnia, from a Commander's Perspective

SIR MICHAEL ROSE[*]

The lessons from the experience of trying to establish peaceful conditions to run a humanitarian operation in the Balkans in the 1990s provide an excellent starting point to reform the way we collectively and individually look at peace support operations for the future. Whilst the attention of the world community still focuses on the aftermath of the civil war, and the creation of new states out of the former Yugoslavia, it should be possible to reform the conduct of such operations in the future. That reforms must be made in the way all international institutions undertake and conduct peacekeeping operations is irrefragable.

The changed circumstances brought about by the end of the Cold War, when we have seen conflict shift from inter-state to intra-state, have provided the impetus to change our thinking and the very basic concepts of operation.

This paper will examine the lessons which, from a commander's perspective, are there to help shape peacekeeping doctrine and policies in the years to come, and will conclude with a look at some recommendations for using these changes to conduct more effective and efficient peace support operations in the years to come.[1] Given that perspective, most comments will focus on the military aspects of peacekeeping, although it is difficult to separate the *military* from all other aspects of such an operation. Indeed, the arbitrary separation of the various aspects of peacekeeping seems to be at the very heart of the doctrinal and practical differences which exist between the United Nations and NATO at this point in time.

---

[*] Gen. Sir Michael Rose (UK), former Adjutant General of the UK Army, was Commander UNPROFOR in Bosnia-Herzegovina from 1994 to February 1995.

Background

In recent years, the reputation of the UN has become tarnished, notably as a result of failure to relate political will and military action in Bosnia and Somalia.

Whether the UN had started to suffer from an excess of expectation, that is, that it could provide the solutions to all types and all sizes of conflicts, or that whilst the end of the Cold War created wider opportunities for peacekeeping, the means and tools by which the new challenges could have been confronted by the UN have not been forthcoming. Unavoidably, this has led to a fundamental questioning of the value of peacekeeping. Yet if we collectively or individually lose faith in either the concept or the undertaking of peacekeeping operations – or both – and if the responses of the international community to the challenges of the new world disorder are to be limited to the extremes of total international non-involvement, or war-fighting, then the world will undoubtedly become a considerably more dangerous place than it is at present.

We are now in the position where the United Nations as an international institution has not yet come to grips with the changing concepts of peacekeeping. It appears that there is no agreement on even the basic definitions of *classic peacekeeping, peace support operations, wider peacekeeping* and *peace enforcement,* and we have seen that policy makers and operators alike have themselves not entirely understood the doctrines of peacekeeping.

Moral dimension

One point which has emerged very clearly from the Bosnian experience is that there has to be a new understanding of the moral basis on which nations have the right to intervene in one another's affairs, for without it, we will have learned nothing from the way the Yugoslav mission was conducted. The level of moral justification underlying political resolve to intervene militarily on the part of the world community in responding to the types of disasters which have increasingly occurred since the end of the Cold War must be clearly understood. What this means is that the international community must determine which crises need a response, and which ones can be ignored. Is CNN to be the policy driver, or should a decision be based on a more reasoned, moral consideration, avoiding a premature involvement which only exacerbates a problem and increases the agonies of the peoples involved? In essence, do we – the international community – simply walk away from or ignore a problem and let the fires burn out? Or should we harness all our efforts towards preventing such situations occurring in the first place? And finally, if we do decide to act, how far should we allow peacekeepers to get involved in peace enforcement? It is only once we have resolved such moral issues that we can then decide upon a strategy and on an effective plan of action.

Lessons from Bosnia

Lesson 1: Requirement for a specific mandate

First and foremost, it is essential that, if we are to draw sound lessons from our experiences in the Balkans, then the UN must be judged on what it has been asked to do, not on what it has *not* been asked to do. It is all too clear that the mandate given by the Security Council to the mission in the former Yugoslavia was – and in many cases is still – not well understood, by the media, by some international observers, by the general public.

In fact, it is not always clearly understood that the mandate of a mission defines not only the aspirations but also the limitations of action of the international community which are governed by the domestic policies of the contributing countries, as well as by the international community at large.

On the one hand there existed at the international level the hope that human suffering in Bosnia could be alleviated, that the state of Bosnia-Herzegovina could be sustained and that the problems could be contained within the confines of the remnants of the Yugoslav federation. On the other hand there was the fear on the part of the international community that other nations could themselves become embroiled in a wider conflict outside their national interests. This concern is understandable and will always be the case when no direct national self-interest is involved.

Right from the beginning there was a clear refusal by the international community to intervene militarily in order to preserve the territorial integrity of Bosnia-Herzegovina.

The wrongdoings of the Serbs might have been universally regarded as being morally reprehensible and politically unacceptable, but common international policy has to be viewed in light of the simple fact that no nation ever declared itself willing to take up arms against those who were deemed to be the aggressors.[2]

Amidst all the distortion and misunderstanding surrounding the UN mission in Bosnia, it is often forgotten that its mandate was not to bring the aggressors to task. Rather, the mandate was simply to sustain the people of that country in the midst of civil war, whilst trying, whenever and however possible, to bring about the conditions necessary for a peaceful resolution of that war. This mission was indeed accomplished in no small way.

One needs only look at the casualty statistics over the years of the civil war which bear this out. In 1992, before the UN deployed to Bosnia, some 130,000 people were killed. In 1993, as the UN started to become effective, some 30,000 people were killed. In 1994, numbers were further reduced, to 3,000.

The figures for 1995, which report about 55,000 casualties,[3] seem to belie these successes. But one must take into consideration that the various offensives of 1995 took a very severe human toll, in spite of the best efforts of the UN and the aid agencies to maintain the impetus of the previous year, and which in fact support the argument that UNPROFOR had been dragged beyond its mandate into a peace enforcement operation, and, for all intents, had ceased to operate in the manner it had been intended.

The best answer to those who say that it would have been better if the UN had not involved itself in the conflict from 1992 is provided by those millions of people whose lives were sustained throughout the war by the presence of the UN: for over 2,000 metric tons of stores a day were delivered to even the remotest parts of Bosnia along roads built by the UN and using airfields operated by the UN. The fact that the opportunities for peace were not taken advantage of by the political leaders of Bosnia and the war lords can scarcely be blamed on the UN.

The mandate in Bosnia was never to impose any political solution by force of arms, to alter the balance of forces, to defend territory, or even to enforce the passage of convoys, although this was done from time to time. These are war-fighting actions and the mission was neither mandated, equipped, trained nor deployed for war-fighting. The mission had to work with general consent from all sides – even if only at the strategic level, for as finally happened in September 1995, it could not survive in the face of sustained opposition by one or more of the warring factions.

Not surprisingly, therefore, the first and most important lesson that can be learnt by the international community for the future is that there must be an unequivocal mandate clearly defining the limits of a peace support operation, and one that is furthermore fully backed by the members of the Security Council in terms of financial and political support. This must be a prerequisite of any future mission.

Similarly, a peacekeeping mission must not allow itself to be hijacked by outside international powers or alliances who may wish to use the presence of peacekeeping forces in a country to change political states or simply to meet its own ends. Where conditions for peacekeeping are not met, but a *peacekeeping* as opposed to a *peace enforcement* operation is mounted anyway, there is the very real danger that the result will be, at best, 'mission creep' in its worst sense, and at worst, paralyzis and accusations of impotence being levelled at the commanders on the ground and at the UN as a whole. At same time, the international community must learn to withstand the propaganda and the manipulation of international opinion, which inevitably surround such situations, from becoming the basis on which international policies are made. The mandate cannot be dictated by ill-informed, sensationalist public opinion or by the need for the international community to assuage its own guilty conscience. This can only lead to the creation of hasty, ill-thought-out missions which will undoubtedly fail due to lack of support and capabilities. An obvious risk exists that peacekeeping forces will be given missions and tasks which they are not capable of achieving, by virtue of their mandate and combat capabilities. The results of this are self-evident, especially in view of what happened in Bosnia.

Lesson 2: Use of force

The use of force, especially in wider peacekeeping or peace enforcement operations where the level of consent on the part of the warring factions may be patchy at best, is a second area where the Bosnian experience points out lessons for NATO as well as the UN.

It is obvious that once a military force has deployed in a humanitarian, peacekeeping role, it will be precluded by the very nature of its deployment and rules of engagement from acting as a combatant. However, if it is to deliver aid, maintain the regime of a total exclusion zone or deter attacks against Safe Areas then it will have to adopt a very forceful approach to peacekeeping indeed. To be credible, a peacekeeping mission must be in a position to escalate, moving if necessary beyond traditional Chapter VI peacekeeping to peace enforcement. To do this, the need to maintain consent and impartiality on one hand, and the need to use force on the other, must be reconciled in the minds of the international community if peacekeeping is going to continue to be a viable option of international conflict resolution.

In traditional peacekeeping missions, where both parties to a conflict have already decided to end their dispute and have invited the UN in to act a mediator, there will be a political process and a high level of consent on all sides. This is the environment in which the UN operated so successfully for the first 45 years of its existence, and in a way reflects the environment in which NATO with IFOR is operating in Bosnia today.

But it is now becoming more and more customary for the UN to be deployed into situations for humanitarian reasons where there is no general consent for its presence, such as in Bosnia and, indeed, Rwanda and

Somalia. In these circumstances, the UN will be obliged to use high levels of force in pursuit of its mandate, which requires a clear understanding about how far force can be used in peacekeeping, whilst still retaining an equally clear understanding of whether the mandate, and therefore the capability of the force, call for peacekeeping or peace enforcement. What is vital is that *war-fighting goals* are never pursued by *peacekeeping forces*.

Retaining a non-combatant status is, needless to say, no easy feat for a peacekeeping force in the midst of civil war. Not only will each party try to draw the UN into taking sides, but inevitably all sides will use humanitarian aid for its own political and military ends. Even the delivery by the UN of basic food and fuel to a besieged population, will be considered as a hostile act by those carrying out the siege.

The central principle governing the actual use of force should be that only *minimum force* should be used to achieve a specific aim. This principle must underpin any UN mandate, equally for classic peacekeeping as for peace enforcement.

It should, of course, be borne in mind that the level of force to be used could well be dictated not by the actual conditions on the ground in theatre, but by external forces which may be summarized as what the 'market' – in other words both the international community as a whole and more specifically the individual troop-contributing nations – will bear. In general, some troop contributors are more likely than others to approve greater levels of force in achieving assigned aims than others, based on national military doctrines and combat capabilities. Naturally, this is an important factor which any commander of a multi-national force will have to keep in mind when determining a course of action to meet a specific situation. A further consideration is that those nations, which have voluntarily contributed their troops to a peacekeeping mission, do not deserve to see their brave young men and women return home in body bags, casualties caused as a result of the inappropriate use of force.

A commander on the ground must nevertheless be given the discretion to use force as and when he sees fit, if he is to remain impartial and keep in control of a situation. It therefore essential that the Rules of Engagement under which he operates must be flexible enough to give him leeway to act. Thus, if, when the mission is first deployed there exists the possibility that force will be required, then the mandate, and resources, will have to clearly reflect this. But if no use of force is anticipated, then a new question will have to be addressed, and that is whether it is appropriate to send in peacekeepers at all, or if armed observers are sufficient to contain the problem.

To use more force than that which is prescribed by the requirements of consent, especially in a pursuit of war-fighting rather than peacekeeping goals, is to cross the line – the 'Mogadishu Line' – which separates non-combatants from combatants. Crossing this line can simply spell disaster for the mission, for a peacekeeping force is neither mandated, deployed nor equipped for peace enforcement or to fight a war. One needs only look to Somalia to see what happens when the line is crossed.

Generally speaking, the fact that UNPROFOR was so lightly armed, consistent with the humanitarian operation, the calling-in of assistance from NATO, initially in the air and then, of course, with NATO's continued role in IFOR and beyond, was in keeping with the maintenance of the *long-term* peace support operation.

There is a pragmatic reason for upholding the principle of minimum force, for undue or excessive use of force could – and did – always act against the programme of aid delivery. In addition, we witnessed in Bosnia how excessive force could place lightly armed peacekeepers in isolated deployments in a highly vulnerable position – a factor of which the Serbs were naturally well aware. They understood only too well the limits of UNPROFOR's combat capabilities and the vulnerabilities of the peacekeepers, and frequently used them to their own advantage.

In Bosnia, UN aid was delivered mainly through Serb-held areas to the minority Muslim peoples living in the enclaves. Since the Bosnian Serbs had a deliberate policy of preventing the build-up of stocks in the enclaves in order to maintain leverage, undue use of force and the consequent effect of shutting off the flow of aid meant that, within days, people began to run short of food and other items essential for survival. The harsh fact remains that, when undue force is used, people start to die of starvation.

The UNHCR and UNPROFOR were always able to restore aid delivery after each occasion when force was used, albeit often at a painfully slow rate, because UNPROFOR was always able to demonstrate to the Bosnian Serbs, at least until the start of the strategic NATO bombing campaign, that in exercising force it remained neutral, impartial and a non-combatant.

Lesson 3: Regional powers – complementary not a substitute

Another important area in which new procedures were developed in the former Yugoslavia concern UN Chapter VIII operations, or the use of regional organizations in support of peacekeeping. Notwithstanding the difficulties encountered, bringing in NATO to support the UN peacekeeping mission was a major step forward in peacekeeping, and indispensable to the continued exercise of the mandate. Without the support of NATO, it is quite clear that the UN mission in Bosnia would have failed.

The presence of NATO airplanes in the skies gave peacekeepers the confidence to deploy in dispersed and remote places, and, of course, it was

NATO that preserved the regimes of total exclusion zones for heavy weapons around Sarajevo and Gorazde. It was also the action and threat of further action of NATO aircraft which in the longer term deterred attacks by the Bosnian Serbs against the Safe Areas.

But there were some highly significant problems with the whole of the NATO involvement, caused by the non-alignment of the NATO and UN mandates. Indeed, to NATO the early involvement appeared to do little more than question the credibility of the whole NATO organization, whilst at the same time the UN felt that its humanitarian mission was endangered.

However, NATO was always forced to remain within the limitations prescribed for the use of force for the duration of the UN peacekeeping mission in the former Yugoslavia, although it has been argued that the 'dual key' arrangement of bringing NATO air power to bear meant that NATO's impact was too little, or too late in bringing peace to Bosnia.

Yet there were, and always will be, obvious limitations on the use of air power in a such a confused civil-war situation as Bosnia, not least as the strategic campaigns were regularly confounded by poor flying weather. More importantly, it is simply not militarily possible to secure Safe Areas or to enforce the passage of convoys by the use of air power alone, especially when peacekeepers are so vulnerable, as they were in Bosnia, to retaliation.

The change in the strategic balance between the warring parties during the summer of 1995, which led to the signing of the Dayton peace accord, come about less from the NATO bombing campaign, although that may have sent a strong political signal to the warring parties, than as a result of the offensive launched by the Croat Army and Federation Forces which threatened much of the land that the Bosnian Serbs needed to trade for peace on their terms.

Lesson 4: Campaign plan: need for...

Another important lesson which can be derived from the experience of the UN in former Yugoslavia is the need for a coherent campaign plan which can ensure the necessary high level of co-ordination that is required between political momentum, security action and the humanitarian aid delivery mission. That such a plan initially was missing is perhaps an indication of the *ad hoc* nature of the UN deployment from the beginning, in keeping with the concerns demonstrated by the unwillingness of the international community to become too deeply involved.

It is obviously easier to deliver aid, rehabilitate health services, make assessments of needs and facilitate the work of the UN aid agencies, the International Committee of the Red Cross and non-governmental organizations in a benign security environment rather than when fierce battles rage. Thus, if the peacekeeping mission through its presence and powers of persuasion can persuade the parties in the war to cease hostilities, or at least to reduce the intensity of the fighting to a level where aid can flow freely, then clearly this will result in improved productivity in terms of the delivery of humanitarian aid.

The agreement of 9 February 1994 between the Muslim and Serb forces which resulted in the withdrawal of the heavy artillery around Sarajevo, and an undertaking not to launch offensive action across the 70-kilometre conflict line which surrounds the city, created just such benign conditions. Following the successful implementation of this agreement, which was brokered by UNPROFOR and backed by a NATO ultimatum to which both the Bosnian Government forces and the Bosnian Serb Army were subject, a second agreement was reached on 17 March by which aid, and subsequently commercial traffic, could enter the city via the airport. As a result, for almost four months, up to 100 commercial lorries per day were arriving in a city which had been besieged for nearly two years. Electricity levels which during the period of siege had hovered about twelve megawatts were increased to 55 as a result of repairs to damaged lines and transformer stations. This allowed trams to run and other services, such as domestic lighting, to be restored. Gas pressures rose from half a bar to six bars. Water pipes were repaired, a Red Cross water pumping station and filtration plant was built, and new wells were drilled. As a result, for the first time in many months water started to be delivered directly into homes. The result was a transformation of life for the 350,000 citizens of Sarajevo.

The point that a peacekeeping operation can only succeed if supported by complementary political action is also well demonstrated by the success of UNPROFOR in implementing the Washington agreement which transformed the lives of millions of people in Central Bosnia, in 1994, in the same way that IFOR is currently doing throughout the remainder of Bosnia today.

This sense of progress is the positive aspect of 'mission creep', where the military operation contributes to a longer-term political solution, which, after all, is the *raison d'être* of any successful peacekeeping mission. To do otherwise is to stagnate and see a mission continuing for years, if not decades, as has happened in Cyprus and parts of the Middle East.

Only UNPROFOR could have provided the necessary infrastructure and confidence-building mechanisms for the stabilisation of the situation and hence advancements in the political arena. The whole exercise which was conducted by the British Commander of the UN Sector proved to be a textbook example of how to turn war into peace, thus laying the foundations for the current NATO mission. Regional and district joint commissions were established, UN forces were interposed, observation posts and checkpoints set up, and joint patrols undertaken in order to implement the agreement. A good deal of work was also done in close co-operation with, and through liaison between, UNPROFOR, UNHCR and other agencies to rebuild the shattered social and economic infrastructure of the region.

Indeed, so much progress was in fact made, that the number of refugees and displaced persons in need of aid was reduced from 2.7 to 1.4 million, and the UNHCR was able to redefine its objectives and move away from the direct provision of aid and concentrate its efforts on looking after and resettling the 430,000 displaced and war-affected people in the area in Central Bosnia.

The main point to be made here is that all the gains made on the security front will be lost, if momentum is not maintained and if political solutions are not found. It is not possible forever to continue successfully a peacekeeping mission in a political vacuum.

Lesson 5: Affect of the media on policy making and peacekeeping

The next lesson concerns the influence of the media on the success or failure of a peacekeeping operation. That the media is a powerful instrument, for good or bad, is obvious to all, as what is reported and seen on TV directly affects policies being developed abroad as well as attitudes within the country where the peacekeeping force is deployed.[4]

If the media falsely shows images of war, exaggerates facts or distorts opinions, then there is of course a very real danger that international policy will become based on propaganda and rhetoric rather than on the reality of the situation in theatre and the advice provided by commanders on the ground.

The reporting and comments of some members of the press corps in Sarajevo came, on occasion, close to becoming identified with the propaganda machine of the Bosnian Government. It is, of course, quite understandable that a government struggling for survival should attempt to suborn the world's media. What is totally incomprehensible is that the international media should permit itself to become part of that effort. Mischievous distortion of reality can only undermine the work of those who are pursuing the path towards peace.

It is essential that major decisions of how and when to deploy on a peacekeeping mission are not driven by the media, especially when media reports are contrary to the reports offered by trained observers and expert political analysts on the ground. A gut reaction on the part of either the UN or interested national governments – or both – could result in the over-hasty deployment of inadequately prepared troops who can do little to resolve the conflict, and who as a result must either be ignominiously withdrawn or who are in danger of being drawn deeper into the conflict with a resultant risk of high casualties.

How the UN deals with the problem of the media in this respect, keeping in mind, of course, that the media have a vital and positive role to play in any international issue, is currently under active consideration in New York, for it is generally recognized that in the high-intensity conflict end of the peacekeeping spectrum, as well as when it is apparent that a mission is moving from a peacekeeping to a peace enforcement posture, a more dynamic and proactive policy is urgently required.

Lesson 6: Leadership

One of the central lessons from Bosnia concerns leadership, and is quite distinct from the management of the campaign. There is a clear difference between management and leadership. Whilst it is true that good leadership must be based on good management, it is also clear that in the dangerous chaotic situations which prevailed in Bosnia, without good leadership at all levels of command, the UN mission simply could not have continued under any circumstances.

It takes a particular level of commitment and skill for a military commander to persist with peacekeeping when all about there is death, destruction and dishonesty, and when even the peacekeepers themselves are being denigrated and accused of condoning genocide. In these circumstances, all leaders from the top to the lowest levels, need to believe in, and understand, the essential humanitarian elements of the mission. They need to understand that it is they, the peacekeepers, who stand on the moral high ground. It is only then that these leaders will be able to instil in everyone a true sense of purpose.

No one in Bosnia who was involved in the humanitarian, peacekeeping or political action ever questioned the value of the mission, although frequently propagandists both within the country and outside did. The reason for this is simple. Keeping entire populations alive and preventing further horrors of ethnic cleansing not only puts the UN on the high moral ground, but also has its own rewards. In the confused circumstances of such a bloody civil war, clearly a leader cannot afford to lose sight of this.

He cannot afford to be beguiled by talk of victim states, but must concentrate his efforts on the real victims of the war, the helpless civilians.

Lesson 7: Maintaining a taut chain of command

Leaders at all levels of a peacekeeping mission can only operate effectively through a taut chain of command, to deal with strategic, operational and tactical issues at once. The three levels of command – the strategic (the UN's New York headquarters, capitals of the troop contributing nations and other international powers, and Brussels), the operational (Zagreb and Naples), and the tactical (on the ground in Bosnia) – will all be compressed and will often issue contradictory advice or orders which must be reconciled quickly, in order to pass accurate information almost instantaneously to subordinate levels of command.

The commanders on the ground were all too aware that an isolated incident was likely to debated within hours in the UN, having been seen on CNN, so were constantly having to react swiftly and effectively, often before detailed guidance becomes available from higher headquarters.

Before 1994, the UN HQ of 580 people in Bosnia was a split organization with its main headquarters outside Sarajevo, some 45 minutes drive away. It was trying unsuccessfully to control the activities of twelve major units as well as fulfil a political function. With the elimination of the main HQ, regional levels of command were established, and the UNHCR and UN political command structure were co-located at each level of command. The performance of the Headquarters improved immediately as did the flow of humanitarian aid.

Deductions on the way ahead

Beyond a shadow of a doubt, if the UN is going to perform better in the future in the face of the new operational circumstances which it is facing, it will not only have to redefine its doctrine, but create new structures, develop new technical capabilities and define new training requirements.

There are five areas, namely planning, the role of the media, doctrine, technology and training in which these reforms could be directed in the years to come, sooner, one might hope, rather than later.

Planning: Headquarters' organization

First of all, the UN at its New York headquarters has already created a far more effective HQ structure than existed previously, adding over 100 people to its strength and allowing proper 24 hour a day/7 days a week coverage so that it could run more effectively the 70,000 troops deployed around the world in peacekeeping operations.

This new operational support is, naturally, in and of itself not sufficient, as the UN also needs to have better contingency planning and intelligence gathering capabilities, if early and timely policies and decisions are going to be made.

Contingency planning and quick response

In looking at contingency planning, the idea of a 'Vanguard' or rapid reaction force – the idea which was proposed by Canada several years ago – consisting of a force of some 5000 soldiers on standby in their own countries with a fly-out HQ was an excellent idea. It would have allowed us to avoid the horrors of somewhere like Rwanda and is, probably, politically achievable.

The Canadian proposal has now been tempered somewhat by the financial and other realities of earmarking troops for peacekeeping in this way on a national level, and has been largely overtaken by events including continued downsizing of military forces in major troop-contributing countries and seemingly never-ending budgetary pressures.

The idea raised a few years ago, and still occasionally referred to, of specially recruiting UN soldiers is too politically unlikely and militarily unsound. Unfortunately, such soldiers, in the end, would not be able to meet changing operational requirements, a problem which will also have to be faced by those nations whose overall military ethos focuses on peacekeeping rather than on general-purpose combat capability.

Media and information management

There needs to be clearer understanding of how propaganda can be handled and the true message that the UN is working for peace put across. The long and the short of it is that, as things now stand, the Public Information Office in New York is incapable of sustaining the long-term strategic argument in the face of short-term disaster. The need to solve immediate problems still has a tendency to overshadow the requirement to find long-term solutions and to resolve the underlying issues which caused the crisis in the first place. There must be some sort of balance between the two: yes, alleviate suffering in the short term, but do not lose sight of the need to find long-term, peaceful solutions.

Doctrine

We also need to further redefine current UN peacekeeping doctrine, including wider peacekeeping, and incorporate these latest lessons from Bosnia into this doctrine. Only through such an exercise will we be able to come up with a common international understanding of even such basic concepts as the limits of classic peacekeeping, and the conditions under which it is more appropriate to deploy peace enforcement forces, at the other end of the scale.

One of the chief lessons to come from Bosnia is that without political momentum, there is not likely to be a lasting peace; the second most important element concerns the use of force and the understanding of how far into peace enforcement wider peacekeeping can go without becoming involved in a war. These concepts must be fashioned into an accepted international doctrine, if the UN is going to be able to react as quickly as it should to meet crises on the scale which we have seen in recent years.

Equally important will be to look at the rationalisation of joint policies, at both the national and international levels, with a view to ensuring that land, air and sea power work to a common end as part of the single mission. That such a common doctrine was missing in Bosnia undermined the impact that the use of other than land forces could have had.

Technology

Next, new technologies in the area of surveillance, communications, mineclearing and in the technology of aircraft need developing, if we are to deal with the complexities of the sort of war we saw in Bosnia.

Training

Finally, we need to define training standards and objectives which relate to the new operational circumstances and then establish an inspectorate for peacekeepers so that those who are offered up by nations for peacekeeping duties are proved capable of performing the tasks given. Ideally, we could tie into this inspectorate an arm which would determine the equipment required by contributing nations, especially those who normally arrive in theatre minus even the most essential personal equipment. Any form of standardization would, needless to say, make the commander's job easier in getting people up and running and trying to fulfil the mandate of the mission.

Perhaps the most important aspect of common training is the minimum level required for staffs sent to headquarters. All staff members must have at least a basic competence in the English language, and must be prepared to work together as part of an international organization, not as individuals working for national headquarters across the globe.

Conclusion

In conclusion, if the Bosnian experience teaches us nothing else, it is that we need to keep faith with the peace process and with the UN as an institution. The world is a global village. We cannot leave it or dissociate ourselves from its problems. We have to understand that, in the final analysis, solutions do not necessarily come from the belly of an aircraft or the barrel of a gun, but from a greater understanding of the process of peace.

Above all, we should strive to make the UN effective in its principal role of peacekeeping, for peacekeepers are, in the words of Dag Hammerskjøld,

> ...the front line of a moral force which extends around the world...[The UN's] successes can have a profound effect for good in building a new world order of which we may all one day be proud.

We need to build on his ideas, not demolish that force.

Notes

1   The views expressed in this paper are my own, based on my experiences as a senior United Nations commander in Bosnia; where there is any divergence from official United Kingdom peacekeeping doctrine, the responsibility is mine.
2   The discussions on the one proposed policy which might be considered to have been a positive contribution, namely the lifting of the arms embargo against the Muslims, contributed very little to the success of the mission, and, in many respects, undermined the impartiality which I and other UN commanders were at such pains to preserve.
3   Stockholm International Peace Research Institute, Annual Report for 1995, Stockholm, June, 1996. The Report also lists a further 10,000 deaths in Croatia for 1995.
4   The media must also resist the temptation to cover only those incidents which will guarantee immediate world attention, whilst restraining themselves from becoming members of what Martin Bell refers to as the 'do-something club'.

10 Start and End of Srebrenica

LARS-ERIC WAHLGREN[*]

General

Among the very clear lessons of peacekeeping learned during my five years as head of the UN mission in South Lebanon during the ongoing conflict there, was the importance of *impartiality*, *separation* of the fighting parties, and *not to co-deploy* UN troops with those of the Parties.

Impartiality has a close connection to preserving freedom of movement for UN. In the field, it means operational impartiality, reacting equally for the same violation towards the different parties. There is, however also a political impartiality, especially important when giving a mandate to the mission and when a new resolution is adopted.

Separation of the fighting parties whenever possible is a must because the mission of the fighting units is to combat the other side whenever possible. To fail to do so has often a devastating effect for the commander of the fighting unit.

Not to co-deploy means that, in the field, it is not possible to mix or deploy units with different operational missions in the same area, e.g. UN units with the mission to keep the peace and national units with the mission to defend their country.

Much has been said and written about the Safe Area concept, but not so much by us who were there in the field and acted day by day when the Safe Area concept was established. It is important to have these simple rules of experience from the field in mind when discussing the start and the end of Srebrenica and include them among the lessons learned from former Yugoslavia.

---

[*] Lt. Gen. Lars-Eric Wahlgren (S) was Force Commander UNPROFOR from February to July 1993. Gen. Wahlgren was earlier Force Commander of UNIFIL (Lebanon).

168

General situation prior to Security Council Resolution 819

The operational situation at the end of March 1993 was, as in previous years, that the Bosnian Government troops had gained some ground during the winter, taking advantage of their superiority in light infantry. Now that winter had ended, the Bosnian Serbs with their heavier equipment had started to advance and, among other things, the village of Srebrenica was increasingly threatened. On 18 March, I met with the Vice-President of Bosnia-Herzegovina, Dr Ganic, who repeatedly stressed the need for an immediate cease-fire.[1] At a meeting in Belgrade, General Mladic had agreed to three UN demands:

1. A cease-fire beginning at noon on Sunday, 28 March

2. Access to Srebrenica for UN relief convoys and freedom of movement on humanitarian grounds out of Srebrenica

3. A meeting between the military commanders of the three parties at Sarajevo Airport on 6 April at 11.00 a.m. to discuss continued cease-fire and other measures.

On the whole, the cease-fire was holding. On 29 March, 2346 women and children were transported from Srebrenica. Many were wounded or suffering from health problems which required medical treatment. Some were to rejoin with their families in Tuzla. About 500 tents were transported into the village the same day.[2]

The Sarajevo meeting on 6 April agreed to extend the cease-fire. However, at the start of the meeting, the Bosnian Presidency delegation insisted on making a statement strongly condemning the Bosnian Serb party. They then walked out, effectively ending the meeting.

At a new meeting in Belgrade on 9 April with the Bosnian Serb Commander, General Mladic, he promised to instruct his troops not to return outgoing fire in the Srebrenica area after 2 p.m. on 10 April even if they were provoked. A new meeting was arranged for noon, 12 April. The objective of that meeting was to discuss the situation in Srebrenica in order to seek a peaceful resolution that was supposed to include an agreement reaffirming the 28 March cease-fire and cessation of all hostilities in the Srebrenica area. The 9 April agreement resulted in a significant reduction in the level of conflict, but before the meeting on 10 April the Bosnian Presidency Commander, General Sefer Halilovic, told me that he would not attend, alleging that there had been Serb attacks on the eastern enclave of Srebrenica. At that time, UNPROFOR observers in the town reported however that Srebrenica was calm. It appeared from later reports that tank-fire from inside the town in the morning was followed by shelling in the afternoon with casualties of estimated 35 dead and 68 wounded.[3]

This was the general situation. The cease-fire was holding throughout most of Bosnia-Herzegovina despite sporadic violations, and the situation in Srebrenica had deteriorated. The Security Council was very concerned about the situation and that the town might fall or be forced to surrender. The media following the situation also asked the Security Council for action.

Staff work on the Safe Area in UNPROFOR HQ prior to Security Council Resolution 819 (SCR 819, 16 April 1993)

When UNPROFOR HQ received the first cable about the draft of SCR 819 on 16 April 1993, and we were for the first time confronted with the term 'Safe Area', I called for my Chief of Staff (COS) and my legal advisers and we discussed whether it was an established conception, such as Safety Zones. But none of us had ever heard of the term 'Safe Area' before and we set a new meeting for the next day, after some investigations. None of us had found Safe Area as an established term, but Safety Zones and Demilitarized Zones were defined in the Geneva Conventions of 12 August 1949. As Article 60 of the Geneva Conventions (see Box 10.1) gave guidelines for the establishment of a demilitarized zone, we decided to follow that article in our further negotiations.

SCR 819 had also:

- Reaffirmed its call on the parties to observe an immediate cease-fire

- Demanded that all parties and others concerned should treat Srebrenica and its surroundings as a Safe Area, which should be free from any armed attack or any other hostile act

- Demanded also to that effect the immediate cessation of armed attacks by Bosnian Serb para-military units against Srebrenica and their immediate withdrawal from areas surrounding Srebrenica

- Requested the Secretary-General with a view to monitoring the humanitarian situation in the Safe Area to take immediate steps to increase the presence of UNPROFOR in Srebrenica and its surroundings. Further,

- demanded freedom of movement, further requested safe transfer of the wounded and sick civilians from Srebrenica, etc.

Under these circumstances, we decided to apply the Geneva Conventions during our negotiations to fulfill SCR 819. The result of negotiations with General Haldovic and General Mladic on 17 April 1993 was reported by the ICRC (see Box 10.2).

Box 10.1 The Geneva Convention⁴ and Demilitarized Areas

1. It is prohibited for the Parties to the conflict to extend their military operations to zones on which they have conferred by agreement the states of demilitarized zones, if such extension is contrary to the terms of the agreement.
2. The agreement shall be an express agreement, may be concluded verbally or in writing, either directly or through a Protecting Power or any impartial humanitarian organization, and may consist of reciprocal and concordant declarations. The agreement may be concluded in peacetime, as well as after the outbreak of hostilities, and should define and describe, as precisely as possible, the limits of the demilitarized zone and, if necessary, lay down the methods of supervision.
3. The subject of such an agreement shall normally be any zone which fulfils the following conditions:

    (a) all combatants, as well as mobile weapons and mobile military equipment, must have been evacuated;
    (b) no hostile use shall be made of fixed military installations or establishments;
    (c) no acts of hostility shall be committed by the authorities or by the population; and
    (d) any activity linked to the military effort must have ceased.

    The parties to the conflict shall agree upon the interpretation to be given to the condition laid down in sub-paragraph (d) and upon persons to be admitted to the demilitarized zone other than those mentioned in paragraph 4.
4. The presence, in this zone, of persons specially protected under the Conventions of this Protocol, and of police forces retained for the sole purpose of maintaining law and order, is not contrary to the conditions laid down in paragraph 3.
5. The Party which is in control of such a zone shall mark it, so far as possible, by such signs as may be agreed upon with the other Party, which shall be displayed where they are clearly visible, especially on its perimeter and limits and on highways.
6. If the fighting draws near to a demilitarized zone, and if the Parties to the conflict have so agreed, none of them may use the zone for purposes related to the conduct of military operations or unilaterally revoke its status.

7. If one of the Parties to the conflict commits a material breach of the provisions of paragraph 3 or 6, the other Party shall be released from its obligations under the agreement conferring upon the zone the status of the demilitarized zone. In such an eventuality, the zone loses its status but shall continue to enjoy the protection provided by the other provisions of this Protocol and the other rules of international law applicable in armed conflict.

Box 10.2 UNPROFOR Agreement on Srebrenica, 17 April 1993

AGREEMENT FOR THE DEMILITARIZATION OF SREBRENICA[5]

At the meeting held at Sarajevo on 17 April 1993, Lt. Gen. Mladic and Gen. Halilovic in the presence of Lt. Gen. Wahlgren representing UNPROFOR, acting as mediator, agreed the following:

1. A total cease-fire in the Srebrenica area effective from 0459 on 18 April 1993. Freezing all combat action on the achieved lines of confrontation including supporting artillery and rocket fire.

2. The development of Company Group of UNPROFOR into Srebrenica by 1100, 18 April 1993. This Company Group is guaranteed safe and unhindered passage from Tuzla to Srebrenica by both sides.

3. The opening of an air corridor between Tuzla and Srebrenica via Zvornik for evacuation of the seriously wounded and seriously ill. The air corridor opens at 1200, 18 April 1993 and continues on 19 April 1993, weather permitting, for as long as it takes to evacuate all of the existing seriously wounded and seriously ill. The helicopters will fly from Tuzla to Zvornik and land for an inspection in Zvornik which will not cause unnecessary delay to the evacuation. The seriously wounded and seriously ill will be evacuated after identification by UNPROFOR in the presence of two doctors from each side and the ICRC. All categories of seriously wounded and seriously ill will be evacuated unhindered by either side. The number of seriously wounded and seriously ill is believed to be approximately 500. This will be verified on 18 April 1993 by UNPROFOR and the result notified to each side.

4. The demilitarization of Srebrenica will be complete within 72 hours after the arrival of the UNPROFOR company in Srebrenica (1100 hours, 18 April 1993, if they arrive later this will be changed). All weapons, ammunition, mines, explosives and combat supplies (except medicines) inside Srebrenica will be submitted/handed over to UNPROFOR under the supervision of three officers from each side with control carried out by UNPROFOR. No armed persons or units except UNPROFOR will remain in the city once the demilitarization process is complete. Responsibility for the demilitarization process remains with UNPROFOR.

5. A working group will be established to decide the details of the demilitarization of Srebrenica. This group will study in particular: the action to be taken if the demilitarization is not complete within 72 hours; the correct treatment for any personnel who hand over/submit their weapons to UNPROFOR. The working group will report to Lt. Gen. Wahlgren, Lt. Gen. Ratko Mladic and Gen. Sefer Halilovic. The first report will be made at a meeting to be held at Sarajevo airport on Monday 19 April 1993 at 1200.

6. Both sides are to submit a report on the minefields and explosive obstacles in the Srebrenica area to UNPROFOR. Each side is to clear its minefields under the supervision of UNPROFOR.

7. Neither side is to hinder the freedom of movement. The UNHCR and ICRC are to investigate allegations of hindrance of movement in Srebrenica and Tuzla in particular.

8. Humanitarian aid will continue to be allowed into the city as planned.

9. The officers and the doctors supervising the demilitarization process are under the protection of UNPROFOR, their safety is to be guaranteed by both conflicting sides.

10. The working group is to make recommendations on carrying out an exchange of the prisoners, the killed and the wounded according to the principle 'all for all' in the region of Srebrenica within 10 days. This is to be under the control of the ICRC.

11. All the disputed issues are to be resolved by a mixed military working group or at another meeting of the respective delegations of the conflicting sides under the mediation of Lt. Gen. Wahlgren.

signed:
Gen. Sefer Halilovic   Lt. Gen. Ratko Mladic

witnessed by:
                              Lt. Gen. Lars-Eric Wahlgren

The 18th day of April 1993

We also knew that we had to use experienced troops with good equipment and therefore deployed very good Canadian troops. The time schedule was met and, after inspection by officers from both sides and a UN officer, it was reported that Srebrenica was demilitarized. General Mladic then complained that too few weapons had been handed over to UN, but I stated that that was not in our negotiations – and could not be. However, he also admitted that Srebrenica was demilitarized as planned, but confirmed no Serb withdrawal. After a lot of trouble, UNPROFOR was able to reinforce Srebrenica and on 21 April it was reported that eight CivPol, six UNMOs, Canadian Coy (150), one UNHCR and three ICRC personnel were deployed there.[6]

We would have preferred a larger Safe Area, but for that, the Security Council Resolution would have had to have been agreed earlier on. At that time, however, the Bosnian Government had presumably not yet accepted the establishment of a demilitarized Safe Area and UNPROFOR had no resources available for a larger area. We knew that we could be isolated, but the earlier executed airdrops, mainly US, had been very accurate, and could be one solution to provide temporary support to our units. We also estimated that a demilitarized area – as of the Geneva Conventions – if attacked, should be seen as a 'grave breach' (§85) of the Conventions and we assumed that it should not be any problem to get support from the international community, for example, close air support to the Canadians, as we had now separated the fighting parties.

Staff work on the Safe Area in UNPROFOR HQ prior to Security Council Resolution 824 (SCR 824, 6 May 1993)

In SCR 819, it had also been decided to dispatch a team of the Security Council to the mission area. This six-person delegation was co-ordinated by the very 'anti-Serb' Mr Diego Arrta from Venezuela. The team members had never been in a peacekeeping war zone before and left a strange impression on most of the mission personnel they met. In their report to the Security Council, they noted:

> Before the agreement of 18 April 1993 the town had been under intense shelling, was surrounded and totally isolated. The situation forced the local Srebrenica authorities to agree to a settlement by which only the Muslim side was to disarm under the supervision of UNPROFOR.

This is how the team saw the situation when the Muslims withdrew and UN took over the responsibility of the town. Further they added:

> The alternative could have been a massacre of 25,000 people. It definitely was an extraordinary emergency situation that prompted UNPROFOR to react...There is no doubt that had this [UNPROFOR] agreement not been reached, most probably a massacre would have taken place.[7]

When the team visited Srebrenica it was calm but as we all knew, the living conditions needed a lot of improvements. UNPROFOR resources were now heavily stretched and for a 'more intensive' peacekeeping, we needed more troop resources to be allocated.

The discussion continued between UNPROFOR and UN HQ, and on 29 April, I sent a memo about our discussions about international humanitarian law and which area-concepts it provides which might deserve the term 'Safe Areas'[8]. However, we noted that when we spoke of demilitarization and entering of UN troops, this was described as 'disarming one side' in the cable from NY.

With SCR 824 (6 May 1993) the Security Council decided that Sarajevo, Tuzla, Zepa, Gorazde, Bihac and their surroundings should, in addition to Srebrenica, be treated as Safe Areas. On 8 May an extended cease-fire agreement was signed by General Mladic and General Halilovic, witnessed by General Morillon. In the UNPROFOR HQ, we had discussed a 'schematic model' of a Safe Area (Figure 10.1). We noted that during a demilitarization operation, there is also a phase in which the strength of forces can be reduced, once the demilitarization is established and the system of control operates smoothly and the risk of external aggression is reduced. The responsibility of the UN for controlling and following-up is an act of balance between the parties. A system for action if the situation deteriorates should also be formulated.

In the Security Council, however, unrealistic thinking about voluntary withdrawal within the war zone prevailed, and UNPROFOR was reinforced with only 50 UNMOs for all of the new Safe Areas.

It must also be remembered that at this time we were all working for implementation of the Vance–Owen Peace Plan (VOPP), which included demilitarization of Sarajevo (under UN administration). However, this was not accepted by the Bosnian Government. The subject of demilitarization was therefore on our minds, but it had only been implemented in Srebrenica, where the situation since 18 April was calm.

Staff work on the Safe Area in UNPROFOR HQ prior to Security Council Resolution 836 (SCR 836, 4 June 1993)

During the whole month of May, a discussion had continued between UNPROFOR HQ and UN HQ NY. As a result of our discussions a realistic Working Paper by the Secretariat on Safe Areas was distributed. The paper was in principle along the lines of Figure 10.1 and also had a discussion of the Geneva Conventions of August 1949. When they analysed troop strength needed for Sarajevo, Bihac, Tuzla, Gorazde, Srebrenica and Zepa, it amounted to 18 Mechanised Recce Coys, 33 Infantry Coys, 3 Engineer Coys, 10 Close Support Artillery Batteries and 12 Aviation Squadrons[9]. We thought that the figures were realistic if our operational concept of demilitarization was accepted.

Figure 10.1 UNPROFOR Safe Area Concept, May 1993

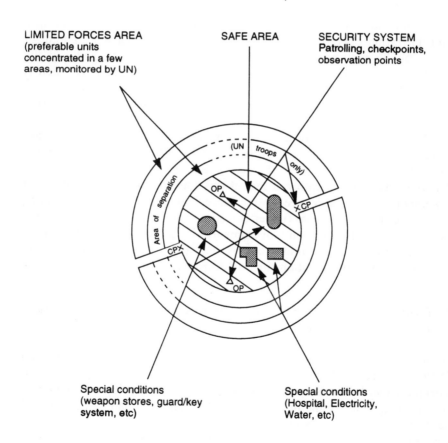

SCHEMATIC MODEL OF A SAFE AREA

(UNPROFOR Concept of Implementation SCR 824, dated 10 May 1993 – Annex of a fax sent to the UNHQ by the Force Commander requiring additional troops to implement the Zones of Separation around Safe Areas)

LIMITED FORCES AREA (preferable units concentrated in a few areas, monitored by UN)

SAFE AREA

SECURITY SYSTEM Patrolling, checkpoints, observation points

(UN troops only)

Area of separation

OP

CP

OP

Special conditions (weapon stores, guard/key system, etc)

Special conditions (Hospital, Electricity, Water, etc)

The situation grew very serious and worse with the SCR 836 of 4 June 1993, however. In para 5 of the Resolution, the Security Council decided

> ...to extend to that end the mandate of UNPROFOR in order to enable it, in the Safe Areas referred to in resolution 824 (1993), to deter attacks against the Safe Areas, to monitor the cease-fire, to promote the withdrawal of military or paramilitary units other than those of the Government of the Republic of Bosnia and Herzegovina and to occupy some key points on the ground, in addition to participating in the delivery of humanitarian relief to the population as provided for in resolution 776 of September 1992.

The resolution also requested reinforcement of UNPROFOR. However, this resolution was in fact the practical end of Safe Areas,[10] because it failed to demand any demilitarization and because it ordered the UN troops to co-deploy with one of the parties. We visualized the prospective situation, with UN soldiers caught between the two fighting parties. Earlier lessons learned had not been heard in the Security Council. The UN administration had not been able to convince the Council (or was there some overruling influence?).

The development in the Safe Area and Security Council Resolution (SC 844)

Developments in the Safe Areas came as predicted. There are no gentlemen in a war. Whenever it is possible to hit the other party, they will do it. The situation in the Safe Areas and especially Srebrenica deteriorated. On 9 May 1994, the Secretary-General reported to the Security Council:

> The army of the Government of Bosnia and Herzegovina has also used the Safe Areas as locations in which its troops can rest, train and equip themselves, as well as fire at Serb positions, thereby provoking Serb retaliation.

The Secretary-General's suggestion was therefore 'full demilitarization by both sides' and 'extensive UNPROFOR deployment' in the Safe Areas. The well-known rule of peacekeeping – separation of combatants – had been shown to be valid. But wishful thinking in New York had been lost to hard reality in the field. The first step towards the massacre in Srebrenica and the disaster for the Dutch peacekeepers had been taken.

It must always be remembered that as the situation develops in the field and incidents occur, you as commander have to make decisions based on what you know then, the information you have at that very time.

Political factor of influence

The idea of providing Safe Areas was raised earlier by the President of the International Committee of the Red Cross (ICRC), Mr Cornelio Sommaruga, talking to the heads of the permanent missions in Geneva, when he suggested setting up protected zones. The aim was to protect vulnerable groups – over 100,000 Muslims – in Bosnia-Herzegovina, who could not be granted asylum in other countries. The discussion in the political groups and the International Conference on the former Yugoslavia (ICFY), which were doing their best to halt the ethnic cleansing, saw in this arrangement a risk that Safe Areas might in a way support and facilitate ethnic cleansing by the Serbs.

It was not expected that either side (Muslims or Serbs) would agree to this concept. No troop contributors were ready to provide troops if needed to defend this area. Since there was no possibility for asylum, the Austrian government also agreed to lifting the arms embargo.

As early as 7 January 1993, President Izetbegovic said to the press in Geneva that the map of the Vance–Owen Peace Plan (VOPP) ratified and legitimized the fruit of ethnic cleansing and effectively prevented the return of refugees. He further said that during the negotiations, he had felt that he had been treated like the president of Czechoslovakia in Munich in 1938. When President Izetbegovic later talked to Mr Vance and Mr Owen, he backed off immediately, but the message was in the media, the damage was done. Asking Bosnian Muslims to compromise was after that often noted as unfair bullying.

The inauguration of newly elected President Clinton was due on 20 January. The new National Security Adviser Tony Lake had given a commitment for the new administration to support the Vance–Owen Peace Plan and that the Bosnians would be urged to accept it. There were, however, also contrary views from people in Washington.

In late January, there was heavy disinformation and criticism of VOPP in the American press, and the Secretary of State's spokesman said that Mr Christopher 'expressed doubts about whether it can realistically be achieved, whether they can in fact, find an agreement'. This was a reverse of the US position and provoked a crisis for the UN, the negotiators and the twelve member states of the European Community. (VOPP had at that time also been supported by the Russian Federation.)

Negotiations for an agreement on the cessation of hostilities went on in Geneva. The recently established Mixed Military Working Group had reached an agreement among the warring military commanders. When the time for signing came, President Izetbegovic however did not want to sign.

It might have been the case that he felt encouraged by the new US attitudes and wanted to hold out for a better deal.

In the beginning of February, Mr Christopher announced a new policy of the US administration – approval for the peace plan. Although the US had no intention of committing troops they had now developed a more coherent and supportive policy. The administration appointed an envoy to participate in the ICFY negotiations and promised that if viable agreement containing enforcement provisions were reached, the US was prepared to join with the UN, NATO and others in implementing it. This announcement, however, became the source of considerable friction across the Atlantic as it became clear that this commitment had been accepted only reluctantly by the administration and that it was questionable whether it would ever be fulfilled.

On 8 March in Brussels, the EC Foreign Ministers stood firmly for the VOPP as a basis for further negotiations even against US policy. ICFY had Mitterrand's assistance in putting heavier pressure on Milosevic to avoid a breakdown of the peace process. In the US, there was no readiness to concede the importance of Milosevic. During these negotiations, the economic arguments and the lifting of sanctions were the decisive questions.

The political discussions went on. The US decided on a 'lift and strike' policy, but was not ready to define what 'lift and strike' was intended to achieve. The Germans, for example, were asking the US if the arms deliveries to be permitted by lifting the sanctions against Bosnia were to help the Muslims fight the Croats in the ongoing conflict in the centre of Bosnia. Would NATO forces strike Croat forces as well as Serb forces? What would be the basis for negotiations? The US said it was only expressing doubts about the VOPP map. They wanted it to be more generous to the Muslims.

However, in a few weeks' time, the US had changed its mind and then said the map should be more generous to the Serbs. After having analysed the situation and its implications, President Clinton made up his mind and the 'lift and strike' policy was dead.

A new US policy had begun to emerge under the heading of 'containment', resulting in the US joining the UN effort in Macedonia to quiet the do-something lobby and to avoid committing US ground troops to Bosnia, but also to ensure that the VOPP was dropped at the same time as 'lift and strike'. On 8 May, the Americans were positive toward border monitoring; the day before, they had been against it.

The above mentioned is a fragment of the political game that was supposed to provide a basis for firm and decisive actions in the field to restore peace and security to the people in former Yugoslavia.

In the mission area, we were not aware of the seriousness and depth of the schism between the negotiating EU, UN and US representatives and the inconstant US politics based on different opinions within the new administration and also the changing influence of the new president. I thought that our many cables from the mission's HQ and assistance by UN HQ administration would be able to convince the various authorities involved of the necessity to follow well-attested experiences of peacekeeping and fully support us along the lines of these principles.

Non-support of UN sanctions and UN resolutions

One of the greatest mistakes of the UN was not to support the UNPROFOR mission with media transmitters from the very beginning. The three parties were free agents in disseminating propaganda to the local population. When we requested support by a UN transmitter, no member country was willing to provide this support. During the communist period the Yugoslav people had been taught to listen to the state-controlled media and so they continued to do so in order to get at least some 'information'. This misinformation made the UN mission much more difficult. General Michael Rose has described this situation very well when he said:

> It is of course quite understandable that a government struggling for survival should have a propaganda machine. It is not understandable that the international media should become part of that machine. Mischievous distortion of reality can only undermine the work of those who are pursing the path towards peace.[11]

When even Western authorities were misled or violating UNSC decisions, it became even more difficult to explain UN impartiality. The smuggling of weapons during the UN embargo was later openly admitted even by UN member states. No wonder that the suggestion of imposing border controls in Bosnia-Herzegovina to slow down the conflict, when suggested by ICFY, was not supported, not even as a limited main road control. President Izetbegovic acknowledged on Sarajevo television that 30,000 rifles and machine-guns, 20 million bullets, 7,000 mines, 46,000 anti-armour rockets, 20,000 hand-grenades, uniforms and boots were smuggled into his area.[12]

Instead of supporting the first demilitarization of Srebrenica according to the Geneva Conventions and UN protection of the civilian people living there, Serb propaganda talked about disarming the Muslims.

Analyses of the course of events

At the end of the winter of 1993, the conflict between Muslims and Croats was intense. The lines of confrontation towards the Serbs had mainly stabilized, but in the eastern part of Bosnia, the Muslims with their larger number of infantry had advanced. In the Spring, the Serbs, supported by their larger number of heavy weapons, started to advance, creating a great number of refugees. The situation in and around Srebrenica became catastrophic. The pressure on the international community to do something was enormous. As described above, the mission to make Srebrenica a Safe Area was then given to UNPROFOR, UNSCR 819 of 16 April 1993. With the limited resources we had and given our mission, the only acceptable solution was to base ourselves on the Geneva Conventions and demilitarize the entire area. The former Yugoslavian army was well aware of the Geneva Conventions.

When we reached agreement on 17 April 1993, it was necessary to deploy a unit well trained in peacekeeping and preferably also in NATO procedures and with good equipment. The Canadian Tow-missiles had earlier been respected and I decided to use this unit. The demilitarization went well. The area was inspected under UN supervision and accepted by the two parties. However, the Serbs complained that only a few weapons had been left behind and stored and guarded by UN. But also General Mladic admitted that the number of weapons was not within the agreement. As always in complicated situations in peacekeeping, it was then a series of problems, but the fighting had now calmed down in the Srebrenica area.

I assumed there was also the political will to fully support this operation, if necessary with airdrops and when needed, close air support against those weapons firing against the UN, in violation of our agreement, and a grave violation of the Geneva Conventions. To fire on the particular weapon or weapons that violate an agreement means that you are still impartial, but have acted in self-defence, in order to fulfil the mission given by the Security Council. (Airstrikes against other installations is mainly a political reaction.)

At the Conference in Athens 1/2 May 1993, all parties to the conflict signed the VOPP and the map. The only remaining step was confirmation of Karadzic's signature by the Serb Assembly in Pale. I was optimistic on leaving Athens and thought that this could be the 'turn of the tide'. After the conference, Lord Owen in the Steering Committee visited Milosevic in Belgrade and gave him the message that if the Bosnian Serbs accepted the VOPP before the deadline of UN Resolution 820, new sanctions would not start. We specifically discussed with Milosevic the road through the northern corridor and the demilitarization zones on both sides.[13]

However, decisive united political pressure from the great powers was not applied on the Bosnian Serb Assembly and the VOPP was not accepted.

When the Security Council decided (UN SCR 824, May 1993) to establish four more Safe Areas, one Ukrainian company was sent to Gorazde, but then we had no more troops available. The UN HQ had estimated that we needed 15,000 men, and I thought that our concept of operation should be accepted for the future also. We would have a robust self-defence component if one of the parties prevented us from discharging our duties within the concept of demilitarization. It is my experience that this could be done within the request of impartiality and without becoming a combatant, if you have a signed agreement with the parties involved.

The fatal blow to the Safe Areas came with Security Council decision (UNSCR 836) of 4 June 1993, deciding that there should be co-deployment in the Safe Areas. In our cables to UN HQ we had predicted what would happen if this occurred and, as one of the rescue workers in Srebrenica said to me: 'During the winter [93/94] it was as much outgoing as incoming fire.'

After nine months, the Security Council changed its mind: the Safe Areas should be demilitarized. But now it was too late. Already in June, UNPROFOR estimated that we needed about 35,000 troops – about the same number as IFOR – to be successful. On 4 June 1993, the Security Council, against all advice, chose an option of only 7,500 troops and on top of that, did not oblige UNPROFOR to continue to seek the consent of the parties, and also forced us to co-deploy.

The decision by the Security Council in March 1994 to reverse itself and to demilitarize the Safe Areas was never possible to carry out. In peacekeeping, you must be very firm in your policy. Often being the militarily weakest part in the conflict, you must apply your firm principles and be ready to defend those principles.

As is well known, the Safe Area of Srebrenica ended with a blood-bath. On 7 July 1995, an Observation Post (OP) of a Dutch company, then deployed in Srebrenica, was attacked by Bosnian Serb tanks. The Dutch Commander requested close air support. This was refused by General Smith – close air support was considered to interfere with ongoing negotiations. The next day the OP withdrew, but was fired on by the Bosnian Government troops and one soldier was killed. Another UN OP was then overrun by Bosnian Serbs, who took the crew hostage. During the Bosnian Serb attack on Srebrenica, a total of 55 Dutch soldiers were taken hostage.

On 10 July, the Muslims, totalling 15,000 men of fighting age and of whom some 3–4,000 carried arms, had – according to the Dutch Government – slipped out of the enclave. Their commander left Srebrenica some days before the final assault. On 11 July the Serbs launched a frontal attack on Srebrenica and after several requests from the Dutch commander, two successful air attacks against Serb tanks were launched. Concern for the hostages called off further air support. On 21 July, the Dutch soldiers were allowed to leave Srebrenica. Some 40,000 Muslims were 'ethnically cleansed'.

UNPROFOR intended in April/May 1993 to take the responsibility for the people in Srebrenica according to our humanitarian mandate. I still believe it would at this time have been possible to do this if we had been given strong, united political support when Srebrenica was demilitarized. The tragic end of Srebrenica shows that co-deployment of two military units with different tasks, is not possible. It shows in particular the importance of separation of the fighting parties in a conflict.

Lessons learned from Safe Areas

Impartiality. From my five years as Head of Mission in Lebanon, I learned by experience that the different parties always want you to support their own side. Thus the UN has to go its own way of impartiality by treating all parties involved in the same way for similar violations. It should have been easier in ex-Yugoslavia, where you mainly had only three parties; in Lebanon there were eight to ten. However, when there was no united political support, the parties were allowed to play not only a double but a triple game. This game involved our Western media.

Security Council. The United Nations is no stronger than the support given to the Security Council by the member states. However, when the member states are not politically united, the Security Council must then be realistic in its rhetoric. It is a must that the members of the Security Council have a good knowledge of how their decisions will impact on the situation in the field. It is also a requirement that they know how their resolutions will impact on the situation in the field, especially when the Security Council has a nasty, brutal war on its hands and makes a decision which is against the advice of the field mission and the UN administration.

The Security Council did not want to hear about a double game when it was played by Muslims, when the latter broke a cease-fire or fired at their own people. Part of this problem can also be found within the UN units.

Self-defence. When the mission started, UN was overstretched with too many ongoing missions. Troops not trained in peacekeeping were sent to the FY mission and occurences, like the killing of Deputy Prime Minister Turajlic of Bosnia in a UN armoured personnel carrier gave the UN a bad reputation. It was not clear for all the UN commanders that, by definition of the Secretary-General, self-defence is:

...the authorized use of weapons in self-defence, to include resistance to attempts by forceful means to prevent it from discharging its duties under the mandate given by the Security Council.

This definition of self-defence gives the local commanders great responsibility and possibility to take action against groups of bandits, etc.

Training and information. There is also a problem with troops not trained and equipped for peacekeeping collecting and transmitting confirmed information. From the very beginning UNPROFOR should have been equipped with trackmode radar to be able to verify, for example, the breaking of a cease-fire. I also asked for, based on my experience in the Middle East, UN-controlled small unmanned surveillance airplanes or drones. It was obvious that the great powers had information which was not given to the UN, presumably for political reasons. This made it even more difficult for the Security Council and also for the media to fully understand and assess the ongoing situation.

New concepts. When the Security Council establishes new conceptions, such as Safe Areas, a very close co-operation with the International Court of Justice is advisable.

Political support. When establishing a new UN mission in the future, the political support of the member states and resources available must be confirmed. However, I firmly believe that even with the very limited resources UNPROFOR was given, the war in Bosnia could have ended much earlier, if the UN had been backed with adequate political support by all the member states.

Notes

1   UN Document, UNPROFOR Press Release, 27 March 1993.
2   UN Document, UNPROFOR Press Release, 29 March 1993.
3   UN Document, UNPROFOR Press Release, 9 and 12 April 1993.
4   *Protocol I (Chapter V, Article 60)*, Additional to the Geneva Conventions of 12 August 1949, adopted 1977.
5   Transcript of the original signed document.
6   Cable, 21 April 1993, Wahlgren to Annan, 'Nations in Srebrenica'.
7   Report of the Security Council, Mission pursuant to Resolution 819.
8   Cables, 29 April and 10 May 1993, Wahlgren to Kofi Annan, DPKO.
9   Cable, 28 May 1993, Safe Areas, Kofi Annan, DPKO, to Stoltenberg for Wahlgren.
10 David Owen writes about SCR 836: 'on 4 June UNSCR 836...the Council embarked on the path of enforcement with no intention of backing it with the necessary resources: the most irresponsible decision taken during my time as Co-chairman and taken by four of the permanent members as part of their JAP.' (David Owen, *Balkan Odyssey*, Chapter 4, Victor Gollancz: London 1995, p. 190.)

11 General Sir Michael Rose, Talk to the Royal United Services Institute, 30 March 1995.
12 Owen, ibid., Chapter 4, p. 127.
13 Owen, ibid., Chapter 4, p. 127.

11 UNHCR in the Balkans

Humanitarian Action in the Midst of War

SADAKO OGATA[*]

Introduction

On 14 November 1991 when the Secretary-General of the United Nations asked my Office to assist displaced persons in the Socialist Federal Republic of Yugoslavia, we had no idea that in the years to come we would be leading perhaps the most complex humanitarian operation in history! There were doubts at my own headquarters about UNHCR's becoming involved in a war zone in Europe. However, I found it inconceivable that we should stand by and not utilize the emergency capacity we had built up earlier that same year during the crisis in northern Iraq.

There was a further prospect of engaging in conflict prevention and mitigation. Boosted by a promising new atmosphere in the Security Council, this was a challenge of early peacemaking and of humanitarian intervention during conflict, reinforced by increasing calls to contain rising refugee figures world-wide. Notwithstanding ample frustration, I do not regret the decision to become involved.

Humanitarian action played a vital and politically significant part in the international response to the fighting and persecution that accompanied the disintegration of the old order in Yugoslavia. I will discuss here the main characteristics of the humanitarian operation and try to draw lessons for future crisis management, which I hope will give the effective protection of threatened populations higher priority than in former Yugoslavia. I will end with some observations regarding the return of refugees and displaced persons as envisaged under the Dayton Peace Accord.

Main features of the humanitarian operation

Humanitarian action in former Yugoslavia was multi-faceted, constrained by unprecedented obstruction and manipulation, and plagued by many dilemmas. It was closely linked to the process of political mediation. An

---

[*]   Ms Sadako Ogata is the United Nations High Commissioner on Refugees (UNHCR).

186

innovative feature was military support for relief delivery. The question of the use of force, to ensure humanitarian access or to enforce protection of the Safe Areas, and its impact on impartial humanitarian action was a subject of continuous debate.

Comprehensive and multi-faceted

The humanitarian operation targeted all populations affected by the conflict, whether they were trapped in besieged towns, on the move inside their own countries, or fleeing abroad. Inside the whole of former Yugoslavia there were 3.5 million beneficiaries, whereas some 620,000 Bosnians fled beyond the region to other countries in Europe and elsewhere.[2] As the lead agency, supported by many other humanitarian organizations, UNHCR adopted an integrated approach to the situation.

These were new elements for my Office. Mandated to protect and assist refugees, i.e. persons fleeing across borders from persecution or war, our involvement with 'internally displaced persons' – those fleeing conflict within their own country – had been exceptional. Organizing the operation according to conventional categories of victims and institutional mandates would, however, have been artificial and ineffective. Artificial, because the protection and relief needs are to a large extent similar. Ineffective, because co-ordination requires leadership that should not be fragmented.

Underpinning the humanitarian operation was the seven-point plan of action that my Office introduced at a ministerial meeting held in Geneva on 29 July 1992. I convened this meeting to mobilize awareness about the disastrous situation following the spread of 'ethnic cleansing' from Croatia to Bosnia and Herzegovina. The plan called for action to ensure respect for human rights, to improve humanitarian conditions, to grant at least temporary protection to those fleeing abroad and to guarantee the right to return home. The response was comprehensive in humanitarian terms, seeking as it did to ensure respect of the 'right to remain', *viz.* not to be forcibly displaced, the right to flee and the right to return. The plan guided UNHCR and our partners throughout the war.

In practice, the operation comprised a multitude of assistance and protection activities throughout the region, and on either side of the front line in Bosnia as well as in Croatia.[3] I should make specific mention of the airlift to Sarajevo, which, starting in July 1992 and ending in January 1996, surpassed in duration the 1948–49 Berlin airlift. The Sarajevo air bridge proved to be a lifeline for the city's embattled people.[4] Made possible by some twenty participating nations, secured by UNPROFOR and run by UNHCR's airlift operations cells in Geneva and Ancona, it provided a remarkable demonstration of international co-operation. The airlift was under constant threat: in 1994 alone there were 102 security incidents and a total of 104 'no-fly' days.

Aid as a weapon of war

The obstruction of the airlift is symbolic of the manner in which aid was used as a weapon of war. It is well known that the humanitarian operation in Bosnia faced a continuous erosion of 'humanitarian space' in an extremely politicized context. The key and interlinked principles of integrity and impartiality, unhindered access and staff security were under constant threat.

In a conflict over ethno-territorial control, starvation was a weapon of war, and obtaining access for relief convoys or flights was therefore a major problem. The definition of relief, be it food, medicine, emergency shelter, agricultural seeds or heating fuel for hospitals and schools, was a pivotal and over-politicized issue in the negotiations for access.

Relief access was not only repeatedly blocked but also threatened by conditions such as *quid pro quo* prisoner releases, reciprocity in aid, ethnically based evacuation and even unconditional surrender. UNHCR refused to entertain any such linkages. A well-publicised example, with which we had great difficulty, was UNPROFOR's agreement with the Bosnian Serb Army to obtain access for relief to and medical evacuations from Srebrenica in return for the evacuation of Serbs from Tuzla. The manipulation of the aid effort went, however, much further. There is no doubt that relief goods were diverted to the military. In a context of active combat and without a clear distinction between civilians and soldiers, monitoring and controlling the end use of aid was often impossible.

The manipulation by the parties was for both military and political ends: humanitarian issues, such as denial of access, ethnic persecution and prisoners, were constantly exploited for political gains in the international arena, or for political posturing at the negotiating table. The Bosnian Serbs and Croats tried to present all sides as equally guilty, whereas the Bosnian government tried to drum up support for large-scale military intervention in favour of the main victims – the Bosniaks. The humanitarian operation was caught in between. We were accused of helping 'the enemy' and perceived to be an obstacle to intervention.

Aid with military support but without enforcement

Military support for humanitarian action was a radical new feature of the operation. Anxious to remain independent and impartial, we were initially less than enthusiastic about the idea of engaging the military in the Bosnian relief operation.

The idea surfaced in the summer of 1992 in reaction not only to concerns about the safety of relief workers but also to reports, including from my own Office, of Serb-run detention camps and of atrocities committed by Serb forces. While there was no consensus in favour of action to halt the bloodshed, Western capitals nevertheless felt that initiatives had to be taken beyond the Sarajevo airlift.

The result was military support for civilian humanitarian action. SCR 770 of 13 August 1992, adopted under Chapter VII, called upon states 'to take...all measures necessary' to facilitate the delivery of relief, and SCR 776 of 14 September 1992 assigned this task to UNPROFOR on the basis of the concept of negotiated safe passage, as contained in the Secretary-General's report.[5] Much discussion in between these two resolutions, including at the London Conference at the end of August 1992, resulted in a rejection of the enforcement option for relief operations, despite calls to the contrary, especially by the Bosnian government. We in UNHCR were relieved. We were – and are – convinced that aid delivery by force would be unworkable, indeed would mean the end of aid deliveries. It would also have dragged UNPROFOR into the war.

Without UNPROFOR, the humanitarian operation could not have achieved what it did. Where UNPROFOR was present, it protected the relief operation and provided logistical support and vital security information. Despite the incremental blurring of mandates under Chapter VI and VII, the Blue Helmets also brokered and monitored local cease-fires, negotiated agreements on civilian freedom of movement and restored essential public services.

For our convoys there were occasions when UNPROFOR's presence seemed to draw rather than to deter fire. But more often military backing helped to gain negotiated passage and to ensure a minimum of safety. An important initial principle was that military assets were used only at our request, and problems indeed arose when this rule was stretched. Over time, because of worsening security conditions, UNPROFOR, with our co-operation, inevitably assumed greater responsibility for deciding when convoys could move, on which routes, and with what type of escort. Finally, by mid-1995, the scale of security problems and obstructions into Sarajevo led us to ask UNPROFOR to provide trucks driven by uniformed and armed soldiers to get food into the city over Mount Igman.

Because of our different operational cultures, co-operation developed slowly, even reluctantly. Still, we have profited from association with the military's planning capacity, while on the other hand, the military has learned to appreciate humanitarian creativity and flexibility. With time, we also identified keys to effective co-operation: joint determination of roles and responsibilities, exchange of liaison officers, establishment of civil-military operation cells and daily meetings of all partners.

Close co-operation with political mediation

The humanitarian response was not only supported by peacekeepers but was also combined with intensive efforts at peacemaking, by the EU (Lords Carrington and Owen), the International Conference on former Yugoslavia (ICFY) and later by the Contact Group. Compared to the Cold War period, this too was new. Humanitarian action was undertaken not in isolation but in tandem with an early search for political solutions. It was even meant to contribute to such solutions.

Following the London Conference, I was asked to chair the Working Group on Humanitarian Issues (HIWG) of ICFY (which had six Working Groups). Benefiting from continuous support by ICFY's Chairmen, the HIWG was an important and inclusive forum for negotiations on humanitarian issues with the Bosnian parties, based on their commitments under the London Programme of Action and their obligations under international humanitarian law. We valued the input and co-operation of the ICRC.[6] The HIWG also served as a platform for larger meetings with donor and other states, human rights and reconstruction actors and of course our humanitarian partner agencies, to set the course in the humanitarian operation, to expose human rights abuses and denials of access in the field and to raise political and financial support. Donor support has on the whole been generous, and indicative of the political significance attached to the operation.

Daunting dilemmas

In describing the main characteristics of the operation, it must also be noted that we had to face agonizing dilemmas. I already mentioned the rejection of linkages for obtaining humanitarian access, however desperate the need for such access was at any given moment. Another acute dilemma was the extent to which humanitarian agencies should assist in the movement of populations.

While we brought many people to safety, especially released detainees and others from Srebrenica and the Banja Luka region, our policy was to evacuate only in life-threatening situations. We did not want to play into the hands of ethnic cleansers. The very people engaged in ethnic persecution went as far as invoking the human right of freedom of movement to justify population transfers and ethnic division. In practice, more important was that had we ceded to these pressures, and started bussing people out of Bosnia, there would have been no end to extorting and manipulating the humanitarian operation. This would have attracted even more persecution. It might also have led to retaliation by the Bosnian army. UNHCR therefore concentrated on making sure that refugees fleeing across the borders with Croatia and Yugoslavia (Serbia and Montenegro) would be allowed in.

The exposure of our staff to harassment and danger was a constant source of concern. Twelve relief staff were killed. When pursuing access for relief convoys, we agonized over how far we should go in challenging the armies and snipers that were shelling and trying to starve the populations of Maglaj, east Mostar, Bihac and other towns. The safety of our staff – especially those located in the many areas where UNPROFOR was not present – was a constant worry, not least because of our media policy. We consciously adopted a high media profile to denounce persecution and denials of access: media exposure was an instrument of protection. It proved its worth on many occasions, but required constant balancing against the interest of staff security.

An assessment: the challenges of effective action in conflict

While it is probably fair to say that relief action was generally as effective as it could have been under the circumstances, the UN's record in ensuring protection to civilians caught up in the conflict could perhaps be described as mixed at best and a failure at worst. The Security Council wanted the UN to engage in relief as well as protection, and moreover to broker peace at the same time. This proved to be an extremely tall order: indeed, almost impossible.

There was tension between relief operations proceeding on the basis of negotiated consent and attempts at ensuring physical security in the six Safe Areas. There was also tension between these attempts and the political process. Unrealistic expectations and blurred priorities, which reflected divided opinion in international capitals, led to much frustration and undermined the credibility of the UN.

I would like to turn now to the main challenges for ensuring effective humanitarian action in conflict.

Protecting civilians in conflict

The notion that humanitarian action is limited to providing material relief is a prevailing misperception. Above all, humanitarian action is concerned with protecting and saving civilians from war and persecution. Its objective is physical protection in all necessary forms. Gaining access and providing food to threatened or besieged populations should be considered a form of protection, especially to counter starvation tactics, but such relief action does not shield them against other abuses or attack. Short of full-scale military intervention, are there tools that can ensure the safety of people, especially those who are trapped behind front lines and cannot exercise their right to seek asylum abroad?

Creating the six Safe Areas in Bosnia was the UN's main attempt at providing physical protection.[7] After issuing several statements and press releases condemning the Serb bombardment and starvation tactics in eastern Bosnia,[8] I wrote on 2 April 1993 to the Secretary-General urging that Srebrenica's inhabitants be either protected *sur place* or evacuated.[9] The alternative was a blood-bath.[10] Fourteen days later, after renewed shelling had killed 56 people during an evacuation attempt, Srebrenica became the first 'Safe Area', followed by the designation of five others in May.

Analyses of the Safe Area protection envisaged by SCR 836 of early June 1993, its ambiguous text and its complicated implementation appear elsewhere in this book. By and large the Safe Areas resulted in a military stalemate. With the disastrous exceptions of Srebrenica and Zepa, the Safe Area policy did help to halt the violent conquest of territory, which the Security Council had repeatedly condemned.

However, from a humanitarian point of view, the fixed front lines and Bosnian government policy not to allow negotiated departures made it virtually impossible for the inhabitants to escape from their predicament. The areas were far from safe. Amidst confusion and controversy about the authorized use of force, UNPROFOR resisted being drawn into the war. Its relations with the Bosnian government, which hoped for intervention, became strained. In the eyes of the Bosnian Serbs, UNPROFOR lost what was left of its impartiality after NATO used air power.

Was the Safe Area concept flawed from its inception? Probably. First, demilitarization was not a clear part of the concept. Second, confusion reigned over whether the Safe Area regime was designed to protect territory or people. It seems both. An important rationale was to promote acceptance of the Vance–Owen Peace Plan, already endorsed by the Bosnian government and the Bosnian Croats, and under which the areas in question would be preserved for the Bosnian government side. The Safe Areas were therefore both a political and a humanitarian instrument, and, as spelled out in SCR 836, meant to be a 'temporary measure'.

Although consistently giving rise to problems, this blurring of political and humanitarian objectives may have been unavoidable given the political circumstances of the time. Application of the various 'safety zones' foreseen under the Geneva Conventions, which aim exclusively to protect people – and must therefore be established by mutual agreement and be neutral – was not a realistic option, because the areas in question were hotly disputed.

Without mutual agreement, willingness to use force to ensure protection appears to be a conditio sine qua non. Depending on local conditions, however, force may be no guarantee of effective physical protection. Only if there is a realistic prospect for a political solution is such protection likely to be sustainable. In Bosnia, the solution was a long time coming. The Safe Area decision and implementation contribute to acceptance of the Vance–Owen and subsequent peace plans.

Preserving humanitarian impartiality and integrity

In order to be effective, the work of humanitarian agencies must be perceived to be impartial, that is, based solely on the humanitarian needs of people without distinction to political or other affiliation. This perception is also critical for staff security. When territory and people are the object of conflict, the image of impartiality is by definition difficult to maintain, because aid is always perceived as assisting the 'other' side. Yet, despite everything, the humanitarian operation survived because the parties had an interest in aid and, although often accusing us of unfair distribution, acknowledged that UNHCR and its partners tried to serve the people of Bosnia without prejudice.

While unable to provide physical protection against attack and persecution, the humanitarian operation managed to prevent deliberate starvation and helped the victims through three winters of war.[11] The parties' self-interest, objective needs assessment, open lines of communication, constant cajoling through negotiations and media pressure, UNPROFOR's support and good inter-agency co-operation were the ingredients for this achievement.

Here, we learned two lessons. The first is that impartiality need not equate with silence over persistent abuses, and should therefore be distinguished from political neutrality in its most rigid form. The second lesson is that close co-operation with military forces that protect some areas against others – and are therefore no longer politically neutral – does not necessarily prevent impartial humanitarian action. The line is admittedly a very thin and fragile one. It is clearly crossed as soon as enforcement action is taken, whether by those same forces or others associated with them, in this case NATO. Civilian relief operations then come under direct threat, at least temporarily.

However, the integrity of humanitarian action requires that this should not be used as an argument to avoid necessary enforcement action where this is the only way to provide protection against systematic attacks against the security of people. As I have argued on several occasions, it is only logical that in such cases the military should take over from civilians. Otherwise, both the military and relief workers risk being put in a frustrating situation in which both the military and the civilian effort could be jeopardized or indeed paralyzed altogether, ultimately achieving very little.

There are other dangers to the integrity of humanitarian action, one of these being the political pressure exerted to force operations to continue despite the flouting of all fundamental principles.

A well-publicized example is the controversy over the partial suspension of UNHCR's operation in February 1993, when the City Council of Sarajevo instituted an aid boycott in protest over Serb actions such as denial of access to Srebrenica. UNHCR's suspension was an act of protest against the politicization of aid by all sides. There were times when we felt that staff security was so threatened that we should consider withdrawal, at least temporarily or from certain regions. Saying 'enough is enough' may moreover be the message needed for parties to change their attitudes.

We learned the hard way that when humanitarian action serves a political purpose and a big military machinery is built upon it, the ability to say 'enough is enough' is severely constrained. The lesson I have drawn here is that, especially in operations combining humanitarian action with military support, we must try from the outset to reach an understanding about the thresholds beyond which the humanitarian imperative of aiding needy populations can no longer be pursued, at least not by a civilian operation.

Toward an integrated crisis response

Former Yugoslavia and especially Bosnia produced the first structured attempt, during conflict, at combined political and humanitarian action. Unlike in former Zaïre since 1994, we never felt alone, although my colleagues in the field sometimes felt there was a gap between the reality on the ground and the peacemaking process in Geneva and New York. Humanitarian and political action supported each other. Already in the Vance Peace Plan of late 1991, UNHCR's role to facilitate the return of those expelled from the UNPAs in Croatia was meant to contribute to a climate conducive to peace negotiations. While agreements on humanitarian issues indeed at times my have had a soothing effect on the political front, their impact should not be overrated. In fact, the political mediators' and Security Council's support for our work was perhaps more vital for us than our actions were for them.

Unintended repercussions in integrated operations are sometimes unavoidable. The political process at times impacted on the situation on the ground, whereas humanitarian crisis situations affected the peace negotiations.[12]

Apart from the lack of decisive political back-up, the mediators also lacked the discreet environment in which their work might have had the best chance of success. On our part, UNHCR's active media policy, to which I referred earlier, was essential both to our operation and to the wider 'need for truth' about what was really happening. At times our public statements caused controversy in political capitals and with our military partners, for example when graphic reports from my staff under Serb bombardment in Gorazde in April 1994, after which NATO threatened air strikes, were at variance with UNPROFOR's assessment of the gravity of the situation. I am, however, convinced that without our active media exposure, the victims would have been worse off. Being able to tell the truth, *a fortiori* when information from local sources is constantly distorted, is vital not just for the integrity of humanitarian action but even to help keep hope alive.

In concentrating on achieving a peaceful settlement, political actors may have a longer-term perspective than concentrating on life-saving needs allows humanitarian actors to have. It is crucial for efficient co-operation that one civilian office or individual in the area of operations is in charge, not only to oversee the military-humanitarian relationship but also to ensure the necessary interface with the political negotiations. The different facets of the UN's involvement were too disconnected before Mr Stoltenberg, Co-chairman of ICFY, also became SRSG and hence chief of the civilian and military operations, followed in this same capacity by Mr Akashi. Mr Akashi, however, was left largely alone to cope with the deteriorating military situation, and eventually the UN's political role was taken over by the Contact Group.

My conclusion is that effective crisis management should not only be comprehensive – political, humanitarian and military, if necessary and feasible – but it should also be integrated. In this way, reconciliation of political and humanitarian priorities and approaches can be better managed.

Peace-building and the return of refugees and displaced persons

When peace was finally pushed through, we had high hopes that at last we could work on solutions for the 2.1 million Bosnian refugees and displaced persons, the last component of the comprehensive plan of action of July 1992. I was grateful to be entrusted under Annex 7 of the Dayton Peace Agreement with the task of designing and organizing the 'early, peaceful, orderly and phased' return of refugees and internally displaced persons to their homes or another place of their choice in Bosnia.

As a UN official, I was saddened by the fact that the outgunned UN troops, who had borne the brunt of easy criticism during a devastating conflict, were now, in peacetime, replaced by a much superior force. At the same time, we felt supported by IFOR's mandate to help refugee returns by creating a secure environment for them. During 1996, 250,000 refugees and internally displaced persons returned, almost exclusively to their homes in 'majority areas'. However, progress toward solutions has been slow, mainly as a result of political obstruction of 'minority returns' and the lack of shelter, because houses had been destroyed or were occupied by displaced persons. Together with our partners we are pursuing every opening for return and are increasing the housing stock, but we remain confronted with the same policies of ethnic division from the same people who tore Bosnia and Herzegovina apart.

It will be extremely difficult to build a stable peace without adequate and fair solutions for all those who have been expelled and uprooted. Although much progress has been made in many areas, peace-building is proving to be as challenging as peacekeeping in conflict. There does not seem to be a genuine agreement on the future make-up of Bosnian society. The issue of population transfers has not been resolved. While it is understandable that Dayton leaves the choice of destination – return home or relocation to 'majority areas' – to the individual refugee concerned, it thus leaves room for policies of ethno-political exclusion. Humanitarian agencies again have to grapple with issues that are in fact highly political.

Concluding remarks

International involvement, however flawed, contained the Bosnian conflict geographically, saved civilian lives, protected refugees and prevented starvation. Had there been no UN, providing the limited protection and more extended assistance that political decision makers allowed it to provide, Bosnia would have disappeared amid even more serious carnage.

However, the conflict in the former Yugoslavia and the difficulty in ensuring refugee return in its aftermath demonstrate that the international community has yet to come to grips with contemporary wars fuelled by territorial and ethnic rivalries. In such conflicts the expulsion of the 'other' ethnic group is a goal in itself and the perpetuation of the results of 'ethnic cleansing' becomes the official policy after the guns fall silent. Despite the international consensus that such policies are unacceptable, there is too little determination to reverse them.

Some will argue that we have reached the limits of what international action may achieve in such conflicts. But have there not been missed opportunities of prevention and early intervention, for example to stop the destruction of Vukovar in 1991 or the initial shelling of Sarajevo? Had there been a common analysis of the nature of the Yugoslav crisis and a convergence of interests among the major powers to halt it, a more viable peace might have been achieved much earlier.

Peace was finally established when the major powers agreed to joint action to bring about a peace agreement. By then, the disunity among major governments and the subsequent approach of poorly supported peacekeeping had become practically unsustainable. In the view of many, this approach and political neutrality in the face of massive human rights violations was wrong from the start.

That is perhaps the most important lesson for the future. The second related and wider lesson lies in the sad reality, *anno* 1997, that reversing 'ethnic cleansing' (like coping with the aftermath of genocide in Rwanda) may be more difficult than preventing it would have been. Yet we must try. To give up now would be to betray both the ideals that have underpinned the UN operation and the memory of those who gave their lives resisting 'ethnic cleansing' or helping its victims.

This leads me, in conclusion, to pay tribute to UNPROFOR as well as to our partners, such as WFP, UNICEF, WHO, the UN Human Rights Centre, IOM, the European Community Humanitarian Office, the European Community Monitoring Mission, ICRC, IOM and countless NGOs, both local and international. Without them, the suffering in former Yugoslavia would undoubtedly have been still worse.

Notes

1   This followed a similar request from the Yugoslav government during UNHCR's annual Executive Committee meeting at the end of October 1991.
2   UNHCR Information Notes, July 1995. The 3.5 million figure covers refugees, internally displaced persons and other war-affected people who benefited from some form of UN humanitarian assistance in former Yugoslavia. Of these 2.7 million were in

198 UN Peacekeeping in Trouble

Bosnia. In Bosnia alone the food deficit, which the operation tried but rarely succeeded to meet with WFP food, was 23,000 metric tons monthly. In July 1995, there were 449,000 refugees and internally displaced citizens in Croatia, including the UNPAs. There were 449,000 refugees in Yugoslavia (Serbia and Montenegro), before Croatia's military offensive in UNPA Sectors North and South during the summer of 1995, 26,000 refugees in Slovenia and 15,000 refugees in former Yugoslav republic of Macedonia.

3   With an extensive network of field offices we concentrated on the provision of essential relief and winterization materials, on ensuring that displaced persons were sheltered and properly treated and on attempts to protect 'minorities' against prosecution. We also organized family reunifications and medical evacuations, traced children and their parents and supported victims of sexual abuse and other trauma.

Refugee protection and assistance was and continues to be a vital part of our work. Ensuring admission – through the UNPAs to Croatia proper – of fleeing ethnic Croats and especially Bosniaks from Bosnia was a priority but often difficult. The refugees were not safe in the Serb-controlled UNPAs, but admission to Croatia proper could increasingly be secured only on the basis of assurances of onward travel or resettlement to third countries. The refugee burden in Croatia was compounded by the suffering of the Croatian nationals expelled from the UNPAs. Together with UNPROFOR, our staff repeatedly had to withstand political pressure by and on these displaced to march back to the UNPAs – which would have caused a blood-bath. Yugoslavia's refugee burden, already receiving too little international attention, became even higher after some 200,000 ethnic Serbs fled from Croatia's 'Operation Storm' during Summer 1995. Attenuating the humanitarian impact of sanctions against Yugoslavia was an increasingly important component of the humanitarian operation, but initially problematic as a result of cumbersome exemption procedures. In both Croatia and Yugoslavia we had to intervene repeatedly against threats of forcible military recruitment of refugees. Pressing Bosnian refugees for organized settlement to third countries was a major and complex undertaking in favour of ex-detainees, victims of trauma and those with protection problems in asylum countries.

4   The airlift carried over 160,000 metric tons of food and medicine, more than 1,100 medical evacuees (who were screened by my Office), as well as numerous official delegations, thousands of journalists and tons of newsprint for the legendary *Oslobodjenje* newspaper.

5   UN Document S/24540 of 12 September 1992.

6   As the custodian of the laws of war and being directly involved with negotiations on prisoner releases and humanitarian access, it participated fully in the Working Group meetings, albeit in an observer capacity.

7   There were other attempts. A rare but positive example of human protection was UNPROFOR's robust preventive deployment in Vares in November 1993 to avert another massacre. Such action should not be left to local initiative but be part and parcel of the humanitarian mandate of future military support forces. Another valid protection measure was the 'protected villages' in the UNPAs in Croatia, where UNPROFOR soldiers guarded small groups of remaining ethnic Croats. UNPROFOR's prolonged absence in Bosnian Serb-held territories was most regrettable for it left UNHCR, the ICRC and some local NGOs alone in exposing ethnic persecution and interceding with the authorities. UN human rights monitors were not accepted either by the Serbs. While our efforts may have moderated some persecution, they could not halt it.

8   UN Document, UNHCR press releases of 12 February 1993 and 18 March 1993.

9   The letter is part of S/25519 of 3 April 1993.

10 For us at the time there was hope that innocent civilians would finally be protected. During an earlier evacuation of some 8,000 inhabitants from Srebrenica, we had been harshly accused, not least by the Bosnian government, of 'facilitating ethnic cleansing'.

11 Fortunately, these winters were relatively mild.

12 It would be interesting to analyse the possible link between lack of progress in the negotiations and intensified shelling, obstruction of access for relief, etc. There also appeared to be a link between territorial shifts in draft peace plans and intensified movements or expulsions of populations living in areas concerned.

Part Three

MILITARY AND DIPLOMATIC VIEWS

Second Section

Concepts of Prevention and De-escalation of Conflict

12 The Incalculable Dynamic of Using Force

and the Dilemmas for United Nations Peacekeeping

JOHN M. SANDERSON[*]

The new global context

The resolution of conflict is one of the most immediate international issues of our time. Around us we see brutality and suffering on a scale unprecedented since the major conflicts of this century. The cost in lives and infrastructure, along with the diversion of finances to arms and military capabilities, continue to detract from prosperity and the social progress needed to alleviate the causes of conflict. Our common humanity demands that we find an escape from this vicious cycle of violence.

While the recent strategic shifts have seen the threat of global nuclear war recede, the end of the Cold War has also removed the restraining hands of the superpowers on their client states and proxies, which, for most of the fifty years since the end of the Second World War, seemed to contain many of the deep ethnic, religious and cultural tensions which have plagued modern history.

In many respects, the post-Cold War world is an extension of the post-colonial world. The Cold War froze the problems associated with colonial frontiers, often drawn for political or administrative expedience, or as trade-offs in nineteenth-century diplomacy in European imperial capitals. The problems of divided ethnic, cultural, religious and economic groups have thus been transported to another age, and have emerged anew to challenge international conflict resolution processes designed for the essential, but very different purpose of preventing a repetition of the two disastrous world wars. The need for leadership is clear, but, confronted

[*]   Lt. Gen. J.M. Sanderson, AC, is Chief of the General Staff of the Australian Army and Commander Joint Forces Australia. During 1991 and 1992 he was attached to the United Nations to complete the planning for the United Nations Transitional Authority in Cambodia (UNTAC). From March 1992 to September 1993 he was Commander of the Military Component of UNTAC.

with these crises, the United Nations has been found wanting in its capacity to assume the full moral authority established in its origins.

The United Nations Charter

Fifty years ago, at the end of the most disastrous war the world has known, the representatives of fifty nations signed the Charter of the United Nations. In this process they recalled the devastating effects of the earlier Great War and resolved that the United Nations would transcend the failure of the League of Nations to prevent conflict during the inter-war years.

The Charter is a framework for reconciliation. Its drafters sought to use the wartime cooperation to build confidence between nations. Through the united strength of Member States they hoped to provide defence against threats to the concepts of sovereignty within recognized frontiers, fundamental rights and the rule of international law.

Recent experiences have shown yet again that the link between civilisation and barbarism is thin. What is certain is that the massive human rights violations, hunger, disease and refugee flows caused by conflicts cannot be ignored. If the prevailing international fraternity is to survive, the central issue is how to intervene in a way which holds the prospect of resolution of a crisis while remaining within the framework of the United Nations Charter.

Strategic objectivity

In the last decade of the twentieth century, the deployment of peacekeeping forces has become the most visible face of the United Nations. This is a contradiction. Peacekeeping operations were never envisaged in the United Nations Charter. They have emerged as an appropriate mechanism within the framework of Chapter VI, The 'Pacific Settlement of Disputes'. Specifically, they come under Article 33, which provides for 'other peaceful means' among a range of peaceful options.

Operations which come under Article 42 in Chapter VII of the Charter, 'Threats to the Peace, Breaches of the Peace and Acts of Aggression', are not peacekeeping. The purpose of Chapter VII is, in essence, collective defence against expansionist military powers, such as the Axis threat of the Second World War. Article 42 legitimises international violence to this end (which is otherwise proscribed by Article 2). The Korean War and the Gulf War provide the only clear examples of Article 42 action.

The United States-led intervention in Somalia in 1992 and the French intervention in southern Rwanda in 1994, are both also ostensibly Chapter

VII actions. Both, however, introduced the contradictory state which plagues modern international policy, of having Chapter VI and Chapter VII actions in parallel in an internal conflict. While not unfamiliar to former colonial powers, this contradiction is at odds with the spirit of the United Nations Charter.

Pure peacekeeping operations seek to resolve lesser disputes without being judgmental about the rights and wrongs of the parties, any international backers they might have, or other states that perceive they have interests at stake. The fundamental building-block for diplomatic responses (outlined under Article 33) which can be most readily agreed is the peaceful settlement of the dispute. Article 2 obliges this and Chapter VI provides the framework for United Nations action.

The dynamics of force

In an environment of excesses and obstacles, the use of force as a preventative measure, to impose a settlement on recalcitrant parties, or to establish order over lawless groups, sometimes emerges as an apparent necessity. Experiences in the United Nations Transitional Authority in Cambodia (UNTAC) and more recent public commentary suggests that, to many, enforcement by peacekeepers is an option. The issues involved are not well understood, and in many peacekeeping operations, this confusion over the necessary constraints on the use of force can make effective command very difficult.

This is why the essence of a successful conflict resolution strategy includes at its core, absolute discrimination in the application of force. It should not occur haphazardly in a climate of passion and raw politics. Nor should it occur as a result of decisions made purely in the glow of television screens. It needs to be borne in mind that enforcement implies that someone does not agree to the role of the enforcer and is therefore likely to resist in a way which quickly moves affairs into a state of reciprocating violence.

The peacekeeping ethos

Peacekeeping is based on consent of all the parties involved, including that of the peacekeepers. This requires, for their own protection, an overt display of impartiality to establish their credentials as 'honest brokers' in the process. This display is totally different to the display required for enforcement, which is warlike and concentrated to establish seriousness of intent.

In true peacekeeping, member states deploy an international force to facilitate settlement, or to inhibit escalation of a conflict. It matters little whether the agreement of the parties in the conflict is due to diplomatic pressure, economic sanctions or exhaustion. The opposing factions want either resolution of the conflict, or at least its suspension while diplomacy proceeds. The peacekeepers are legally protected by the agreement; their legitimate purpose is confidence building and there are clear limits to what they can do while retaining the consent of the parties.

The peacekeepers' neutrality gives them their unity and their strength. They are constrained to limit the use of force to self-defence. If peacekeepers move beyond their inherent right of self-defence, experience shows us that they will almost invariably compromise their neutrality and become another party to the conflict. When this occurs, their unity is shattered and they are stripped of their strength.

Self-defence in peacekeeping

Regrettably, the confusion is exacerbated by a wide interpretation of the meaning of self-defence among contributing countries and analysts. For example, responses among UNTAC contingents ranged from some troops allowing themselves to be disarmed when threatened, to others opening fire with all available weapons at the slightest provocation.

This confusion owed something to the fact that the Cambodian operation was conducted in a country which had suffered a quarter of a century of civil war and genocide. Despite the pledges of the Parties to the Paris Agreements, the UNTAC peacekeepers and civilian components eventually had to deploy into a climate of escalating violence, demanding 'go' or 'no go' decisions. The ultimate decision to follow through on the UN mandate, of necessity, had to comprehend the need for self-defence.

From the point of view of the UNTAC Force Commander, self-defence meant defence of anyone going about their legitimate business under the Paris Agreements – nothing more. In this context self-defence is passive – it does not include actively seeking combat. At the same time, self-defence not only meant an individual's defence of self alone – it meant collective responsibility and collective action. In particular, the UNTAC mandate automatically implied custodial responsibilities on the part of the UN forces for the security of disarmed troops and collected weaponry. To this end, some company-level defensive battles had to be fought. But it is important to understand that where these engagements occurred, the use of force by peacekeepers was never offensive – only those actually using force against mandated activities were engaged, and then only to the extent necessary to provide protection. While the majority of the UN military units were eventually mentally and physically prepared to do this, it remained important that their operations were seen to be conducted strictly within these constraints.

Defending the mandate

In Cambodia, the fundamental act of the mandate was the Cambodian election. The key element in its success was the readiness of the people to vote. This depended in a large part on the perceived commitment of the United Nations to that end, and the Cambodian conviction of that commitment.

At the outset the delayed start by UNTAC eroded much of the hard-won opportunities provided by the Paris Agreements. Adding to this, the Khmer Rouge claimed that UNTAC was not implementing the Agreements fairly and that the people would reject the UNTAC process. They said that the violence in the countryside, including the massacres of innocent civilians, was a manifestation of the people's anger. On the other hand, the Phnom Penh faction claimed that UNTAC lacked the will to prevent the Khmer Rouge from subverting the peace process. How to respond was the dilemma the United Nations faced.

On a number of occasions, in response to atrocities, the Force Commander was called on, by people both within and outside the United Nations, to use the peacekeeping forces for the conduct of operations against the Khmer Rouge. There is no question that these operations would have been *offensive* – no one could draw any other interpretation. But what was most astonishing was the passion with which the use of force was espoused. Often, the most fervent advocates of violence were those who would otherwise declare their total opposition to war!

Enforcement would have required a force several times larger than the one provided by the United Nations, one structured and equipped for a protracted conflict, and at a significantly greater cost. Such a mission would have spelt doom for the Cambodian peace process, even if it had been given wide international support. The many years of diplomatic effort and a huge expenditure of international funds would have been wasted.

Enforcement is, after all, war by another name. It is only if there is almost universal consent that a particular party is in the wrong that international support for enforcement will follow. There has to be interests of severe magnitude at stake before the consensus within the contributing countries will reach the necessary fervour to provide the forces and funds for war-fighting, and possibly to accept casualties on a significant scale.

A critical issue in such considerations is that of sustainment. Can a coalition response be sustained once it comes under such stress? Anyone who thinks they can bluff their way through these things with a mandate and troops designed for peacekeeping has little understanding of the nature of conflict and the consequences of the use of force.

The political imperative

If the mission in Cambodia was to proceed, it was critical for UNTAC to retain the peacekeeping ethos under the prevailing political circumstances. There were strong strategic reasons why enforcement was never an option. While the Khmer Rouge was usually seen as the recalcitrant party, there were deep divisions internationally, within the Security Council and within UNTAC, about where the guilt lay. There was no broad consensus within UNTAC, or among the international supporters, for offensive action against any party. Both UNTAC and the essential international unity which had been built up behind the Cambodian peace process and scrupulously guarded would very likely have been shattered had it been tested with enforcement.

The difficulty here lies in ensuring that everyone understands the purpose of peacekeeping operations, why the peacekeepers are deployed to these volatile areas in the first place, their objectives and what they are legally entitled to do. The issues of consent and jurisdiction are the key themes here. The only way to avoid the need to consider peace enforcement, with all its consequences, is to generate and maintain consensus on the steps for peaceful resolution of the conflict.

To do this, everyone has to have something at stake, and the benefit of complying with an agreement has to exceed the consequences of not complying. While there may have to be an element of coercion in this, it must be done with a complete comprehension of the dynamic nature and effect of the use of force at the international level. Closely related to this is the need to understand the effects of the use of force by peacekeepers on the credibility of United Nations peacekeeping generally, as well as on the activities of all United Nations personnel and non-government organizations in the mission area.

In Cambodia, the command assessment had to be that, although there was a climate of violence, it was manageable, provided UNTAC did nothing to contribute to it, while containing it to the extent possible through negotiations, and moderating its effects through diplomatic efforts. The long-term objective of the mandate had to be the focus.

The civilian components had their mandated responsibilities, and humanitarian agencies and non-government organizations had their programmes aimed at alleviating the suffering of the people. For most, this included extensive field work. In their interests, UNTAC had to avoid conflict as much as was reasonably possible. But at a critical point UNTAC also had to stay and defend the essential element of the mandate – the electoral process. It was a case of bluff in which the risks could only be taken where UNTAC could be relatively sure of its support and the commitment of its own people.

It was only in the context of self-defence that this outcome could be reasonably certain. Self-defence in support of the mandate was only possible with cohesion in the Security Council and consensus in the countries contributing troops to the peacekeeping mission. The two issues are synergistic; each depends on the other. When they are drawn together, diplomacy is concentrated to support action. Once again, this emphasizes the need for absolute discrimination in the use of force.

Jurisdiction

Even if an agreement is broken, or in the case of these humanitarian missions where peacekeepers might be deployed without a formal agreement being reached between recognizable political authorities, it is difficult to argue that anyone has the right to kill or injure people in their own country without proper sanction under either international or domestic law. A mandate which draws its authority from a Charter designed to defend the sovereignty of states and to promote and encourage respect for human rights, cannot comprehend hostile intervention against any party within a state! And if responses are not firmly based within the framework of the Charter, how can the United Nations Commander issue lawful and sustainable orders to soldiers of another member state, or indeed of his own country? Where does that leave the soldier who might have to make the choice between obeying or disobeying those orders, and bearing the consequences?

In Cambodia, there was no legitimate authority to engage in offensive operations, since all the Parties to the Paris Agreements had not acceded to it. The appropriate response was the one taken, namely, to fulfil the mandated responsibility of establishing a recognizable legitimate authority which was then capable of exercising sovereign jurisdiction.

This is not to suggest that there are no enforcement options. But force has to be lawful, and the significantly greater demands it imposes, planned for and resourced. In this respect, where there is active debate about transition from Chapter VI peacekeeping to Chapter VII enforcement operations, the difficulties for the Force Commander in maintaining a peacekeeping climate escalate rapidly. Most of the force is neither equipped nor trained for such a transition, and the wavering international support for whatever new objectives are chosen makes the command weak and vulnerable. This is no way to go to war!

Standing armed forces for the United Nations

If it is accepted that peacekeepers are the preferred diplomatic instrument and they are to be constrained accordingly to the use of force only in self-defence, ready sources of suitably qualified troops need to be assured. Various options have been suggested over the years to strengthen the United Nations capacity to intervene, including standing armed forces.

The idea of a standing United Nations force is not new. Suggestions to this effect were made as early as 1948 by Trygve Lie, the First Secretary General of the United Nations. They have been made on numerous occasions since. In 1990 member states were requested to indicate what military personnel they were, in principle, prepared to make available for United Nations service. In his *An Agenda for Peace* of June 1992, the Secretary General Boutros Boutros-Ghali stated that:

> Stand-by arrangements should be confirmed, as appropriate, through exchanges of letters between the Secretariat and Member States concerning the kind and number of skilled personnel they will be prepared to offer the United Nations as the needs of new operations arise.

In his *Supplement to An Agenda for Peace* of January 1995, the Secretary-General took this further to propose the formation of a 'rapid reaction force', which would be under his 'executive direction and command', and which would act as the Security Council's 'strategic reserve' for emergency intervention in crises. Studies to this effect have since been undertaken by a number of Member States. In all cases these studies have come up against the realities of consensus and jurisdiction as outlined in the preceding paragraphs.

Objectivity and military command

The capacity of peacekeepers to effect their mandate impartially are often compromised from the outset by the fundamental contradiction between the diplomatic compromises needed to gain the mandate, and the essential requirement for objectivity in the development of effective military operations.

While military operations cannot be an end in themselves, as has been alluded to previously, commanders will always be confronted with circumstances which require action, which will in turn generate a reaction. Without objective direction, there is a strong probability that those actions will disconnect from diplomatic action, thereby corrupting the mission and causing its failure. The resulting tendency of the involved actors then to blame each other will affect the credibility of the structures provided by the United Nations, causing erosion of confidence in the organization. The critical issue here is not who might be to blame, but that peacekeepers need to be actively supported by diplomacy.

It is also critical that objective decisions are passed to those charged with their implementation in a way which focuses their actions, This requires an effective command structure. The military doctrine of most countries identifies three levels of command; strategic, operational and tactical. These have different functions and nature, but all three have the common purpose of passing objective directions to their subordinates, and ensuring that they are empowered and resourced to do the tasks.

If one of these levels is deficient, or their roles become merged, the capacity of the others to function effectively is severely limited. If the strategic level becomes involved with tactics, it is likely to lose its broad perspective and diminish the power of commanders on the ground. At one and the same time, tactical actions, which are not focused appropriately, can impact adversely on the strategic plan. The operational level both separates and binds the strategic and tactical levels, ensuring that tactical actions are co-ordinated to achieve strategic objectives.

Co-operating for peace in Cambodia

By way of example, these levels of command were represented in UNTAC from 1992 to 1993, as follows:

- The strategic level was the United Nations Security Council in New York, supported by the United Nations Secretariat and the state structures of Security Council members, with their links to the national capitals of interested states and the highest level headquarters of involved agencies of the United Nations or non-government organizations.

- The operational level was the United Nations Headquarters in Phnom Penh, with its links to the leadership of the Cambodian parties, the diplomatic community and the most senior authorities of the various agencies in-country.

- The tactical level was the military units, civilian groups and elements in the field, co-ordinated by regional headquarters, normally located in provincial capitals.

The key issue is that the three levels are mutually supporting and are complementary elements which form an effective whole. Each functions in the light faced by the realities of the others. Much of the success achieved in Cambodia was due to the operational level, despite all sorts of interventions, being able to achieve an effective harmony between all levels and to maintain it up to the end of the mandate.

Although the Cambodian operation is acknowledged as a United Nations success, it was clear that all three levels were deficient in some way. From the outset, there was no strategic co-ordination in UNTAC. Each component survey team developed its own plan in isolation, lacking the benefit of even a co-ordinating conference beforehand to determine the strategic direction. The bringing together of these plans only occurred when the Secretary-General's report was prepared for the Security Council in the period January to February 1992. Few component leaders participated in this process.

The first co-ordination at the operational level between those component heads who were available, occurred en route to Phnom Penh from Bangkok the day UNTAC was established. Some component heads were not available to the mission until five months later. Among them all, only the Force Commander had participated in the preparation of his component's plan. None of them had participated in the negotiations which had preceded the Paris Agreements on which the strategy for the United Nations mission in Cambodia was based. The initial strategic disconnect was severe.

Within the mission, harmonising the activities of the various elements of UNTAC was always problematic. Senior staff meetings were held regularly, chaired by the Special Representative of the Secretary-General (SRSG), or his deputy and attended by component heads and other key senior staff. But there was a tendency for meetings to become bogged down in matters of detail which were more appropriately the concerns of the tactical level. This was almost certainly contributed to by the lack of formalized co-ordinating structures at lower levels – a common UN failing.

In the absence of strategic direction, co-ordination was achieved through component heads networking as problems arose. There was no UNTAC-wide operations centre. To some extent, the civilian logistics organization assumed a directing role in the early period of the United Nations presence. But the logistics staff, being constrained by United Nations procedural matters, were, for the most part, deterred from focusing on outcomes. By the end of 1992, the Military Component's Plans Branch became the focal point for a planning and control alliance between the Military and Electoral Components, and Information and Education Division, for the critical voter registration and electoral phases.

At the same time, at the tactical level, the Military Component's ten Sector Headquarters, spread throughout Cambodia, adopted the co-ordinating role. This eventually drew in the liaison mechanism put in place to work with the Cambodian military and police of the Parties supporting the UNTAC-sponsored elections, as well as the UNTAC Civilian Police and the other civilian components. These cooperative arrangements were sufficient to see the UNTAC-sponsored elections of May 1993 through to their successful conclusion.

These observations are not intended to denigrate the United Nations effort in Cambodia, nor to suggest that such shortfalls have not been addressed. Rather they highlight the systemic problems of command and control which have plagued many United Nations missions.

In fact, success in UNTAC could not have been achieved if there had not been unity at and with the strategic level. The Paris Agreements, on which the Cambodian operation was based, were an objective document which had been long in gestation. Following their signature in October 1991, by the four Cambodian Parties and 18 interested countries, including the Parties' main backers, they defined the legal relationship between the signatories and the United Nations. In the initial absence of an early comprehensive and authoritative United Nations presence, a diplomatic body, the Expanded Permanent Five (EP5), had been set up in Phnom Penh soon after the signing of the Paris Agreements. This grouping drew around the Ambassadors of the Permanent Five members of the Security Council, those of Australia, Germany, Indonesia, Japan and Thailand. India and Malaysia joined subsequently. The EP5 served to remind the Cambodian parties of their obligations under the Paris Agreements during the five months between their signing and the establishment of UNTAC, as the Parties, and some countries, sought to exploit the new dynamics created by the Agreements. It continued to support UNTAC throughout the mandate. The EP5's relationship with the SRSG and the Force Commander was a corporate one. They met regularly and the EP5 was briefed often.

The EP5 mirrored a grouping in New York known as the 'Core Group'. Contact between these two groupings ensured co-ordination between the operational and strategic levels, through the policy processes in the capitals of the nations concerned. This meant that Security Council resolutions on Cambodia, drafted in the face of major obstacles as the mission progressed, were achievable and reflected the realities on the ground. Without this support UNTAC could not proceed to implement its mandated responsibilities, confident of its jurisdiction.

Command, control and the Charter

In multi-national operations of the complexity of the one in Cambodia, nothing is a set piece. International sentiment generated by media coverage, will ensure that those responsible cannot wait for everything to be put in place. Decision makers must be able and prepared to act in pursuit of the defined objectives and to account for their actions.

To discriminate in this requires a highly responsive command and control system. And there is the dilemma for the United Nations. It does not have a responsive command and control system. It is a simple fact that deployed operational level UN commanders do not have a superior headquarters which anticipates and is responsive to their needs. Responsiveness at the highest level requires a strategic headquarters which is purpose-designed to this end. Among other things, it requires a deep intelligence process in order to be able to make valid judgements in the light of all the issues involved. Unbiased and independent analysis is the key here.

Reinforcing the Charter through enhanced command and control

Under Article 43, all Member States undertake to make armed forces available to the Security Council for operations within the framework of the Charter. In recent times, governments of many Member States have issued policy directives or guidance defining the circumstances under which they will commit forces to United Nations operations. In essence, the purpose of these have been twofold:

- To reassure their own people that any national commitment will be justified by the realistic prospect of the potential ends justifying the risks. And

- to signal to the United Nations Organization that it must get its house in order if it expects governments to be able to generate support from their domestic constituencies.

Apart from protecting the interests of the states concerned, the definition of a framework for involvement reflects a demand for strategic objectivity on the part of the United Nations which includes a requirement for morally sustainable responses. Mandates which are framed with objectivity and aimed at the accomplishment of realistic goals are more likely to generate sustained consensus, confidence and commitment to provide resources, including forces. The settlement of the dispute, in a way consistent with the objectives of the Charter, must be the aim.

The best starting point in reforming these processes is the United Nations Charter itself, which has already been agreed by the Member States of the United Nations. The Security Council has specific responsibilities under both Chapters VI and Chapter VII and its central role as the strategic authority designated by the Charter must not be eroded. In this regard it is critical that risks of perceived bias in Security Council decisions are avoided. The United Nations Secretariat has the critical role of ensuring that the deliberations of the Security Council members maintain their objectivity. This places the Secretary-General and the SG's staff in an onerous position of responsibility.

Regardless of this essential role for the Secretariat, it has always been recognized that it would not be capable of providing comprehensive military advice, nor of controlling complex military operations. This is why the role of the Military Staff Committee was established in Articles 46 and 47 of the Charter for Chapter VII operations (see Figure 12.1). Security Council resolutions must be informed by institutionalised military advice, and this advice should emerge from the structures responsible for the implementation of those operations mandated by that advice.

Given the complexity of latter-day Chapter VI operations, the Military Staff Committee should therefore be empowered to perform these responsibilities for both Chapter VI and Chapter VII operations. This would require discrete secretariat services to enable co-ordination of the separate national military advice to form agreed collective advice, plans and directions. Broader representation would probably be needed to generate the necessary climate of trust in these extended activities of the Military Staff Committee, but this is also catered for under Chapter VII.

Conclusion

Reconciliation strategy. Reconciliation is the basis of all successful strategies. This is the underlying theme of the United Nations Charter. The United Nations brings together most of the sovereign states on earth which, by their ratification of the Charter, establish the moral authority of the organization.

Moral authority. When a United Nations mission is mandated it thereby assumes a measure of the moral authority from the Charter, the extent depending on the purpose of the mission, the objectivity with which the mandate is framed and the consensus upon which it is based. Throughout the mission, successes consistent with the mandate can contribute to that moral authority, while failures will erode it. If the initial mandate is flawed, that erosion can be rapid. More to the point, if the dynamics of the sustaining UN resolutions do not engender a clear understanding of the relationship between the international objective and the application of force then disaster is sure to follow.

Perception of success. In a media environment where the passion of the moment becomes a marketable product to be flashed around the world as events unfold, successes are likely to be less obvious than failures. Sustaining an international commitment in the light of this reality requires a comprehensive public relations strategy based on a firm understanding of the moral authority of the United Nations. Moral authority is generated through the belief which the peoples of the United Nations have in it. That belief is variable and is the sum total of the perception of successes and failures of the United Nations at any point in time. Where the perception of success is high, so is the faith in the organization. The commitment to both its principles and activities is therefore likely to be strengthened. This desirable outcome is not possible unless UN coalition operations are developed and controlled by a discriminating and responsive system of integrated command.

Box 12.1 The United Nations Charter, Articles 46 and 47

Article 46

Plans for the application of armed force shall be made by the Security Council with the assistance of the Military Staff Committee.

Article 47

1. There shall be established a Military Staff Committee to advise and assist the Security Council on all questions relating to the Security Council's military requirements for the maintenance of international peace and security, the employment and command of forces placed at its disposal, the regulation of armaments, and possible disarmament.

2. The Military Staff Committee shall consist of the Chiefs of Staff of the permanent members of the Security Council or their representatives. Any Member of the United Nations not permanently represented on the Committee shall be invited by the Committee to be associated with it when the efficient discharge of the Committee's responsibilities requires the participation of that Member in its work.

3. The Military Staff Committee shall be responsible under the Security Council for the strategic direction of any armed forces placed at the disposal of the Security Council. Questions relating to the command of such forces shall be worked out subsequently.

4. The Military Staff Committee with the authorisation of the Security Council and after consultation with appropriate regional agencies, may establish regional subcommittees.

13 Developing the Peace in Central Bosnia – 1994

The Role of the Joint Commission

ANDREW RIDGWAY[*]

The conflict develops

The conflict in Bosnia erupted in 1992 and its development over subsequent years has been well documented. The results of the extensive ethnic cleansing from Prijedor, Banja Luka and elsewhere became increasingly apparent in Central Bosnia, especially in towns like Zenica where large numbers of displaced persons were accommodated amongst the largely Muslim population. International attention early in the conflict focused upon the situation in Sarajevo and particularly upon the conflict between the Bosnian Serbs and their primarily Bosnian Muslim adversaries. The international community responded in the autumn of 1992 with a major deployment of United Nations forces to support the humanitarian efforts of the UNHCR and the many affiliated non-governmental organizations. The situation on the ground then stabilised and by the end of 1992 a static confrontation line between the parties to the conflict had been established.

During this period the British contingent of a battalion group based on 1st Battalion The Cheshire Regiment deployed into the area and established bases in a selection of locations in Central Bosnia. The situation on the ground then changed dramatically. The uneasy alliance between the Bosnian Croats and Bosnian Muslims collapsed and a bitter war broke out between the former allies. Fanned by atrocities such as those at Stupni Do and Ahmici this fighting developed into some of the most bitter of the entire conflict with neighbour turning against neighbour in an orgy of destruction and killing.

---

[*] Brigadier Andrew Ridgway (UK), is Director of Operational Capability at the British Ministry of Defence. He was Commander of the 7th Armoured Brigade and UNPROFOR Sector South West.

218

The cease-fire

In February 1994 the situation in Central Bosnia changed dramatically once again. Generals Roso and Delic, the commanders of the Bosnian Croat and Bosnian Muslim armies, agreed a pact which led to the signing of the Washington Treaty – an agreement not only to stop the fighting between the two sides but for them to join together and form a unified federal government. While it had never been clear what precisely had led to the original eruption of fighting between the Bosnian Muslims and Bosnian Croats, it was far less clear what had prompted the agreement to the uneasy truce between two adversaries who had been involved in such bitter fighting for more than twelve months. There was clearly a good deal of American influence in encouraging the parties to cooperate, but there was precious little enthusiasm for any meaningful measures to work together and give substance to the emerging Federation.

British General Sir Michael Rose had taken command of UN forces in Bosnia in December 1993 prior to the signature of the Washington Treaty. He was, inevitably, focused on the continuing conflict with the Bosnian Serbs which dominated the attention of the international community and the world's press. He immediately appreciated the significance of the pact between the other parties to the conflict and decided that its implementation could not be conducted alongside his overall responsibilities for Bosnia-Herzegovina from his headquarters in Sarajevo. Consequently, he accelerated his plans to establish an intermediate level of tactical command in Bosnia and directed the creation of three Sector Headquarters, Tuzla – Sector North East, Gorni Vakuf – Sector South West and Sector Sarajevo. The responsibility for the implementation of the peace treaty between the Bosnian Croats and Bosnian Muslims fell to the UN troops in the new Sector South West which included the pockets of Bosnian Croats around Vitez, Konjic and Kiseljak as well as the confrontation line between the largely Bosnian Muslim region of Central Bosnia and the self-styled Bosnian Croat Republic of Herceg-Bosna. This chapter describes how this fragile peace in Central Bosnia was nurtured and developed and demonstrates how the previously warring factions were encouraged to work together in pursuit of a lasting settlement. It focuses on the crucial role played by the Joint Commission in encouraging the peace process and suggests that there are lessons that can be drawn from the experiences of the UN in Central Bosnia in 1994 for similar attempts at peace implementation now and in the future.

The new UN Headquarters Sector SW was formed within days of the signing of the Washington Treaty and formed up in an old factory in Gorni Vakuf, right on the confrontation line and in a location already occupied by the British battalion responsible for escorting humanitarian aid through the area. The commander of the Sector was the British Brigadier John Reith, a Parachute Regiment officer who had previously been Chief of Staff of the British 1st Armoured Division during the Gulf War. His Headquarters was based initially upon the Headquarters of the British 4th Armoured Brigade which had been based in Divulje Barracks, Split as the British national contingent headquarters. This British staff core was rapidly reinforced by contingents from Spain, Canada, Malaysia and elsewhere to form a truly multi-national headquarters.

The mission of the new Headquarters Sector SW was clear – to implement the Roso/Delic pact and stop the fighting between the two partners in the new Federation. This was an awesome task with no enthusiasm for reconciliation apparent between the parties and continuing fighting by both sides with the Bosnian Serbs, the third party to the conflict. The degree of success was quite remarkable and has been described by General Rose as being a copybook example of this type of peacekeeping operation. A Joint Commission was established in Gorni Vakuf with the military commanders of both factions represented. At regular meetings, chaired by the Sector Commander, the delineation of the Confrontation Line was agreed and a Buffer Zone established; Heavy Weapons were identified and Exclusion Zones defined; and excess weapons were corralled in Weapon Collection Points. The particular difficulty of restricting the use of Heavy Weapons against each other whilst continuing to prosecute the war with the Bosnian Serbs was overcome by the establishment of Active Weapon Sites where UN Artillery monitors ensured that the weapons were only fired against Bosnian Serb targets and not used against their Bosnian Croat or Muslim allies. This was a delicate process which always ran the risk of being misinterpreted by the Bosnian Serbs as active UN support for the Bosnian Muslims and Bosnian Croats but which was merely a recognition of the fact that the Muslim/Croat cease-fire was the only one in force at the time. The process of restoring utilities to the local population was also started so as to generate some sort of peace dividend. The whole operation was a remarkable success and laid the foundations for the subsequent attempts to consolidate the situation and develop it into a wider peace throughout the region.

Peace development

It was at this stage in the operation that the British 7th Armoured Brigade took over command of Sector SW and became responsible for the development of the fragile peace in Central Bosnia. The Sector SW area covered most of Central Bosnia-Herzegovina from Maglaj in the north, to the outskirts of Sarajevo in the east and right down to the border with Croatia in the south. The UN force of some 8,500 peacekeepers consisted initially of five infantry battalions; two from Britain and one each from Spain, Malaysia and Canada, plus a British Engineer Regiment and a Belgian transport company. During the summer this force was reinforced by a Turkish mechanised infantry battalion, a British recce regiment and a large mechanised infantry company from New Zealand.

An initial analysis of the mission given to the Sector revealed that there were three key components of this complex task:

- The conditions in which to allow the distribution of humanitarian aid had to continue to be created. The relief of suffering was, after all, the reason that the UN force had been deployed to Bosnia in 1992 and, despite the Washington Treaty, nearly 3 million people across the region still relied entirely upon UN aid for their very existence

- The fragile peace between the Bosnian Muslims and Bosnian Croats had to be nurtured, protected and developed. Success in this task would inevitably assist in the task of distributing humanitarian aid

- Wherever possible the new peace in Central Bosnia was to be extended to include the Bosnian Serbs with whom the war continued.

The unifying purpose of these tasks was the creation of the conditions necessary for the achievement of a wider peace throughout the region. The UN troops in the Sector had made an excellent start. The cessation of hostilities between the Bosnian Muslims and Bosnian Croats had dramatically improved the flow of humanitarian aid, removing the need to negotiate the movement of each convoy across the many confrontation lines. However, road communications remained tenuous, the only road access into Central Bosnia and onwards to Sarajevo and the enclaves of Srebrenica, Zepa and Gorazde was on Route Triangle, a mountain track that had been converted into a major two-lane highway and kept open through the depths of two Bosnian winters by teams of British Royal Engineers. This was one of the most remarkable feats of the whole campaign.

However, the key to improving the flow of humanitarian aid lay in reopening the low-level route along the Neretva River known as the 'Lifeline Route' and which had been closed in 1993 by the blowing of the road bridges at Bijela, north of Mostar. A Slovakian ferry service around the blown bridges had been established by the UN but it could not begin to cope with the demand and a better solution was urgently needed. A multi-national UN operation involving engineers from Britain, Spain and Slovakia built a floating bridge and carved a huge by-pass out of the rock face to reopen the route and allow the aid convoys to flow along the Lifeline Route once again. The effect on aid deliveries was dramatic, a ten-fold increase during the summer of 1994. The access provided by the new route and the cessation of the fighting opened Bosnia up to all manner of commercial traffic once again. In fact at one stage during 1994 it was possible to buy petrol in Sarajevo more cheaply than in Germany! The real problem during much of this period lay in maintaining the flow of humanitarian aid amongst the increasing levels of commercial traffic that clogged the roads throughout the region, and in overcoming the constraints imposed by bureaucracy and corruption, rather than in overcoming military interference with aid operations. By the autumn of 1994 the first of the Sector's mission components had really been completed. The conditions to allow the delivery of humanitarian aid had been created, it was merely a matter of maintaining them. The practice of providing UNPROFOR escorts to aid convoys within the Sector had virtually ceased and this allowed the UN troops to focus on the other two components of the mission.

Despite the improving relationships with the Bosnian Muslim and Bosnian Croat factions, relations between UNPROFOR and the Bosnian Serbs in the Sector remained difficult. And yet without a good relationship with the Bosnia Serbs, built on trust and mutual understanding, there was little prospect of achieving the wider settlement necessary to a lasting peace in the region. The Bosnian Serbs had a well-developed hierarchical structure both politically and militarily. There were few opportunities for independent action on the part of Bosnian Serb subordinate military commanders or politicians. Consequently real progress with the Bosnian Serbs was only ever going to be made at the highest levels and this was the main focus of effort at General Rose's headquarters in Sarajevo. This limited the activities of the Sector in this regard to attempts at confidence building and in particular to establishing liaison and trust with Bosnian Serb commanders so that when the settlement came, which it inevitably would, a framework of trust would already have been created which would help facilitate the peace process. Progress was patchy. The Canadian battalion worked wonders and developed an excellent relationship with the Bosnian Serb brigade around Ilias, north-west of Sarajevo, which led to the stationing of a complete Canadian company on Bosnian Serb-held territory – the only UN troops so stationed at the time. The Spanish battalion was also extremely successful and established close liaison with the Bosnian Serb Herzegovina Corps. This led to regular meetings at Sector

Commander level with General Grubac, the corps commander. Elsewhere the Sector was less successful, there was deep suspicion on the part of many of the Bosnian Serbs; and the Bosnian Muslims resented any UN contact with the faction that they regarded as the aggressor and they took every opportunity to frustrate attempts at closer liaison. Despite this there was evidence of regular contact between the Bosnian Croats and Bosnian Serbs, especially if mutually beneficial trade was involved. The Sector occasionally used these links to establish contact with the Bosnian Serbs but such links were very sensitive and were closely protected by the Bosnian Croats. Despite these difficulties the development of relationships with the Bosnian Serbs was an important component of the mission and remained so throughout the period.

However, the main focus of the Sector and the main effort of the UN contingents was the third of the key mission components, the nurturing and development of the fragile peace between the Bosnian Muslims and Bosnian Croats. The maintenance of this peace agreement seemed to be the key to the success of the mission as a whole. If the peace in Central Bosnia collapsed, the fighting would restart, the vital aid operation would be disrupted and there would be little prospect of the wider involvement of the Bosnian Serbs in the peace process. There were three sub-components of the task.

The separation of military forces had to be completed. Despite the remarkable success of the early days of the peace, the two factions remained in considerable strength around the confrontation lines. The lack of trust was palpable and led to widespread reluctance to reduce force levels, dismantle defences and commence the lifting of mines. Force levels were at their greatest in areas such as Mostar, Vitez and Gorni Vakuf where the fighting had been most intense and where the parties felt that they had most to lose in the event of a breakdown in the peace process. The UN contingents maintained relentless pressure on the military commanders to implement painstakingly agreed force reductions. Gradually confidence in the ability of the UN to monitor and ensure parallel implementation of the various agreements grew and military force levels on the confrontation lines were progressively reduced. However, there was another more subtle danger in this process. The factions came to be more and more reliant on the UN for their security. They were content to remove a defensive position or a checkpoint provided it was replaced with a UN observation post.

Anyone who has visited Cyprus will understand the dangers in encouraging such reliance on the UN in these circumstances. The status quo can rapidly become established as a goal in itself and subsequent attempts to achieve reconciliation between the parties to the conflict can become more, rather than less, difficult as a result of the presence of the

UN which then becomes part of the problem rather than part of the solution. To overcome this danger a dynamic approach to this aspect of the campaign was adopted. Wherever there was a danger of a UN checkpoint or observation post becoming too permanent it was moved; whenever the factions began to expect the presence of UN troops, the deployment routine was changed. The aim was to give the factions confidence in the overall ability of the UN to implement the agreements without becoming dependent on the UN at every potential flashpoint. It was, after all, their peace agreement, not the UN's; they themselves had decided to stop the fighting and form a Federation.

The strategy was not without its difficulties; it was high risk and had the potential to go badly wrong on a number of occasions thus jeopardising the whole process. It depended crucially on the judgement of UN battalion commanders as to where and when to disengage and where the risks were unacceptable. This was initially a difficult concept for some contingents to embrace, particularly those with experience of other UN operations where a more static approach to the problem is encouraged. However, by the autumn of 1994 all contingents were actively involved in the process and it was encouraging to see the individual portacabins that the UN had put in position for the benefit of each of the factions being removed from checkpoints so that the factions had either to share the same facilities or get cold and wet. It also dramatically reduced some UN contingent's enthusiasm for erecting enormous white observation towers at every opportunity as they knew they would be invited to move them within a few weeks.

Although the separation of forces was, of course, critical to the peace process, as it generated confidence and reduced the risk of an incident on the confrontation line escalating into a return to hostilities, it was only part of the solution. The conflict between the Bosnian Muslims and Bosnian Croats had suddenly erupted in the winter of 1992/93, equally suddenly, a year or so later it had ended; not just with a cease-fire, but with the formation of the Federation. None of the issues that prompted this bitter struggle had really been identified let alone resolved and there was a real danger that the conflict would flare up again. Consequently the second crucial sub-component in the process of nurturing the peace agreement was the undermining of the will of the population to return to conflict. This was a complex psychological process in which the Sector tried to give the population something that they really did not want to lose. In early 1994, before the peace agreement, Central Bosnia was an awesomely depressing place. It was cold and dark, no vehicles moved other than UN convoys, many of the towns lay in ruins, the economy had collapsed, the men spent their days in the trenches and the women scrabbled around by night to find food and heating materials. When the peace agreement was signed in February 1994 the fighting stopped but initially little else changed. The immediate imperative was to make a real difference to people's lives, including offering some advantages rather more tangible than the creation of a Federation with erstwhile enemies. A campaign of emergency reconstruction was initiated, concentrated as far as possible on those centres of population most at risk of a return to fighting. The aim was to provide water and electricity, to clear some of the debris, and to reopen the schools and medical facilities. Clearly this was not a task that UNPROFOR could attempt unaided but the UN troops helped to focus and co-ordinate the activities of the various aid agencies and in particular the British Overseas Development Administration (ODA), now retitled Department for International Development (DfID). The ODA played a major part in the operation to generate electrical power. The vital operation to re-establish an electricity distribution system to the towns and villages was run by an outstanding young British engineer called John Adlam who almost single-handedly re-established the electricity supply to most of Central Bosnia. Many other agencies were involved in this emergency reconstruction programme and the UN contingents played a major part in building bridges, encouraging freedom of movement, clearing mines and even in devoting their free time to reconstruction projects such as schools and hospitals. This often had the effect of galvanising some overwhelmed and ineffectual local authorities into self-help action and, as a general rule, unless such participation was forthcoming the focus of UNPROFOR effort was shifted elsewhere.

The result of all these efforts was a major transformation of life in Central Bosnia. In a few short months many roads were opened and a degree of freedom of movement was re-established water and electricity were returned, the process of replacing roofs on homes had begun, schools and hospitals were reopened and the first steps towards a return of normality were taken. This transformation of life for the population was all very gratifying but it was not an end in itself. The real purpose of all this activity had been to demonstrate that a better life was possible and that a return to fighting would result, not just in more death and destruction, but in the loss of the newly returned water and electricity supplies and in the closure of the newly reopened schools and hospitals.

Figure 13.1 Freedom of movement through UN checkpoints in the Lasva Valley, February to October 1994

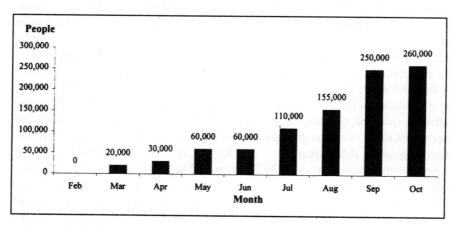

Improvements in freedom of movement were not universal and areas like Mostar remained difficult throughout the period but in the Lasva Valley, the scene of some of the most vicious fighting, the change was dramatic. The rate of return of water and electricity to houses in the Lasva Valley during 1994 can also be shown in the following graphs drawn from the HQ 7 Armd Bde Post Operation Report issued in November 1994:

Figure 13.2 Distribution of water in the Lasva Valley, February to October 1994

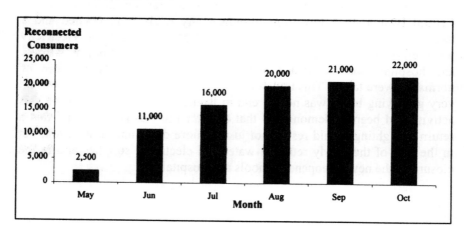

Figure 13.3 Distribution of electricity to Bosniak areas in the Lasva Valley, February to October 1994

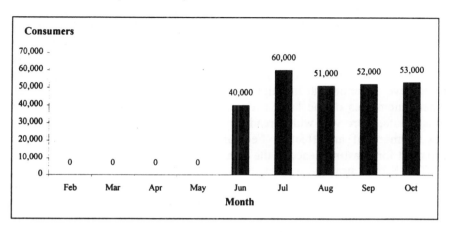

Figure 13.4 Distribution of electricity to Croat areas in the Lasva Valley, February to October 1994

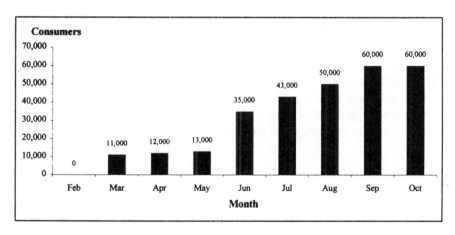

The traditional response of aid agencies in these sort of circumstances is to delay reconstruction effort until an overall peace settlement has been achieved. The Sector line was that waiting for an overall peace settlement risked losing the potential gains of the agreement between the Bosnian Muslims and Bosnian Croats and that risking some resources in this early reconstruction effort was the most valuable contribution possible to the overall peace process. Fortunately many agencies accepted the logic and made enormous contributions.

However, separating the forces and undermining the will of the population to return to war were still not sufficient in themselves to secure the peace process in Central Bosnia. The real challenge, and the third sub-component of this task, lay in encouraging the implementation of the newly created Federation. It was very clear on the ground that the Washington Agreement was a marriage of convenience with precious little sign of any sort of love affair between the parties. It was difficult enough for the parties to achieve agreement at the highest level in Sarajevo; but at a local level, where memories of the last year's fighting and destruction were at their most acute, there was widespread opposition and obstruction. And yet the development of an effective Federation seemed to offer the only real prospect for a lasting peace in the area, if it could be achieved!

The Sector strategy was to promote the Federation and its emerging structures at every opportunity, encouraging co-operation between the parties and refusing to deal with local politicians who were unacceptably obstructive. Many of the local political leaders were almost uniquely unhelpful combining all the worst, post-communist characteristics of a reluctance to accept responsibility and a refusal to delegate authority with some pretty widespread corruption and the sort of antipathy bred by the recent fighting. The ability to focus the emergency reconstruction effort was crucial to the process. Towns whose politicians were prepared to work across the ethnic divide received a priority for the investment of reconstruction effort thus demonstrating the real and immediate benefits of co-operation. This approach was reinforced by the work of the UN Civil Affairs staff who were actively involved at a local political level facilitating the first faltering meetings of the emerging Federal structures. The UN military contingents also played their part in this process by providing secure venues for meetings and providing transport for delegates.

The Joint Commission

The prosecution of the peacekeeping campaign in Central Bosnia at this stage in the process can therefore be seen as a complex activity in which there are three clearly definable lines of operation:

Military – the separation of forces so as to reduce the risk of military conflict

Civilian – the targeting of aid and reconstruction effort so as to undermine the willingness of the population to return to conflict

Political – the encouragement of the development of new political structures so as to reduce the possibility of future conflict.

The simultaneous prosecution of all three lines of operation was a complex business involving many diverse agencies as well as the military and political leadership of the parties to the conflict. The necessary co-ordination of activities was achieved through the Joint Commission that had originally been set up so successfully by Brigadier John Reith as a largely military structure to initiate the separation of forces in the immediate aftermath of the signing of the Washington Agreement. The Joint Commission evolved considerably during the year.

Figure 13.5 The structure of the Joint Commission

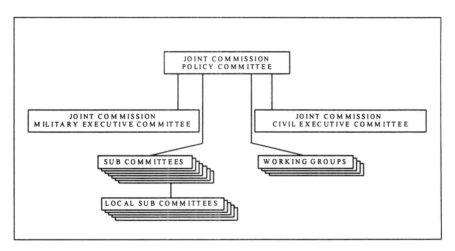

At the head of the Joint Commission was the Joint Commission Policy Committee (JCPC). The JCPC was chaired by the Sector Commander and contained military and civilian members of both parties. The military representatives were delegates from the Headquarters of the Commanders in Chief of the ARBiH, the Bosnian Muslim Army and the HVO, the Bosnian Croat Army, and they were authorised to speak on behalf of their commanders. Once the new Federal Army structures began to develop in Sarajevo they were represented by General Roso, the commander of the Federal Army Headquarters (and a previous commander of the HVO), General Muslimovic, the Chief of Staff, and several of their staff officers from both factions. The civilian delegates changed several times during the year as the focus of the Joint Commission changed and the development of the civilian and political lines of operation began to dominate. They were initially delegates from the political leaderships located in Sarajevo for the Bosnian Muslims, and Mostar, as the capital of the self-styled Bosnian

Croat mini-state of Herceg-Bosna, for the Bosnian Croats. Once the Federal Parliament met and elected the members of the Federal Government they officially became the delegates from the Federal Government in Sarajevo. In the autumn of 1994 an attempt was made to refine the membership of the JCPC to reflect the emerging Canton administrations. This was part of the process of encouraging the development of Federation structures but the initiative proved unpopular with the Bosnian Croats who were reluctant to surrender any authority from Mostar – a situation which persists today!

The JCPC also included UN representatives, particularly the Sector head of UN Civil Affairs as the focus of the political line of operation and Lane Visser the UNHCR liaison officer as the focus of the civilian line of operation. Thus it can be seen that the complete spectrum of operations of the Sector, across all three lines of operation and including the military and political leadership of the targets of this activity, could be brought together in a single committee to advance the peace process. The role of the JCPC was to make policy, to decide the direction of the campaign and to broker agreement to initiatives. Agreements reached in the JCPC had the authority, not only of UNPROFOR, UN Civil Affairs and the UNHCR; but also of the military and political leaderships of both parties to the conflict – at least in theory! Inevitably, achieving agreement in a policy committee is rather easier than implementing the policy on the ground. Consequently the Joint Commission had a network of sub-committes and local sub-committees that cascaded down into every town and village across Central Bosnia. The UNPROFOR battalion commanders chaired the sub-committees in their own areas of responsibility with ARBiH Corps and HVO Operations Group military commanders and local political leaders as the delegates and with their own UN Civil Affairs officers and UNHCR liaison officers as delegates. At a lower level the UNPROFOR company commanders chaired local sub-committee meetings in each town with brigade commanders and local mayors as the delegates. In this way the policy decisions of the JCPC were communicated right down to the lowest levels and attempts to frustrate their implementation could be dealt with rapidly. Some issues did not lend themselves to such a hierarchical structure, particularly in the field of emergency reconstruction. Electricity supply lines and the telecommunications networks criss-cross battalion boundaries and were best dealt with by Working Groups set up for a particular purpose and with appropriate representation, but answerable to the JCPC. Despite the authority for the work of the sub-committees stemming directly from the JCPC and from there to the highest military and civil authorities in the Federation there were many attempts to frustrate progress. Clausewitzian friction was certainly alive and well in Central Bosnia!

To address the inevitable difficulties and to avoid getting the JCPC bogged down with the detail of execution rather than policy, two Executive Committees were formed – the Joint Commission Military Executive Committee and the Joint Commission Civil Executive Committee. These were standing committees in permanent session. They met every day and were charged with the active resolution of problems on the ground. The Military Committee was led by Major Miles Brown of the Royal Artillery. The members of his committee were officers from the ARBiH and HVO and they acted with the authority of the JCPC. They toured Central Bosnia relentlessly demanding compliance with policy decisions of the JCPC and troubleshooting when situations threatened to get out of hand. The Civilian Committee was chaired by John Ryan, an Irish lawyer and highly successful Head of the Sector's UN Civil Affairs office. He was assisted by Wahid Wahidullah from Afghanistan and Victor Bezruschenko from the Ukraine. With their varied backgrounds they had an unrivalled perspective on conflict and the difficulties inherent in its resolution. This was just as well as their committee seemed to attract the most difficult and recalcitrant of local politicians as delegates and they spent long days debating the implementation or formulation of policy for the JCPC. They were absolutely crucial to the success of the Joint Commission.

In the early part of 1994, immediately after the signing of the Washington Agreement, the Joint Commission represented the only real authority in Central Bosnia other than that exercised by local warlords. Even when the Federal Parliament had been formed in Sarajevo and authority had been vested in Federal Ministers there was no machinery to exercise this authority. Members of the Federal Government were seldom able to travel outside the capital and, as relations with the Bosnian Serbs deteriorated during the summer and the fighting around Sarajevo intensified, so the ability of the Federal Government to exercise its authority was reduced. Initially there was much suspicion within the Federal Government about the activities of the Joint Commission and a feeling emerged that the UN was attempting to supplant the authority of the legal government. However, over time and following endless liaison visits to Sarajevo, they became reconciled to the fact that the Joint Commission was a significant force for good in the region and was the only means by which the peace process could be taken forward in Central Bosnia.

The operation of the JCPC

The key to the operation of the Joint Commission was the JCPC. It met routinely at Sector Headquarters every 14 days throughout the summer and autumn of 1994 although additional meetings were convened at different times and in different locations to address specific issues, such as the lack of freedom of movement in Mostar. The JCPC meetings were the focus of all efforts to take the peace process forward in Central Bosnia and thus were an extremely important part of the work of the UN in the Sector. The success of the Joint Commission depended on a number of key factors.

Authority. If the delegates to the Joint Commission were to be expected to take the work seriously it was important that they felt that they were part of an important institution. A special room was set aside in the Sector Headquarters which was decorated with maps and flags, a special Joint Commission table was built by the Royal Engineers, delegates were given special Freedom of Movement passes which authorised them to cross confrontation lines throughout the area. The authority of the Joint Commission was boosted whenever possible by the presence of important visitors such as the US Ambassador to Bosnia-Herzegovina, or by the publication of declarations of support for the work of the Commission from visitors such as Ambassador Holbrooke. As well as giving the Joint Commission authority as an institution, it was essential that delegates had real authority to make decisions on behalf of their military and political leaders. This was not easy to achieve and was only maintained at the insistence of the Sector Commander and as a result of regular visits to the Commanders in Chief of the armies and to the President and Vice-President of the Federation and their key Ministers.

Discipline. It was very easy for the meetings to degenerate into recrimination sessions or into endless debates over minor points of detail. After one particularly rowdy and unsatisfactory meeting some ground rules were established which were then rigidly imposed:

- Only those sitting at the table could take part in discussions

- There would be no breaks for smoking or delegate conferences during the meetings

- All contributions would be through the Sector Commander's Interpreter

- Only one delegate could speak at a time

- There would be no tape recording of proceedings.

Once the rules were established they led to much more productive meetings and became self-regulatory as old hands disciplined new delegates who broke the rules. One significant improvement was to replace the square Joint Commission table, where the factions confronted one another from opposite sides, with an oval table where they sat on the same side opposite the UN delegates. It became clear that it was significantly more difficult to have a heated argument with someone alongside you than with someone across the table. This psychological process was further developed by sitting the civilian delegates from both factions together and similarly the military delegates side by side. The military delegates, in particular, got on extremely well especially as many had served together in the Yugoslav armed forces before the war, and this tended to break down factional positions with the military delegates from both factions often siding together in the face of civilian intransigence.

Initiative. New initiatives for the Joint Commission were addressed in different ways. It was sometimes best to achieve broad agreement in the Civil Executive Committee before bringing a proposal to the JCPC for formal endorsement. This worked well with less contentious issues. The more difficult proposals were best bounced upon an unsuspecting JCPC with no warning. Delegates were then given no opportunity to prepare counter-proposals and were keen to avoid being seen to be deliberately obstructive. While this tactic was unlikely to achieve immediate success it often allowed agreement in principle to be achieved which could then be refined over time by one of the Executive Committees. However, the best and preferred technique was to gain agreement to a proposal in advance with each party separately. The initiative could be presented to each party in terms most favourable to themselves who then felt that their points of view were receiving special attention. Whatever method was selected to introduce a subject, the key was always to maintain the initiative. Just when the parties were becoming comfortable with a particular course of action, another initiative would be produced so that they were always reacting to events and were never given the opportunity to dominate the proceedings. Maintaining the initiative by staying inside the decision cycle of the factions was vital to the progress of the peace process.

Communication. It has already been explained that the whole structure of the Joint Commission was established to facilitate communication of decisions from the JCPC right down into the towns and villages. So that subordinate UN commanders could talk with authority at sub-committee meetings, the UN battalion commanders all attended the JCPC meetings as observers and similarly the UN company commanders all attended the sub-committee meetings chaired by their battalion commanders. There was also a need to communicate the results of Joint Commission meetings to the population. It was very important to prevent unfounded rumours spreading and to identify publicly those local political leaders who were deliberately obstructing progress. An information campaign was conducted over the heads of the local politicians. Posters were distributed in local towns and villages, regular press releases were issued and press conferences were often set up to take place immediately after potentially difficult JCPC meetings to encourage compliance during the meeting and, if that failed, to give politicians the opportunity to be asked by the media to explain to the local population why they were blocking a particular initiative.

Preparation. Perhaps the most important factor in achieving success in a JCPC meeting was preparation. The preparation for the next meeting started as soon as the previous meeting had been completed. The JCPC planning group, containing all the key Sector staff including the Spanish Chief of Staff, Colonel Manalo Borra, the Russian Sector Administrative Officer, Colonel Vitaly Petronov, the Canadian Chief Operations Officer, Lieutenant Colonel Walt Natynczyk and the Russian Chief Military Observer, Lieutenant Colonel Nikolai Rumyantsev, would meet to agree the strategy for the next meeting and how the various lines of operation were to be progressed. The Executive Committees were tasked, media plans were prepared, documents for signature at the next meeting were drafted, and pre-meetings with key political and military leaders in Sarajevo and elsewhere were planned. Then the whole JCPC meeting would be war-gamed. Every conceivable response to the various initiatives would be considered and reactions planned. Alternative drafts to the documents for signature would be prepared to cover as many eventualities as possible. Major Andrew Sharpe, Military Assistant to the Sector Commander, had the special responsibility for adjusting plans during the JCPC meetings and, if necessary, leaving the table to produce alternative drafts to documents in time for signature before the end of the session. Delegates were never allowed to leave the table until documents had actually been signed.

Loose ends. Despite these preparations it was impossible to forecast accurately how every aspect of a meeting would go and consequently how the peace process would develop. There were some issues that were never really satisfactorily addressed and which plagued the workings of the Joint Commission throughout the period.

War crimes. Joint Commission meetings were often disrupted by allegations and counter-allegations about alleged war crimes. The UN had no effective machinery to investigate war crimes or even to collect evidence for later investigation. This failure is still hampering some of the current trials at The Hague and certainly hampered the workings of the Joint Commission at the time.

Civil disobedience. While the Joint Commission had considerable influence over the factions military and political leaderships, it had no authority over the civilian population. Local police forces were generally inadequate and even minor incidents of civil disobedience, such as blocking roads to traffic, had the potential to bring the peace process to a halt. The

UN Civil Police force was neither resourced nor mandated to assist in such incidents.

Criminal activities. It was always difficult to define precisely what constituted a return to normality and it was important not to apply Western European standards to the judgement. There was a particular difficulty over some criminal activity. In some respects the bringing of peace to Central Bosnia made it safe to continue with normal pre-war activities such as banditry. In some areas the collection of unauthorised taxes and tariffs to allow the passage of freight was institutionalised and was an important part of the local economy. The UN in general and the Joint Commission in particular, faced a dilemma over the extent to which this sort of activity could and should be condoned. Despite the difficulties it was possible to take measures to reduce incidents of banditry. In the British battalion area joint police patrols were conducted with the local police alongside the Royal Military Police. This gave the local police the confidence to operate in high-risk areas and reduced the opportunities for police complicity in incidents. The results of this initiative were quite startling especially as this sort of crime was increasing elsewhere.

Figure 13.6 Reported banditry in Central Bosnia, May to October 1994

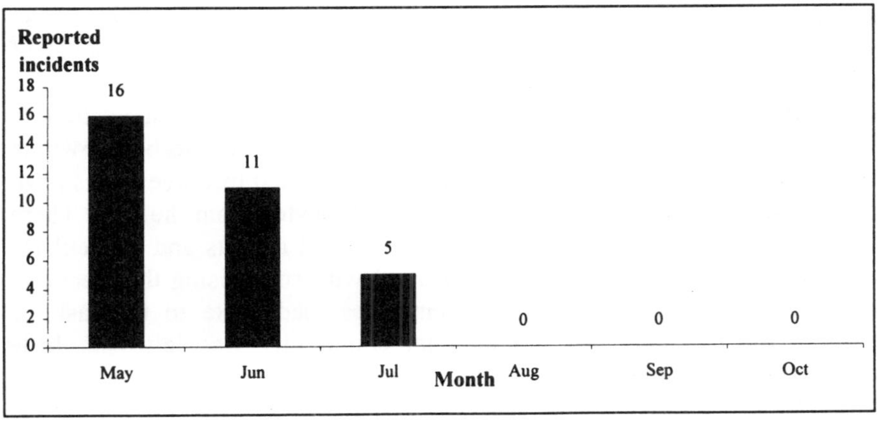

A model for IFOR

Throughout 1994, the fragile peace between the Bosnian Muslims and Bosnian Croats grew stronger and life in Central Bosnia returned to some sort of normality, but despite this the situation remained dominated by the continuing war with the third party to the conflict, the Bosnian Serbs.

Despite hopes for the creation of a Federal Army, or at least for some active co-operation on the ground between the ARBiH and HVO, there was little sign of real progress. The situation changed dramatically during the following summer with the rout of the Krajina Serb Army and the ethnic cleansing of the Krajina Serb population from Croatia. The subsequent NATO bombing and UNPROFOR Rapid Reaction Force shelling campaign and the land offensive by the ARBiH and HVO supported by the Croatian Army culminated in a cessation of hostilities and the signing of the Dayton Agreement. The situation on the ground at this stage was remarkably similar to that which had prevailed in Central Bosnia 18 months previously. The fighting had stopped but the armies in the field had not been defeated and confrontation lines were still manned in strength; a political agreement had been reached which had not really addressed many of the key issues which started the conflict in the first place, and there was deep cynicism and mistrust between the former warring factions.

There was a clear need to make progress on each of the three lines of operation previously identified in Central Bosnia in 1994: military, civilian and political. However, the very structure of the Dayton Agreement made the co-ordination of these activities difficult to achieve. Success in military aspects was clearly uppermost in the negotiators minds; at that stage no one could have known just how compliant the factions would be on the ground and there was a clear wish not to take any chances. The military annex was well drafted with clear objectives and tasks which reflected the level of underlying agreement. The same could not be said of the civilian aspects of the treaty. Carl Bildt, as the High Representative, derived his mandate both from the UN Security Council and from a reformed ICFY to be known as the Peace Implementation Council. Organizational and resource issues have dogged the implementation of civil aspects of Dayton from the start. There have been similar difficulties over some political aspects and particularly over the elections. The OSCE was charged with supervising the elections but once the parties had proved themselves inadequate to the task of running the elections, the international community was left with little option but to intervene and this compounded the OSCE's funding difficulties.

However, the real difficulties were experienced on the ground. The ARRC was keen to implement a Joint Commission on the lines of that adopted in Central Bosnia in 1994 but there was a pronounced US aversion to any NATO military involvement in the civil aspects of the Agreement. Consequently, separate Military and Civil Joint Commissions were set up to deal with their own aspects of implementation. The under-resourcing of the High Representative hindered his initial progress and he decided to focus his attention onto Sarajevo and subsequently the important cities of

Banja Luka, Mostar and Brcko. Progress in the military implementation was quick and efficient with all Dayton military objectives achieved broadly to plan. However, the lack of a truly Joint Commission meant that it was difficult to refocus effort onto the civilian and political aspects of implementation as they became progressively more significant. The reallocation of the UN Civil Affairs officers from the Sector Headquarters to the IPTF without replacement created a major gap in capability which has not been satisfactorily filled and which continues to hamper the establishment of municipality government. The desire to limit the involvement of NATO in civil issues is understood, particularly as the dangers of mission creep had been all too apparent during the UN operation. However, the satisfactory resolution of many of the civil and political issues was always going to be on the critical path for early military disengagement and a failure to address these issues early enough may have made their resolution more difficult to achieve.

With less than a year to go before the planned withdrawal of SFOR the situation is uncertain. On the surface there has been tremendous progress; the fighting has stopped, reconstruction is underway, over 250,000 refugees and displaced persons have returned to their homes, elections have been held and some common institutions have been created. However, a deeper analysis is less positive; ethnic divisions have remained and communities have become more polarised, very few refugees and displaced persons have returned home across the old confrontation lines into minority areas, the Inter-Entity Boundary Line risks looking progressively more like an international border, and freedom of movement is severely restricted. Municipal elections seem set to be dominated by nationalist parties and there has been slow progress in the establishment of many of the more difficult central institutions. There is a danger that partition will become the new reality on the ground and this would seem to be a pretty unsatisfactory result of nearly six years of UN and NATO engagement in the region. The failure to establish a truly Joint Commission to progress the peace process may yet prove to have been a costly omission.

14 Preventive Peacekeeping as a Model for the Prevention of War

American Lessons Learned in Macedonia

HOWARD F. KUENNING[*]

Introduction

I was a 'typical' American peacekeeper. That is, I joined the United Nations Preventive Deployment (UNPREDEP) in Macedonia straight from a US Army position, on temporary duty, lacking experience or training with either the UN or peacekeeping operations. That deplorable lack of preparation was typical, especially for individual assignments such as mine (rather than one with a unit). Increasingly, US infantry and other units assigned for UN duty are being well trained in peacekeeping tactics and other important skills (notably, force protection measures), but experienced peacekeepers know that expertise in tactics only begins the transformation of 'warriors' into skilled peacekeepers, whose effectiveness results from blending tactics with proper attitudes, beliefs, values, expectations and hard-won experience, all in short supply in US forces, with their intense war-fighting focus. However, Americans are learning valuable lessons from experiences such as mine, and not just about the impact of an American presence in PKO. These remarks are intended to offer a new perspective on both that presence and the important new initiative of preventive peacekeeping.

---

[*] Col. Howard F. Kuenning is Chief, Special Programs/Plans & Policy, AFSOUTH, Naples, Italy. He was COS of the UN Preventive Peacekeeping Operation in Macedonia from October 1993 to March 1994. Views and opinions expressed in this contribution are personal and do not represent official views.

The American presence

American peacekeeping has been a reality since 1992 in Macedonia, where over 500 US soldiers serve with Nordic comrades to fulfil the UN's first preventive peacekeeping mission. Placing American soldiers alongside Nordic peacekeepers was an inspiration. Nordic and American people have deep cultural and historical bonds. Most Americans lack foreign language skills, but most Nordic peoples speak English well. And, like Americans, Nordic soldiers are professional, competent, technically sophisticated and proud.

An important factor in the continuing US presence in Macedonia involves the trust placed by all levels of the American chain of command in the Nordic General Officers Commanding (GOC). This begins at the highest levels of the US government, and I saw its personal expression in the relationships between my GOC and two of the three Commanders-in-Chief directly involved in this mission: General Joulwan, SACEUR and CINC, US Forces in Europe; and Admiral Smith, CINC, Allied Forces South and CINC, US Naval Forces Europe. Senior US leader reliance on the qualities of the GOC directly affects how that mission operates daily, and has been key to keeping USBAT in Macedonia. US leaders must be confident that the UN commander is competent and will co-operate with them. Senior US leaders closely scrutinized this important mission, indicating the sensitivity and care with which it is being managed and watched by the American administration.

This intense command scrutiny played out ironically against the command's tactical situation, which during my tour was almost routinely 'calm and quiet'. The peaceful, relatively static environment allowed for an undistracted analysis of the US presence, especially valuable in contrast to the high-profile, high-tension Bosnian mission. In Macedonia, the UN's preventive mandate is modest and clearly stated, the commander's military mission is achievable, and he has adequate and appropriate resources. UNPREDEP's mission is not confrontational. The UN and the US are accepted by all parties. In fact, the primary threats to Macedonian stability from the first have been non-military, but political, social and economic. The mission is tailor-made for successful American involvement in a UN mission, in sharp contrast to the infamous, much-analysed Somalia mission, which is often cited as reason for the US to avoid peacekeeping operations.

In the long history of US military doctrinal development of what we now call 'Operations Other Than War' (OOTW), one hot topic addresses the proper balance between using powerful military force and protecting US soldiers in vague military missions that tend to 'creep', or change in unpredictable ways. All military leaders, but especially Americans, tend to express frustration with the vulnerability of US combat units which are placed under strict political control, with severe limitations on the use of military force. These mission restrictions usually are dictated by complex regional issues. Examples include the Philippines, the Dominican Republic, Korea, Vietnam, Lebanon, even Desert Storm. Recently, Somalia, Panama, Haiti, Guantanamo and Macedonia continue the discussion. In faraway Macedonia during a visit in 1994, General Joulwan addressed the tensions in US operational doctrine, telling UN leaders and USBAT soldiers to 'Forget OOTW! Operations are operations, and missions are missions. Everything you do must be done as a military mission, with all the discipline and skill you bring to a wartime mission'. He was attempting to clarify the infantry soldiers' role in a non-traditional mission.

Thus, Macedonia is a good test-bed for evaluating the US presence in PKOs. The questions raised are many, far beyond the scope of this short article. How well does a US combat unit perform? How do other peacekeepers and regional parties relate to US peacekeepers, and vice versa? What are the domestic American repercussions of direct UN involvement? Can American political and military leaders continue to place US soldiers in this inherently vulnerable position? Are American soldiers too vulnerable, too high-profile, to be effective peacekeepers, no matter their skills? Can Americans be peacekeepers and NATO peace enforcers in the same theatre? Should American combat units be reserved for UN peace enforcement missions? These questions beg significant other questions, but they illuminate the complexity and significance of this quiet but important UN peacekeeping mission for an American combat unit.

Although I had no specific instructions from any US commander or staff chief involved in supporting the US unit, the unofficial role of the Chief of Staff as the senior American officer 'on the ground' plays an important role in the continued success of USBAT. The Nordic GOC probably will have an American Colonel as Chief of Staff while USBAT stays. (The utility of this 'burden sharing' principle is clearer to me now that I serve in a NATO staff.)

The Chief is in a position to monitor and help manage the complex command relationships surrounding USBAT (known in US circles as 'TFAS' – Task Force Able Sentry). Several commands and departments monitor or direct USBAT: the UN GOC, the US Liaison Office in Skopje, Joint Task Force Provide Promise in Naples (which at that time commanded and controlled all US military involvement in the former Yugoslavia), US European Command (parent command of the JTF), and US Army, Europe, the Task Force parent command. The Chief of Staff helps the GOC and the US commanders in Naples and Germany understand each other's concerns, systems and policies. He can reduce misunderstanding and help co-ordination and co-operation among these commands. I accomplished this primarily through passing information via fax and telephone, almost always with the full knowledge of the General Officer Commanding or the senior US official involved. The only exceptions, and they were few, involved temporary delays when American classified information was involved.

I also focused on reducing the pressures placed on the USBAT commander. This lieutenant colonel, because of the uniqueness and sensitivity of his position and the resulting high visibility, at least in 1993 and 1994, was forced to juggle almost impossibly competing demands. He felt he was allowed no mistakes by his American commanders. His behavior was as if he had been ordered to eliminate all possibility of risk. He often had to choose among his loyalties – to his UN Commander (a one-star Dane, Norwegian, Finn, or Swede), to the Joint Task Force Commander (a four-star Navy Admiral), to his chain of command in Europe, and sometimes to the US State Department, represented by the Head of the US Mission, who was also the senior US official in Macedonia. These pressures seemed out of proportion to the seriousness of the threat or the level of the problems involved, but I believe they are an inevitable accompaniment of US involvement in peacekeeping. Yet the senior leaders with whom I worked, both UN and US, recognized that the stress was too much, and we all worked to lower it. However, the battalion commanders I observed continued to suffer from too many demands, too many visitors, too many operational limitations. I believe this is an important lesson learned about US involvement in peacekeeping.

National perspectives of the US presence

What follows is a personal understanding of the impact of the American presence, and of the perspective of the Balkan parties, the UN (basically a Nordic entity in Macedonia), and lastly of the United States itself.

Generally, all parties clearly recognize the significance of US presence in the Balkans. The mere presence of a US infantry battalion demonstrates the obvious interest of the United States. However we might want to treat USBAT as just another peacekeeping battalion, we cannot ignore the great weight it adds to the UN presence. We cannot ignore the significance of placing a US combat unit in a peacekeeping command, whether it turns out positive or negative, and whether it is their proper role. There were other US units in UNPROFOR, such as the hospital in Zagreb, but their presence does not have the military-political significance of USBAT/TFAS.

Why did the US place a battalion in Macedonia? It seems obvious that the United States wanted in 1992 to be part of the solution in the Balkans, not then as a member of NATO, which was slowly coming to terms with the Balkan war. US leaders may have felt they could not place US soldiers too close to the fighting in the former Yugoslavia, for many reasons – to avoid US entanglement in a regional war, and to avoid domestic sensitivities over US casualties. Macedonia was the relatively quiet, safe place to be part of the Balkan solution.

But, to give credit where it may be due, there is a deeper aspect to the Macedonian situation. Many peacekeepers and diplomats wiser than I argue that Macedonian stability is the key to Balkan stability and regional peace, in 'negative' terms. That is, failure of the Republic of Macedonia increases risks of a wider war than the Balkans suffered, including possible conflict between NATO allies. Thus, the US has placed its soldiers in the more critical part of the Balkans, where the international community must draw the line. If we did not understand that in 1992, we do now. The continued bilateral relationship between Macedonia and the United States proves that US leaders understand the importance of Macedonia. US bilateral involvement must be measured against other nations' interest in Macedonia, such as Turkey and Russia.

The Macedonian and Serbian perspectives of the US presence

The Balkan nations recognize the importance of the American involvement. Although UNPREDEP was emplaced between the potential adversaries of Serbia (FRY) and Macedonia, it is interesting that their security concerns are congruent: both desire stability in the southern Balkans, both want to be seen as co-operative with the UN and the US, and both play off of the UN and the US for regional positioning with their neighbours (including each other). Both are concerned with defining their common border, wish diplomatic recognition, share problems of ethnic tensions and both share the economic impact of embargoes and sanctions. These factors cause both countries to use the presence of a US unit to improve their position in the international arena.

Serbia's reaction to USBAT ironically both raised and lowered tensions in Macedonia. Especially early in the mission, they distrusted the motives behind the US deployment. Their understandable observation of new UN activity in the border area combined with US fears of confrontation and casualties to raise tensions. On the other hand, their clear desire not to provoke more condemnation from the US and international community encouraged them to act with extreme restraint and caution in the disputed border area. On the other hand, Macedonian officials eagerly welcomed the US unit, and any American team that arrived to discuss bilateral activities.

United Nations (Nordic) perspective

The insights on American peacekeeping that I gained from my Nordic colleagues was invaluable. However, it was always tempered by this *personal* perspective. There is much good surrounding the USBAT involvement. Young soldiers and officers are learning much from the UN. There are exchange programs. The Americans work among the Macedonian people, and they gain invaluable experience in peacekeeping operations. When my Nordic colleagues expressed their frustrations, I often would remind them that USBAT had many advantages – it is professional, disciplined, well led, well equipped and well supported, and trained to perform the mission.

However, there are problems worth addressing, some procedural and some operational. The central administrative problem involves the six-month rotation of the battalion task force. The turmoil that results is worsened by the lack of UN training and experience, especially in administration and logistics. USBAT is formed from active duty infantry battalions from USAREUR, which rotate under six-month US Temporary Duty (TDY) procedures, including the commanders and staff. TDY procedures are not simply administrative; they are based on US legal restrictions on the employment of soldiers with strict time limitations, involving pay and privileges, family support and soldier reassignments. Perhaps the US will develop peacekeeping units similar to the NORBAT model, but only if we become much more involved in peacekeeping operations.

Until then, I'm afraid we will continue to suffer the discontinuity inherent in this semi-annual rotation. There is some discussion about assigning the American officers at the UN HQ for one year; that would help. At least as important would be attendance by key leaders and staff officers at Nordic UN training courses.

A second common critique from experienced UN peacekeepers is that the battalion is relatively isolated, cut off. This perception results from the extensive force protection measures built around Camp Able Sentry, the personnel management measures that prevent US soldiers from free movement outside the camp, and from the rapid rotation of personnel, who always seem to be arriving, or leaving, or looking to Germany for much of their support.

However, the operational limitations on the use of USBAT are the most difficult challenges in this mission. From the US point of view, the battalion is under the limited operational control of the General Officer Commanding. The Commander of the Task Force was the Commander of Joint Task Force Provide Promise, at the time Admiral Smith. (Since then, command arrangements have changed.) Strict US command and control is mandated by the US Congress, and rigorously monitored by State and Defense Department civilian leadership. By US law, US command takes primacy over UN command. There is some truth to the argument that all nations retain significant command lines to their units in UN missions, often, this situation has little practical effect. However, these specific limitations on USBAT caused the two GOCs I worked for to question whether the unit was performing its mission or would be effective in a crisis:

-   Soldiers could not be placed on one particular observation point (Hilltop 1703), where the most tense Serbian-Macedonian confrontation occurred in the summer of 1994

-   Soldiers could not approach closer than 300m to the UN-defined border (NLAOO, or Northern Limit of the Area Of Operations) in their sector

-   Soldiers could not patrol at night

-   Soldiers could not deviate from their patrol route/plan.

NORBAT, on the other hand, had none of these restrictions, and seemed even to me from the UN HQ to be generally more involved and co-operative in most operational, administrative and logistical matters. The disparity created a definite tension in the command which no one was comfortable with – all military professionals want full cohesion and operational effectiveness.

United States perspective

In terms of military command and control, it became clear to me that all US commanders wanted the UN mission to succeed and were not comfortable with all restrictions on USBAT operations. They desired that USBAT be able to respond fully to the UN commander. They recognized the importance of the mission, and in fact argued that the battalion's presence represented a major investment of US forces in Europe. Since 1990, US Army forces in Europe have dropped from nearly 250,000 to about 65,000.

There are six infantry battalions left in the two divisions of USAREUR, and at any time, three are involved in Macedonia. One is on the ground, one is 'recovering', in administrative and training terms, and the other is preparing to go.

I had only occasional insights into the relationship between the Commanders-in-Chief and the US leaders in Washington, but their decisions indicated that the political risks of US casualties or even embarrassing incidents was so high as to warrant policies and risk-avoidance that they in other missions as military leaders would not have accepted. The driving force of most controversial decisions surrounding USBAT involved protecting American soldiers from being targeted in any way. The fact that the threat in Macedonia was almost nil did not prevent the US giving an overwhelming priority to force protection.

American memories are vivid, and sensitivities strong, about their soldiers being singled out as targets. Combine that sensitivity with resistance to any involvement with the UN by some US politicians, and with misperceptions about the UN's role in the disaster in Somalia, and the decisions in Macedonia make more sense.

Is preventive deployment a success?

UNPREDEP's history proves that deploying soldiers before conflict occurs can help stabilize an area of potential crisis, but it hints also that the concept may be troubled by doctrinal contradictions and a lack of international will for spending on prevention. How the UN commander and his military peacekeepers interpreted the military mandate and supported the broader diplomatic mandate reveals the dynamics of a preventive mission, especially how traditional peacekeeping principles must be adapted for a preventive context.

Using soldiers under UN mandate to prevent conflict seems to be a new use of military force, by applying timely early warning and military monitoring resources along with diplomatic talent within the parameters of traditional peacekeeping – consent, impartiality, and the non-use of force except in self-defence or defence of the mandate.

As early as September 1988 a Soviet Deputy Foreign Minister was calling for preventive military force, with UN observers stationed along 'frontiers within the territory of a country that seeks to protect itself from outside interference at the request of that country alone'. This proposal anticipated UNPREDEP's mission; the command deployed at Macedonia's invitation to monitor its troubled borders with Serbia and Albania.

Discussion about preventive deployments early on thus raised questions about *partial consent*, whether peacekeepers could be a deterrent force or a monitoring and reporting force only, and question of sovereignty, all of which have affected the Macedonia deployment in some way. These issues begin to distinguish preventive deployment from traditional peacekeeping.

The UN and the US struggle with similar problems: how to select among competing crises, less willingness to deploy fewer forces, and budget shortfalls. In this environment, preventive concepts hold a weak hand. Major powers tend to deploy soldiers only where they have important or vital interests, yet UNPREDEP shows that pre-crisis diplomacy and preventive deployment are cost-effective.

Has UNPREDEP prevented war in the southern Balkans? There is a problem with identifying preventive success – 'A deterrent (preventive) threat is difficult to evaluate, because when it succeeds, nothing happens.' Analysis of UN work in Macedonia, however, proves that statement false; much has happened. But before discussing UNPREDEP's successes, it must be said that other factors also contribute to the absence of conflict in Macedonia, including:

- US and other diplomacy and policy in the southern Balkans, including international sanctions against Serbia

- The work of many international agencies, such as OSCE, ICFY, UNHCR, ICRC

- Relatively moderate behaviour by Macedonia's neighbours – they may not be helping, but also not threatening military action. And

- Macedonian efforts to maintain and encourage a viable multi-ethnic society.

All of these are important. But the UN command enhances stability also, in important ways. First, it focuses international and regional attention on the issue of Macedonia's stability. Second, it reduces the risk of conflict due to border tensions and the lack of diplomatic relations between Serbia and Macedonia. Third, it moderates internal political friction. I will mention with respect to the last only that the military peacekeepers greatly magnify the SRSG's (Special Representative of the Secretary General) ability to monitor and moderate internal Macedonian affairs, such as the controversial census and elections in 1994, and dangerous attempts by ethnic Albanians to establish a so-called Albanian-language university in Tetovo.

The effect of 'being present'

Woody Allen, the American filmmaker and comedian, said 'Half of life is showing up'. So true. Of course, the other half is to do something once there, but simple presence is one powerful aspect of prevention, well worth emphasizing to politicians and other leaders willing to send troops and money only to help bloodied survivors of a conflict that might have been prevented.

First, UNPREDEP's presence serves notice to regional parties that the continued peaceful existence of the Republic of Macedonia enjoys international support. Particularly in the Balkans, where grotesque misinformation is a routine diplomatic and political tool, the presence of a respected international agency as a source of accurate information moderates destabilizing words and activities.

The world notices Macedonia in ways it would not without UNPREDEP. The media pay little attention to 'calm and quiet' situations, yet the UN headquarters focuses some attention on the potential crisis in Macedonia. Ambassadors and embassy officials, most notably Turkish and American officials, meet frequently with the UN commander and SRSG. The UN headquarters hosts co-ordination meetings for international organizations. The Command regularly briefs diverse international visitors. The importance of providing an objective political-military analysis of the situation cannot be overstated.

UNPREDEP also regularly monitors the military, economic and social situation, and then confirms, counters or balances the reporting of other agencies. For example, in 1994 US State Department officials identified as a significant risk the potential for a mass exodus of ethnic Albanian refugees from the Kosovo Province in Serbia through Macedonia to the Greek border, leading to conflict between Greece and Turkey. But UNPREDEP concluded that the risk is low, and reported its assessment regularly to UNPROFOR and to the US and Nordic governments through their unit national chains of command, and to visitors.

A second example – the proximity of the war in Bosnia and the international reputation of the Serbs caused many observers to assume that military tensions in the southern Balkans were high. In March 1995, two experienced journalists, from the *Boston Globe* and *The New York Times*, asked me how many Serb units were 'Massed against the border'. Other visitors to UNPREDEP shared their surprise at learning the truth – none. The link between Bosnian conflict and the southern Balkans was at this time entirely theoretical.

UNPREDEP also helps stabilize the region through border identification and verification. Macedonia's borders with Albania, Bulgaria and Greece are undisputed, but the boundary with Serbia long had been a disputed boundary between the two republics of the former Yugoslavia.

The Nordic battalion monitored the ethnically sensitive situation along the Albanian border, where Orthodox Macedonian police dealt with Muslim Albanians who frequently crossed the border for various personal and illicit reasons. These examples illustrate that preventive military presence, and actions of oversight and advice in the early stages of small crises and tensions, can prevent a cumulative effect that could add up to more dangerous instabilities.

Early on, the UN Commander faced a challenge; how to perform his mandate to 'establish a presence below the disputed border' without a clear boundary? Initially, the Macedonians and Serbs refused to co-operate with his requests for border data. Promising secrecy, the commander and his staff obtained and used the differing border traces to propose an administrative UN boundary at first called the 'Northern Limit of the Area of Operations' (NLAOO) but now called the 'UN Line'.

In July 1994, both parties accepted this boundary as the northern limit of UN patrolling. That Macedonian and Serbian patrols also tend to respect this boundary indicates that the UN solution to a practical mission problem established a *de facto* buffer between potentially hostile parties.

From August into October 1994, the UN mission also reduced tension resulting from smuggling, an activity often observed and well understood by UN outposts. Macedonian border police were using deadly force both to enforce the law and to profit by robbing the smugglers. Several incidents heightened border tension. The shooting death by Macedonian border police of a fleeing smuggler who turned out to be a Serbian army officer was followed by the cold-blooded shooting of an ethnic Albanian Macedonian smuggler by Serbian soldiers. The UN commander used his influence with the Serbian and Macedonian general staffs to urge restraint. Since Macedonian officials informed him that the presidents of the two countries had informally agreed to lessen tensions in the border area, the UN has monitored only minor incidents related to smuggling.

Active conflict de-escalation

The military mandate clearly ordered a presence within Macedonia to protect Macedonia. However, early in the command's history, General Trygve Tellefsen, GOC in 1993–94, established contact with the Serbian General's staff in Belgrade. His broad interpretation of the preventive mandate allowed him to clarify among all parties the UN's mission, thus exercising the traditional peacekeeping principle of 'transparency'. He felt it urgent to explain to the Serbs the planned deployment of the US contingent from a reserve posture to relieve a departing Swedish contingent along the border.

The Macedonian government complained that 'their' UN commander should not contact the potential enemy. Their concern highlights a potential problem, host-nation 'ownership' of a preventive force. None the less, the commander in March 1994 began meeting with Lieutenant General Kovasevic in Belgrade.

Initial visits uncovered Serbian suspicions that the UN force, especially with its US battalion, foreshadowed a major deployment of US and NATO forces. The Commander's personal diplomacy, bolstered considerably by generous sharing of information, turned Serb suspicion into trust and established a UN bridge of communication between the two governments. For example, in October 1994, I observed General Tellefsen carry to Belgrade the good wishes of the Macedonian Minister of Defence and the Chief of Staff of the Macedonian Armed Forces. He reported on UN monitoring in the border region, explained plans for the December rotation of a new US infantry battalion, and delivered a map of the UN deployment, with all unit headquarters and observation posts plotted. In return, Lt. Gen. Kovasevic reported on plans to shift border units and the state of their preparations for border commission work, and sent his good wishes to his Macedonian counterparts.

These visits bore fruit almost immediately. In June and July of 1994 a dangerous military confrontation in the US sector, between Serbia and Macedonia, was defused when the commander intervened, brought both General Staffs to the area, and mediated a Serbian withdrawal from an incursion into Macedonia. Had the UN not been there, the confrontation could have escalated.

Military leaders in both governments found in UNPREDEP a reliable, neutral, non-confrontational form of communication. The UN contact confirmed non-hostile intent, finessed the lack of diplomatic recognition between governments, and lessened the chances for destabilizing confrontation. In March 1995, the Force Commander, General Engström, began visits with Albanian officials and regularly travelled to both Belgrade and Tirana.

Conclusions

Do these successes of UNPREDEP illustrate the potential value of preventive deployment to moderate the same tensions that in Croatia and Bosnia erupted in civil and ethnic war? Here are some insights.

Peacekeeping principles

The UN command in Macedonia uses traditional peacekeeping principles and structure, but the similarity between traditional peacekeeping and preventive deployment breaks down with the question of consent. The UN commander essentially developed his own consent with the Serbs and acted in an even-handed way to overcome perceptions of partiality.

But, if one function of preventive deployment is to deter aggression, we must recognize that *deterrence* differs substantially from traditional peacekeeping roles of helping co-operative parties maintain a cease-fire or implement a peace agreement. Parties who are being deterred and who presumably do not consent to the deployment will view it with suspicion. Without consent, tensions may rise rather than fall after the deployment. In fact in Macedonia, they did.

Both Albania and Serbia perceived partiality in the UN's deterrent posture. Albania complained that the peacekeeping force was not necessary along a stable, historically peaceful border. I understand that their sensitivity influenced the deployment of the force, so that a significant portion of the Albanian border is monitored not by peacekeeping soldiers, but by unarmed UN military observers, a less provocative presence.

The Serbs, for their part, responded to the deployment with increased patrols, observation posts and even a MIG fighter flyover into Macedonian airspace to take a close look at a US Black Hawk helicopter flying in support of US peacekeepers. This action alarmed the US, already under intense pressure to avoid international incidents and domestic criticism of its foreign policy.

The success of the UN force in negotiating an end to the confrontation crisis in the US sector and the simultaneous acceptance by the parties of the UN boundary was the happy ending to a major problem that may be typical of preventive deployments. Through aggressive interpretation of the mandate, the UN created its own consent with the Serbs. Another commander, with a more cautious approach, might not have been successful. Had General Tellefsen not resisted Macedonian complaints, and had he not followed the instinct to create consent, UNPREDEP's success might be much less clear. Some argue that 'peacekeeping forces are not designed to create on the ground the conditions for their own success. Those conditions must pre-exist for them to be able to perform their task.' Although disproved in Macedonia, the statement may be true elsewhere; whether consent can be created in more volatile crises remains to be seen.

Peacekeeping force structure

A second issue with respect to preventive deployments is that a traditional peacekeeping force structure may not meet preventive requirements. Here we discover the debate over whether peacekeepers also can be peace enforcers. There are at least two theoretical designs for a preventive force.

First, a fact-finding/monitoring force would have small teams with sophisticated surveillance technologies. This force would have no explicit deterrent function, but would be designed to assist preventive diplomacy and improve 'military transparency' between potential enemies. The teams would be capable of quick escape from a hostile situation.

A second option is a brigade-sized 'deterrent deployment' with combat capability, that 'represents the will of the international community to oppose aggression, and could call upon substantial military backup in a pinch. Such deployments – the tripwire force together with its backup – might affect an aggressor's calculations'.

UNPREDEP tries to do both, in a way. Its mandate orders fact-finding ('monitor and report') but also implies deterrence ('essentially preventive'), but the command's capability compromises on both. It is basically brigade-sized but has little combat capability to deter, and no plans to fight. Mobility is restricted to small-unit patrolling. No combat forces are earmarked for reinforcement, although endangered peacekeepers presumably could count on rescue from NATO. Withdrawal plans assume a permissive environment. Nor does UNPREDEP meet the standards for high-tech, stand-off surveillance. Soldiers monitor with binoculars and foot and helicopter patrols. UNPREDEP's blended approach performs a new mission with an old force structure. It places a peacekeeping force in what could require enforcement capability.

But the fact that UNPREDEP is not a perfect example of theoretical prevention, that it finds itself in the middle of debates about peacekeeping versus peace enforcement, should not detract from its very encouraging success. War in the southern Balkans would be a catastrophe we can ill afford.

Winston Churchill said that, 'The UN was not created to create heaven on earth – just to save it from hell.' That comment leads me to a quotation from the Bible, which I find appropriate to UNPREDEP's work. In the Book of Acts:

> And a vision appeared to Paul in the night; a certain man of Macedonia was standing and appealing to him, and saying, 'Come over to Macedonia and help us.' And when he had seen the vision, immediately we sought to go into Macedonia. (Acts 16–9)

I am not implying that the Secretary-General stands up to the status of the great Apostle, but there was a call for help, and we did go into Macedonia!

15 UN Media Policy

Lessons to be Learned to Counter War Propaganda

JAN-DIRK VON MERVELDT *

Introduction

From the outset I must state that the views and opinions expressed in this contribution are personal and have no official standing or sanction and do not represent the views of my government or the UN. Neither do I wish to imply criticism of any organization or individual. I have been out of Bosnia since April 1995 and things I raise here may have later been overtaken by events or have been rectified.

I came to Bosnia in September 1994 as the Bosnia-Herzegovina Command Liaison Officer (BHC LO). This wide-ranging portfolio gave me the opportunity to involved myself in everything, meet a lot of people and travel very extensively throughout Bosnia-Herzegovina.

In late Autumn 1994 I suddenly found myself standing in as the Senior Military Press Spokesman for Bosnia-Herzegovina Command (BHC) in Sarajevo. Having been the BHC LO and travelled extensively throughout the mission area I was able to bring a mission-wide perspective to the job of the military spokesman, something I was very grateful for as I had got to know the area and made very useful UN civil, military and media contacts, an opportunity my predecessors were not able to enjoy. It also helped me to understand and hopefully project the difficulties UN troops were experiencing on the ground. Sadly I never really mastered the correct expression of all the geographical and personality names.

Apart from a 48-hour hand-over from my predecessor I had no form of central UN media induction, orientation or guidance for this appointment. My tour of duty as the military spokesperson started just as the Bosnian Serbs counter-attacked onto the so-called 'Bihac Safe Area' after a previous Bosnian government forces breakout from the Bihac Pocket into Bosnian Serb territory.

* Lt. Col. Jan-Dirk von Merveldt (UK) is Chief Public Relations Officer of the British Forces in Germany. From September 1994 to March 1995 he was the BHC LO at UNPROFOR and for part of this period the UN Military Press Spokesman in Sarajevo.

The Bihac crisis – Autumn 1994

The Bihac crisis turned out to be one of the UN's early and most intense media crises, which ran at high intensity for about six weeks, in fact until Mr Jimmy Carter arrived quite unexpectedly and created the condition for a (temporary) cease-fire. In Sarajevo the long-established UN practice was to hold a daily press conference with a civil affairs, a military, a UNHCR and a Red Cross spokesperson. The only consistent factor here was that the military spokesperson was always there, the others only some of the time.

During the Bihac crisis we on various occasions lacked our Civil Affairs spokesperson. During this time we were confronted on the daily, often hour-long press conferences, by about 30 television cameras, 40+ microphones and tape recorders and about 55 international correspondents quite apart from the numerous local journalists and observers.

All the journalists, most of them international household names on television, radio or on paper, told us that our job, at that particular time, was far more difficult than the job of the military spokesmen during the Gulf War and that they would not want to do it themselves. They also told us that they could not think of any other organization that had to give such high-profile press conferences on a daily basis with such weighty world-wide and international, political, military and humanitarian implications that got little or no help from above.

During the latter part of the Bihac crisis the whole UN mission in Bosnia was in imminent danger of breaking up and a recommendation to withdraw from Bosnia, as stated by General Rose publicly at a press conference, at The Residency, at the height of the crisis, was only a matter of days away, as the cost of continuing involvement in the conflict was in danger of outweighing any possible gains or benefits.

Credibility and media

The primary role of UNPROFOR was to create the conditions in which the parties to the conflict could negotiate their own peace. The mission was not well understood by the outside world and even when it was understood it was often abused for political purposes. Added to this the mission was immensely complex and involved international relations, humanitarian aid, human rights and military affairs at the very highest international level. The cost of the whole of this UN operation in 1994/1995 was estimated at about 2 billion US dollars annually.

In the late Autumn of 1995 the whole concept of UN peacekeeping and NATO and international credibility was threatened. Whatever we and others were saying at the daily press conference in Sarajevo was crucial to the international perception of what was happening in Bosnia, but more importantly our reported words appeared to influence the continuing unity and credibility of the UN and NATO and appeared to influenced the decision process not only in New York at the UN, but also in Brussels with NATO and in many other capitals of the world. We were a bit part actor in the 'CNN effect'. We found ourselves answering questions, often live on TV or radio to a world-wide audience on an hourly and often minute by minute basis, questions, which should have been answered in New York, Washington, Brussels, London and Paris and not in Sarajevo by us.

The UN information back-up system at that time for its media staff in Sarajevo was, in my opinion, wholly unprepared for the intricate media war in Bosnia. The words guidance, press line, line to take, preparation, preplanning, key issues guide, questions & answers (Q & A) analysis or anticipation, were not something that at that time the UN information system appeared to be familiar with and were not there for the UN Press Officers and national contingents commanders and press officers in the field to draw on. As a result we all felt that we were often left out in the cold on major political, military and policy issues and decisions with no back-up, guidance or line to take when having to answer questions which were impossible to avoid. In Sarajevo we were not able to effectively or comprehensively monitor the major international media output on a real-time basis.

This meant that we were often confronted by a third party, with something that had been said on CNN, Reuters, AP, CBS, NBC, RTL, SKY or the BBC World Service or written in a major international paper and which was difficult to react to in detail and in a timely manner because one had not actually seen, heard or read it at first hand. This was especially so with utterances on Bosnia from UN HQ in New York or Zagreb, NATO in Brussels or Naples and the major capitals of the world. We were not even in receipt of a comprehensive UN international press cutting service and had to rely on our own national in-house material from United Kingdom sources.

UN media resources

Our UN media technology and resources in Sarajevo were inadequate, outdated and underfunded and was no match for what the media in Sarajevo had access to, or at their disposal. In my first two weeks in Sarajevo I shared the same phone with the Commander's MA and ADC, which incidentally was the only one with an international dialling facility.

Our only wire service was a Reuters receiver, loaned from Reuters, with an inadequate screen (on loan from a British Signals Unit) and a poor-quality printer.

We were not in receipt of the daily international press cuttings from UN HQ in Zagreb. If we did get cuttings from the UN they were always from the US papers. There appeared to be no comprehensive UN monitoring of UK, French and importantly other contributing nations media. I felt that local media monitoring was inadequate with no proper assessment or analysis facility. In theatre there was no co-ordinated UN effort to counter the very effective and professional propaganda being churned out by the warring factions. Although countering propaganda is not necessarily a prime task of a UN media agency, it affects the media and is certainly interrelated and of high priority. We also lacked an overall mission-wide and co-ordinated campaign to inform the population. Only belatedly was there a move to inform the local community what the UN was doing to restore peace to the region; regrettably this was not co-ordinated at a theatre level and relied more on the local initiative of the military sector information officers and unit information officers.

To be fair some Sectors, notably Sector SW, did their own thing with local radio, television and the papers. Sadly, none of the local media was impartial so they often restricted what they took from the UN in the sectors. To my mind, a fundamental requirement of peacekeeping is co-ordinated unbiased information for the local population. This sadly was totally lacking as the UN did not have its own uncensored output facilities for radio, television or print and thus failed to use effectively major and vital tools of peacekeeping.

One of the most infuriating aspects of my job were the many other 'spokespersons' from various UN and other agencies who would pop up and give their assessment without ever letting us know what they were going to say, or giving us the opportunity to contribute the correct military and political input. The head of civil affairs in Bihac was continually on the line to CNN and SKY giving emotional and in my opinion one-sided reports, which were not necessarily substantiated by the UN military on the ground, but of course were very difficult to refute publicly, especially if one did not want to give the impression of a split within the overall organization by categorically denying another UN agency statement. This proliferation of autonomous UN and other organizations, with their spokespersons, was an aspect that the mission could well have done without.

National media

One aspect which was much underestimated by the UN, in my opinion, was the media input of the national contingents. National contingent commanders and their unit press officers were continually being interviewed and quoted by their own national media. Some countries had permanent media teams deployed with their contingents who were producing material on a daily basis which in turn was influencing perceptions in the contributing nations' capitals. Quite naturally national contingent commanders were asked and were expected to answer questions on all manner of subjects not necessarily appertaining to their units but to events in the mission area which they would be expected to know about.

Due to the total lack of UN media guidance to these outlets their answers were often, through no fault of their own, in conflict with the official UN line (which they were often not aware of) and which as a result could be interpreted as less than impartial. Lack of overall central UN guidance also reinforced unfounded media suspicion that certain national contingents, UN and NGO agencies were running their own agenda because what they were saying was not necessarily what was being said in Sarajevo, Zagreb or New York. In short the UN needs to be aware of the ever-present contributing nations' national interests in the activities of their contingents and ensure that they are furnished with the UN line in order that it is projected correctly to their respective audiences.

The tyranny of real-time information

There was in my opinion a fundamental failing within the mission area and at UN HQ in understanding the dynamics of the real-time impact of the news media. For us it was impossible to keep abreast of what was being reported from the theatre, what was being put out by the warring factions and what was being said and discussed in open forum by interested and influential parties world-wide, effectively all this passed us by. In order to react, correct and influence this, the UN, in my opinion, needs to alter its whole approach and attitude to the media and the rapid handling, timely and co-ordinated release and management of accurate information.

In a UN environment there is no restricting the media as there has been in other campaigns such as the Gulf War. The UN therefore has to be equipped and trained both mentally and technically to keep up with the media and indeed stay ahead. This in turn of course requires money, resources, manpower, monitoring facilities, a media strategy/policy and above all direction, co-ordination and planning.

Although the UN has television, radio, print and analyses resources with very talented people, it appeared to be unable to get its act together and to get them to work towards a common aim in UNPROFOR. The days of 'No comment' to the media are over, especially in this era of modern technology and when much is done live from attaché-size, hand-held, digital, satellite communications equipment.

Many of the journalists I met in Sarajevo had been there continually since the start of the war, some indeed had been responsible for getting the UN there. Many had seen far more action than many of the UN soldiers. Others rotated on a two, three, six, or eight-weekly basis and others only came when there was a big event, or their editors thought they could find blood on the streets.

However, the majority of the journalists were very professional and a large number of them have been very brave. By the time I left I was told that over 75 journalists have been killed in this war alone. If given the facts, the resident 'reptiles', as my distinguished successor called them, reported them correctly. It was better to give information than withhold it, because if it did not come from us it would be obtained from another source. I was absolutely amazed at the sources and access to information and communication resources which the journalists in Sarajevo had. Not only did many of them have the latest satellite and camera technology, mobile editing suites and direct access to the wire services and their own head offices, in Sarajevo they also openly monitored the UN radio nets and had their own stringers with radio communications, in various parts of the town and at known hot spots.

One news agency employed no less than 15 radio-equipped stringers in Sarajevo, who on a daily basis would rove or monitor all hot spots. As a result, and because of the very effective pool system established by Martin Bell of the BBC, the media often had information long before we had it. Basically our problem was that our information had to be accurate and stand up to prolonged scrutiny, whereas what the journalist writes is often forgotten after it is printed or broadcast. We were therefore frequently at a disadvantage, as one was battling with speed of release of information, versus confirmed accuracy of information, which is difficult enough if you are working in a purely national one language environment. But if there are some 19 other nationalities involved, as there were with the UN in Bosnia, it all gets a bit difficult. The different international time zones and the military habit of reporting 24 hours retrospectively for the just past period from midnight to midnight did not help us in the real-time news environment with instantaneous communications.

In spite of working for the UN many of the contributing nations' military units were reluctant, or refused to give information to us, the UN

Press office, about events which were ongoing or had already happened, and to a greater or lesser extent were already in the public domain through other means. This sort of attitude did not help the credibility of the UN in Bosnia in what was supposed to have been a transparent organization.

In early February 1995, I visited both Bihac town and Vilika Kladusa at the northern end of the pocket where Mr Abdic was then the local warlord. Here I found that much over-reporting and dramatisation of events in the Bihac area had gone on. Whilst I was there reports of massive starvation were circulating in the world media but proof of which was certainly nowhere to be found on the ground. Damage to buildings and infrastructure was much over-exaggerated and in general confined to areas near military installations and to the edge of Bihac town.

Extensive exaggeration was the norm as it was put about by the local propaganda machine and is unwittingly supported by, in my opinion, well meaning but often naïve aid workers. Unfortunately the UN was unable to get its act together sufficiently, to counter outrageous and inflammatory statements. By this I do not mean control of the media but certainly a system that enables it to correct information instantaneously and counter very obvious propaganda or one sided reporting. Only making UN transport available sparingly to the media was a self-inflicted wound as many of the positive UN activities went unreported as a result.

Although I may have dwelt a little too much on the less perfect elements of the UN media aspects in the former Yugoslavia the story of the UN's presence is not all negative. There were many very positive things that occurred because of the UN presence in the former Yugoslavia. Much of it did not attract any attention. Sadly the negative events always grabbed the headlines because no one in the UN was tasked at the beginning or later specifically with publicising the positive contributions of the UN and the many other agencies and brave individuals which were involved in this mission.

Summary of lessons learned

The following lessons might be useful for future UN operations or other multi-national missions:

1. *Key issues guide*. Comprehensive guidance from top to bottom on key issues affecting the mission. Updated on a regular basis. Continual updates on current issues with lines to take. Widely distributed in the mission area and in the languages of the main mission area and of the contributing nations.

2. *Media orientation.* Media orientation for all newly arrived senior UN staff and media personal, aid agencies and senior commanders of national contingents and their spokespersons.

3. *Informing the local population.* Information to the local population on the aims and achievements of the mission needs to be co-ordinated and continual and through a medium which can be receive locally and uncensored.

4. *Countering propaganda.* Propaganda from all sides and specifically against the mission needs to be countered professionally and timely. The local endemic attitude to propaganda and the media needs to be planned for, especially if the mission is in a former communist country. The influence of propaganda on the mission needs to be neutralised.

5. *The spokespersons.* These need to be of high calibre, in the 'pocket' of their commanders, fully briefed and in touch with all elements of the mission and policy appertaining to the mission, and have immediate access to commander and other UN spokespersons.

6. *Co-ordinating all spokespersons' output.* All agencies, national contingents and aid agencies spokesperson's output needs, to be co-ordinated, directed, controlled, monitored and at times corrected.

7. *Monitoring of the media and reacting to it.* Local and international media output needs to be effectively monitored and professionally reacted to by the mission. Everyone needs to be aware of the influence of the media (and propaganda) not only in the mission area but also on the contributing nations.

8. *Other nations' media* needs to be given equal prominence. Less emphasis needs to be put on American media comment and more notice needs to be taken of other contributing nations' media. News agencies need to be given a high priority.

9. *UN media equipment and personnel.* UN media equipment and technology needs to be ahead in the technological loop. UN media cells need to be properly staffed.

10. *All mission aspects* need to be brought to the media's attention. A professional attitude needs to be taken towards the media and all aspects and areas of the mission need to be brought to their attention. Media tours and facilities need to be organized.

11. *Transport for the media.* The media needs to be helped to have access to parts of the mission area where they would not normally be able to get to.

12. *The same media handling rules for all mission participants.* All mission participants need to adopt same media handling rules. This will often mean that national military rules for media handling need to be reviewed in order that they do not contradict or go against the mission's media policy.

13. *Unrestricted UN access to local media output.* SOFAs need to include unconstrained and uncensored access to local media and information outlets. The mission area should have its own frequencies and transmission capabilities for radio and television which needs to be budgeted for.

14. *A mission 'Information Campaign'.* Each mission needs an 'Information Campaign' which starts at the earliest possible time and before the mission commences. This information campaign should constantly send a coherent and co-ordinated message to the chosen audience, be it in the mission area, internationally or to opinion formers.

16 International Humanitarian Law, Protected Zones and the Use of Force

JEAN-PHILIPPE LAVOYER[*]

Introduction

Appalled by the horrors of recent conflicts, the international community is wondering what can be done to curb violence and secure respect for international law. Many proposals to that effect have been made in the last few years and several practical measures have been taken. A new vocabulary has come into being as a result of attempts to safeguard civilian populations by bringing them under a regime of special protection. Phrases such as 'security zones', 'safe havens', 'Safe Areas', 'safety zones', 'neutralized zones' and 'protected areas' have been coined. In this debate on an extremely complex issue it may be noted that these expressions have often been used in very different ways and that the same term is sometimes used to convey very different notions.

The purpose of this short study is to dissipate the present confusion, clarify the concepts involved, outline their main features and offer some pointers for the future. It will start by briefly describing the protected zones provided for in international humanitarian law and go on to consider the conflict in the former Yugoslavia. It will examine the protected zones established there, both under humanitarian law and by the Security Council. The latter, as will be seen, followed a logic of quite a different kind.[1]

Protected zones under international humanitarian law

As the reader will be aware, international humanitarian law, also known as the law of armed conflict or the law of war, comprises treaty or customary

---

[*]   Jean-Philippe Lavoyer is a legal adviser at the International Committee of the Red Cross (ICRC). He has been working for the ICRC since 1984 and has spent several years in the field. The opinions expressed here are those of the author and do not necessarily reflect those of the ICRC.

rules limiting the use of force in time of armed conflict, by protecting all persons taking no part or no longer taking part in the hostilities and imposing restrictions on means and methods of warfare. In short, the use of force is limited to what is necessary to defeat the enemy. Humanitarian law is a very practical kind of law which takes into account the demands of humanity as well as military necessity. That is precisely what explains its universal acceptance.[2]

International humanitarian law, which has constantly adapted to the changing face of war, is composed mainly of the four Geneva Conventions of 12 August 1949 and their two Additional Protocols of 8 June 1977. The Geneva Conventions have long since achieved universal adherence,[3] and three-quarters of all States are already bound by the Additional Protocols[4]

Today's world is beset by a rash of civil wars, and it should be pointed out that Article 3 common to the four Geneva Conventions of 1949 and the provisions of Additional Protocol II of 1977 apply precisely to internal armed conflict.[5] It should also be noted that international humanitarian law and human rights law apply at one and the same time. Humanitarian law, however, addresses very specifically the dangers and the humanitarian needs arising from war.[6]

The primary purpose of humanitarian law is to protect the civilian population against the effects of war. In particular, it prohibits attacks on civilians and indiscriminate attacks, protects objects indispensable to the survival of civilians, and prohibits forced population movements. In order to improve this protection still further, it provides for the establishment of *zones under special protection*. These are dealt with below.

The Geneva Conventions of 1949

Article 23 of the First Geneva Convention[7] provides for the establishment of 'hospital zones and localities' so organized as to protect from the effects of war wounded and sick members of the armed forces. This provision mentions that the parties to the conflict may conclude agreements with each other; for this purpose they may implement the provisions of Annex I to the Convention. The parties to the Convention must regulate access to the zones, which may not be used in the war effort and are to be marked by means of the red cross or red crescent emblem. Protecting Powers and the International Committee of the Red Cross (ICRC) are invited to lend their good offices in order to facilitate the institution and recognition of such zones.

The Fourth Geneva Convention[8] contains two provisions relating to protected zones. Article 14 relates to 'hospital and safety zones and localities' so organized as to protect from the effects of war the following members of the civilian population: wounded, sick and aged persons, children under 15, expectant mothers and mothers of children under seven. As is the case for the zones provided for in the First Geneva Convention, the parties to the conflict may conclude agreements on the basis of Annex I to the Fourth Convention, and here too Protecting Powers and the ICRC are invited to lend their good offices. Persons in these zones may not perform any work directly connected with military operations, and the Power establishing such a zone must take all necessary measures to prohibit access to all persons who have no right of residence or entry therein. Hospital and safety zones are to be marked by means of oblique red bands on a white ground, and if reserved exclusively for the wounded and sick may be marked by means of the red cross or red crescent emblem.

Article 15 of the Fourth Geneva Convention offers the possibility of establishing 'neutralized zones' to shelter from the effects of war wounded and sick combatants and non-combatants, civilians who take no part in the hostilities and who, while they reside in the zones, perform no work of a military character, and the personnel responsible for organizing and administering the zones.

This provision expressly requires that neutralized zones shall be the subject of *written agreement* between the parties to the conflict. Such agreements specify the geographical position, administration, food supply and supervision of the zone, and fix the beginning and duration of its neutral status. The zones may be established either by direct negotiation between the parties or through a neutral State or some humanitarian organization. Article 15 does not provide for the zones to be marked in any particular way; this means that the parties to the conflict may agree among themselves on the way in which neutralized zones are to be made visible.

The Additional Protocols of 1977

Additional Protocol I introduces two types of zone under the heading 'localities and zones under special protection'.

Article 59 relates to 'non-defended localities'. A party to the conflict may declare any inhabited place to be a 'non-defended locality' on condition that it is not used for military purposes. This implies that all combatants and military equipment must be evacuated, no acts of hostility may be committed by the authorities or population, and no activities in support of military operations may be undertaken. Another important point is that these 'non-defended localities' are to be open for occupation by the adverse party. A party to a conflict which receives a declaration of a non-defended locality must acknowledge its receipt and respect the zone unless it has not been demilitarized. Parties to the conflict may conclude agreements, notably relating to the signs to be used to indicate the exact area of the locality so protected.

The 'demilitarized zones' provided for in Article 60 of the Protocol offer more extensive protection, on condition that an express agreement is concluded by direct negotiation between the parties or through a Protecting Power or impartial humanitarian organization.[10] Like non-defended localities, demilitarized zones may in no circumstances be used for military purposes. Above all, therefore, it is imperative that combatants, weapons and military equipment be evacuated. The parties agree among themselves as to the way in which the zones will be marked.[11]

Protected zones in practice

It has to be admitted that the zones under special protection provided for in the Geneva Conventions and their Additional Protocols have not really yielded the results expected. Indeed, the number of zones actually established under these legal provisions or at least inspired by them is still very small. How can this be explained?

To begin with, not all the zones described above are equally important in practical terms. Those provided for in Article 23 of the First Geneva Convention and Article 14 of the Fourth Geneva Convention are of limited scope (they apply only to the wounded and sick and a few categories of civilians). They are undoubtedly less important than the neutralized zones described in Article 15 of the Fourth Geneva Convention or the demilitarized zones provided for in Article 60 of Additional Protocol I, which cover the entire civilian population. As stated above, such a zone can be established only by *agreement between the parties*. This is precisely what causes problems in practice. It is obviously not easy to conclude agreements in the heat of action, when tension is running high and the mentality is all too often one of 'total war'.

Yet the agreement of the parties to the conflict is essential, for protected zones under humanitarian law require a climate of trust and cooperation between those parties. The minimum degree of trust necessary to establish the zones relates above all to their *demilitarization* which, as we have seen, is a basic principle. Protected zones therefore have to be strictly regulated by the parties to the conflict, which usually distrust each other to such an extent that none of them is prepared to take risks because it anticipates from the start that the adverse party will not keep its word.

As regards protection of wounded and sick, under the Geneva Conventions and their Additional Protocols civilian and military *hospitals* and *medical transports* as such already enjoy neutral status. In time of armed conflict they are marked, with the permission and under the control of the relevant authorities, with the red cross or red crescent emblem. *Personnel* looking after the wounded and sick enjoy the same protection.[12]

It is as well to make clear here that the zones provided for in humanitarian law relate only to international armed conflicts. Neither Article 3 common to the four Geneva Conventions nor Additional Protocol II of 1977 contain any provision for protected zones. Nevertheless there is no reason why parties to an internal conflict should not apply, by analogy, the rules pertaining to international armed conflicts.[13]

As has been seen, the ICRC, as a neutral and independent intermediary, may be invited to lend its good offices for the establishment or administration of protected zones. Where it is not expressly named, it is at least covered by the term 'humanitarian organization' mentioned as a possible intermediary between the parties. The ICRC, however, has often played a far more significant role. It has several times taken the initiative of setting up neutralized zones and placing them under its own supervision, first making sure in all cases that all the parties agreed to its doing so and only then taking control of the zones in question. Because this last task in particular is always an onerous one, and bearing in mind its limited resources, zones declared neutral by the ICRC have been comparatively small in area. They have generally been only a single building, such as an hotel, or a compound. There is no room in this brief study for detailed enumeration of all the protected zones established by the ICRC.[14]

One case should be mentioned here, however, because it illustrates very clearly the limitations of protected zones set up under international humanitarian law. In 1979 several protected zones were established in Nicaragua, including the *zona franca* near Managua airport, shortly before the Sandanistas seized power. An unusual feature was that they even harboured combatants who had laid down their arms, notably members of Somoza's personal guard. These people believed that their presence in a protected zone granted them amnesty, but the purpose of humanitarian law is to provide protection against hostilities, not to offer political, let alone legal, protection. A protected zone gives no protection against capture or prosecution. This experience showed how important it is to make the limitations of protected zones perfectly clear, especially to the persons directly concerned.[15]

The conflict in the former Yugoslavia

The fluctuations of the armed conflict in the former Yugoslavia had a direct bearing on the use of 'protected zones'. During that war not only protected zones as provided for in international humanitarian law but also 'Safe

Areas' ordained by the United Nations Security Council were used. These two types of zone should be considered separately, for the reasoning behind them was quite different.[16]

Protected zones set up under international humanitarian law

The armed conflict in Croatia led to the establishment of several protected zones that were in conformity with international humanitarian law. It is surprising to note that they were set up with an attention to legal formalities that was unusual, if not unique, although the prevailing climate was one of extreme tension.

From the very beginning of the war the extent to which humanitarian law applied to the parties to the conflict was in doubt. Was it an international or an internal armed conflict? As the promoter and guardian of international humanitarian law, the ICRC took upon itself to bring the protagonists together at the same negotiating table, so as to ensure application of the greatest possible number of rules of humanitarian law.[17] Several agreements on the application of humanitarian law were concluded in this way.

Here we shall focus on the *Memorandum of Understanding* signed in Geneva on 27 November 1991 by the plenipotentiary representatives of the Federal Executive Council, the Republics of Croatia and Serbia and the Yugoslav People's Army, under ICRC auspices.[18] Point 7 of this agreement concerns the establishment of protected zones, and is worded as follows:

> 7. Establishment of protected zones
> The parties agree that for the establishment of protected zones, the annexed standard draft agreement shall be used as a basis for negotiations.

The *Standard draft agreement relating to protected zones* contained references to Article 23 of the First Geneva Convention and Articles 14 and 15 of the Fourth Convention. It stated that the zones were to be marked with the red cross emblem and placed them under the supervision and control of the ICRC. Access to the zones was to be restricted to the following categories of persons (subject to alteration in specific cases):

- Sick and wounded civilian and military personnel
- Civilian persons not taking part in the hostilities
- Medical and administrative personnel
- ICRC delegates.

No weapons were permitted within the zones and all military equipment had to be removed. The agreement also stated as follows:

> No persons residing in or visiting, in whatever capacity, the protected zone shall perform any work directly connected with or contributing to the military operations...In no circumstances may the protected zone be the object of attack. It shall be respected and protected at all times by the parties to the conflict.

The Osijek protected zone

Subsequently, on 27 December 1991, an 'Agreement relating to the establishment of a protected zone around the hospital of Osijek' was signed at Pècs, Hungary, under ICRC auspices.[19] This text, which comprised no less than 18 articles, was based on the above-mentioned framework agreement concluded on 27 November 1991. There were, however, some differences: the range of beneficiaries was more limited than in the framework agreement, the following persons being allowed to stay in Osijek hospital:

- Sick and wounded civilian and military personnel
- Family members visiting patients recovering in the hospital
- Persons aged over 65 years, children under 15, expectant mothers and mothers of children under seven, taking no part in the hostilities
- Medical and administrative personnel of the hospital of Osijek
- ICRC delegates and ICRC local staff.

This list derives from a combination of the 'hospital zones and localities' under the First Geneva Convention and the 'hospital and safety zones and localities' mentioned in Article 14 of the Fourth Geneva Convention. The following clause is also noteworthy: 'The parties in particular reaffirm that hospitals even if not situated in a protected zone may in no circumstances be the object of attack or be used to commit hostile acts.' This passage is important as a reminder of the general immunity of hospitals.

The agreement also stipulated: 'The protected zone will be placed under the supervision and control of the ICRC', and 'There will be ICRC delegates permanently present in the zone.'

The agreement of 27 December 1991 came into effect at midnight on 3 January 1992, and Osijek hospital remained a protected zone until 30 June 1992.

Osijek hospital was in fact composed of several buildings. Its pre-war capacity was 1,600 beds. When the protected zone was set up, 500 beds were available in the basements, and 800 people were working there. The zone was under the control of ICRC delegates, hospital security personnel and a few members of the Croatian police. A team of Croatian Red Cross volunteers also helped with the task. The hospital was marked by means of large flags bearing the red cross emblem.

The Osijek protected zone had its problems – it was hit by shells more than a dozen times. Formal representations concerning these violations were made to the parties concerned.[20] Following certain incidents the parties met at Pècs on 9 April 1992 under ICRC auspices and strengthened implementation of the agreement of 27 December 1991 by adoption of an additional provision.

The Osijek protected zone was certainly the most well organized, but it was not the only one. A very brief review of other protected zones is given below.

Here we cannot fail to mention the tragic events in Vukovar, which in fact prompted the establishment of the Osijek protected zone. Everything possible had to be done to prevent a similar disaster. As regards Vukovar itself, the belligerents gave their oral agreement in Zagreb on 19 November 1991 to conferring neutral status on the city's hospital as from 8 p.m. the same day. The agreement referred to Article 15 of the Fourth Geneva Convention, placed the hospital under ICRC protection and made provision for its demilitarization. The agreement never took effect, however, for on the following day, 20 November, a number of patients were taken away from the ICRC and forcibly removed to an unknown destination. It is believed that they were later executed. An agreement providing for the evacuation of the wounded and sick had already been concluded on 18 November.

In view of the scale of the hostilities in the Dubrovnik area, at the end of 1991 the ICRC proposed to give neutral status to the Franciscan monastery and Medarevo hospital. This was done on 6 December 1991, on the basis of a locally negotiated agreement. The status of the hospital as a protected zone formally ended on 15 July 1992.

At one time or another it was proposed to protect other hospitals, in particular Zagreb military hospital, Karlovac hospital and the Kosovo hospital in Sarajevo.

Successes and failures

What successes and failures should be ascribed to these protected zones established in accordance with international humanitarian law?

First of all, it may seem surprising that a hospital should be declared a protected zone, for, as stated above, hospitals are already protected and given neutral status by international humanitarian law. Nevertheless the ICRC, having observed that the parties to the conflict tended not to respect the immunity of hospitals, felt that their existing legal protection needed to be reinforced.

As for the protective effect of such zones, experience has shown that this is often difficult to gauge with any certainty. Although Vukovar was a tragic failure, it has to be admitted that the other zones certainly helped provide more effective protection for victims. It cannot be ruled out that without these protected zones events might have taken a much more disastrous turn. Very probably the process of negotiating the protected zones, as well as the agreements concluded, helped to reduce tension between the parties.

Inconsistent decisions by the UN Security Council

Now we shall turn to the Safe Areas set up in Bosnia-Herzegovina, which may be regarded as another type of protected zone.[21]

From the start of the war in Bosnia-Herzegovina the civilian population was ill-treated and suffered appalling atrocities. In particular it fell victim to the policy known by the sinister name of 'ethnic cleansing'. Under this policy civilians became the very object of the conflict, in flagrant violation of the most fundamental principles of international humanitarian law. The international community, wondering how to put an end to a situation that was totally unacceptable from the humanitarian point of view, cast about for some means of offering effective protection to this terrorized and persecuted population. Could it, for example, shield the most vulnerable population groups by establishing protected zones?

An ICRC initiative

Faced with this ongoing tragedy and the magnitude of the needs, at the end of October 1992 the ICRC proposed to set up zones of this kind, first of all in northern Bosnia-Herzegovina where protection was most urgently needed. The President of the ICRC appealed to the international community to take action to save tens of thousands of civilians in the region whose lives were in danger.[22]

The ICRC stated: 'The present situation calls for the creation of zones adapted to its specific requirements and, in particular, which need an international protection.'[23] Indeed, it seemed out of the question to leave such zones under the sole responsibility of the parties controlling the territory on which the zones were likely to be set up, as provided for in international humanitarian law. Obviously their establishment was far beyond the capacity of the ICRC.

The ICRC made known the conditions which in its view had to be fulfilled. It was convinced in particular that the parties concerned should agree to the establishment of such zones and that international forces such as UNPROFOR should be responsible for their security. The ICRC also offered its services in helping to set up and administer the zones, and in restoring contact between members of separated families and providing relief supplies.

The Security Council for its part invited 'the Secretary-General...to study the possibility of and the requirements for the promotion of Safe Areas for humanitarian purposes' (Resolution 787 of 16 November 1992).

In view of the worsening plight of the civilian population, especially those considered as ethnic minorities, in December 1992 the ICRC launched a new appeal to the international community for the establishment of protected zones and again denounced the policy of 'ethnic cleansing'.[24] The ICRC pointed out that 'the purpose of protected zones could not be to protect besieged towns', saying that in its view other ways of doing this – such as the cessation of hostilities – would have to be found. Repeating its proposals of 30 October, the ICRC suggested that United Nations forces or other forces not involved in the conflict should be deployed in all towns in Bosnia-Herzegovina in which minority groups – whether Muslim, Croat or Serb – were at great risk. It furthermore proposed that displaced populations should be given temporary protection in these zones.[25]

The ICRC again stressed that these zones should be based on the agreement of the parties, that they should be only a temporary expedient, and that for practical reasons they should be comparatively small. It also pointed out that:

> the above measures could in no way be regarded as contributing to the policy of 'ethnic cleansing', since they would involve, in the first case, protection of minority groups in their places of residence and, in the second, aid to people who are already displaced.

Evidently, even if these protected zones were not quite those provided for in international humanitarian law, they were nevertheless very similar, especially because they had first to be accepted by the parties concerned. In making clear that protected zones such as these could not serve to protect besieged towns (that is, zones disputed by the parties to the conflict), the ICRC was taking into account the limitations of protected zones under international humanitarian law, whose sole purpose is to give protection against the effects of the fighting. The ICRC's proposals were, however, not adopted, in particular at the meeting of Foreign Ministers held in Geneva on 16 December 1992. It is noteworthy that the Office of the United Nations High Commissioner for Refugees (UNHCR) expressed strong reservations, feeling that safety zones should remain 'a last option'.[26]

Inconsistent decisions by the UN Security Council

Later, the United Nations Security Council took practical steps to set up safety zones in Bosnia-Herzegovina. First, invoking Chapter VII of the United Nations Charter, by Resolution 819 of 16 April 1993, it established a 'Safe Area' in and around Srebrenica. In Resolution 824 of 6 May 1993 it extended the 'Safe Area' concept to the towns of Sarajevo, Tuzla, Zepa, Gorazde and Bihac 'and their surroundings', and to 'other such threatened areas', again invoking Chapter VII of the Charter. Subsequently, Resolution 836 of 4 June 1993 extended the role of UNPROFOR.

These zones call for comment in several respects. First of all, the purpose of the Security Council's 'Safe Areas' were intended to protect minorities against the 'ethnic cleansing' policy. It was not just a matter of offering protection against the effects of fighting, as in the case of zones under special protection provided for in international humanitarian law; the aim was to enable the minorities concerned to stay on the spot. This was an entirely strategic objective. In establishing these 'Safe Areas' the Security Council was attempting *to influence the very course of the conflict*, and hence directly involved the United Nations in the armed conflict. These zones thus had more in common with *jus ad bellum* than with *jus in bello*, that is, international humanitarian law.[27] The Security Council's decisions were not without ambiguity, however, for apparently the States concerned were very anxious not to become involved in the conflict and wanted to avoid any confrontation, preferring traditional peacekeeping to peace enforcement.

It has to be recognized that the parties concerned had protected zones thrust upon them, even although from a purely formal point of view they may have been in (temporary) agreement. At least, the fact that Chapter VII of the Charter was invoked seems to support that theory. It was only too obvious that no agreement had been concluded between the parties (with the exception of the agreement for the demilitarization of Srebrenica, see hereafter). The armed conflict in Bosnia-Herzegovina being what it was, one can hardly believe that agreement was possible. As it happened, the lack of any *genuine* agreement meant that the forces assigned to protect the enclaves had to be large enough and sufficiently well equipped to repel violent attacks. What is more, they still had to be authorized to use force.[28]

In this respect, one question that should be addressed is whether such forces, if they find themselves in a position in which they use force (to enforce their mandate or acting in self-defence), become a party to the conflict and are bound by international humanitarian law, and in particular by the Geneva Conventions of 1949 and their Additional Protocols of 1977. There has been a long debate on this issue. The main problem is the following: if forces under UN command are considered a party to an armed conflict, they would then become a legitimate military target; they could also be captured and detained until the cessation of active hostilities. Such an option is of course not at all acceptable for the forces concerned, and the Convention on the Safety of United Nations and Associated Personnel, adopted by the General Assembly on 9 December 1994, aims precisely at improving their protection.

However, it would seem reasonable to believe that forces under UN command and control, whether involved in peacekeeping or enforcement operations, cannot act in a legal vacuum: if confronted with a situation of violence, there is no doubt that they would have to abide by the rules of humanitarian law. In concrete terms this would mean in particular that they would always have to make a distinction between civilians and combatants, that they would have to respect the rules prohibiting or restricting the use of certain weapons and methods of combat, that they would have to provide medical care to the wounded and that they would have to treat captured combatants in accordance with the Third Geneva Convention relative to the treatment of prisoners of war.

As a consequence, it would be appropriate if the ICRC would be given access to such detained persons. In addition, the United Nations have argued that, because the UN is not a State, it would not be able to become a Party to the Geneva Conventions and their Additional Protocols. However, the United Nations have undertaken long ago to respect the principles and spirit of international humanitarian law. The ICRC has tried to specify the rules and principles of international humanitarian law that should apply to forces under UN command, taking into account their particular situation and status. It should be added here that the contingents from various countries are of course also bound by the commitments made by their respective States.[29]

As already stated, the withdrawal of combatants and military equipment is another essential condition for the establishment of protected zones under international humanitarian law. This question also arises as regards the zones ordered by the Security Council. Resolutions 819 and 824 did not require their demilitarization, but Resolution 836 demanded it unilaterally.[30] In any event the presence of armed forces in the zone was bound to prompt attacks – perfectly legitimate ones, considering that combatants and their equipment are a military objective. Demilitarization of the enclaves would probably have made their protection easier.

In this connection it is interesting that an agreement for the demilitarization of Srebrenica was signed on 17 April 1993 by representatives of the Bosnian Muslim forces, the Bosnian Serb forces and UNPROFOR.[31] This agreement, although a step in the right direction, was never fully applied, and the failure of this 'Safe Area' to provide protection is, alas, only too well known.

Concluding remarks

During the armed conflicts in the former Yugoslavia two kinds of protected areas were established: those directly based on international humanitarian law and those imposed by the Security Council.

Clearly, both encountered considerable problems, but it was the very ambitious Safe Areas established by Security Council resolutions that had tragic consequences and prompted more public discussion. Tremendous hopes were raised only to be dashed, and this just made matters worse for the civilian population.

The most striking thing of all is that the Security Council adopted a policy on this question without having adequate means to carry it out, since there was no real political will to take effective action. It is highly regrettable that the reputation of the Security Council and of the United Nations in general was tarnished in this way. It is indeed important that States accept their responsibilities, and it would be unfortunate if the experience in the former Yugoslavia would make States more reluctant to take practical steps to address crisis situations which threaten international peace and security.

That being said, it is not easy to find a way through situations as extreme as those in Bosnia-Herzegovina, where human rights and international humanitarian law were flouted far too often. It has to be admitted that in such situations, where the civilian population has become the main object of the conflict, protected zones as envisaged by international humanitarian law offer no more than a temporary remedy of very limited scope.

Lastly, it is perhaps worthwhile to think in general terms about the most appropriate response to large-scale violations of human rights and humanitarian law. One could hazard a few suggestions in broad outline, but obviously the best way to protect the civilian population in time of war is a matter that calls for further discussion and more focused consideration.[32]

Some pointers for the future

1. First of all it must be remembered that in armed conflict situations the parties to the conflict are under an obligation to respect international humanitarian law, in particular the Geneva Conventions and their Additional Protocols. Moreover, States not party to the conflict are under an obligation to contribute to such respect.[33]

2. If it is necessary to protect the civilian population against the effects of war, protected zones as provided for in international humanitarian law may be used, bearing in mind that their purpose is only a limited one. They must be the subject of an agreement between the parties, and they must be demilitarized. Although such zones may offer protection during long-range bombing and shelling, it is much more difficult for them to provide protection when there is heavy fighting on the ground. Ultimately, protected zones under international humanitarian law will always depend on the political resolve and goodwill of the parties to the conflict.

3. If large-scale violations of international humanitarian law and human rights occur and it therefore becomes necessary to intervene in the conflict to put a stop to such violations and avoid further massacres, the community of States should mobilize and take action using appropriate means. From the viewpoint of international law, these situations probably constitute a threat to international peace and security and therefore justify intervention on the basis of the United Nations Charter.

4. If there is no alternative to imposing protected zones, States must realize that the troops sent to the spot will probably have to use force and thus take part in the armed conflict. It is therefore particularly important that those troops should have a clear and precise mandate, particularly as regards the use of force. Furthermore, zones imposed on the parties need considerable resources in terms of manpower and equipment. If at all possible, they should be demilitarized; this requires strict supervision but at the same time makes it much easier

to establish them. Lastly, international troops having to use force must respect international humanitarian law. Everything possible must be done to avoid creating a false sense of security among the civilian population or, worse still, placing it in a situation it perceives as a trap, as decisions are taken with a view to enhance its protection, whereas they do not at all permit to achieve that aim for lack of consistency and available resources.

5.   It must always be borne in mind that humanitarian action has its limits, and that when there are large-scale violations of human rights and humanitarian law, States cannot unload their political responsibilities on to humanitarian agencies. The latter can carry out their tasks with full impartiality only when States have created the necessary 'humanitarian space'. It would certainly facilitate the provision of protection and assistance for all victims if a clear distinction were drawn between political and military activities on the one hand and humanitarian action on the other.

6.   In any event it is of crucial importance that no protected zone should be established if it would be detrimental to the protection of the civilian population as a whole. The belligerents must not be given the impression that only the population within the zone is entitled to protection. The principle of the general immunity of the civilian population must always be stressed.

Notes

1   For practical reasons, other zones under special protection, such as those in northern Iraq (1991) and Rwanda (1994), will be not be discussed in this paper.
2   For an introduction to international humanitarian law, see Gasser, Hans-Peter, 'International humanitarian law: An introduction', in Hans Haug (ed.), *Humanity for all: The International Red Cross and Red Crescent Movement*, Henry Dunant Institute/Paul Haupt Publishers: Geneva/Bern, 1993; Frits Kalshoven, *Constraints on the waging of war*, ICRC: Geneva, 1991. On the subject of the implementation of humanitarian law, see Pfanner, Toni, 'Le rôle du CICR dans la mise en oeuvre du droit international humanitaire', in *Le droit face aux crises humanitaires*, European Commission: Brussels/Luxembourg, 1995.
3   As of 15 August 1997, there were 188 States party to the four Geneva Conventions. It is widely recognized that the provisions of the Geneva Conventions represent customary law.
4   As of 15 August 1997, there were 148 States party to Protocol I and 140 to Protocol II.
5   In non-international armed conflicts or internal armed conflicts, armed opposition groups are bound in the same way as government authorities. This has no effect on the legal status of the parties to the conflict.

6   On the subject of the relationship between human rights and humanitarian law, see Louise Doswald-Beck and Sylvain Vité, 'International humanitarian law and human rights law', *International Review of the Red Cross (IRRC)*, No. 293, March–April 1993, pp. 94–119.

7   Geneva Convention for the Amelioration of the Condition of the Wounded and Sick in Armed Forces in the Field, of 12 August 1949.

8   Geneva Convention relative to the Protection of Civilian Persons in Time of War, of 12 August 1949.

9   It should be noted that the ban on attacking non-defended localities was already laid down in Article 25 of the 1907 Hague Regulations: 'The attack or bombardment, by whatever means, of towns, villages, dwellings, or buildings which are undefended is prohibited.'

10 Unfortunately, the term 'demilitarized zone' gives rise to confusion, for it is used to cover very different concepts, ranging from zones provided for in peace treaties or international agreements to buffer zones set up following an armistice. The purpose of the zones described in Article 60 of Protocol I is purely humanitarian, that is, to protect the civilian population within the zones from attack.

11 It should be noted that under Article 85, para. 3(d), of Additional Protocol I, making non-defended localities and demilitarized zones the object of attack constitutes a grave breach of the Protocol and is therefore a war crime. Under para. 3(a) of that Article, the same applies to attacks against the civilian population in general.

12 This protection dates as far back as the 1864 Geneva Convention. For detailed rules on the use of the emblem, see Jean-Philippe Lavoyer, 'National legislation on the use and protection of the emblem of the red cross and red crescent', *IRRC*, No. 313, July–August 1996, pp. 482–495.

13 Common Article 3 invites even parties to a non-international armed conflict to 'bring into force, by means of special agreements, all or part of the other provisions' (of the Geneva Conventions).

14 An overview of protected zones and ICRC action can be found in Yves Sandoz, *The establishment of safety zones for persons displaced within their country of origin*, Multi-choice Conference on International Legal Issues arising under the United Nations Decade of International Law, Doha/Qatar, 22–25 March 1994, pp. 119–136. Neutralized zones were for example established by the ICRC in Dacca (1971), Nicosia (1974), Saigon and Phnom Penh (1975), Nicaragua (1979), during the Falklands/Malvinas conflict (1982), in Sri Lanka (the hospital in Jaffna, since 1990). More recently the ICRC acted as a neutral intermediary in Mexico: see Béatrice Mégevand, 'Between insurrection and government: ICRC action in Mexico (January-August 1994)', *IRRC*, No. 304, January–February 1995, pp. 94–108. For steps taken in relation to the former Yugoslavia, see the next section.

15 For a general description of ICRC activities, see Marion Harroff-Tavel, 'Action taken by the ICRC in situations of internal violence', *IRRC*, No. 294, May-June 1993, pp. 195-220.

16 For ICRC activities in the former Yugoslavia, see Jean-François Berger, *The humanitarian diplomacy of the ICRC and the conflict in Croatia (1991-1992)*, ICRC, Geneva, 1995; and Michèle Mercier, *Crimes without punishment*, Pluto Press, London/East Haven, 1995.

17 For further details see Yves Sandoz, 'Réflexions sur la mise en oeuvre du droit international humanitaire et sur le rôle du Comité international de la Croix-Rouge en ex-Yougoslavie', *Revue suisse de droit international et de droit européen*, 4/1993. The question of the legal nature of the conflict assumed particular importance in relation to the prosecution of war criminals by the International Criminal Tribunal for the former

Yugoslavia: see Cherif Bassouni and Peter Manikas, *The law of the International Criminal Tribunal for the former Yugoslavia*, Transnational Publishers, Inc., Irvington-on-Hudson, New York, 1996, pp. 441–479.

18 See ICRC Press Release No. 1695 of 27 November 1991.

19 See ICRC Communication to the press No. 91/53 of 31 December 1991.

20 See ICRC Press Release No. 1710 of 24 April 1992, issued after the hospital had been hit by several shells the previous day. Following this violation the President of the ICRC sent messages to the Presidents of Croatia and Serbia and to the highest federal authorities.

21 The United Nations Protected Areas set up in Croatia are not discussed here.

22 Statement by the President of the ICRC to the heads of the Permanent Missions in Geneva, 30 October 1992.

23 ICRC position paper of 30 October 1992, 'The establishment of protected zones for endangered civilians in Bosnia-Herzegovina'.

24 *Protecting vulnerable ethnic minorities in Bosnia-Herzegovina*, ICRC paper, 14 December 1992.

25 On the subject of population displacements under humanitarian law, see Jean-Philippe Lavoyer, 'Refugees and internally displaced persons: International humanitarian law and the role of the ICRC', *IRRC*, No. 305, March–April 1995, pp. 162–180.

26 'Safe areas for humanitarian assistance' (SC res. 787), Position of UNHCR, 14 December 1992. UNHCR particularly emphasized that any safety zones established 'should not affect freedom of movement nor *ipso facto* frustrate the right to seek asylum'.

27 The distinction between *jus ad bellum* and *jus in bello* is fundamental. *Jus ad bellum* is concerned with the extent to which it is legitimate to use force. That aspect of an armed conflict is regulated by the United Nations Charter. It must be dissociated from *jus in bello*, which is international humanitarian law.

28 Security Council Resolution 836 of 4 June 1993 authorized UNPROFOR 'acting in self-defence, to take the necessary measures, including the use of force, to reply to bombardments against the Safe Areas by any of the parties...'.

29 The ICRC recently drew up, in close cooperation with a group of experts, a set of guidelines for forces under UN command 'when in situations of armed conflict they are actively engaged as combatants', applicable to both peacekeeping and enforcement operations, where the use of force is authorized either in self-defence or in pursuance of a mandate of the Security Council. See: *Symposium on Humanitarian Action and Peacekeeping Operations*, Geneva, 22–24 June 1994, ICRC, 1995; and *Humanitarian Action and Peacekeeping Operations*, Keynote address by Cornelio Sommaruga, UNITAR/IPS/NIRA Conference, Singapore, 24 February 1997.

30 '5. Decides to extend...the mandate of UNPROFOR in order to enable it...to deter attacks against the Safe Areas,...to promote the withdrawal of military or paramilitary units other than those of the Government of the Republic of Bosnia and Herzegovina...'.

31 Agreement for the demilitarization of Srebrenica, signed by Lt. Gen. Mladic and Gen. Halilovic, as well as Lt. Gen. Wahlgren, representing UNPROFOR. The main elements of this agreement were: a total cease-fire in the Srebrenica area, the deployment of UNPROFOR into Srebrenica, the evacuation of the seriously wounded and sick, the demilitarization of Srebrenica within 72 hours, the submission of reports on minefields and the clearing of mines, freedom of movement, the provision of humanitarian aid, and the establishment of a working group that would decide the details of the demilitarization and make recommendations for the exchange of prisoners, the dead and the wounded under ICRC supervision.

32 Among recent contributions on the subject of protected zones, see Maurice Torelli, 'Les zones de sécurité', *Revue générale de droit international public*, No. 4, October–December 1995, pp. 787–848; and Karin Landgren, 'Safety zones and international protection: A dark grey area', *International Journal of Refugee Law*, Vol 7, No. 3, 1995, pp. 436–458.

33 Article 1 common to the four Geneva Conventions of 1949 reads: 'The High Contracting Parties undertake to respect and to ensure respect for the present Convention in all circumstances.' Article 89 of Additional Protocol I of 1977 reads: 'In situations of serious violations of the Conventions or of this Protocol, the High Contracting Parties undertake to act, jointly or individually, in co-operation with the United Nations and in conformity with the United Nations Charter.' It is most regrettable that States only very partially live up to this important responsibility. See Condorelli, Luigi and Boisson de Chazournes, Laurence, 'Quelques remarques à propos de l'obligation de 'respecter et faire respecter' le droit international humanitaire 'en toutes circonstances'', in: *Studies and essays on international humanitarian law and Red Cross principles in honour of Jean Pictet*, ICRC/Martinus Nijhoff Publishers: Geneva/The Hague: 1984, pp. 17–35; Umesh Palwankar, 'Measures available to States for fulfilling their obligation to ensure respect for international humanitarian law', *IRRC*, No. 298, January–February 1994, pp. 9–25. In regard to the relationship between the United Nations and international humanitarian law, especially its implementation, see 'The United Nations and international humanitarian law', in Luigi Condorelli, Anne-Marie La Rosa, Sylvie Scherrer, eds, *Actes du Colloque international à l'occasion du cinquantième anniversaire de l'ONU (Genève, 19, 20 et 21 octobre 1995)*, Pedone: Paris, 1996.

Part Three

MILITARY AND DIPLOMATIC VIEWS

Third Section

'Learning from Doing' Peacekeeping – Political and Practical Implications

Part Three

MILITARY AND DIPLOMATIC VIEWS

17 The Situation in UN HQ

Ready for the Challenges?

CEES VAN EGMOND*

Introduction

Peacekeeping has experienced an enormous evolution since the early 1990s. Many more, much larger, much more complex and greatly varying operations were launched and executed, without a proper doctrinal foundation. Peacekeeping was, directly after the Cold War, seen as the panacea for the problems in the world. But new missions were created without adequate understanding of how to deal with the. problem. Unclear mandates were the consequence. Quite often, the mandate offered insufficient guidance to the leadership in missions, being unclear about 'what to do' whilst the implementers in the field had great difficulty in defining 'how to do' it in view of unclear direction, the lack of doctrine and the lack of appropriate experience. At UN Headquarters in New York, this evolution came similarly unexpected and had to be dealt with by a staff that was largely inadequate in view of all the challenges involved.

The situation in 1991

In early 1991, the UN was carrying out eight field missions, most of them 'traditional', long-standing and a result of inter-state conflicts. Many of these missions were Cold War-related, when containing certain problems was of great importance. Without belittling the difficulties encountered in the field, it is fair to state that many of these peacekeeping operations (PKO) were relatively simple and had to a large extent the character of observer missions: 1) they were static, where operations and logistics became fairly routine and predictable, 2) the parties in the conflict were kept at bay by the superpowers, who had every interest in containing the problem, 3) civil life in the mission area experienced little disturbance from

---

* Col. Cees van Egmond is an officer in the Royal Netherlands Marine Corps. He was Chief Mission Planning Service of the UN DPKO (Department of Peacekeeping Operations) from December 1993 to March 1997.

the conflict, and most often, there was no complex humanitarian need in the area.

During the 1960s and 1970s, there were also more complex PKOs like the one in the Congo (ONUC), the UN operation in the early phase of the Cyprus conflict (UNFICYP) or in Southern Lebanon (UNIFIL). Like the conflict in the former Yugoslavia, UNIFIL was an operation to a civil war-like conflict involving several states and a variety of national and religious factions which affected thousands of refugees and was a complex humanitarian challenge for the UN. Relief organizations operated under extremely challenging conditions.

However, during the Cold War, such complex operations were more the exception rather than the rule. The military staff in UN NY, as part of the Department of Peacekeeping Operations was small, but sufficient to look after these ongoing missions. Most tasks were routine and most issues were dealt. with in the field. As a result, the military staff faced few real operational challenges and had become a hardly distinguishable part of the Bureaucracy. The logistic side was run by the Field Operations Division (FOD), which belonged to the Department of Administration and Management.

In 1945 the Secretariat was created to support the legislative bodies of the United Nations. This is, in essence, an administrative role, that allowed the General Assembly, the three Councils and the Committees to function. The Rules and Regulations for the Secretariat were designed to facilitate precisely that role. Almost all operational functions performed by the UN were dealt with by the specialized agencies such as UNDP, WFP, UNHCR, etc.

The only exception was peacekeeping, which was politically and operationally looked after by the Under-secretary for PKO and his staff. The obvious shortage of staff in HQNY and the very limited capabilities for contingency planning and mission follow-up was reported from the field over decades. Unfortunately, no major improvements took place. Most missions were financed through the regular budget. Monitoring the ongoing operations was merely an extension of the administrative function already performed.

The situation since 1991 – demands

This situation changed dramatically in the second half of 1991. A new role was envisaged by many for the United Nations to fill the void that had come to exist after the Cold War. The nature of the problems the UN now had to deal with had changed from generally inter-state conflicts to intra-state conflicts and the number of Security Council resolutions on these issues increased sharply, many of them establishing peacekeeping operations in these areas (El Salvador, Somalia, Mozambique, Cambodia, former Yugoslavia). The Secretary-General was now facing the daunting task of translating these mandates into effective peacekeeping operations with an organization that neither had the structure, the experience, nor the culture to launch huge, complex operations in the field.

The military staff was completely inadequate in numbers, but also in experience and background. FOD still belonged to the Department of Administration and Management, which did not facilitate co-ordination. Further, the Secretary-General did not possess any of the means or assets to carry out peacekeeping operations – troops and the equipment to support them – so for the provision he had to completely rely on the Member States. A last obstacle for the Secretary-General was the process of funding. Upon the acceptance of a mandate by the Security Council no money was available to get a mission started. The General Assembly decided over the budget, a process that sometimes lasted many weeks, if not months. Without the budget approved in time, this resulted in substantial delays in mission start-up.

Mission preparation

A solid, well-thought out plan should be the basis for any operation. In light of the above, it may be clear that such plans were not available for most missions. Developments in the world took place so quickly and the demands on the Organization were so high that the Secretariat hardly had time – quite aside from the capacity – to perform contingency planning. The staff could only react on an *ad hoc* basis to decisions by the Security Council. There was no capacity or time to follow a normal planning process of mission analysis, development of courses of action, task deduction, formulation of a concept of operations, specification of the requirements, and so on. Instead, planning started on the basis of the numbers of troops and observers authorized in the Security Council resolution. It concentrated mainly on logistical issues: how to get the troops in place and how to support them. As a consequence, much of the above-mentioned planning process had to be done in the field by the Force Commander or the Chief Military Observer (CMO) and their staff. (In observer missions, Chief Military Observers (CMOs) were sometimes used as equivalent to the Force Commanders (FC) in PKOs with military units.)

Unfortunately, the mission staffs were not a model of effectiveness and efficiency either. Staff officers came from all over the globe, without previous peacekeeping experience, common procedures, doctrine and with inadequate language knowledge. The lack of structure and staff effectiveness as well as the lack of up-front funding that accompanied mission start-up made it almost miraculous that missions got started at all, and that many were performed with considerable success. The leadership in the field, many staff members in the field but also at UNHQ, deserve great credit for their willpower, dedication and above all common sense.

Nature of peacekeeping

'Peacekeeping is not a job for soldiers, but only soldiers can do it.' This remarkable statement was made by the second Secretary-General of the United Nations, Dag Hammerskjøld, one of the founding fathers of peacekeeping. Much has changed since the creation of the first peacekeeping mission, UNEF I, in 1956. Peacekeeping nowadays is by far more complex than it used to be. The situations which require peacekeeping forces are often also humanitarian emergencies. Great numbers of refugees, internally displaced persons, famine and serious health problems are part of the deteriorated situation.

As a consequence, the problems in a mission area are not only of a political and military/operational nature, there are significant humanitarian and economical dimensions too. The military operational component in peacekeeping missions must be facilitative and supportive to the other components, by creating an environment in which the country involved can get back on its feet again. This is true during all phases of the peace process, be it during preventive diplomacy, peacemaking or post-conflict peacebuilding, each phase making different demands on the 'facilitators'.

This role is new for most in the military (except perhaps in some traditional 'peacekeeping countries'). They are used to preparation for war-fighting situations, in which everyone is subordinate to the military authority. Many other characteristics of modern peacekeeping are in contrast to our traditional military upbringing. The absence of an enemy, no victory in the traditional sense of the word, the different applicability of the principles of war, the emphasis on de-escalation, no unity of command in the mission, are just a few of these problems. Military forces that are not prepared for these changes may seriously hamper the operation. Proper preparation and training for these challenges is of the utmost importance. Focusing on war-fighting is not enough. Serious attention should be given by military units to the requirements of peacekeeping prior to participation in peacekeeping operations. Sticking to Dag Hammarskjøld's statement most often prevents such attention. Only an attitude: 'If only soldiers can do peacekeeping, they'd better consider it to be part of their job' will provide properly prepared contingents with the proper mind set in peacekeeping missions.

Problem areas and potential remedies

Multi-functionality/complexity

During the tremendous increase in number and size of peacekeeping operations, staff and troops lacked proper peacekeeping training and experience. As a result, the various components in a mission (political, military, humanitarian) acted in an uncoordinated way, each heading into different directions, creating one of the major deficiencies in most missions. Co-ordination to reach a common goal should, however, not start during mission execution. It is a fundamental element during the planning process. In the absence at UNHQ of a proper planning capacity and a planning process earlier in this decade, political/humanitarian/military-operational co-ordination was non-existent. This problem has since been addressed through the 'Framework for Co-ordination', which describes the co-ordination requirements between the Departments of Political Affairs, Humanitarian Affairs and Peacekeeping Operations in the whole process of mission development, from the reception of early warning signals until the closing out of a peacekeeping mission.

This 'Framework' has, over the last few years, improved co-ordination between the departments substantially. This change was, like all change, hindered by the organization culture, which had to be transformed from an 'information guarding' to an 'information sharing' culture. The 'Framework for Co-ordination' is a very important first step, but it requires structural amendments in the UN Secretariat and in missions in the field, not leaving the process to chance or individual goodwill. Responsibilities for this process must be assigned to appropriate parts of the Organization.

Command and control

A major problem area is *command and control* (C&C). Originally, a military term, command and control is widely misused and as widely misunderstood. Command designates the authority a person (or an institution) has to order subordinates into actions with adequate resources, to achieve a defined goal. Control assesses the feedback and prepares additional directives for the command authority to issue, in order to optimize the process. This ongoing process requires a continuous link between the command and the control function. The command authority has full responsibility, is fully accountable for the actions ordered. How does this all relate to the various levels in UN peacekeeping?

Limited authority of the UNSC. The Security Council issues orders in the form of mandates. It could be argued, that the Council has strategic-level command authority. Mandates quite often do not define the desired goal or endstate and do not always include provisions that allow a comprehensive approach in the political, humanitarian and economical areas. Even if the mandate should include all these provisions, the Security Council does not have the authority over the assets required, or the budget necessary for the operation. These assets must come from the Member States and there is no guarantee that Member States will comply. The General Assembly, in eventually authorizing the budget, scrutinizes the budget proposal and eliminates all those costs, that do not directly relate to the political/military operation. In sum, the Security Council has restricted authority, coupled with a virtually non-existent accountability.

The control function was originally meant for the Military Staff Committee, but this body has never functioned as intended. At best, it can be argued, that the Secretariat is now performing that function. The link with the council, however, is sporadic and 'layered'. The new Secretary-General has gone to great lengths to improve this. The quality of feedback to the Council has improved substantially. For instance, the Military Adviser, who now disposes of a substantial analysis capacity, provides military advice, which is in undiluted form presented to the Secretary-General and subsequently to the Security Council. Resolutions have since become more realistic and achievable, although they always will have a strong element of compromise. Yet, the desirable interweaving of the command and the control function is not fully established.

The role of the UNSG. The Secretary-General is tasked with the execution of the mission. As such, he is the Chief Executive Officer, acting on behalf of the Security Council, thereby remaining at the same strategic level. For UN peacekeeping operations, he does not have a command-authority by himself, nor does he have authority over the finances for the mission. The SG must simply make things happen, within a set of often very restricting boundaries (mandate, UN Rules & Regulations). He can be placed in a virtually impossible position with a formidable mismatch between 'mission' and 'tools', which raises the interesting question, whether the SG could say 'no' if ordered to act in such a situation. Over the last few years such situations have come very close, especially in the Great Lakes Region in Africa. Perhaps the situation in Rwanda in April 1994 was more than close.

The Secretary-General is often seen as the 'Commander' of Peacekeeping Operations. In view of the above, this is not correct. Besides, the SG does not have an adequate staff to fulfil the duties of a higher headquarters, and is deprived of the control function needed to exercise the command function. In essence, the SG provides executive direction to the Head of Mission.

The role of the Head of Mission. This official should logically perform the command function at the operational level in a mission. Unfortunately, not all the mission components, especially on the humanitarian side, are always formally placed under the Head of Mission, who, at most, has co-ordinating authority, which does not greatly facilitate the comprehensive policy required during the peacemaking and post-conflict peacebuilding process. This situation is aggravated by the lack of resources, since the peacekeeping budget may only be used for sustaining the politico/military mission and its direct functioning.

Often, the Head of Mission is a Special Representative of the Secretary General (SRSG). Most of these individuals have a diplomatic or academic background and lack the management experience to lead complex missions. This expertise should be added in the form of a qualified Deputy-SRSG, who will run the mission – integrating the various components – leaving the overall political process to the SG.

The role of the Force Commander. The Force Commander has to implement a substantial part of the orders and directives, but cannot often exercise the command function. Up to now, there has been no formal transfer of authority from Member States to the UN, so it is unclear what the Force Commander can actually order. Most often, contingent commanders make execution of orders dependent upon approval by their authorities in their capital. This is disastrous if contingents perform an essential role in a comprehensive plan, jeopardizing the entire peacekeeping operation and introducing unacceptable risk for others. In complex military operations, a commander not only orders troops around, but also takes command decisions concerning the assets for support. Not so in a peacekeeping operation, where the Force Commander does not have command authority over the support assets. These conditions are unacceptable in enforcement operations. They provide a vital argument for the UN as an organization not to become involved in enforcement operations and to delegate such tasks to a 'coalition of the willing', as happened in the Gulf War.

Changes in the UN HQ. At UN HQ a system is now under development to formalize the participation of Member States, establishing C&C definitions and a 'Transfer of Authority' mechanism. The logistic command problem has been partly addressed through the creation of an integrated support structure in missions where the military and civilian logistic component work side by side, so that priorities can be properly set.

Although this facilitates the process, the fundamental flaw addressed above can only be overcome if the UN rules and regulations are changed. This, unfortunately, has not happened during the last few years!

In the past, the leadership of field missions have had problems in communicating their concerns to NY HQ. Only during regular working hours (US Eastern time!) could officials be reached, which was quite inconvenient, since most of the missions took place in time zones with six to twelve hours' difference. To solve this problem and to streamline the information flow to and from the field, the Situation Center was created, providing a 24-hour communication capacity, linking the field with senior officials in New York in case of urgency or emergency.

Due to the complexity of missions, most leaders are ill-prepared for their tasks. They are exposed to hitherto alien cultures and getting acquainted with them in the field does not facilitate an effective start. With the help of some Member States, future SRSGs, Force Commanders and leaders in the humanitarian and administrative field are now trained and familiarized with the other areas. This ensures optimal co-operation when they are actually deployed in the future.

In conclusion, C&C in the UN is at minimum confusing, while basic principles of command and control do not apply. Perhaps it is best to avoid the terms at the strategic level, and speak about the mandating authority of the Council and executive direction for the SG. What is more important however, is that the Member States take a serious look at the 'resourcing' of peacekeeping operations, realizing, that mission and tools must be matched and that the interweaving of the various components should be facilitated by 'all covering budgets'.

Peacekeeping vs. peace enforcement

Another problem area is the issue of peacekeeping vs. peace enforcement. The Secretary-General has stated in the *Supplement to an Agenda for Peace* that enforcement actions should be performed by groups of Member States or through regional organizations.

The reasons why the UN is not suited to execute peace enforcement operations are three-fold. First, the command and control arrangements as described above are insufficient to guarantee proper execution of enforcement operations. Second, in a multi-complex operation many other actors are present. Among them, the humanitarian community strives to maintain complete impartiality. Humanitarian organizations do not want to be associated with other parts of the UN, that do not observe their strict neutrality and impartiality. However, enforcement actions do not violate impartiality *per se*. Parties in a conflict may equally expect action against them by an enforcement force if their actions are in violation of conditions set out in the mandate. This 'impartiality towards the mandate' is often not perceived by the humanitarian community and combining humanitarian aid and an enforcement mission under the one blue UN flag remains difficult. Thirdly, enforcement operations may lead to more offensive actions, especially when there is non-compliance with the conditions spelled out in the mandate. Prolonged offensive actions demand combat logistic support, which the UN is most often unable to provide.

However, in practice, those coalitions of the willing, groups of Member States, or regional organizations mentioned above are not always available, capable, or especially willing to carry out enforcement actions. In their absence, the problem is dropped in the lap of the Secretary-General.

Enforcement elements to back up UN peacekeeping

Because of this circumstance, the UN is executing peacekeeping missions with a substantial enforcement back-up. The best example is the operation in East Slavonia, UNTAES. The SG's view has been that this operation should be part of IFOR. In particular, the US view, for domestic political reasons, was different. So eventually, the Security Council decided to mount and execute a 5,000-strong UN operation under Chapter VI of the Charter, but with an enforcement mandate to, a/o guarantee freedom of movement. No 'coalition of the willing' could be found, no regional organization was prepared. IFOR had used most of the potential resources. The search for a lead nation was in vain. Eventually, a force was structured along traditional UN lines, however, with a few exceptions. One NATO country was asked and was willing to provide the Force Commander along with a trained and prepared staff, thus eliminating some of the command and control concerns. All participating Member States provided a higher form of logistic self-sustainability than ever before. 'Force multipliers' like tanks, artillery and armed helicopters were added and the support of IFOR air assets was secured, should the need arise.

Mission preparation and force structuring

Planners at the UN face a few additional problems compared with national planners:

-   Planning starts almost in a vacuum, when little concrete direction is available. The mission statement will only formally be known from the Security Council mandate. The international community then expects instant reaction by the Organization. So advanced, assumption-based planning, is started early

- The United Nations, unlike Member States, does not own any of the assets needed for mission execution

- The lack of a budget and advance spending authority, as already mentioned

- The mission is planned virtually without the input from its executors, the Force Commander, Chief Military Observer or their staff

- Considerable efforts have been made to overcome these difficulties.

The Planning Division in the DPKO. The creation of a Planning Division in the Department of Peacekeeping Operations has reversed the pre-1991 situation drastically. Planning now follows a traditional pattern and is based on doctrine as it has developed over the years. The division provides a core function of integrated mission planning, with specialized input in all the areas of peacekeeping. Interdepartmental co-ordination is provided through the 'Framework for Co-ordination', which also includes the specialized UN-agencies on a need-to basis. Operational planning starts after a period of monitoring a specific situation in the world, and subsequently develops options or contingencies.

Proper analysis will lead to an operational concept and a force structure, suitable to address the situation, including the threat that parties may pose. Substantial difficulties are often encountered in the process of translating the paper force-structure into a real-life force. The proposed structure identifies several units, indicating a combination of numbers and capacities. Similar units may differ substantially in capacity and size among Member States. It is a painstaking and time-consuming process to match Member States' offers with the required capacities within Security Council dictated overall numbers.

Stand-by Arrangements. The system of Stand-by Arrangements introduced in 1993 has brought considerable relief in this process. Member States can pledge whatever national assets they – in principle – are willing to participate in peacekeeping. The pledge is conditional and requires a Member State's explicit approval upon a specific request for participation by the SG. The advantage of the Stand-by Arrangement system – which is the next best thing to a (politically unrealistic) standing UN force – is that the force-structuring process is greatly helped. Pre-arranged offers can be matched with the requirements, facilitating the identification of the most suitable contributing nation for a new mission. It also greatly helps national preparation for peacekeeping. Sixty-five Member States have joined the system in the last three years and the system has been used in the establishment of all new missions since 1994.

Contingent-owned equipment system. Another helpful new tool in the force-structuring process is the new system for reimbursement for contingent-owned equipment. It identifies, prior to deployment, the total assets a Member State should bring in and defines, based on standard costing, the amount the Member State is reimbursed for its contribution. A Contribution Agreement is made up prior to deployment. Cumbersome, lengthy reimbursement procedures, sometimes years after mission close-down, are now a thing of the past. The reimbursement may even take place during mission execution, provided there are funds in the UN treasury. This system may also have a positive effect on the perceived Member States' donor fatigue.

These initiatives put Member States on a much better footing to prepare their contingents and leaders for peacekeeping. Requirements are spelled out in detail and Member States are provided with a wealth of training information as to how and to what standards to prepare the units. United Nations Training Assistance Teams (UNTATs) are available to help train the trainers. At the same time, doctrine development has continuous attention at UN HQ, so that all directives are in full support of the current doctrinal approach.

Missions are still almost entirely planned without the input from their implementers. A Force Commander is appointed late in the process, since selection depends on which Member States will participate. Likewise, the composition of the staff, reflecting various national contributions, is likely to be known only shortly before mission start. For that reason, several issues, that are normally in the domain of the Force Commander, are now addressed by the planning staff in New York. These include detailed plans, including logistics, command and control arrangements, drafting of Rules of Engagement, all to avoid delay in mission start-up.

Rapid Deployable Mission Headquarters. An extra help in this process is the Rapid Deployable Mission Headquarters (RDMHQ) which is in the process of being established in New York. A total of 60–80 personnel, to perform key tasks in a mission staff during the start-up phase, are pre-identified at UNHQ and will perform all the necessary preparation, including training activities for the entire RDMHQ. This headquarters will provide the Head of Mission with a hitherto unknown start-up capacity, completely focused on the job ahead, with full knowledge of the UN system and how to make that work to the mission's advantage.

Rapid deployment

Situations for which a peacekeeping operation is mandated often require a quick response to avoid further deterioration. The UN Organization is not particularly good at responding rapidly. The reasons have been mentioned: budget, Rules and Regulations, lack of assets, etc. The budget and the rules can only be addressed by the Member States collectively in the General Assembly. It is hard to be optimistic in this area, considering the lack of action by the GA over the last four years. So other solutions must be sought.

The resources that the UN lacks are available with Member States. Rapid deployment is possible, provided Member States step forward to contribute what is needed. Rapid deployment is the result of a combination of actions/provisions, although many see it as the result of high readiness. But there is more to it than that. To start with, Member States have to respond rapidly. This can only happen if:

- Forces maintain a high degree of readiness

- Political decisions are made rapidly

- All the administrative procedures, like Contribution Agreement for COE reimbursement are finalized quickly.

If sufficient strategic lift and logistic sustainment capabilities are added, rapid deployment will be the result.

The UN Organization has often been blamed for lack of responsiveness. It should be clear, that the organization is severely hindered by factors beyond its control. Member States, however, do have the key to success in this area in their own hands:

- Simplify the political decision-making processes

- Prepare 'Draft Contribution Agreements' well in advance, based on contributions to the Stand-by Arrangements

- Provide strategic lift, by using the vast amount of naval/amphibious shipping that is around

- Provide a military logistic capability, allowing the UN sufficient time to build the UN logistic support system, which takes, due to the budget and mandatory bidding procedures, three to six months to establish.

If Member States are really serious about the issue of rapid deployment – and the large size of the group called 'Friends of Rapid Reaction' indicates so – they should individually and collectively work on the elements described above. They have all the tools to make it work.

Conclusion

The drastically changed demand on the United Nations Organization in the area of peacekeeping has led to major changes within the organization. Capacities have been built, organization parts were added and much has improved over the last few years. Many valuable lessons have been learned. But the UN can only do so much in translating these lessons into workable applications for the future. The United Nations is a collective membership, so the Member States must play a vital role in implementing the necessary improvements. Looking at the various indicators, it seems that Member States are not always sufficiently aware of their role therein:

- Even before the added capacity in the Department of Peacekeeping Operations has come to full growth, the Secretariat is under pressure to minimize or downsize these new capacities

- The fact, that many military officers, now serving to provide that basic capacity, are 'on loan' from their governments, is a thorn in the flesh of several Member States. Yet, efforts to create sufficient UN-paid positions have been futile. Actually, the number of UN-paid military posts were reduced by the General Assembly in June 1996

- The much criticized Rules and Regulations have not changed one iota over the last years. The emphasis in the process is less on achieving the goals then on abiding by the rules. The focus of the internal and external auditing processes only reinforces that approach. Hence, confusing effort with achievement is often the result.

In conclusion, effectiveness and efficiency can be substantially enhanced, but it requires a combined approach from Member States and the UN. The new Secretary-General has the support of the Member States and all staff members in the organization have complete confidence in him. Metaphorically, it must be realized though, that a tree, that was allowed to grow in one direction for 45 years, having several sides shielded from the sun, cannot grow in another direction, simply by changing the gardener. Severe pruning, exposing all sides to the sun and above all, the provision of nutrients and water must help the new gardener in his efforts.

18 UN Peacekeeping and New Challenges in a New World

Danish Lessons Learned from UNPROFOR

HANS HÆKKERUP[*]

Introduction

When I first visited the Department of Peacekeeping Operations in New York, it had a staff of 38 persons. Now, approximately 400 persons are occupied dealing with the day-to-day operations and the conceptual development in the DPKO. I do not mention this as an example of UN bureaucracy, but as a concrete picture of the dramatic changes that the UN system has had to adapt to. The conditions for UN involvement in conflict resolution have changed immensely in recent years – not only quantitatively, but also qualitatively.

Denmark, along with the other Nordic countries, was involved from the very beginning of UN peacekeeping. Since the First United Nations Emergency Force in the Sinai in the 1950s, many other peacekeeping operations followed. Most of these missions were simple operations that demanded good and solid peacekeeping skills like monitoring cease-fires. Some, like ONUC (Congo), or UNFICYP (Cyprus) and UNIFIL (Southern Lebanon) were more complex and challenging due to civil war-like circumstances, but not of a dimension like the UN operations in Cambodia or in the former Yugoslavia.

The crucial breach of this peacekeeping tradition came after the breakdown of the Warsaw Pact. We have seen that the new security environment that evolved from 1989 both meant the release of a number of pent-up conflicts, but also involved new possibilities of international joint action. The UN Security Council was enabled to act without the constant interference of the use of the veto. But the conflicts that emerged, many of ethnic origin, also required far more demanding operations. In most of these conflicts, many warring factions were involved, and the internal systems in the conflict areas were broken.

---

[*] Hans Hækkerup (DK) is Danish Minister of Defence since 23 January 1993.

These complex conflicts created the need for another kind of international involvement. Monitoring and supervising elections, assuring delivery of humanitarian relief and assisting in the reconstruction of governmental or police functions became part of peacekeeping operations, and the mandates from the UN developed from being based only on Chapter VI of the UN Charter to those involving Chapter VII.

The UN-mandated peacekeeping operations in the former Yugoslavia have shown this development into a new multifunctional type of peacekeeping operations. They – and not least UNPROFOR – are therefore very important experiences in the process of assessing future demands for peacekeeping operations.

Requirements evolved and lessons learned since 1992

UNPROFOR can be described as a peacekeeping mission that was caught in the middle of war. The causes for this turn of events have already been widely discussed and will without doubt be further discussed in the years to come. Lessons learned from the more than three year long UN engagement in the former Yugoslavia are now emerging and are being carefully analysed. When we examine the validity of the lessons learned from UNPROFOR, however, we have to identify the underlying causes and assess whether they are specific for UNPROFOR, thus being of a temporary nature, or whether they can be seen as general trends for peacekeeping operations in the future.

Because UNPROFOR was deployed in the middle of ongoing and continuing fighting, the lessons learned to a very high degree concern themselves with the UN troops' ability to cope with this fact and to establish the capability to fulfil their mission under very unfavourable conditions. UNPROFOR's mission – in short, to provide the basis for a durable cease-fire and for the delivery of humanitarian aid – proved to be very difficult and extremely dangerous under the prevailing circumstances. The war in the former Yugoslavia was extremely dirty, often with intimidation and violation of civilians and ethnical groups as objectives for military and paramilitary action. This of course meant that the fulfilment of a highly visible and important part of UNPROFOR's mission – providing the basis for the delivery of humanitarian aid – was not always in the interest of the various fighting groups, and thus more often than not met with various kinds of obstructions, in some cases even the implied threat of armed opposition. Even so, UNPROFOR succeeded in alleviating many of the consequences of war for thousands of people, a feat which can only be subscribed to an enormous effort by UN troops.

A large number of factors influenced UNPROFOR's ability to fulfil its mission. The time that lapsed from the initial decision to establish UNPROFOR until the peacekeeping troops were deployed led to continued fighting between the warring parties. This changed the basis upon which the peace plan for Croatia that the UN troops were deployed to supervise had been negotiated. The preconditions in military terms related to the cease-fire were no longer valid when the troops finally arrived. In addition, UNPROFOR evolved incrementally through a substantial number of Security Council resolutions over the years. This was especially the case for the operations in Bosnia-Herzegovina, where the international community through a succession of Security Council resolutions tried to harness – or even just to keep up with – developments on the ground. With each change, new tasks were added to UNPROFOR's overall mission. Sometimes, but not always, the new tasks were accompanied by an allocation of additional troops in order to make ends meet for UNPROFOR. But, although the new tasks were expected to be executed immediately, a considerable amount of time often passed before the required additional troops became available, if ever. This again resulted in an almost permanent imbalance between troops and tasks.

The profusion of Security Council resolutions also made it painfully apparent for all involved, including the warring factions and UNPROFOR itself, that there was no clear political consensus on how to deal with the conflicts in the former Yugoslavia. Subject to strategic ambiguities, UNPROFOR had to muddle through without consistent political guidance or objectives and, because of this, without the necessary political credibility in the eyes of the warring factions.

For UNPROFOR, the hostile conditions put a premium on the ruggedness of the force as such, and on the robustness of the military units assigned. Due to the continued fighting and incessant obstructions by the warring parties, fulfilment of UNPROFOR's mission was hampered by what became an almost prevailing lack of essential operational prerequisites such as freedom of movement and ultimately also freedom of carrying out the UN mandate.

Freedom of movement and freedom of action did not disappear all at once; they were gradually undermined, until the possibility to act or move freely no longer existed. The UN troops were, time and time again, faced with minor infractions or obstructions of a seemingly innocuous nature, which in total, however, undermined the military credibility of the whole force in the eyes of the combatants. The hesitation in using force was partly due to the possible military and political repercussions following the use of force to uphold these important principles. The vulnerability of the troops, which were not altogether configured to operate in a hostile environment, made resolute action difficult and thus also played a role in the gradual 'imprisonment' of the UN forces.

Given the general purpose of the operation, the civil-military relationship was very important. Many organizations and agencies were engaged, requiring military commanders at all levels to set up cooperation arrangements or to participate in different co-ordinating fora. Military as well as civilian and humanitarian organizations had to adapt to this complex situation by working together with civilians from agencies and NGOs. If UNPROFOR did not generally succeed, the positive civil-military cooperation did affect, at least at the local level, the material and human resources of the inhabitants. Emergency aid was successfully distributed to those who needed it. A lot of lives were saved.

UNPROFOR provided a number of valuable lessons learned which appear to be relevant for future peacekeeping operations. Among these, especially three stand out and merit further discussion:

First, a peacekeeping operation should be timely. This implies an ability to react rapidly when a decision is made to launch a new peacekeeping operation, or for that matter to reinforce an existing mission with additional troops. An ability to react promptly presupposes an 'early warning' capability by the UN in order to be able to draw attention to potential trouble spots before an actual crisis builds up or erupts into open conflict.

Second, the strength of the peacekeeping mission should correspond to its mandate and be sufficiently robust in the broadest sense of the word. This implies military units and troops that are well led, trained and equipped; troops that are prepared and motivated to take on what can potentially be a very challenging and perhaps even dangerous task, and a sufficient number of troops to carry out its tasks according to the mandate.

The weaponry available should reflect likely scenarios, and the rules of engagement should be clear and precise and make it possible for the troops to take timely and necessary steps in case of an incident that warrants the use of force to defend UN troops and their mandate against armed attacks. Troop protection and quality-of-life endeavours are equally essential. The deterrent value, and thereby the passive protection – and even in some cases active protection – extended by heavy weapons should not be underestimated. This was clearly demonstrated when the Danish tank squadron that joined UNPROFOR in 1994 was able to ward off the shelling of an observation post near by Tuzla in April 1994 by opening fire on the assailants.

Third, because peacekeeping operations are multi-national in nature, the capability to conduct highly complex peacekeeping operations presupposes a level of prior preparations and training to take place in a multi-national context. The more preparation the better.

UNPROFOR also introduced a number of interesting concepts for peacekeeping. Most prominent among these was the 'protected areas' established in Croatia in 1992 and the 'Safe Areas' established in Bosnia and Herzegovina in 1993. The two names imply that UN troops would guarantee the safety and integrity of the areas and would resist any kind of military action against the areas. This protection never materialized, and seen retrospectively, the concepts appear to have failed. One could also argue, however, that the concepts themselves are not unsound and that the lack of success was due to flawed mandate, resources and implementation. An acute shortage of UN troops capable to implement the Safe Areas was one of the major problems. In Bosnia, the UN troops were eventually not mandated to demilitarize the Safe Areas, and the UN Force Commanders did not receive the ground troops and equipment necessary to protect them. The concept of preventive deployment of UN troops has come out of the Balkan conflicts as a winner. The UN-operation in the Former Yugoslav Republic of Macedonia, first as a part of UNPROFOR and later as an independent mission, has managed to stabilize and turn around a potential critical development in this area from 1993 and onwards. The concept of preventive deployment could be further strengthened by putting into place mechanisms enabling the UN to catch future conflicts in the embryonic stage. Thereby, it may be possible, by the deployment of a preventive force, to forestall a lot of the killing and bloodshed that makes reconciliation in a conflict area virtually impossible afterwards. Such mechanisms include early warning capabilities, appropriate consultation and decision-making mechanisms as well as rapid deployment capabilities.

UNPROFOR was a mission where Command and Control issues became subject of heavy discussions because of the dual-key decision system concerning the NATO-led airsupport. The need for a clear line of Command and Control was therefore yet another lesson learned from UNPROFOR.

Where do we stand today?

In December 1995 the NATO-led Implementation Force (IFOR) took over from UNPROFOR in order to implement the Dayton Agreement. Now IFOR has been replaced by the somewhat smaller Stabilization Force (SFOR). Upon deployment, IFOR comprised some 60,000 personnel and a large number of armoured units, heavy weapons and sophisticated weaponry such as attack helicopters. The contradiction in relying on the lightly-armed UNPROFOR to provide the basis for a durable cease-fire and negotiations about a peace agreement, and then having a war-fighting force implement the peace agreement when a cease-fire has been obtained, is obvious. This view, however, appears to be over-simplified. Instead, one could argue that the deployment of a strong and robust force like IFOR was required in order for the warring parties to overcome the mutual mistrust and embark upon the path to peace.

With IFOR, and now SFOR, the military capabilities deployed in the former Yugoslavia greatly surpasses what UNPROFOR could ever have been brought in a position to muster. This is, however, not an expression of a new set of standards for peacekeeping in terms of capabilities required. There is still a broad scope for peacekeeping operations to be conducted directly under the command of the UN and utilizing forces configured for peacekeeping and not war-fighting.

Initiatives launched

Rapid deployment capability

A substantial amount of time went by from the beginning of the conflict in the former Yugoslavia, and until a peacekeeping force was deployed and in place. Part of the reason for this simply was that only a portion of the troop-contributing nations had troops available immediately after the decision to launch a peacekeeping operation was made in the Security Council. The slow reaction was a contributing factor to the loss of momentum in the peace process. Only in the former Yugoslavian Republic of Macedonia was a relatively small force deployed in a timely way and thus succeeded in preventing this conflict from spreading.

For a number of years, actually since the Secretary-General's *Agenda for Peace* from 1992, the UN has tried to make the organization capable of deploying UN troops rapidly to potential conflict areas, thereby being able to contribute actively to prevent conflicts from arising or escalating. Consequently, the UN established a pool of military units and other resources available for peacekeeping operations at high readiness, to which member countries can enrol force contributions, the so-called UN Stand-by Forces Arrangements. However, the stand-by arrangements system has so far not reached the intended operational level.

In his *Supplement to an Agenda for Peace* from January 1995, the Secretary-General recommends that the UN should consider the idea of a rapid deployment force. In the Spring of 1995, Denmark and a number of other countries with similar experience in peacekeeping operations met in a working group to discuss the possibility jointly to establish a high readiness brigade. In a report from August 1995, the working group concluded that it would be possible to establish a high readiness brigade for peacekeeping operations within the framework of the UN Stand-by Forces system. When established, such a brigade could be used for rapid deployment with 15 to 30 days' notice. The force should be stationed in a crisis area only for a period of up to six months, after which an 'ordinary' peacekeeping force could be deployed to take over if necessary. The decision to take part in actual operations can still be made at the national level – but more rapidly because the basic work has already been done.

It has been decided to move the project forward, and the brigade, which is called the Multinational UN Stand-by Forces High Readiness Brigade or SHIRBRIG for short, is expected to be operational by 1999. In the Spring of 1997, a small planning staff for the brigade was established in Denmark. The planning staff will consist of a few officers from each of the participating countries, and the staff will prepare joint procedures and carry out minor training exercises. The troops will be stationed in their own countries, but they will be trained according to the same basic procedures and standards. This will help create a joint understanding between different units and soldiers, ensuring both a rapid deployment capability and improved operational proficiency within realistic economical limits. A Contact Committee will be established in New York in order to provide information promptly on possible missions. The basis for the political decision on deployment will then be available at a very early stage.

Besides the SHIRBRIG initiative, a Rapid Deployable Mission Headquarters (RDMHQ) concept has been developed on a Canadian initiative. Initially this was done among a group of countries called 'Friends of Rapid Reaction' and later within the UN. The idea is that the UN at mission level should have at its disposal a headquarters unit, which could be immediately activated. In 1997, a permanent element consisting of eight officers was set up in the UN headquarters. This element will in case of activation be augmented by personnel within the UN Secretariat as well as personnel provided beforehand by supporting countries.

Together with SHIRBRIG, a preplanned mission headquarters at a high readiness will improve the UN's ability to respond quickly. An early response to an emerging crisis is necessary to avoid human suffering and could be accomplished efficiently with less troops than would be needed (and could often not be available) to contain or even stop a fully developed conflict.

More peacekeepers

The three Baltic states regained their independence in 1991 and they had to build up their defence forces from almost nothing. Since they were very keen on participating in peacekeeping operations, they realized that if they should contribute to the UN peacekeeping with a substantial force, it was necessary for them to co-operate in setting up a battalion-sized unit. Therefore Estonia, Latvia and Lithuania in 1993 decided to establish a joint Baltic peacekeeping battalion. Together with the United Kingdom, the Nordic countries in 1994 in a Memorandum of Understanding committed themselves to support the battalion. Later the US, the Netherlands, Germany and France joined. The supporting states have provided the battalion with peacekeeping training and equipment before its actual deployment to UN peacekeeping missions.

This work is complemented by bilateral co-operation between different countries and the three Baltic states. For the time being, a Lithuanian company is deployed as a part of a Danish battalion in the NATO-led Stabilization Force in Bosnia. The lessons learned from this arrangement are very positive. It shows that under certain circumstances, depending on the overall situation in the mission area, it is possible to mix troops of different nationality even within battalions. However, it demands thorough preparation and training. After this posting, the company will have completed its training and will be ready to be a part of the joint Baltic battalion, the so-called BALTBAT. It is planned that the battalion will be fully operational in 1998. This is a unique example of a regional co-operation in the field of peacekeeping between small countries, which well might serve as a source of inspiration for other regions.

Training of peacekeepers

The multifunctional peacekeeping operations have put great emphasis on the training of the peacekeepers. The need for supplementary training and specialists is obvious and the high degree of multi-nationality as seen in the former Yugoslavia calls for standardized training. Common standards will help improve the soldiers' ability to work together, thereby increasing both the efficiency and the safety of the troops. It should also be taken into account that an overall common attitude and approach to solve the different problems in the mission area will give the forces higher credibility.

The work in the UN and the NACC/PfP to develop common training standards is therefore highly appreciated and needed. Training of specialists in peacekeeping operations along with the ordinary training is a huge task involving many resources. The Nordic countries have a long tradition of sharing this burden. With the establishment of a Clearing-house in Denmark, a catalogue of available peacekeeping training courses is distributed to all the NACC/PfP countries, thus providing the opportunity to share the overall burden of preparing for peacekeeping operations. Other countries outside of Europe also benefit from the Nordic courses. For instance Denmark and the other Nordic countries are supporting efforts in the Southern African Development Community (SADC) to create their own peacekeeping capacity.

The Nordic co-operation on peacekeeping matters is constantly being updated. At the moment, ways to further develop the Nordic co-operation on peacekeeping have been agreed upon. Training is one of the main issues.

Future challenges

The UNPROFOR operation provided us with some valuable lessons learned for future peacekeeping operations. These lessons were drawn upon when preparing the ongoing IFOR/SFOR operation in Bosnia. And these lessons should be drawn upon when forming future peacekeeping policy. Ideally, the UN as the overarching impartial world-wide organization should be responsible for carrying out global conflict resolution over the entire spectrum of peacekeeping operations. In reality, however, the UN has neither the capability nor the resources to do so. The limitations in the UN's capabilities are particularly pronounced in the most complex military operations. These kinds of operations will, in many cases, have to be carried out by proxy, on a UN mandate – like the present NATO-led Stabilization Force in Bosnia.

I have mentioned some of the initiatives – in which Danish defence is involved – aimed at providing the UN with a better capability of dealing with peacekeeping operations. Rapid deployment is a key capability in preventing a crisis from developing or escalating. The current endeavours to establish a Rapid Deployable Headquarters Element in the Department of Peacekeeping Operations (DPKO) at UN Headquarters in New York complements the multi-national UN Stand-By Forces High Readiness Brigade that we are establishing with a number of other countries. Other efforts to strengthening the DPKO should be made. The financial situation of the UN, however, sets out certain limitations.

An obvious area to further develop in order to improve the conditions for future UN peacekeeping operations is the conceptual area. The increasing complexity and scale of peacekeeping operations combined with the UN's dire economic situation dictate that proxies will have to be used.

In my view, this stresses the clear need to set out an overall political-military framework covering the key aspects of the international peace support operations, including the new so-called multifunctional or wider features. This should be done under the auspices of the UN. The framework should provide a comprehensive strategy for conflict resolution comprising the whole string of measures from diplomatic and economic measures, preventive deployment, peacekeeping, possible peace enforcement, and post-conflict nation-building. And it should provide a clear picture of the division of labour between the different players involved in its implementation. Hereby an all-encompassing package would be planned for a conflict area.

Below the level of the overall strategy, the UN should continue trying to develop a peacekeeping doctrine as its tool to ensure that peacekeeping operations are conducted in accordance with the principles and purposes of the UN – no matter whether the peacekeepers take part in a UN-led mission or a mission led by a proxy.

19 Lessons Learned for the OSCE

Options of a Regional Organization to De-escalate a Civil War-like Conflict

MAX VAN DER STOEL[*]

Introduction

Yugoslavia, Nagorny-Karabakh, Abkhazia, Chechnya – these and other cases show that conflict can take place not only between states but also within states. Intra-state conflicts are nowadays a more important threat to peace and security than purely international tensions. These internal wars have the potential to destroy Europe, if not its body then at least its soul. Who can forget the images coming out of Bosnia, just one year ago? There are situations in Europe with such an explosive potential that a whole region may come aflame and be destroyed.

After the Cold War, we failed to recognize that the dictatorship established in the name of communism had only hidden, not eradicated, internal and international tensions in central and eastern Europe and their destructive aspect. The ensuing disputes and conflicts were not anticipated by the international community, and it did not know how to prevent them.

This, however, is not the entire story. Although it sometimes seems as if all of Europe is a battlefield, we should realize that there are many regions where tensions have not turned violent. Although, in some of these cases violent conflict is already smouldering, they must and can be prevented from bursting into flames.

However, one aspect should be very clear: states must have an open eye for longer-term developments with a view to anticipating future crises and not only pay attention to already existing conflicts. The success of preventive diplomacy ultimately depends on the concrete political and other support they are prepared to invest in it. Of course alarmism and precipitate actions have to be avoided. But it is never too early for a realistic

---

[*] Max van der Stoel (NL) is OSCE High Commissioner on National Minorities.

assessment of worrisome developments. If we devote our attention only to the wars of today, we will have reasons to mourn again tomorrow.

In spite of this clear need for early responses, one cannot escape the impression that individual states or the international community as a whole are rather slow in their reactions. Probably the Foreign Ministries have the necessary information at their disposal and they employ competent analysts who know to assess it. But do their reports and analyses get the necessary attention at the decision-making levels in time? One gets the impression that this is not always the case. Equally, it appears that the states as a group are not always able to come sufficiently quickly to effective decisions.

Roots of ethnic tensions

As OSCE High Commissioner on National Minorities, I am specifically mandated to work towards the prevention of ethnic tensions. Such tensions can lead to immense violence as we have seen in Yugoslavia and elsewhere. Indeed, it is my impression that most if not all of Europe's current and potential conflicts have, at least in part, an inter-ethnic dimension.

At this point, I should emphasize the political nature of many of these conflicts. Most of them are not 'natural' or 'inevitable' occurrences but are the result of extremist politics including radical nationalism. In an increasingly polarized environment, extremists can more easily gain support. Moderates may be forced aside or will adopt more radical positions to avoid that happening. Thus, the threat of violence may quickly grow. One of the aspects of conflict prevention, then, is to prevent radicals from gaining the upper hand. These radicals are a relatively small group and we should not equal them and their behaviour with the entire group which they purport to represent.

If radical groups, religious, ethnic or other, do seem to acquire a certain following among the population, one should ask why they have success. More often than not, the root causes of radicalisation trends lie within states, and they may have many facets.

Issues concerning human rights, democracy and the rule of law are often critical components. Violations of human rights often lead to tensions, to societal conflicts and distrust, including at the international level. Especially if large groups such as minorities are affected, the stability of states or even a region may be at risk and kin-states may become involved.

Economic factors matter, too can play an important role. At present, quite a number of European states are engaged in a process of transforming their economic order from command economies to free-market economies.

However, in some countries economic developments have taken a sharp downward turn which may lead to social tensions and people may become more open to authoritarian and even xenophobic influences. Even if economic factors in themselves are not the direct cause of tensions, they will often exacerbate matters.

Moreover, for these and other reasons states may feel insecure, both in their international relations and domestically. Bad memories of past inequities, real or imagined, often play a role as well.

Political options

Finally, even if the threat of a large-scale military conflict in Europe has receded considerably, the military factor is still of great importance. International arms control and the continued use and improvement of the regimes of military transparency remain essential.

Effective conflict prevention requires that all these aspects be taken into account, involving various time frames. Short-term conflict prevention aims at the prevention or containment of an immediate development towards escalation. The durable prevention of conflict in Europe, however, requires a long-term perspective, involving *inter alia* building a viable democracy and its institutions, structuring the protection and promotion of human rights and respect for minorities. It also requires the peaceful transition from a rigid state-commanded economic order to a flexible market-oriented system.

Effective conflict prevention requires international assistance in many of these areas. Undeniably, it is the individual states themselves which carry primary responsibility for the processes on their territory, including the economic one. At the same time international assistance is essential. Expertise, financial help and political support may all be necessary.

Military options

In the context of a project on peacekeeping, one cannot avoid briefly addressing the question of possible military options. Military measures are politically and psychologically in a category different from other conflict-preventive activities. The case of former Yugoslavia is quite illustrative of the possibilities and limitations of such measures. One could add the case of Rwanda. Above all, we should realize that it is states which decide whether and to what extent such measures may be used and not international organizations.

Military limits. The coercive use of military force will often prove not to be a viable option. The Gulf War was obviously an exception. Peace enforcement therefore appears improbable, at least for the foreseeable future. Peacekeeping operations, although more of an acceptable option, also know many restrictions and can only be effective under very particular circumstances. At any rate, they do not contribute to solving the tensions at hand but can only provide a breathing space for parties. If parties are not interested in reaching a settlement, peacekeeping operations cannot be a substitute for that.

Preventive peacekeeping. A few words to the possibility of preventive deployment, of which the deployment of foreign troops in the Former Yugoslav Republic of Macedonia is the prime example in Europe. Preventive deployment involves the positioning of troops, military observers and related personnel between parties to a dispute or where there is an escalation towards conflict. It has the primary aim of deterring the escalation of such situations into armed conflict. A related task will be the performance of monitoring functions. How credible preventive deployment as a deterrent is, will depend essentially on the perceived likelihood in practice of a strong international reaction if there is any resort to violence by one of the parties.

Preventive deployment should not be lightly considered. It belongs to a category quite different from preventive diplomacy. However in certain circumstances it may be the only effective method to keep an already unstable situation from deteriorating into war. Still, preventive deployment in itself is not enough to defuse tension, let alone address the underlying issues. It should be part of a comprehensive preventive diplomacy strategy to contain and resolve a dispute.

Role of the OSCE

Many-faceted as the problems are, they need a plurality of answers and many different instruments may be of use in addressing them. To which organizations should we look to provide us with these instruments? Organizations like NATO, the Council of Europe, the European Union and the OSCE all have their specific characteristics, each with its own aims and its own competencies and means. Whether or not their strengths are used depends almost exclusively on their member states.

As the High Commissioner on National Minorities is an institution of the Organization for Security and Co-operation in Europe (OSCE), *I* would like to concentrate on the possible role of the OSCE. The OSCE combines a broad membership with a comprehensive approach to security, and an emphasis on co-operative implementation of its political norms and activities with a large degree of institutional flexibility. Arguably, it is best placed to concentrate on conflict prevention in the wide sense.

In the past few years, we have already witnessed the increasing role the organization is playing in this regard. Furthermore, the OSCE should also deal with conflict prevention through peace-building in post-conflict situations, such as in Bosnia-Herzegovina. Even if violence has come to an end, very often the underlying causes which led to the conflict have not been removed. Such 'post-conflict conflict prevention' will of course, have to be fully integrated in and co-ordinated with a more general strategy of peace-building which is required in post-conflict societies.

20 Experiences from UNPROFOR – UNCIVPOL

HALVOR A. HARTZ [*]

Introduction

Experience gained when starting up a mission

With reference to the opening of the UNPROFOR mission in March 1992, we experienced a few basic problems. Many police monitors being brought into the mission area were incapable of gaining an initial foothold due to:

- Lack of basic knowledge of the mission language (English)
- Little or no knowledge of the conflict itself
- Little or no briefing received in the mission area before they were deployed into their specific areas
- Complete absence of SOP (Standard Operational Procedures) from the UN describing how to set up and start an initial monitoring mission in a hostile or war-torn area
- No knowledge of how to perform the most basic monitoring
- Little or no information on the local police structure and judicial system
- The lack of logistics of all kinds
- Lacking basic experience in driving motor vehicles.

A quality review made in UNPROFOR in 1992 showed that 48 per cent of incoming monitors did not speak English, and 43 per cent were not able to handle a vehicle. After many expensive repatriations, the situation improved somewhat. However, this is still one of the main problems in the missions and hampers the operations.

---

[*] Halvor Hartz is UN Co-ordinator in the Norwegian Ministry of Justice. He served as CivPol Chief of Staff UNPROFOR in 1994/1995.

311

During events like this, it is easy to discover how the different police forces are organized and trained throughout the world. In some police forces, one will find members trained and allowed by their system to undertake command initiative and responsibilities above and beyond their ranks; others must wait for orders from their superiors.

Working in an operation like this, one has to be aware the fact that police forces of the world sometimes only have the name 'Police' in common.

Another fact that everybody should bear in mind is that the police monitors deployed into the mission are not monitors by profession, but police officers.

It is to be expected that they do not know their new task, and that some information has to be provided. This applies every time new monitors arrive in the mission area.

Administrative support from the UN system was not in place when the mission started up. There was a lack of vehicles, communications, computers, contracts, finance, maintenance, etc. Even the command structure was built up in the field, after the deployment. Given that there is no international ranking system for the police, this task created a lot of additional difficulties in a very crucial period of a mission just starting up.

Despite all the experience gained in CIVPOL during the earlier phase of the missions in former Yugoslavia, I still see the same mistakes being made over again. When new mandates are given and new areas are to be monitored, the UN and the mission management have not been able to obtain advantages from lessons learned. The focus is solely on the specific number of police monitors which is suggested for each of the missions. Very little attention is paid to the qualifications of the monitors.

First a vast number of monitors are deployed, then the command structure is built. Finally, logistics and support arrive. Because of the emphases on the number of monitors more than on their quality, skilled monitors must spend their time organizing, training and watching unqualified monitors, rather than working with local police.

When CIVPOL was given a specific task, it was of utmost importance to put in place an overall command and control structure that would work. But only the head of the CIVPOL unit, the Police Commissioner, was appointed by UNNY, allowing him to select his senior staff. Today, 1997, this privilege has been taken away, and the commissioner of the International Police Task Force (IPTF) has senior officers appointed by UNNY, where the national balance is the overriding concern. Unfortunately, prior UN mission experience is not compulsory for CIVPOL senior staff officers.

Too often the monitors who arrived were recruited from police forces which are educated and trained on a level that could not be compared with those being monitored. The mission can only succeed if local police feel they are being monitored by police officers of their own standard or above.

General experience

Personnel. General qualifications are laid down by UNNY with reference to police officers. Unfortunately, some countries are supplying missions with personnel who do not meet the requirements; I believe the system is about to initiate some action to improve this situation.

A Training Unit that has been established in the mission area, which certainly is an improvement. It provides a one week induction programme for incoming monitors.

As mentioned earlier, the police officers coming to the mission area are not monitors, but police officers. That is a great difference. The incoming personnel have to be taught the fundamentals of their new role on site. The DPKO is working hard on developing standard training programmes, and to make them available for the contributing nations.

I will also touch on the inter-racial as well as the inter-cultural aspect. I experienced little, if any, tension related to these factors. Boiled down to the basics, people from around the world are not that different. I also feel that there does, under circumstances like UNPROFOR, exist a feeling of an international police-officer community.

It is important to avoid sending unqualified personnel to the mission area. There is a mental stress in being repatriated, and repatriation represents unnecessary costs to the UN and the home country.

Information. It is of paramount importance that the mandate for CIVPOL is known to the local population as well as the local police, at all levels. It has been my experience that, in conflict areas, the population is misinformed, and one can not rely on the information sources controlled by the warring factions. In UNPROFOR, the UN Press and Information Unit managed to some extent to inform the international press, but failed, despite many good efforts, to inform the local population. The reason for this was that the UN went into the mission without a formally signed agreement with the parties to the conflict, an agreement which could have stated that the UN was granted access to specified frequencies for radio and TV transmissions.

Operations. The Cyrus Vance Plan stated 'The CIVPOL is to be collocated with the local police'. The fact is that, in any mission, the UNCIVPOL will without any doubt be greatly outnumbered by the local police. What sort of collocation we are looking at, depends on the situation.

It is, however, necessary to establish a close and daily (frequent), contact with the key persons of the force we are to monitor and preferably on a personal basis. We rely heavily on relationships built on confidence. We must never forget to consider what it is, and how it feels, to be monitored. Therefore, our presence must be a balance between efficiency and understanding for the force monitored. In my opinion, it is time to look at our organization with this in mind.

Traditionally, CIVPOL has been organized with a centralised HQ, and with decentralised elements of sectors, down to station level with all known components. This organization works, but the question is how efficiently.

After the war in May and August 1995 in Croatia, forming teams was tried out, but with the continuation of a central HQ as well as sector HQ. By organizing the duty in teams, we could cover a bigger area, and the tasks became more challenging and interesting for the teams. We could do more with less personnel than we had been able to so far. CIVPOL could more or less do away with the traditional station and its staff functions. However, doing this requires monitors with a level of experience above the average of the current monitor of today.

The model now being used in UNTAES is very interesting. A CIVPOL monitor is present at all times at the local police station. This monitor is able to find out what is happening in this district, and is, via radio, able to direct CIVPOL patrols directly to the scene. This procedure became possible due to the stronger mandate imposed on the parties as a result of the Erdut/Dayton Agreement on Eastern Slavonia.

As long as CIVPOL does not execute police power, its personnel must remain unarmed. I have noticed some doubts about this issue among colleagues coming for the first time to a CIVPOL mission. However, at the end of their duty, the CIVPOL officers share the understanding that our best protection is that we are unarmed.

Violations of human rights, in particular those being committed by the law enforcement agencies that CIVPOL is monitoring, must be the overriding concern for the CIVPOL monitor at all times. This is the main reason why CIVPOL should be present in the mission area in the first place. Unfortunately, there is a lack of understanding of this mandate within the CIVPOL organization, as well as in the management of the missions. For the monitor, it can be difficult to stand up against local officials. Much too often, I saw monitors busy doing the comfortable part of the mandate, distributing humanitarian aid, instead of sitting on the backs of the local police.

As the UNPROFOR mission went on, CIVPOL as well as the other UN agencies, experienced 'creeping mandates'. As a result of UN Security Council resolutions, bilateral agreements, or interpretation of the mandates, additional tasks were given to CIVPOL. CIVPOL found themselves doing several kinds of investigations and executive police work. By doing so, they interfered with the local authorities, leaving both them and the contending sides in the conflict to criticise CIVPOL's work.

One should bear in mind that, at all times, it is the responsibility of the local authorities to do proper police work within their own legislation and within international minimum standards. The moment CIVPOL leaves the monitoring role and starts to operate as police, they let the local law enforcement agencies off the hook. The UN must leave them on the 'hook' with their responsibilities, and monitor, guide and report their behaviour.

Another experience gained was that, while CIVPOL was continually changing its personnel, the local police forces more or less remained the same. In the monitoring process, the local force gained experience all the time, whilst the incoming CIVPOL personnel have to gain their experience during their tour of duty, leaving the local police force with the upper hand.

I do not recommend that the forces should mix in the performing of their daily duties. CIVPOL is initially looked upon as an outside, objective force, and should remain so. The opposing sides will always use any given opportunity to discredit the UN force.

Logistics. The logistical situation appeared to be adequate, as time passed by. There will of course always be a need for vehicles, but it seemed like we survived in spite of accidents, as well as a very high rate of hijackings. It was a problem, however, that around 30 per cent of the assigned vehicles were out of order all the time. The main reason for this was that the UN was not able to pay the companies that supplied our workshops with spare parts. Consequently, the vehicle fleet became more and more worn out. CIVPOL was supplied with computers, not the latest models or programs, but they were functional.

However, the main problems are not so much in the logistical system, but on the human resource side.

Recommendations

Personnel. UNNY must continue to issue common training programmes for UN Police Monitors, distribute them to the personnel-contributing nations, and require that all monitors be trained according to these programmes in their home countries prior to departure for any mission. A mission-specific induction programme must be given immediately after arrival in the mission area.

Prior to departure from their respective home countries, monitors should be tested in the English language and in driving skills. Today, DPKO provides Selection Assistance Teams to contributors with large contingents. This has saved a lot of expenses, avoiding unnecessary repatriations.

Personnel should be accepted only from forces which are of a professional standard, equal to or above the force which is going to be monitored. In order to also ensure the quality of the monitors with respect to their past records, only police officers recruited by authorities of the contributing country should be accepted. If the requested numbers of monitors cannot be reached applying this criteria, one should seriously consider keeping the number down instead of increasing it with monitors who will have problems with fulfilling their tasks.

When UNNY asks for police officers, it should also include ranks and qualifications of some kind, in order to obtain at least some qualified seniors.

Press and information. The optimal solution would be that the UN backs up their forces with a well-orchestrated information strategy conducted by professional press people who are able to spread information throughout the mission area using television, radio, leaflets, etc.

CIVPOL must, at an early stage of the mission, be able to hand out leaflets in the local language explaining the mandate of CIVPOL. It is of the utmost importance that the CIVPOL mandate is understood by all the agencies involved, the parties to the conflict, and the local population, enabling realistic expectations to be met about CIVPOL's work.

Operations

The CIVPOL commissioner must report directly to the SRSG (Head of Mission) and never be under operational command or control of the Force Commander, Head of Civil Affairs, or anyone else.

DPKO should plan for new missions by appointing a professional and experienced Advance and Advice Team and keep it 'on stock'. This team should contain an experienced Police Commissioner, Deputy, Chief of Staff, and a handful of senior staff officers and region commanders. They should have for their support a number of UN civilian international staff members, tasked to provide initial logistic and administrative support. This team should be first in, kick-start the mission, act as consultants to the regular CIVPOL force, and withdraw after a few months.

Logistics and support. It is recommended that CIVPOL be provided with an independent communication system, so they do not find themselves in the situation where they have to rely on local communication systems or UN-military. Satellite telephones and VHF radios are 'musts' and crucial factors for success.

It is necessary with a certain basic supply in order to fulfil the most basic functions. A stationary box (e.g. small container) equipped with lap-top computers, paper, envelopes, etc. should be designed, kept in stock, and made available for the team that is first in.

Endnote. The DPKO, through its CIVPOL Unit, Training Unit and the Lesson Learned Unit, has lately made tremendous efforts to improve the situation described in my lecture. Having worked closely with these units mentioned throughout the last two years, my experience was that the diagnosis made in UNNY was correct. DPKO was aware of the problems and the bottlenecks. They are today trying to provide the right medicine. One of their major problems is that they receive more requests for seminars and more academic interest from the world society than practical support. It is of paramount importance that the contributing nations be willing to give their full support to peacekeeping operations in general and to the important peacebuilding element of CIVPOL in particular.

21 UN Military Observers' Role in De-escalation of Local Conflict

Lessons Learned from a Soldier's Perspective

SØREN BO HUSUM[*]

Introduction

UNMOs – the nature of our task

As there was no general peace to keep in the former Yugoslavia, our tasks in this peacekeeping mission had to be adjusted according to the actual situation, which could vary a lot from areas where a cease-fire was in effect to areas ravaged by war. Although sometimes our assignments were ordered and specific, on many occasions, it was left to our own imagination and judgement to create suitable tasks on the spot. These could be of both military and civilian origin, all depending on the situation in the area we were stationed. One duty we always carried out, however, was patrolling of the different front-line areas, in order to stay informed on the situation.

In this article I describe four assignments carried out by UNMOs as follows:

- UNMOs as the eyes and ears of the UN

- UNMOs as mediators between the warring parties

- UNMOs as confidence builders for the local population

- UNMOs as actors against atrocities.

---

[*] Søren Bo Husum is a captain in the Danish army. He served in former Yugoslavia as UN Military Observer (UNMO) in 1993/94. He was deployed in Mostar, southern Croatia, the Medak Pocket in Serb-Krajina (Croatia) and the Bihac Pocket.

These tasks are illustrated by practical examples showing how important it was that each and every UNMO tried to adjust quickly to a new and sometimes grotesque situation. Flexibility, imagination, patience, self-control and courage were qualities needed to be a good UNMO in the former Yugoslavia.

The daily life of an UNMO was in addition greatly affected by the constant dangers of being exposed to mines and the effect of well-organized propaganda blaming and discrediting the UN. This latter subject is covered in chapter 15 of this book.

UNMOs as the eyes and ears of the UN

Because UNMOs were unarmed and worked in small teams of two to four officers, we were not considered as 'threatening' to any party. This often made it possible to be present in very tense situations, observing and reporting what was going on. We could be considered as the forward eyes and ears of the UN.

The Medak Pocket in Serb-Krajina (Croatia) – Autumn 1993

The war that took place in Croatia in 1993 was, with the exemption of incidents such as the attack on the Medak Pocket, fought with long-range artillery cannons. I use the term 'war' deliberately knowing that a peace agreement did actually exist. But being there made it quite obvious that even though the front-line hardly moved, this peace was worth very little in reality. Hostilities certainly still existed.

In September 1993, the Croatian army conquered a small Serb-held 'pocket' (called the Medak Pocket) in the Krajina area. After international pressure and intense negotiations, the Croatian Government agreed to let UN forces take control of the area.

The whole operation took place in a very tense, hostile environment. The Canadian UN soldiers whose mission it was to take control of the pocket were often provoked by Croatian soldiers who, on numerous occasions, tried to delay the takeover through such means as shooting and blocking the roads with tanks. The Canadians, on the other hand, pushed constantly forward, especially after it was found out that the Croats destroyed everything they left behind. There were numerous situations in which the Croats and the Canadians were very close to getting into actual combat.

Reconnaissance prior to the deployment of Canadian UN soldiers in a new area was vital, but for them to do it themselves – armed and behind the Croatian lines – was not possible because of the tense situation. We – the

UNMOs – were therefore in this operation tasked as liaison and reconnaissance teams, which meant that we went into the area to find suitable positions from which the area could be controlled and to then give a 'green light' to the Canadians after having made sure that the Croats were not present. We could complete the reconnaissance for the Canadians without making the Croats feel that their authority was being threatened. I feel certain that the presence of UNMOs in this operation prevented both Croatian and Canadian lives from being lost.

Unfortunately – as a result of our reconnaissance – we were often the first witnesses to the massive Croatian destruction of Serb property that took place. Altogether, in the areas I was deployed, more than 300 houses and barns were destroyed or burned. And worse than that, some civilian Serbs who did not escape in time were found dead, some of them had been assaulted.

The Bihac Pocket – Winter 1993/94

In the Autumn of 1993, Fikret Abdic, a Muslim member of the Bosnian presidential council who disagreed with President Izetbegovic about the terms of making peace with the Serbs and Croats, had declared the Bihac Pocket for the 'Autonomous Province of Western Bosnia'. A part of the 5th Corps of the 'Armija BiH' (the official army of Bosnia-Herzegovina) supported him, while the majority stayed loyal to the government in Sarajevo. Fighting broke out and soon, an internal front-line between the two Muslim factions was a reality. Fighting soon became fierce, often taking place in and around small villages, trapping civilians in between.

We UNMOs were located on both sides of the internal front-line. One of our tasks was to patrol areas of fighting on a daily basis. It was expected of us that at any moment we would be able to give an updated description of the situation in our area of responsibility. By observing from near or far, talking to commanders, soldiers and locals, we soon got a solid perception of what was going on in the area. The parties knew we patrolled on a regular basis searching for information from various sources.

Both parties very often complained about the bad treatment of the civilian population by the other side. Accusations of using civilians as 'human shields' and other atrocities were numerous, making it difficult for us to investigate these incidents and meaning that we had to go to the forward line, jeopardizing our own security.

I especially remember one incident of this kind. The higher command of Abdic's side complained that a unit from the 5th Corps had infiltrated their lines during the night, attacked a small village at dawn and withdrawn, taking civilians as hostages. We were asked to go there in order to confirm the information. While approaching the village, said to be 2–3 kilometres behind the front-line, I suddenly saw soldiers in trenches and seconds after, civilians taking cover. Shortly after we heard projectiles hitting the ground and houses around us and we then realized that we were not 2–3 kilometres behind the front-line, but at the front-line itself, caught in a crossfire together with many civilians. We took cover behind a steep rise in the middle of the village, but it did little to help as mortar grenades started to explode around us. We were caught in that village for one hour before we were able to get out without having had a chance to confirm the information given to us. This incident made it quite clear to us that we had to take our own security into consideration as an important factor when approaching the front-line. So, even though we were expected by our authorities to be up-to-date on the situation, we had to accept that there was also a limit to where we could go or what we could see.

Having said that, it is on the other hand important to stress that we actually did see a lot that would otherwise not have been noticed by anyone from the outside world. As an example, I remember a visit to the village of Buzim, which was the home-base of one of the brigades on the 5th Corps side. This brigade was notorious for treating its prisoners poorly and at the same time it was very reluctant to corporate with the UN. Once we had visited the village, we witnessed two soldiers beating up another soldier in front of the prisoner cellblock. When they saw us they became very embarrassed and put a lot of effort into explaining to us that he was just one of their own who had been drunk and insulted a woman. They of course knew that we didn't believe them, that we would report what we saw and that we would be back to check on them another day. Shortly after, we were allowed access to the prisoner cellblock in order to see for ourselves that prisoners were not beaten on a regular basis. We were however still not impressed by the way they treated their prisoners.

I remember another incident in which we acted as forward representatives of the UN and found ourselves right on the spot. During a morning patrol, we talked to a local commander who informed us that the village of Todorovo had been attacked earlier that morning. Todorovo was not on our schedule for that day but we quickly changed our patrol plan and went straight to the village. While approaching the area, we realized that something was definitely wrong. Straggling groups of women, children and old people were on the road, bent under the weight of bags, sacks and miscellaneous items from their homes. But not only people from the village itself were on the run. People from the whole area were trying to escape in case the attack went into their neighbourhood. As fighting was still fierce, we had to observe from a high spot just outside the village and via the radio, we kept our HQ informed of what was going on.

Fighting went on for weeks with Abdic's forces trying unsuccessfully to recapture the village.

UNMOs as mediators between the warring parties

The presence of UNMOs alone did not in general reduce hostilities. But by being present, we not only encouraged the conflicting parties to co-operate with the UN, we were also sometimes able to calm down the situation and make the parties talk to each other.

Mostar – Summer 1993

In the city of Mostar in southern Bosnia-Herzegovina, heavy fighting between the former allied Muslims and Croats had broken out in May, 1993. A front-line, following more or less the Neretva River, divided the city into two parts leaving some 35,000 Muslims on the eastern bank besieged on all sides and regularly bombarded from the gun positions on the hilltops surrounding the city. The situation on the eastern bank, an area not bigger than 6 square kilometres, became more and more desperate, as the Muslims did not have any running water, electricity, medical care or enough food.

UNPROFOR initiated a local peace plan to put an end to the fighting and start negotiations. Both parties agreed to negotiate and our Senior Military Observer (called SMO, head of the UNMOs in a Sector) was appointed as chairman of the 'Joint Commission Committee' as it was called.

For three weeks, the SMO carried out tough daily negotiations assisted by us, the regular UNMOs, whose duty it was to report on the situation at the front-line. It was obvious from the beginning that both parties, especially the Croats, had not gone into the negotiations wholeheartedly. They saw Mostar as the capital of their republic of 'Herceg-Bosna' which they were unwilling to share with the Muslims. It therefore seemed that both parties had made up their minds to find a solution on the battlefield. Nevertheless, we kept trying to bring them together, in order to at least keep the hope of local peace alive. At the same time, chairing the committee gave the SMO and thereby the UN authority in the city. As long as the negotiations went on, we couldn't be avoided.

Unfortunately, we did not succeed in establishing a lasting cease-fire as we had hoped. There was simply too little will to achieve a peaceful solution to the disagreements. Fighting intensified, and after three weeks, negotiations ended.

It can as a result be asked: 'Wasn't it meaningless to keep persuading the parties to negotiate for three weeks when it ended in failure?' In my opinion, absolutely not! We kept the possibility of a local peace alive for three weeks, which is far better than giving up on it beforehand. These weeks taught me to accept that in the former Yugoslavia, you had to value partial success, and this lesson I kept in mind the rest of my tour.

After the breakdown in negotiations we, the local UNMO team, continued to held daily meetings with both parties. In this second phase of our presence in Mostar our task was more or less just to keep our headquarters informed about the situation in the city. But the daily meetings meant that we remained a factor in Mostar in case of sudden changes in the situation.

The Bihac Pocket – Winter 1993/94

After Abdic had declared the Bihac Pocket autonomous, he made a separate peace with the Krajina-Serbs, the Bosnian Serbs and the Bosnian Croats. This agreement made it possible, among other things, to transport all kinds of goods from Croatia via Krajina into the besieged pocket. Abdic was even supported by Bosnian-Serbian artillery in the internal war.

One of the major problems Abdic tried to solve right after the peace agreement was that of Bosanska Bojna, a small area in the northern part of the pocket where the Serb majority had been expelled at the beginning of the war. In April 1993, these Serbs, heavily supported by the Krajina-Serb army, recaptured the area. For the months to follow, this area remained a major problem in the otherwise relatively peaceful relationship between the Muslims and the Krajina-Serbs. The peace agreement made Bosanska Bojna a demilitarized zone (DMZ) controlled by French UN soldiers. It didn't work out well. Among other problems, the Serbs violated the agreement by carrying weapons in the area. Abdic didn't have the power to stop this violation and the French didn't have the will to do it by force.

Instead, a UN-initiated commission was established to solve the problem by negotiations. This commission was headed by a UN general who was chief of Sector North in Croatia. The UNMOs attended these meetings as observers. In between the meetings, daily problems arose, jeopardizing the fragile local peace. In this context, the UNMOs played an important role. We could, and did, take immediate action in resolving conflicts as soon as they arose by clarifying what was sometimes only a misunderstanding, or persuade the parties to meet at a local level. Although this daily work didn't solve any of the overall problems, it reduced some of the tension. By offering our assistance when needed any time of day, we furthermore gained considerable respect as representatives of the UN. It was quite obvious that they appreciated our presence.

At the internal front-line, several attempts were also made to arrange a meeting between the parties. Both parties were, however, quite inflexible in this respect. Abdic would only agree to negotiate directly with Izetbegovic, who on the other hand demanded that Abdic negotiate with the commander of the 5th corps of 'Armija BiH'. We also tried several times to arrange local cease-fires in order to evacuate civilians or calm the situation. But our efforts were 'grounded' because of the lack of will from both sides. One example remains especially clear in my mind. The Abdic supreme command had for weeks asked us to arrange a cease-fire for the internal front-line. We tried more than once without luck. The 5th Corps commanders were reluctant, according to Abdic, because they wanted only a military solution. Then, by a stroke of luck, the Corps command suddenly proposed an overall cease-fire themselves. This offer was at once forwarded to the Abdic command, which seemed to be pleased. But, to our great surprise and disappointment, Abdic personally refused to accept the cease-fire. Only a local one for Todorovo (where he was in trouble!) could be agreed and only until women and children had been evacuated. We tried through all means possible to convince Abdic of the fact that this was his only opportunity to establish peace, but our efforts proved unsuccessful. It was then that we found out that Abdic was just as eager to seek a military solution as he accused the 5th Corps command of being. At the end of my tour, we did finally succeed in arranging a cease-fire leading to direct negotiations chaired by a representative of the UN. This calmed down the situation considerably for several weeks. Unfortunately, the parties couldn't agree on any terms to establish permanent peace. Fighting broke out again, leading to the defeat of Abdic's forces.

UNMOs as confidence-builders to the local population

UNMOs were often accommodated in private houses among the local population close to the different front-line areas. This created confidence and goodwill and gave us the opportunity to explain our mission to a lot of people who did not really know what the UN was doing in the former Yugoslavia. At the same time, however, living day by day among the locals demanded that each officer keep in mind the importance of maintaining his impartiality.

Mostar – Summer 1993

The war in Mostar was vicious, especially in that the Muslims and Croats were fighting each other with little mercy. Civilians often became the victims of the fighting as a result of sniper or mortar fire directed at them and their houses. The situation soon became so tense that almost all international organizations had left the eastern bank, leaving the UNMOs present 24 hours a day. It was then our responsibility to be the impartial witnesses to what was going on. In this situation, we carried out a lot of work not strictly related to 'normal' UNMO work. In short, we did everything we could to help the locals who found themselves trapped in a particularly bad situation. This was a task we invented ourselves, knowing that if we didn't do it, no one else would. Staying there jeopardizing our own security and doing what we could to help the people gave us considerable respect.

On one occasion, we received an emergency request from the under-equipped hospital in East Mostar. The unborn child of a pregnant Muslim women had died, endangering the life of the woman. There was no way that the necessary operation could be carried out at the hospital in East Mostar, so if the woman was to survive, she had to be moved to the western part immediately. We then crossed the front-line, made contact with our Croatian liaison officer, got his approval, contacted the Spanish UN platoon located in East Mostar and had them to transport her in an APC. Missions like these of course, helped the overall situation very little. But, we made a difference where we could, and it actually meant that we were considered as the reliable and conscientious representatives of the UN.

On another occasion, civilian Muslims driving a small bus had been visiting relatives in the western part of Mostar and were left behind, unable to cross the front-line and frightened of what would happen to them. (This was in the early days of the Muslim/Croat war, where some very strange phenomena took place. It was at this stage for example possible to cross the front-line and visit relatives in the other part of the city, at the same time as the two parties were fighting a brutal war.) After finding the bus, we simply told the chauffeur to follow us. We then crossed the front-line as soon as there was a pause in the fighting. We were welcomed with tremendous gratitude by the worried families upon our arrival to the main street of East Mostar.

But not only the Muslims asked for our help. Once, our Croatian liaison officer asked us to locate an elderly Croat woman living in East Mostar in order to make sure that she was not being mistreated by the Muslims. We found the elderly woman who was grateful for our concern although uninterested in leaving her home in East Mostar.

The Bihac Pocket – Winter 1993/94

That winter, the UNHCR distributed large amounts of food aid to the population in the Bihac Pocket. The food was made available by local distribution offices located all over the region. Although the UNHCR wanted to make sure that the food was given to those in need and in the right quantities, they didn't have the manpower to check this themselves. The UNMOs were then asked to assist by visiting several local families each week throughout the area. This assistance brought us in close contact with families in the most remote villages, almost completely isolated from the outside world. In most cases, we were welcomed warmly and spent up to an hour together with the family. Our overall impression obtained from numerous visits, was that the food aid did actually reach those it was intended to help. The two armies each took a share, but then again, they too had a lot of mouths to feed.

These visits gave us a unique chance to explain to people the mission in general and our work in particular. Their previous knowledge of our role in their country was very limited. This convinced me even more of the importance of these visits. Furthermore these visits made it clear to the families that we, and thereby the UN, cared about their situation. This is perhaps the most important issue in confidence building. However, it was not only to the benefit of the UN that we tried to build the confidence of the locals. It was certainly also in order to protect ourselves. Many locals didn't understand our mission. This sometimes created very bad rumours that jeopardized our security. I especially remember one incident in this respect. Fierce fighting was going on just north of the village of Skokovi. In this key area, the 5th Corps was trying to cut off Abdic's forces. We observed the situation from a short distance with occasional mortar impacts very close to our position. Suddenly, a man came running towards us from the nearest house, looking desperate. He was stammering from fear and smelled heavily of slivovic. He feared for his family and begged us to bring an end to the 5th Corps' attack. Suddenly he pulled a revolver, waving it wildly in the air and screaming, 'but they won't get me! I will shoot the bastards when they come!'. As the shelling intensified and we feared that the fighting would cut off our way back, we decided to take off. This made the man even more desperate and the last thing he asked us was whether or not it was true that we (UNPROFOR) were supplying the 5th Corps with weapons! Rumours like this were (as it can be imagined) dangerous to our security, and the incident made it clear to us that it was not only preferable, but absolutely necessary, to talk to the locals in order to establish confidence and trust.

UNMOs as actors against atrocities

UNMOs were very mobile and thereby able to go into areas of tension on short notice. The warring parties were often aware of our presence and knew that we would report what we saw. So even though atrocities (especially towards the civilian population) were numerous and the UNMOs did not have any physical means of intervening, I am convinced that the mere presence of UNMOs did prevent a lot of atrocities from taking place.

Mostar – Summer 1993

After the breakdown in negotiations between the Muslims and Croats, fighting seemed to intensify day by day. The war was fought without any respect for the Geneva Convention whatsoever. As a consequence, we made it a part of our task to try to prevent the worst atrocities and at least to inform the UN command of the current circumstances.

One of the worst atrocities I experienced was the killing of a 7-year-old Muslim girl, shot by a sniper while playing in front of her house. I personally examined the body and could confirm that there was a small entrance hole in her forehead, leaving little doubt that she had been killed deliberately. We went straight to our Croatian liaison officer, facing him with what we had just seen. I think it's easy to imagine the self-control that we required when the liaison officer claimed that it was the Muslims who had shot her themselves, in order to create bad publicity for the Croats. (I later learned that such an accusation was almost a 'standard procedure', so to say, used by all three parties involved in the war in cases like this.)

We made it quite clear to both parties that the killing of that girl was a war crime under terms of the Geneva Convention, and that we would report not only this case but every single one that we found out about. We finally requested that both sides let us know immediately, if something like this should ever occur again. We witnessed many other atrocities, but that was the first and only time during our time in Mostar that we saw a child killed by a sniper.

Evaluating whether or not our presence in Mostar reduced the numbers of atrocities is, of course, difficult, as one never knows how it would have been had we not been there. It is, however, my belief that by being present, showing the flag, patrolling, talking to the parties and confronting them with our observations, we prevented at least some atrocities from taking place. The war in Mostar continued as perhaps the most brutal of all of the wars in the former Yugoslavia. But I am sure that the presence of UNMOs did make a difference.

Zadar, Croatia – Autumn 1993

As mentioned earlier, hostilities still continued between the Croatians and the Krajina-Serbs in this area, even though the parties had officially agreed on a cease-fire.

According to the peace agreement, we were supposed to investigate every violation and thereby every mortar or artillery impact. But with up to 6,000 impacts a day in our sector alone and only about 80 UNMOs, that was impossible. We therefore had to concentrate our efforts, which we did by investigating every impact reported in urban areas, making bombardment of important installations and front-line violations second and third priority. Both parties knew that every impact in urban areas was investigated and reported through our system.

Shelling a town was usually the last act in a series of retaliations from both sides. We knew this from experience, so as soon as the parties started to shell anything else than front-line positions, our 'alarm went on' as we followed the situation carefully in case of deterioration of hostilities. This happened quite regularly during this period. And as soon as it did, contact was made to both parties. Our UNMO team in Zadar contacted the Croatian command, and our sector headquarters in Knin contacted the Serbs. We then tried to arrange a cease-fire in order to calm the situation and stop the shelling of various towns.

Although we normally succeeded, the time it took to get both parties to believe that the other would uphold the cease-fire could vary from half an hour to several hours, depending on what had already been shelled or what had happened prior to the shelling. Sometimes the reason for shelling various towns was something out of our 'domain' so to say. One example, however, was the shelling of Zadar on the same day as that Croatian army attacked the Medak Pocket. To stop this shelling demanded action taken at a much higher level than ours. So, until a solution was found we were left almost as spectators to what looked like the outbreak of a new full-scale war in southern Croatia.

On one occasion, shelling had been going on throughout the day along the front-line. For some reason, hostilities escalated and both parties started to shell towns. The situation was put on edge shortly thereafter, when the centre of Zadar suddenly received numerous impacts within a few minutes. Our Croatian liaison officers next door asked us to pass on the information that if this shelling did not stop immediately, 'This is going to be a day to remember in Knin' – the 'capital' of Serb-Krajina – as it was formulated. Our colleagues on the Serb side were asked to pass the same kind of threats. I clearly remember standing in the UNMO office in the centre of Zadar with grenades impacting all over the place, communicating with the

UNMOs in Knin in order to set up a cease-fire fast. We did, and soon the shelling of Zadar and other towns stopped. After bringing an end to the shelling, our next job would be to investigate, and unfortunately often confirm, reports on casualties, which brought us in close contact with human tragedy.

What made it even more unpleasant was the fact that we, the forward representatives of the UN, were often the first to be blamed for not having stopped the shelling sooner! Fair or not, this was the daily life of an UNMO.

22 Peacekeepers Facing Horrors of Civil War-like Conflict

Danish Lessons Learned in Preparing and Taking Care of Soldiers

Introduction

Danish armed forces – in particular the Army – have gone through a major transformation to the new complex of tasks. This has meant new challenges, but also considerable burdens on the permanent personnel.

The work in the peacekeeping missions has been followed with great interest by mass media and politicians. From the start, the focus has been not merely on the value of the peacekeeping effort, but also on the costs, for instance in the form of psychological strain and possible consequences for the mental health of deployed and discharged soldiers.

Since the first major deployment to UNPROFOR in 1992, the development has been characterized by a great will to learn from experience and continuously to adjust the guidance, both in terms of equipment and personnel, and with regard to organization, leadership and command. Right from the first deployment to the former Yugoslavia, the Psychological Division of the Defence Centre for Leadership (PSD/DCL) was asked to assist in collection of experiences of the Danish personnel. PSD carried out studies on the experiences of the soldiers in the field and also of the relatives during the deployment. Since then, follow-up work has continued, with studies of the Danish IFOR and SFOR soldiers.

These studies have been significant in the development of the Danish concept of prevention and treatment of mental health problems from deployment in international missions.

---

[*] Dr Sten Martini (DK) is Director of the Psychological Department of the Danish Armed Forces Centre for Leadership in Copenhagen, Denmark.

Psychological reactions to war and war-like conditions

Psychic reactions to military fighting have presumably been known as long as soldiers have existed; but we have to proceed to the First World War before work was dedicated to these phenomena. Through the ages, there have been very differing opinions of their nature and they have been ascribed to many different causes. This, in itself, is an interesting subject in cultural history, which reflects the view of various ages and various cultures on human beings and the various comprehension of the responsibility of society to the individual.

Eight million soldiers died during the First World War. The soldiers were locked up in the trenches – confined and powerless, they often witnessed the death or mutilation of close fellow soldiers. They broke down in growing numbers. It has been estimated that 40% of the injured British soldiers fell victim to what in those days was called 'shell shock', because initially, it was considered that the condition was a result of some sort of concussion after shell explosions. However, eventually it became relatively clear that the reactions were caused by psychological components and the causes behind the reactions should be sought in defects of personality, lack of development, and unadaptiveness. This was the prevailing view during the entire inter-war period. During these years, thousands of veterans merely drew their disablement pension – nobody cared about the possibility of treatment.

As the Second World War broke out, it was the opinion that 'shell shock' among the soldiers could be avoided by sorting out the psychologically unfit types of personalities. A great effort was made, among others at the medical boards, to carefully diagnose and remove unstable and mentally unadapted persons from the armed forces. As a logical consequence of this effort, it was considered that the special psychiatric field hospitals which had been set up during the First World War no longer were required and consequently they were abolished.

Therefore the shock was great when it turned out, already a few months into the war, that a large number of combat casualties were of a psychological nature. At the very heavy fighting at Guadalcanal 50% of the total casualties were soldiers with psychological injuries. This was repeated over and over again – in North Africa, on Sicily, in Normandy. The condition was now understood as exhaustion and was called 'Combat Exhaustion'. And – what is important in this connection – it was noted that, in the long run, all personnel would be affected in this way. From this comes the expression 'every man has his breaking point'. Even the most resourceful soldiers broke down after 200–240 days of combat.

During the Second World War, quite a number of very valuable experiences were gained about treatment and prevention. Thus, it was – and still is – clear, that the frequency of psychologically-caused combat casualties is to a large degree connected with social relations and the cohesion between group-fellows and with matters of leadership. The subsequent wars in Korea, Vietnam and in the Middle East have further consolidated and extended this knowledge.

It has been a characteristic of the two world wars, as well as the Korean War, that the public very rapidly lost interest in the veterans, their sufferings and their mental well-being. It was not until the period after the Vietnam War, that the public, i.e., through the media, became more interested in this topic.

The American psychiatrist J. Hermann ascribes this situation to the fact that the veterans got organized and no longer accepted being disregarded.[1] Thus, the problems became political. After the Vietnam War, a number of psychiatric initiatives were implemented, among them, therapeutic groups among the injured veterans. Bit by bit, it was understood that the phenomena had to be considered as particularly striking cases of the reaction patterns which also follow other violent and dramatic experiences in civilian life, such as disasters, major accidents, etc. In 1980, these post-traumatic conditions were recognized under the designation of PTSD (post-traumatic stress disorder) and were accepted in the American list of diagnoses. However, it is important here to point out that PTSD is a serious disorder which is approaching the extreme point of a continuum. There can be stress reactions of a less extreme character which threaten mental health, are very troublesome, and reduce the quality of life of the individual.

Stress and coping in time of civil war-like conflicts

Deployment to international missions is not active combat service, even if participation in military action sporadically can occur. The situation is rather something in between, not war and not peace. But where do we find the strain?

Upon repatriation in August 1993, the personnel of DANBAT batch 3/UNPROFOR were questioned about their individual experiences.

The table below shows that it is not merely the everyday experiences that characterise deployment to an international mission. 37% of the force had none or only a few of the 18 types of experiences listed below; 50% had an average number, whereas 13% had experienced many of them.

Table 22.1 Affirmative replies (in per cent) among 514 Danish soldiers to questions about their experiences during the mission

Distress		*Threat*	
Witness to excesses	33	Were threatened by arms	65
Saw hunger and distress	66	Were in crossfire	38
Saw wounded and dead	45	Saw mate get threatened	58
Took part in body exchange	18	Were fired at	44
		Have fired themselves	25
Anxiety		Threatened by locals	41
Afraid of physical injury	28	Scorned by locals	71
Feeling life endangered	41		
Insecure outside camp	28	*Powerlessness*	
Insecure in camp	9	Circumstances beyond control	26
		Unable to cope	44
		Mission hopeless	77

Straining experiences in themselves do not lead to stress reactions. Many other circumstances play a role. This will be dealt with below. First, the concept of stress which is the basis of the Danish effort to prevent mental health problems will be described in more detail.

The everyday use of the word 'stress' is both imprecise and ambiguous. It is used about positive as well as negative situations. Stress occurs when there is an imbalance between the demands on the individual and the individual's resources. If the demands are not too great, they are experienced by the individual as a challenge (positive stress). If, however, the demands are greater than the resources, negative stress occurs, and the individual has an experience of being unable to cope with the tasks (or being unable to flee from them). If the imbalance continues, the individual ends up in a state of stress and will show psychological and/or physical stress reactions (symptoms). After some time, there is a risk that physical and mental health will suffer.

The basic understanding is that states of stress and stress reactions develop as a natural reaction to straining and abnormal situations.

Stress reactions can occur both after a sudden violent incident, such as being taking hostage, and after a long-lasting strain of less intensity, such as many of the experiences from the UN duty mentioned above. In other words, there is a distinction between traumatic and cumulative stress. Duration and strength are each important aspects, but it is worth remembering that repeated traumatic stress also has a cumulative effect and makes people psychologically more vulnerable. This means that states of stress have a sensitising effect: when sensitivity is being increased, the stress threshold is being reduced. The consequence of this is, that it is not immediately possible to train stress resistance unless special measures are taken to prevent cumulation. This is of far-reaching importance in military education. The essence of this view is, that if the demands on the individual soldier are increased, his resources will have to be increased in parallel, before further strain can be introduced. Another consequence is that prevention becomes important.

In a state of stress, the individual reacts both physically and mentally. A vast number of physiological (hormonal) processes are started and the individual responds with stress reactions – physical, psychological and behavioural. In his state of stress, the individual attempts in various ways to master the situation. The individual uses a number of coping strategies, both cognitive and emotional, which individually and isolated can be more or less appropriate and more or less successful. When the strain has ended, but the coping process has not been completed, or has been carried out in an inappropriate and unsuccessful manner, a number of after-reactions may occur. These after-reactions can be interpreted as expressions of the individual's attempts to finally handle what has happened.

Table 22.2 Ordinary after-reactions

Physical	*Psychological*
Headache	Tiredness/low spirits
Palpitation	Sleeping problems (e.g. nightmare)
Breathing problems	Reliving the stress situation
Sickness/vomiting	Hypersensitivity (e.g. sounds)
Stomach ache	Irritability
Tenseness of the body	Gloom
Dizziness	Self-reproaches
	Problems with ability to concentrate
	Indifference
	Isolation from others

It is common to have psychological stress reactions after straining incidents. In the study mentioned earlier, only 17% of the soldiers had no reactions for up to six months after the repatriation and 44% had one or several reactions during the whole six-month period. Despite the fact that only a minority reported that they have no reactions at all, the study shows that the great majority (70%) were not largely affected by reactions in their everyday life. However, in some cases, the reactions are of a character which implies that the persons concerned must be assessed as strained after their duty. A small number (7%) can be designated as particularly strained, whereas the remaining 23% can be assessed as being somewhat strained.

These results correspond very well to similar studies from the deployment of peacekeeping forces by other nations. However, it should be kept in mind that the individual missions have been very different concerning strain. The quantity and the type of strain also depends on the functions carried out by the soldiers. By way of comparison, it can be mentioned that in the Norwegian UNIFIL study,[2] it was found, that 5% of the veterans from the 1978–91 period showed post-traumatic symptoms in average 6.6 years after the repatriation. Also from the UNIFIL mission, a Dutch study similarly showed, that 5% were suffering from psycho-social after-effects.[3] Among American forces, it was noted that 11% had to be diagnosed as suffering from PTSD according to the American list of diagnoses.[4] However, a Swedish study of medical and logistic personnel in UNFICYP showed that stress symptoms were not found in great numbers – only about 0,5% were suffering from a 'nervous breakdown'.[5] Also, a study covering German medical personnel in Cambodia (UNTAC) showed correspondingly small figures.[6] All in all, it can be noted that about 5% of the personnel in the majority of peacekeeping missions suffer from mental health after-reactions to an extent that they create considerable inconvenience and cause reduction in the quality of life.

Therefore the growing interest in mental health problems caused by strain is not unfounded. Considerable interest is attached to reducing the number of soldiers who are struck by such symptoms. Many countries have paid attention to the problems and developed techniques and procedures in order to counter effects of this nature. Despite the fact that most nations have a common understanding of the problem and share the common base of existing knowledge and research results, there are differences among the nations as to attack things in practice. Further research is still needed, both in theory and based on experiences, before a more complete fund of knowledge can be obtained to be placed at the disposal of the decision makers in peacekeeping operations.

The Danish concept to counter stress reactions during and after deployment to an international mission

The Danish concept has gradually been developed on the basis of the knowledge, which at any time has been available. Most of it has been pieced together from many sources: traditional combat psychology, knowledge about disasters in civilian life, social counselling, psychiatry, clinical psychology, social psychology, etc. The concept has been developed in close co-operation with the operational decision makers and experts from the above mentioned areas.[7]

Box 22.1   The Danish Armed Forces policy concerning countering of psychological after-reactions

'The target group is discharged and serving personnel of the Armed Forces and their relatives, who are threatened by, or are suffering from mental health problems caused by traumatic incidents during their service. It is the policy of the Armed Forces, that within the framework of the Armed Forces, an offer of support shall be made to those personnel and relatives who are suffering from reactions of this kind, which substantially affect their everyday life. The emphasis in this effort shall be put on prevention. It shall also be ensured, through careful selection and training, that personnel to the greatest extent possible can master straining situations.

A basic principle of the offer must be voluntary participation and it is important that the attitude towards seeking assistance in case of mental health problems is characterised by frankness. In the same way, it is central to deal with negative attitude formations in the area.

To the extent support is offered within the framework established up by the Armed Forces, the offer is open to all and is given free of charge, taking into account an assessment of the need in the individual case.'

In 1992 an informal working group was set up to describe and analyse the offers and activities available to the units and individuals. In the light of this work, the Army Operational Command implemented a number of initiatives to counter stress reactions among personnel deployed to UNPROFOR. In 1993, further measures were implemented, and resources, both in the form of personnel and finances, were provided for this area in particular. Most recently a working group, especially set up, has examined the entire area with the aim of formulating an overarching policy, evaluating existing measures and, if required, making proposals for change.

The Danish model is based on the so-called Solomon principles: 'Proximity' (staying at the front with one's mates), 'Immediacy' (early assistance when symptoms are recognized) and 'Expectancy' (expectation of rapid normal function and resumption of the work). The assistance is further based on flexibility and many-stranded support. It has been considered most appropriate to set up the effort in a way that it can be adapted to changing needs.

The activities can be divided into three principal groups: 1) preventive measures, 2) assistance and counselling in connection with major incidents in the area of mission, and 3) follow-up effort, including assistance to persons with after-reactions.

Preventive measures

Research results indicate that knowledge about stress symptoms and coping is important to reduce anxiety and increase the soldier's abilities to cope and arrive at an appropriate adaptation to the situation after stressful events. It is of importance to mastering the problem that all aspects of the experiences come out into the open in terms of thoughts, feelings and behaviour. Fellow soldiers and the functional group becomes central in this connection. Sets of group norms have to be developed, which make symptoms legal and permit discussing emotions. Thus, the study of the Danish forces in UNPROFOR mentioned earlier could document that in the groups where the mutual social relations were good, a substantially smaller number of soldiers had psychological after-reactions than in the groups with poor contact among the soldiers. In those cases where anxiety had also been experienced, the importance of good contact in the peer group increased still further.

The basis of the preventive effort is that these reactions are normal reactions to abnormal situations. The frame of reference is taken in a personal-psychological orientation and, in addition, in a social-psychological frame of comprehension, where the emphasis is put on the group and the broader social system, of which the group is part. The reactions are not seen as any kind of illness, which must be diagnosed and treated, as this involves a risk of developing passivity and helplessness and dependence on a professional set-up of therapeutic personnel.

In accordance with this, education in psychological reactions to serious incidents is carried through at all levels in the Danish forces.

On the level of privates, a brief education in reactions and psychological first aid is given.

A training programme of about ten hours is carried out in the education of non-commissioned officers (NCOs). The main aim of the course is to strengthen training on the lowest level of command concerning knowledge about reactions to strain in the service as well as knowledge on how a commander can intervene and counter possible stress reactions. During the course, the following topics are dealt with:

- Typical stress in connection with normal service with troops, international duty in areas of conflict, and circumstances in a war or combat situation
- Generally occurring physical and psychological reactions to critical events and stressful situations
- Means employed to manage stress reactions

- Prevention of stress reactions.

Education consists of brief presentations, exercises on the base of concrete examples, showing of video films and ensuing group and plenary discussions.

In the education of platoon commanders (basic training of officers), modules in combat and crisis psychology are accomplished as part of the general education in psychology. At the subsequent further education, a ten to twelve-hour course in stress management is carried through. The aim of the course is to provide future commanders with a broad knowledge and insight into the use of various psychological tools to remedy stress-related problems. The course gives the participants knowledge on following topics:

- Stress and the background of occupying oneself with this
- Particularly straining situations during service with troops, duty in international missions or in combat/war
- Ordinary reactions to serious strain
- Intervention against stress reactions, including focusing on the commander's role and options of action.

Education consists of presentations, group and plenary discussions and practical exercises closely attached to practical duty.

Since January 1994, courses on commander's activities have been carried out for commanders and others before deployment to the mission area. The educational content of these courses includes stress management training lasting about nine to twelve hours. The aim is to provide the participants with knowledge on and understanding of how the commander through his own conduct of stress management can prevent and remedy the consequences of strain or assure that this takes place. The focus is particularly on:

- The aim of stress management
- In which situations, there is a special need for this – and why
- Which methods or tools can be used for intervention – and by whom.

The content of the course is not only a general presentation of existing knowledge on stress, strain, stress reactions and stress management in international operations, but also practical application of this knowledge in relation to various typical situations and methods of intervention in case of critical incidents. In particular, the situation of the relatives is given special attention.

The form of training is, here too, mainly based on activation of the participants as a prerequisite to the future practical work as a commander.

Prior to each deployment, all units are given a mission-oriented training, which includes education in the fields of psychological strain, stress factors and options of assistance. The education takes two to four hours and is normally carried out as a briefing, where personnel who have earlier served in international missions are involved. In addition to this, social workers, chaplains, doctors and nurses are included if required. In connection with the briefing the personnel are given written material with more detailed information.

It is a general characteristic of these activities and is emphasized at all levels, that it is normal to react with stress symptoms to serious incidents. It is sought to influence negative attitudes and change obsolete ideas of what the characteristics of a good soldier are. This is a prerequisite for the working through of the experiences in the group. However, it is also characteristic that leaders and commanders have been assigned the task of ensuring that discussions of this nature are taking place. It is our observation that the commanders live up to this. Based on the feedback we have received, it can also be assessed that this approach works. Most of the major and minor incidents are handled at the local level in a way advantageous to the soldiers.

Thus, most incidents can be handled by the resources that are available in the units. In several cases, soldiers also draw on medical personnel and the deployed chaplain. However, serious incidents can occur, and the psychological strain can become very heavy and/or it includes many persons, e.g. by major accidents or perhaps fighting proper. In such cases, local resources are insufficient. The local commander can then – after consultation with the medical experts – ask for professional assistance from Denmark.

Emergency assistance

Since the deployment of Danish forces in 1992, some situations have occurred where a special effort was required, e.g., when in the Autumn of 1995, peacekeeping units were involved in fighting during the Croatian conquest of the Krajina province. In such situations, special personnel trained in handling of crises and disasters have been deployed to assist the units. So far, such teams have been made up *ad hoc* and have consisted of psychologists and psychiatrists. The feedback received has in general been positive.

With regard to ensuring preparedness, both in terms of quantity and quality, mental health support activities have largely been satisfactory under 'normal' conditions both in Denmark and to the troops deployed. However, it has been assessed that the Armed Forces in future must have proper emergency teams at their disposal which, in accordance to need, can be composed of doctors, psychologists and nurses. These should be teams, which can be deployed to the area of mission at short notice. How to put this into effect is currently being worked out.

It is the intention that a deployment of this nature should be able to take place at a notice that guarantees that the team (or the person) can be active in the area of mission within 72 hours. The composition of the emergency team will depend on the character and extent of the incident. Decision on composition of the team is decided after consultation between the head of medical duty in the Army Operational Command and the head of the Psychological Division in the Armed Forces. Decision about deployment will be made by the operational commands after consultation between the same two persons.

In emergencies of this kind so far, it has been an important task to conduct psychological debriefings in groups. The debriefing gives an opportunity to process the events by putting words to the impressions and reactions which the accident has caused. In addition, the psychological debriefing clarifies which resources the group and its members possess. In this way, a basis of strengthening the group cohesion can be created employing the 'self-healing' resources of the group. Similarly, it offers a possibility of getting an impression of the need for special support to individuals.

Follow-up

It is the policy of the Armed Forces that the Armed Forces' responsibility for physical and mental health damage inflicted on the personnel during duty does not end with repatriation and subsequent discharge. Therefore, a number of resources are spent on preventing after-reactions and, if these should arise, on assisting with the necessary treatment.

A number of initiatives can be implemented in accordance with the strain a unit has been exposed to. Prior to deployment contact has been formed between the unit and a psychologist with special training. During the entire course of events, the psychologist will function as liaison between the unit commander and the psychological support readiness of the Armed Forces. The measures which should be implemented are decided upon after recommendation from the commander and the liaison psychologist.

Homecoming and reception

Immediately after their return, the soldiers go on leave for some days to meet with their families. After a couple of days, they meet at the barracks to accomplish return procedures before they are discharged. They go through a medical examination and a number of briefings. In particular, they are informed about possible psychological after-reactions and on the possibilities of receiving psychological assistance if required. Also the soldiers' close relatives are briefed on symptoms, so that they can pay attention to later negative developments. In connection with this, written material is distributed which describes procedures and addresses in case of special need for assistance. In those cases where it is assessed that a unit have been exposed to a particular strain, further initiatives can be implemented in connection with its return, e.g. group discussions *may* be carried through with assistance from the corps of military psychologists of the Armed Forces.

The establishment of the present structure has taken place after thorough review. The possibility of an offer of psychological examination as part of the return procedure together with the medical examination has been discussed. Included here is also whether such an examination should be mandatory for the individual soldier. Two facts in particular have been of importance in the decision to conduct the above mentioned orientation as a mandatory minimum.

First, acknowledgement of having stress reactions is still a somewhat taboo topic. There is a considerable risk that some soldiers partly will repress their reactions, partly will object to receive an offer of help in 'the presence of all the others'.

Second, the reception phase is characterised by an 'ecstasy of reunion', so that possible problems are overshadowed by positive feelings. Frequently, symptoms and inconveniences do not appear until some time after the discharge, when the daily chores again have become a routine. The results mentioned earlier from the Danish study of the soldiers' after-reactions document that reactions after three months were more extensive than at the time of the homecoming and that they were still present to a considerable extent after six months.

On the basis of Dutch experiences, it has been decided to issue a questionnaire to the soldiers about six months after their return.[8] The aim of this is to be able to identify persons who are in need of help and to offer them assistance.

In addition to this, it is possible to hold a so-called homecoming gathering after three to four months for those units who have a special need for processing their experiences.

Psychological counselling and treatment of individuals

In case of injury, Psychological Division will, by request, assist with psychological counselling and crisis relief to the injured person and his/her relatives. In case of death(s) as a consequence of accidents, crisis intervention is also offered to the bereaved on request. Any soldier, serving as well as discharged, can in addition on his/her own initiative approach Psychological Division to receive help and assistance to master mental health problems from incidents in the service.

In recent years, Psychological Division has used some resources on formerly deployed personnel, who up to several years after the deployment, need psychological assistance in order to cope with after-reactions following traumatic incidents.

The psychological assistance most frequently consists of individual talks with the person hit by the crisis, possibly by involving this person's close relatives. In this connection, there is no limit as to how 'old' the traumatic events may be, as long as they concern after-reactions in connection with the service.

The Psychological Division has at its disposal nine especially trained psychologists, who form part of a 'readiness force' during normal duty hours. In addition, they can also be reached by phone within a couple of hours on evenings, weekends and holidays.

In addition to their occupation with the psychological support area, the psychologists are connected with the other spheres of the division. This means that they have a broad interface with the Armed Forces through studies, selection, consultancy work, etc.

Also available are a group of psychologists working at time rates, who are attached to the division in connection with other jobs. They have accomplished basic military training and are trained in stress and crisis psychology, which makes them able to assist in connection with major accidents.

To assist personnel who have settled inconveniently far away from Psychological Division, a network of psychologists in private practice with clinical education can be called on. These psychologists offer short-term therapy after previous examination by a psychologist in Psychological Division. For this group, a basic education in military subjects of relevance for rendering assistance to military personnel, is planned in the near future.

Other circumstances

In addition to what has already been mentioned, a number of activities are carried out for the relatives of the deployed personnel. However, a description of these, is beyond the scope of this presentation.

The importance of avoiding deployment of people who have a special risk of developing psychological after-reactions appears from general experiences and has been documented in several studies. For instance, it has been demonstrated that people with strained family backgrounds, previous adaptation difficulties, weak capacity for social contact and a tendency to introvertness are particularly in danger. In selecting personnel for an international mission, attention is being paid to such circumstances. The decision about deployment is made by the officer in charge. For a number of reasons, it has been found unnecessary to supplement the selection with special competence, e.g., in the form of assistance by psychologists. However, it is also beyond the scope of this presentation to deal with this issue in more detail.

Concluding remarks

The Danish concept is based on the understanding that stress symptoms are normal reactions to abnormal situations. They are not an expression of illness. This does not mean, however, that after-reactions in a more or less untreated form cannot lead to a substantially reduced quality of life and real illness. But turning the person concerned into a patient should be avoided, as this can imply dependence and passivity.

It is also the understanding that the Armed Forces should primarily base their efforts on resources found locally in the units. Only when it turns out that these resources are insufficient should the professionals intervene. This concept demands the effort of a number of authorities, with subsequent co-ordination, co-operation and assurance of a reasonable uniformity in providing additional help. The psychologists of Psychological Division have an important role to play here. In addition to individual counselling and treatment, the division spends many resources on preventive activities. In this sense, a number of training activities are carried out for personnel who are going to accomplish the tasks in the primary contact with the troops.

The concept is based on offer of help and voluntary participation. It is essential that the responsibility and integrity of the individual is respected. Coercion and encirclement must be avoided.

Heavy strain and subsequent psychological short- and long-term reactions can hardly be avoided in enforcement or peacekeeping missions. Through careful preparation and preventive initiatives, we can reduce the price of participating. For those who are hit after all, we must make the price as low as possible. We can never make the experienced inexperienced or the happened not-happened, but we can assist, so that the person integrates his experiences in an extended identity and contributes to the making of a new platform to continue his life.

However, a basic question is, whether we do get in contact with everyone who needs help. We do get hold of many – probably most of them – but not all. We are still working with the remnants of macho attitudes, ignorance and fear of registration. It is our experience that we achieve fine results as regards units and major groups of personnel. As for individual soldiers on rotation or small groups, our experience is that the present concept still holds a risk of some of them slipping through the net and thus not receiving the relevant offer of help.

From time to time, psychological crisis intervention is criticised. It is maintained that it is exaggerated and is employed for any minor incident that everybody should be able to cope with by himself. Particularly concerning soldiers, fear has been expressed that the soldiers may become soft and unable to cope with the strain of war. The latter statement can be repudiated, among other things, with reference to the efforts of the Danish soldiers in the former Yugoslavia, where they had to use their weapons several times.

Which incidents the individual person must be able to bear unaided is an existential question. However, the answer is culturally strongly accentuated; it is different from one culture to another and has changed through the ages. In the pre-industrial societies of western Europe, the majority of the population had to put up with starvation and hunger as part of the conditions of life. Illness and suffering, death and disasters were facts that the individual just had to endure. In today's welfare society, things are quite different. The Armed Forces are part of that society. As a part of that society, the Armed Forces must have to subscribe to its basic values and attitudes.

Notes

1   Hermann, J. L., *Trauma and Recovery*, Basic Books: New York, 1992.
2   Weisæth, L., Aarhaug, P., Mehlum, L. and Larsen, S., *The UNIFIL study, Positive and Negative Consequences of Service in UNIFIL Contingents* 1-XXVI, Report part 1, Results and Recommendations, Norwegian Defence Command Headquarters, The Joint Medical Service: Oslo 1993.

3 Knoster, J. P., *Traumatische Ervaringen en ex-UNIFIL Militarien*, Doc. nr. GW 89-12, Vrije Universitet, Amsterdam, 1989.
4 Friedman, M. and Ehtlich, P., 'Psychological Sequelae. Associated with UN Peacekeeping Operations in Somalia', in IV E.C.O.T.S. *Fourth European Conference on Traumatic Stress*, Paris, 1994.
5 Lundin, T. and Otto, U., 'Swedish UN Soldiers in Cyprus UNFICYP: Their Psychological and Social Situation', *Psychotherapy and Psychosomatics*, No. 57, p. 187 ff, 1992.
6 Schüffel, W. and Schade, B., *Erste Ergebnisse der Untersuchung zur Belastung und der Streßreaktionen von Sanitätspersonal im Humanitären Hilfseinsatz in Kambodscha*, Marburg, 1994.
7 AG/PSYKSTØT, *Redegørelse vedrørende Bistand til Personel der lider af Psykiske Efterreaktioner*, FOK, Vedbæk, January, 1997.
8 Willigenburg, T. and Alkemade, N. D., *Aftercare in the Royal Netherlands Army*, Dept. of Behavioural Sciences, doc. nr. 96–02: The Hague, April, 1996.

Part Four

CONCLUSIONS

23 After Dayton

Write off the UN?

WOLFGANG BIERMANN and MARTIN VADSET

Introduction

Peacekeeping is nearly as old as the United Nations, and it started in the Balkans. The first use of military personnel by the UN occurred in 1947 under the Consular Commission in Indonesia and the Special Committee on the Balkans, UNSCOB (1947–1951). As the personnel participating in these bodies were members of national delegations and not under the authority of the UNSG, the mission is not formally counted as United Nations Peacekeeping Operations.[1]

Fifty years later, another mission in the Balkans, the NATO-led Implementation Force (IFOR) and its subsequent Stabilization Force (SFOR), are also not referred to as United Nations peacekeeping operations.

The fact that NATO took over responsibility for peacekeeping in Bosnia after the Dayton Peace Agreement unavoidably leads to the question of the future of UN peacekeeping: why couldn't the UN do the job? In future crises, is NATO in and the UN out? These questions are beyond the operational peacekeeping issues that were the main subject of this book. But we have some comments that appear relevant.

Our project started as an investigation of UN peacekeeping in civil war-like conflicts, mainly in the former Yugoslavia. The reader of this book has had the opportunity to review some of the lessons learned from the UN peacekeeping operation to the Balkans, UNPROFOR. Through surveying the views of former peacekeeping officers and through presenting conclusions of key civilian and military UN practitioners about the lessons learned from their experiences, we hope to have contributed to the *collective memory* of the United Nations Lessons Learned from the former Yugoslavia.

In this final chapter, we want to discuss some operational lessons learned which may be relevant for the new context of European security after the Cold War.

350 UN Peacekeeping in Trouble

The Chapter VIII option[2]

In *An Agenda for Peace* (1992), the UN Secretary-General referred to Chapter VIII of the UN Charter and to the potential benefit of an agreed division of labour between the UN and nations or groups of nations in the regions of the world. In his view, the Cold War 'had impaired the proper use of Chapter VIII', while the post-Cold War UN had 'encouraged a rich complementary effort' for a division of labour in handling regional crises with 'flexibility and creativity'.[3] Boutros-Ghali saw a new era of opportunity for regional arrangements and agencies 'if their activities are undertaken consistent with the purposes and principles of the Charter, and if their relationship with the United Nations, and in particular the Security Council, is governed by Chapter VIII'.[4]

On 28 October 1992, the UN General Assembly formally welcomed the Organization for Security and Cooperation in Europe, the OSCE, as a 'regional arrangement in the sense of Chapter VIII of the Charter of the United Nations'.[5] In 1993 the OSCE and the UN signed a 'Framework for Cooperation and Co-ordination', and the OSCE received observer status at the UN. This was followed by intensified co-operation between the two organizations in various activities in the field of conflict prevention and crisis management.[6] The OSCE is open to all states in the region from the Atlantic to the Pacific Ocean, including all European nations, the USA, Canada and all former Soviet republics. The OSCE 'as a regional organization under Chapter VIII of the UN Charter, can perform many functions normally expected from the United Nations'.[7] NATO, on the other hand, is a regional defence organization, a military alliance that is not open to all countries, responsible only for its members and does not consider itself a regional organization or arrangement[8] under the terms of Chapter VIII, although it has agreed that it could accept peacekeeping assignments from the UN or the OSCE. But it cannot, outside its own area, give other organizations or itself such a mandate according to the UN Charter.

This distinction between collective security and collective defence organizations might look formalistic, but it became relevant because of tensions between the UN and NATO over the use of air power in the former Yugoslavia. In his study, *Supplement to an Agenda for Peace* of 1995, the UNSG came to the conclusion that there are certain risks in division of labour between UN peacekeeping and NATO enforcement in one operation:

> Much effort has been required between the Secretariat and NATO to work out procedures for the co-ordination of this unprecedented collaboration.

This is not surprising given the two organizations' very different mandates and approaches to the maintenance of peace and security. Of greater concern...are the consequences of using force other than for self-defence, in a peacekeeping context...There is also a danger that states concerned may claim international legitimacy and approval for forceful actions that were not envisaged by the Security Council.[9]

There are more aspects to be discussed here. However, the main task of this book has been to analyse the experience of UNPROFOR as a peacekeeping operation under UN command and control. In this context, NATO was considered only in a limited way as regards its role of providing air power to UNPROFOR and also when our study compared *capability gaps* and *feasibility gaps* of both UNPROFOR and IFOR/SFOR as seen by military officers in the field.

However, NATO's successive involvement in the former Yugoslavia in the form of IFOR, SFOR, and a probable successor requires separate evaluation beyond the scope of this book. NATO's involvement should also be seen in the wider context of the evolution of European security. The fall of the Berlin Wall in 1989 and the end of the Warsaw Pact, has opened the door for a new debate about collective security in Europe,[10] for a search for new forms of co-operation and new institutions of European security and, last but not least, for NATO enlargement. The evolving all-European co-operation among various institutions in Europe has become a 'test case for a less violent world'.[11] NATO itself views IFOR as the 'first real test case' for multifunctional peacekeeping.[12]

NATO's new role in peacekeeping

NATO is a newcomer in peacekeeping. Starting in December 1995, the Alliance has for the first time been carrying out a 'peacekeeping operation', IFOR and then SFOR, based on a UN mandate to implement the Dayton Peace Agreement.

At the Oslo Ministerial Meeting in June 1992, the Alliance officially supported a proposal to seek for the OSCE (then the CSCE) status as a Regional Organization under Chapter VIII of the UN Charter. NATO cautiously declared its readiness to 'support' peacekeeping activities under the responsibility of the CSCE. With respect to UN peacekeeping, NATO only 'welcomed' participation of NATO members in UN peacekeeping.[13] However, six months later in December 1992, NATO confirmed its readiness to 'support' peacekeeping operations 'under the authority of the UN Security Council, which has the primary responsibility for international peace and security. We are ready to respond positively to initiatives that the

UN Secretary-General might take to seek alliance assistance in the implementation of UN Security Council resolutions'.[14]

Five months later, NATO was involved in *supporting* peacekeeping rather than in *carrying out* peacekeeping, through providing resources and capabilities such as communications, logistics and infrastructure in former Yugoslavia. NATO's role included tasks not necessarily typical for peacekeeping: monitoring and enforcing the UN embargo in the Adriatic, enforcing the no-fly zone over Bosnia-Herzegovina, providing close air support to UNPROFOR and carrying out air strikes.

At the Athens Summit in Summer 1993, both the ministers of defence of NATO and of the former Warsaw Pact together adopted peacekeeping guidelines and definitions. These were basically in accordance with traditional UN peacekeeping concepts.[15] Athens was an important element in the process of changing East–West relations and in the establishment of the Partnership for Peace.[16] NATO also provided personnel and equipment to establish a command and control element for UNPROFOR headquarters in Bosnia-Herzegovina and it developed contingency planning for the implementation of a possible UN peace plan as well as for support in the case of withdrawal of UNPROFOR.

This means that NATO had become much more closely involved in the UN operation in the former Yugoslavia than the public might have recognized at that time. The gradual involvement of NATO led necessarily to increasing co-operation between the UN and NATO at the military as well as the political level, in particular between the Secretary-Generals of the two organizations. However, as shown in contributions by UN force commanders to this book, there were many tensions resulting from the different philosophies, doctrines and experiences of NATO and the United Nations. Although the political primacy of the UN as the lead organization defining mandates for peacekeeping 'has never been contested by NATO',[17] one result of NATO's involvement was heavy dependency on NATO by the UN. It is a curious phenomenon that leading nations sometimes took contradictory positions, depending on whether they were acting as permanent members of the UN Security Council asking NATO for support, or as members of the North Atlantic Council (NAC) reacting to a request from the Security Council.[18]

However, what looked like a deep split between the UN and NATO, was in reality more complex.

First, there was an important conflict of *interests* between countries contributing troops on the ground and those not doing so. Second, there were *conceptual* conflicts due to divergent traditional objectives of NATO and the UN, also between NATO countries having a long record of participation in UN peacekeeping, like Denmark and Norway, and others without or with limited UN peacekeeping experience, like the US and Germany. In this sense, at the special meeting of the NAC on 2 August 1993, the US was prepared to act alone if NATO itself was not prepared to decide in favour of air strikes against the Bosnian Serbs, while those NATO governments with troops on the ground stressed the risks involved for UNPROFOR personnel and the humanitarian side of the operation.[19] For example the Danish NATO ambassador asked how the US would decide if they, like Denmark, had 1,500 nationals on the ground.[20]

Third, on the *operational level,* there were tensions between NATO and the UN, particularly in the field of command and control. While political leaders of NATO pushed for the use of force and airstrikes, the military commanders on the ground, often UN officers from NATO countries, were reluctant. This divergence constantly threatened to undermine the authority of UN leadership and contributed to making the Yugoslav conflict also a 'battleground' of conflicting views and interests of the international community. At the same time, the warring parties and their war propaganda utilized those differences for their own war aims.

Balanced participation and impartiality of troop contributors

NATO's support for UNPROFOR was initially requested by the United Nations because the UN had several military capability gaps arising from the fact that UNPROFOR was being deployed in the midst of an evolving war.

This *division of labour contributed* to conceptual conflicts between the UN and NATO. While the UN has decades of experience in preparing and carrying out peacekeeping, NATO had decades of preparation for the collective defence of western Europe and North America by means of war-fighting. As a result, the division of labour between the UN and NATO evolved according to the principle that each should do what it could do best.

However, a division of labour where one partner is responsible for peacekeeping and the other solely for providing enforcement actions is problematic. This situation promotes diverging concepts, interests and manifold opportunities to the conflicting parties to play peacekeepers and 'peace-supporters' against each other. In addition, unity of command is as stressed as unity of policy. Consequently, this division of labour between those who keep peace on the ground and those who enforce from the air is not sustainable.

One of the lessons suggested by UN mediators in this book is that those deciding in the UN Security Council about military action should themselves also provide military personnel on the ground (Stoltenberg), because otherwise, their decisions might ignore the risks involved for the troops on the ground.

To observe strict impartiality is one of the most important rules in peacekeeping. Therefore, in the past, the UNSC preferred the P5 not to contribute national contingents and that an 'equitable geographical representation is desirable'.[21]

In a few cases, traditional peacekeeping did envisage the possibility of troops contributed by members of the Security Council and powers with interests in the area of operation. UK troops participated in UNFICYP in Cyprus, French troops in UNIFIL in Lebanon. 'Old'-line peacekeepers tend to have reservations in these cases, because troops of the P5 could have divergent interests in the same conflict; this could create 'frictions between contingents'. They fear that major powers would be 'less likely than smaller nations to respect the international character of the force'.[22] On the other hand, major power participation may be useful if the major powers can 'balance each other' and that the motive from having their own troops deployed could make the major powers 'become more committed to the mandate of the peacekeeping operation'.[23]

As shown in Chapter 3, 'Setting the Scene', in some cases, UNPROFOR too benefited from the balanced participation, as was the case after the NATO ultimatum of 9 February 1994, when Russian troops reassured the Bosnian Serbs while others, French and British troops, reassured the Bosnian government through interpositioning around Sarajevo. With respect to conflicting interests between the US and Germany and those countries who contributed troops to UNPROFOR, IFOR has had the advantage of having all the major nations, e.g. Russia as well as the US, committed with troops on the ground.

As a general rule, the composition of a peacekeeping force has to be evaluated in each case, based on the experience of UN peacekeeping operations. A key element in establishing consent of the parties has been to get agreement on who should contribute to a mission. In this respect, participation of troops from neighbouring nations and the P5 with interests in the area should be carefully balanced.

Impartiality of IFOR/SFOR. Experience shows that participation on the ground can promote an attitude of impartiality on the part of troop contributors, because direct daily experience increases knowledge of the conflicting parties and reduces the influence of their propaganda. Propaganda fuelling tensions among major nations was a major problem for UNPROFOR. As a result of this process, the UN was frequently criticised for its impartiality towards the Serbs. It had neither the media resources nor a coherent media policy to meet the criticism. IFOR/SFOR however, rigorously follows the principle of impartiality and openness, unchallenged by major powers on the sidelines.[24] IFOR Press and Information Officers saw their role as 'to deliver objective information and not to go to the muddy warfare of local policy'.[25]

Some examples can illustrate the view that after US and German peacekeepers were deployed with IFOR/SFOR on the ground, impartiality became the prevailing attitude towards the parties.

After violent events and exchange of fire between Muslims and Serbs in Gajevi on 12 November 1996, Russian and American troops separated and disarmed the fighting sides. While the Bosnian Muslims accused Russian IFOR peacekeepers of having done nothing to prevent Serb attacks on the Muslims, NATO accused the Bosnian government of provoking violence by sending Muslim refugees back into Bosnian Serb areas without prior consultation and co-ordination with the UNHCR and IFOR.[26] Another example was a search action for illegal weapons against the Bosnian Army Headquarters on 20 December 1997.[27] Western criticism or even action against the Bosnian Muslim leadership would have been unlikely during UNPROFOR. In the UNPROFOR period, Germany and the US had no troops deployed in Bosnia, but they were in the forefront of politically siding with the Muslim-led government in Sarajevo and the Croatian government in Zagreb while criticizing UNPROFOR's impartiality to all three groups including the Bosnian Serbs.

Now, SFOR press conferences regularly report about actions against non-compliance by all parties and about actions against violations, irrespective of whether they were committed by Bosnian Muslims, Croats or Serbs.[28]

The German government, Croatia's 'protector' in the beginning of the conflict, has since participating in IFOR/SFOR shown significant impartiality in its information policy by reporting about wrongdoing and crimes of all the warring parties, for example now confirming Croat police actions in 1991 when about one hundred Serbs in Gospic and 280 in Pakrac were killed in order to reduce the 'percentage of Serbs in the area of Pakrac and Gospic'.[29]

NATO as a peacekeeper in Bosnia

Though NATO has only a few years of indirect and then direct involvement in peacekeeping operations, the alliance has a structure and resources, which enable it to collectively evaluate lessons learned. In our view, NATO has learned many lessons from the UNPROFOR mission and the operational demands facing it and has adapted to the task of managing peacekeeping, developing a doctrine for IFOR and SFOR that closely resembles UN peacekeeping doctrine.[30]

For NATO, IFOR delivers a 'textbook of multifunctional peacekeeping operations',[31] under conditions that UNPROFOR peacekeepers could only have dreamed of:

- A Peace Agreement and the consent of the former warring parties as a precondition for deployment, including a Status of Forces Agreement according to the 'Convention on the Privileges and Immunities of the United Nations'[32]

- A clear mandate limited to 'territorial and other militarily related provisions'[33] in a clearly defined zone of separation and territory to control

- Full political backing of the international community, i.e. a maximum of *unity of policy* by major international players

- *Unity of command* of an international force rather than a frequent struggle about dual key procedures

- Strong financial and material resources for the troops

- The rules of engagement are robust, but as in the case of a classic peacekeeping force, based on impartiality and on self-defence, which includes the right to defend the mandate

- A fully articulated liaison system with all the parties through joint commissions and other structures facilitating the re-establishment of consent if it is challenged

- A clear responsibility of other international organizations (UN IPTF, EU, OSCE) for the civilian part of the mission.

The last point makes the mandate clear and in principle easy to handle by the NATO-led military forces. In distinction to multifunctional PKOs under UN command, Dayton leaves the main responsibility for the co-ordination of very complex civilian implementation to the Office of the High Representative and the other international agencies, which have far fewer resources than are available to the military force. This imbalance can lead to conflicting aims and interests.

IFOR/SFOR officers perceive their mission according to our questionnaire interviews, as a great success with respect to the implementation of the military provisions of the Dayton Agreement. However, the survey shows their strong scepticism concerning IFOR/SFOR ability to enforce the most prominent political and humanitarian aims of the Peace Agreement. Fewer than half of the officers find it realistic to expect the NATO-led force to manage the return of refugees, to reverse ethnic cleansing, or to create conditions for a permanent political settlement. Only a third of them believes that war criminals will be arrested, and only a little more than one in ten believes that it is a realistic task to restore Bosnia as a single multi-ethnic state.[34]

The limits of power

Looking at IFOR/SFOR compared to a traditional peacekeeping force, we feel compelled to say that, in practice, IFOR's approach is close to the principles applied by UN peacekeeping forces. But there is a huge difference in size and military efficiency in favour of IFOR. This difference is highly important as a deterrent and *show of force* posture, familiar to some extent also to traditional PKO. Military power may however be less relevant for a variety of tasks to be carried out in peacetime. Statistical analysis of the IFOR/SFOR survey revealed a considerable *feasibility gap* of the NATO-led force in handling conflicts, a condition also quite familiar during UNPROFOR.

While UNPROFOR was often blamed for its lack of success in carrying out the UN mandate due to lacking military resolve, NATO has daily experienced that military efficiency and strength is an important deterrent against restarting open war, but not necessarily a sufficient recipe for making peace in Bosnia.

The daily joint IFOR/SFOR press conferences are full of reports about non-compliance including provocations against SFOR and other agencies. However, reactions by IFOR/SFOR and the civilian agencies normally do not go beyond usual peacekeeping practices. Let's look more closely at some examples.

Provocations against IFOR/SFOR. SFOR has repeatedly faced protests and civil unrest directed against SFOR or people representing the international community.[35] Other incidents of violence were directed against civilians, e.g. desecration of cemeteries or violence against refugees returning to their homes, incidents similar to those UNPROFOR had to handle frequently.[36] There were also more sophisticated provocations like stealing key components from a Bosnian Serb TV (SRT) transmitter guarded by the SFOR, somehow making SFOR look more like 'UNPROFOR' rather than like a strong military force led by NATO.

Harassment of civilians and local violence. SFOR is only to a limited extent prepared to react to civil unrest and harassment of civilians. The UN mandate is limited to the implementation of military provisions of the Dayton Accords and to assist in creating a 'safe environment'. The IFOR/SFOR force has been given additional tasks, such as to 'assist in the observation and prevention of interference with the movement of civilian populations, refugees and displaced persons, and respond appropriately to deliberate violence to life and person'.[37] However, these activities are guidance for possible emergencies, rather than day-to-day implementation tasks given to IFOR/SFOR by Dayton and the UN mandate.

Consequently, public statements by SFOR, similar to those of UNPROFOR, reflect the limitations of peacekeeping rather than the greater capabilities of an enforcement operation. This is illustrated by SFOR's reaction to incidents in Mostar:

> SFOR joins the rest of the international community in condemning, in the strongest terms, yesterday's violent confrontation during a gravesite visit in Mostar. SFOR remains in the area, patrolling in co-ordination with and in support of the IPTF to help prevent any further violence…SFOR's position remains clear, the control of criminal elements in Mostar is the responsibility of the federation.[38]

Such types of problems and reactions are similar to those UNPROFOR experienced earlier. UNPROFOR often used armoured vehicles to protect civilians in situations of harassment.[39]

Also very familiar to UNPROFOR's experience are frequent bomb attacks against the other ethnic group, preferably against religious targets. For example, a car bomb caused damage though no injuries in Croat-held western Mostar on New Year's Day 1998. During the days preceding the incident, a group named 'Organization of Active Islamic Youth' distributed leaflets in Muslim-controlled eastern Mostar to urge Muslims not to celebrate New Year together with their Croat neighbours. The same organization circulated leaflets in Sarajevo in early December 1997 to call on 'Muslims not to celebrate Christmas'.[40]

Provocations against international civilian organizations. Civil agencies are also the target of daily provocations, and have to react with whatever means are available to them, often with little or no success. Some examples may illustrate the point:

- A few days before elections for the National Assembly of the Bosnian Serb republic in November 1997, Judge Lynghjem of the OSCE Election Appeal Subcommission detected SDS posters presenting Mr Karadzic. Lynghjem criticised in a letter to the first candidate on the SDS's list, Alex Buha, 'the same methods and form of propaganda...[as] the Nazi dictatorship'. He declared an ultimatum for removing the Karadzic posters. Each day that this order was not complied with, 'additional candidates will be stricken off the list'.[41] However, neither compliance nor reaction was reported

- The High Representative states that he was 'extremely concerned at the pattern of harassment and intimidation of the political opposition in Bijeljina...He condemns this failure unequivocally. He will continue to monitor the situation extremely closely'

- Journalists asked for reactions to Srpska's President Plavsic's statement that 'she personally ordered that a plane should not land at Banja Luka Airport carrying Muslim and Croat representatives. She described it as an act of possible sabotage of the political process in Republika Srpska'. The answer by the OHR speaker, Simon Haselock: '...If that is the case, it's extremely disappointing.'

We draw the conclusion, from these examples of daily events in the NATO-led operation, that the daily challenges to SFOR are related to public order in a deeply polarized society, and to a political process in a country where parts of the political establishment are continuing a war with other than military means. However, these challenges cannot be managed by overwhelming military force, and are familiar to traditional peacekeepers.

The *Peacekeeper's Handbook* has for many years drawn the following lessons for those UN troops deployed to 'to meet ethnic conflicts': they require 'military forces that are able to reduce tensions and to provide "conflict treatment"...Demands for national and ethnic identity where majority and minority societies exist side by side often provide the propulsion of violence...Enforcement has no flexibility; based on the power of weapons, it provides few if any choices of action'.[42]

What is new with NATO peacekeeping and what is success?

Operational aspects. As in any complex UN peacekeeping operation, the mission is vulnerable to escalation. Therefore, from an operational point of view, IFOR/SFOR, like a UN peacekeeping force, has been cautious in using force to handle civil conflict because doing so could jeopardize the whole mission. The main factor in determining whether a NATO-led force or a UN force will be capable of managing problems resulting from the implementation of a peace agreement in the former Yugoslavia is the extent to which the force succeeds in creating confidence among the parties and in enabling them move towards a political solution of their conflicts.

As decades of United Nations peacekeeping experience have shown, the question of success is always a relative question. A common argument is that UN peacekeeping operations in Croatia and Bosnia, in Cyprus and in Lebanon have failed, because they have only frozen the conflict and did not fulfil the mandate of bringing about an enduring peace.

Indeed, if the criterion of success is the full implementation of a UN mandate, then UNPROFOR, UNFICYP, UNIFIL and IFOR/SFOR have one thing in common: they all have 'failed'. IFOR too has failed to fulfil the mandate because it has not provided the secured environment for a sustainable peaceful development within the mandated one-year period. And by having decided in advance about a follow-up force to SFOR after Summer 1998, NATO has anticipated that SFOR will fail in the same way as IFOR, in particular because civilian components of the Peace Agreement remain far from being fulfilled.

Similar arguments were repeatedly presented *vis-à-vis* the other operations mentioned above, and contributing nations were frequently under domestic pressure to withdraw because of failure.

However, such arguments are inappropriate and unfair to those who carry out peacekeeping mandates. This is especially so from a humanitarian and from a political point of view:

For example, UNFICYP, often criticized for freezing the conflict in Cyprus, has also separated the fighting parties, stopped the massacres that happened before the deployment, and hindered restarting the war, protected minority enclaves and probably reduced the risk of a military confrontation between the proxy armies of Greece and Turkey in Cyprus.

UNIFIL, often blamed for being powerless, has rendered continuously humanitarian help in Lebanon and has created conditions enabling several hundred thousand refugees to return to the UNIFIL-controlled areas with safety and an economic basis for living and for re-establishing a civil society.[43]

There are more aspects of UNIFIL which may be worth comparing to UNPROFOR.

UNIFIL was also deployed into a situation of civil war. As in the former Yugoslavia, unbelievable destruction and gruesome atrocities were committed. In Lebanon, and especially in South Lebanon, thousands of the local population were repeatedly forced to flee out of the war zone and Palestinian refugees also in thousands were seriously affected.

In Lebanon too, consent of the parties to the deployment of a UN peacekeeping force was fragile; it existed in reality only on the part of one party to the conflict. The government of Lebanon was the only party that fully wanted and supported the establishment of a UN peacekeeping force. It took some time to establish working relations with Israel, the PLO and neighbouring Arab countries. Not all factions or minor groups involved in the conflict by far accepted the UNIFIL presence. Nevertheless, the UN force continuously and progressively tried to establish links to all parties in the area of operation.

In the former Yugoslavia, there were numerous obstacles to overcome from the very beginning. In fact, senior UN officials repeatedly warned against a UN peacekeeping deployment up to February 1992, when the Secretary-General was forced by circumstances to recommend the deployment of a peacekeeping force, UNPROFOR, in Croatia.[44]

It can therefore be said that, both in Lebanon in 1978 and in the former Yugoslavia in 1992, one vital precondition for UN peacekeeping – that all the parties to the conflict genuinely wanted the help of the UN to solve their problems – was missing.

However, even in such circumstances, it would be contrary to the spirit of the UN Charter not to react – as long as there is sufficient international political support for a UN involvement.[45]

In the case of former Yugoslavia, international political support was lacking and the UN peacekeeping force became the target of direct criticism. The will of the parties to contribute towards peace was absent and, until Summer 1995, the world community was not prepared to accept that any viable peace agreement is usually a result of a compromise and not a capitulation by one side.

Although there was no peace to keep, UNPROFOR saved the lives of many thousands, contained the war, and reduced violence in many areas. Several contributors in our book document this fact. UNPROFOR backed up various cease-fires – with mixed success – and the Washington agreement of 1994 with great success.

IFOR/SFOR too may be criticized for not having been able to implement many important political parts of Dayton, but the force has separated the fighting parties, and assures that the guns remain silent. Its deterring effect hinders potentially aggressive neighbours from seeking to divide Bosnia for their benefit. Together with the OHR and the other international organizations, SFOR facilitates a process which has the possibility of rebuilding a civil society step by step – even if it starts with a separated society which may grow more slowly together than many would prefer.

Write-off UN peacekeeping?

It is beyond the scope of this book to assess whether NATO as the world's strongest defence alliance continues to have a crucial role in peacekeeping or not. The decision whether a NATO-led force or a UN force should be deployed, is in the light of the evolution of European security institutions apparently no longer an issue of principle, but instead a question of political practicality.

In the minds of many, the NATO-led force has greater prospects of success than a UN-led force because it has the capability to react with overwhelming force against anyone who may challenge the Dayton Peace Agreement. We have no reason to underestimate the role of NATO's military power in deterring potential challengers. However, we want to call to mind another factor which may be at least as crucial as the military power: the political factor. In the present situation in Bosnia, there is, unlike the case of UNPROFOR, unanimous political support for the continuation of NATO's military presence in the Balkans. One of the most important factors with this regard is the presence of the United States, which also seems crucial for continued presence of other allies.

Former Force Commander General de Lapresle articulated a central difference between NATO and the UN which obliges NATO to success: The UN can politically survive humiliations 'without lethal damage, NATO would probably not.' And in the present historic situation, where NATO is preparing for enlargement in Europe, the Alliance has no other choice than to do everything possible to make Dayton a success.

This requires unity of political support. However, we remind readers that, when there was unity of support, UNPROFOR too succeeded–with respect to the Washington Agreement of March 1994, a story which seems to be forgotten. UNPROFOR successfully implemented the cease-fire agreement between the Bosnian Croats and Muslims which had been signed in Washington. Similar to Dayton, the Washington Agreement was a compromise mediated under the strong leadership of the United States, not by American planes, but by American – and other – diplomats.

As with Dayton, the Washington Agreement received unchallenged international support. But in distinction to Dayton's political provisions, the Washington Agreement was successfully implemented by the UN force in Bosnia, UNPROFOR. Brigadier Ridgway provides in Chapter 13 of this book, an impressive record of the effort to make peace between two parties who fought a fierce war against each other, with destruction of East Mostar by Croat troops at least as brutal as the bombing of Sarajevo by the Bosnian Serbs. As happened later with the NATO-led troops, UNPROFOR did not change hostile attitudes, but it stopped the daily killing and created a minimum of co-operation among the parties.

We can conclude from the successful implementation of the Washington Agreement by UNPROFOR that, even more than the capacity to use military power, political unity among the governments directing the effort is the precondition for successful peacekeeping. In particular, American support is as crucial for a UN peacekeeping operation as for a NATO-led Implementation Force. Concerning the reluctant role of the US *vis-à-vis* the UN efforts at the beginning of the Yugoslav crisis, it may even be argued that if the US as the main force both in NATO and the Security Council had engaged its power and prestige at the beginning to bring the parties to a reasonable compromise, we could have had a Dayton at the outset, successfully implemented by UNPROFOR.

As shown in the chapters written by two non-European authors, Yasushi Akashi and General John Sanderson,[46] also the case of UNTAC in Cambodia has proven that a complex UN peacekeeping operation can be successfully carried out under command of the United Nations if the US and the major powers stand together in giving joint political support.

The parallel between peacekeeping and détente

Politically, peacekeeping has been developed during the Cold War, based on the spirit of the UN Charter. It evolved as a concept to keep and make peace. The main principles of peacekeeping are similar to the policy of détente, which was often denounced for being unprincipled *realpolitik*, although this policy e.g. by means of the CSCE process had contributed substantially to the peaceful revolutions in central and eastern Europe and the end of the Cold War.[47]

- Renunciation of the use of force except in self-defence
- Handling conflicts peacefully
- Providing security through co-operation rather than confrontation
- Respecting the reality in order to free political forces for changing the reality
- Pragmatic dialogue, including circumventing of issues of principle and status, in order to allow practical solutions
- Agreements on the basis of face-saving rather than defeat, in order to get agreements on principles referring to human rights.

After the Cold War, it looked as if the dream of building a New World Order based on a powerful world community might become a realistic option, also with respect to handling civil war-like conflicts. But what looked like a process of transcending *realpolitik* and entering into the New World Order, an international arena ruled by UN-sanctioned enforcement actions, turned out to be only a period of transition. After a phase of belief in enforcement action, it seems that the limits of what can be achieved through military power have again been seen to apply to peacekeeping too.

'Old' peacekeeping principles and 'new' peacekeeping

This book has focused on evaluating the impact of the three traditional peacekeeping principles – consent, impartiality and use of force in self-defence only – in the context of the UN peacekeeping operations in the former Yugoslavia. Some researchers and politicians strongly emphasize the need of a new generation of peacekeeping operations, however, often more in terms of using military power rather than of managing the complexity of conflict.[48] Civil war-like conflicts as in the former Yugoslavia do require new answers, in particular since the end of the Cold War facilitates joint efforts of the international community to work together in managing crises and peacekeeping operations. However, because these operations are so complex, involving various international organizations and agencies, they are highly vulnerable to escalation.

Our analysis confirms the UNSG's correction of some excessive expectations over the benefits of enforcement raised by his *Agenda* of 1992 and of his conclusion in his *Supplement to an Agenda for Peace* of 1995. The application of 'old' peacekeeping principles of consent, impartiality and non-use of force continues vital for success. The dynamics of combining peacekeeping with enforcement are 'incompatible to the process that peacekeeping is intended to facilitate'.[49]

We may summarize as a result that, in civil war-like conflicts, the peacekeeping principles continue to provide valuable guidance for the performance of the troops, to use any chance to diffuse tensions and to de-escalate local conflict. Even in extremely adverse conditions, like those in Bosnia where a cease-fire is not holding throughout the area, application of the classic principles on a local basis brought valuable partial results.

Training of peacekeeping troops and civilian staff is more than ever a key to success, in particular the need to learn to understand the local culture and politics as well as training the ability to handle civil unrest and provocations. In these areas the survey of SFOR officers, indicates the existence of a considerable feasibility gap in handling such challenges.[50]

Without this training, there is a risk that troops may act and react in a combat mode rather than according to UN standards and, as in Somalia, that their response to attacks or provocations may involve disproportionate and excessive use of force, which jeopardizes the mission.[51]

There are new elements in the application of 'old' principles in those missions where peacekeeping forces have had to be deployed in a civil war-like conflict without a sustainable cease-fire, while the UN mediators continue in their attempts to broker a peace settlement.

However, classic peacekeeping principles are vital for success, and, as shown by statements of former peacekeepers in this book, not a hindrance when operating under hostile conditions:

Consent. Is not a given precondition. Consent of the parties to the mission and to agreements has to be strived for daily and on all levels. It is not sufficient to rely on agreements with the political leaders.

Impartiality. Strict impartiality of the peacekeepers to all parties to a conflict is the precondition for action by peacekeepers against violation of human rights and other forms of non-compliance.

Self-defence. Only in exceptional cases of self-defence can robust reactions as, for example close air support, be a valid means in a peacekeeping operation. Use of air power aimed at 'punishment' against one side goes beyond self-defence and impartiality. It frequently led to disastrous consequences in Bosnia. Therefore it is not a valid concept for peacekeeping operations.

A missing dialogue

There is a further lesson from the UNPROFOR and IFOR experience: patience is needed to keep peace and assist the Balkan peoples in solving their many conflicts in a peaceful way and in the spirit of the United Nations Charter. The lesson seems to be reflected in the 'complete reversal' of the Clinton Administration's policy into an 'an open-ended peacekeeping mission in Bosnia-Herzegovina with no exit strategy', as was reported in March 1998.[52] Civilian implementation and reconciliation take time, as is known also from other conflicts.[53] This process can be protected and facilitated, but it cannot be imposed by an international force.

The religious and cultural divide between the Catholic, Orthodox and Islamic world was imposed on the Balkan peoples by shifting empires over the centuries. In each of these wars, this division served Balkan political leaders as an instrument for mobilizing their people against each other, while at the same time using their religious and cultural identity as a device for persuading potential international allies to take sides with them.

One final comment: since the end of the Cold War, ideological orientation has lost its attraction. However, in many social, economic and political crises, religious affinity has taken the place of earlier ideologies and become an important factor sometimes exploited by political leaders. We mention this not to open a new debate on Samuel Huntington's theory of the clash of civilizations.[54] But there still remains one gap to be closed in all the peacebuilding efforts of international organizations in the former Yugoslavia: the need for intensive dialogue aimed at reconciliation, in particular between the religious leaders and their communities.

Such a dialogue has the global dimension of preventing Huntington's nightmare from becoming reality. In the context of former Yugoslavia, it should be part of an effort to stimulate moderate political forces and protect the human rights of those who dare to stand up against the established leadership.[55]

Notes

1 *The Blue Helmets*, 2nd edition, United Nations: New York, 1990, p. 8.
2 A comprehensive interpretation of Chapter VIII of the UN Charter is given in *The Charter of the United Nations, A Commentary*, edited by Bruno Somma, pp. 679–756.
3 *An Agenda for Peace*, ibid., p. 63.
4 *An Agenda for Peace*, ibid., p. 64.
5 UN Document A/RES/47/10 of 28 October 1992, 'Cooperation between the United Nations and the Conference on Security and Cooperation in Europe'. See also: *OSZE-Jahrbuch 1997 – Band 3*, Institut für Friedensforschung und Sicherheitspolitik an der Universität Hamburg, Nomos Verlag, Baden-Baden, 1997, p. 404.
6 See UN Document A/RES/48/5 of 13 October 1993, A/RES/48/19 of 16 November 1993, A/RES/49/13 of 25 November 1994 and A/RES/51/57 of 27 January 1997.
7 Holbrooke, Richard, 'America, a European Power', in *Foreign Affairs*, March/April 1995.
8 Leurdijk, Dick A., *The United Nations and Nato*, ibid., p.1.
9 *Supplement to An Agenda for Peace*, Position Paper of the Secretary-General, ibid., p. 29.
10 See Dean, Jonathan, *Ending Europe's Wars, The Continuing Search for Peace and Security*, The Twentieth Century Fund Press, New York, 1994; Jaberg, Sabine, *Systeme Kollektiver Sicherheit in und für Europa in Theorie, Praxis und Entwurf. Ein Systemwissenschaftlicher Versuch*, Baden-Baden, 1998 (Demokratie, Sicherheit, Frieden, Nr. 112); Bahr, Egon and Lutz, Dieter S. (eds), *Unsere Gemeinsame Zukunft–Die Europäische Sicherheitsgemeinschaft (ESG)*, Nomos: Baden-Baden, 1994/95; Biermann, Wolfgang, 'Möglichkeiten und Grenzen internationaler Organisationen (UNO und OSZE)', in Pax Christi, Dt. Sektion (ed.), *Ultima Ratio ?–Schriftenreihe Probleme des Friedens*, KOMZI Verlag (Germany), 1996, pp. 129–141. There are numerous contributions to this debate, among them the series of publications in the *Hamburger Beiträge zur Friedensforschung und Sicherheitspolitik*, published by the Institut für Friedensforschung und Sicherheitspolitik, Hamburg (Germany); Forndran, Erhard and Pohlmann, Hartmut (eds), *Europäische Sicherheit nach dem Ende des*

Warschauer Paktes, Nomos Verlag, Baden-Baden, 1993; Lucas, Michael R. (ed.), *The CSCE in the 1990s: Constructing European Security and Cooperation*, Nomos Verlag, Baden-Baden, 1993.

11 See Dean, Jonathan, *Ending Europe's Wars*, ibid., p. 333ff.

12 Lightburn, David, 'NATO and the Challenge of Multifunctional Peacekeeping', *NATO Review*, No. 2, March 1996, pp. 10–14 (NIDS Publication).

13 *Final Communiqué*, Ministerial Meeting of the North Atlantic Council in Oslo, 4 June 1992.

14 *Final Communiqué*, Ministerial Meeting of the North Atlantic Council NATO HQ, Brussels, 17 December 1992.

15 Ministerial Meeting of the North Atlantic Cooperation Council Athens, Greece, 11 June 1993, *Report to the Ministers by the NACC Ad Hoc Group on Cooperation in Peacekeeping*, Press Communiqué M-NACC-1 (93)40.

16 See Dean, Jonathan, ibid., p. 380 ff.

17 Leurdijk, Dick A., *The United Nations and NATO in Former Yugoslavia*, Netherlands Atlantic Commission and Netherlands Institute of International Relations Clingendael, The Hague, 1994.

18 Leurdijk, Dick A., *The United Nations and NATO in Former Yugoslavia*, ibid., p. 15.

19 Leurdijk, Dick A., ibid., p. 47.

20 *Atlantic News*, 2547, 4 August 1993, quoted in Leurdijk, Dick A., ibid., p. 47.

21 Skjelsbæk, Kjell and Rikhye, Indar Jit, *The United Nations and Peacekeeping*, ibid., p. 47.

22 Rikhye and Skjelsbæk, ibid.

23 Rikhye and Skjelsbæk, ibid., p. 65 f.

24 NATO/NACC/PfP unclassified: *Seminar on Public Relations Aspects of Peacekeeping*, 10–11 April 1997.

25 'The experiences of P&I section of the Nordic-Polish Brigade', by Arthur Golawski, *Seminar on Public Relations Aspects of Peacekeeping*, ibid.

26 Rüdiger, Michael, *Den Frieden in Bosnien erhalten*, IFDT, Information für die Truppe, No. 1, January 1997, p. 15.

27 'SFOR Raids Bosnian Army Headquarters', *RFE/RL NewsLine* Vol. 1, No. 184, Part II, 22 December 1997.

28 Transcripts are daily distributed via the Internet through NATO's Integrated Data Service (NIDS).

29 *Chronologie des SFOR-Einsatzes unter besonderer Berücksichtigung des deutschen Kontingents*, 1 September 1997 (edited by the German MoD, http://www.bundeswehr.de /sicherheitspolitik/sfor-einsatz/sforchron-sep.htm).

30 *BI-MNC Directive for NATO Doctrine for Peace Support Operations*, 11 December 1995, NATO PfP unclassified.

31 Lightburn, David, ibid.

32 'Agreement between the Republic of Bosnia and Herzegovina and the North Atlantic Treaty Organization (NATO) Concerning the Status of NATO and its Personnel', Appendix B to Annex 1-A, in: *Proximity Peace Talks*, ibid.

33 Annex 1-A, Article 1, in: *Proximity Peace Talks*, ibid.

34 See Chapter 6 of this book for more details.

35 Press briefing transcript for 10 January 1997, NIDS. According to a random search civil violence was discussed in more than 30 SFOR press conferences between February and October 1996.

36 SFOR LANDCENT Transcript, 11 February 1997, Press Conference held on 11 February 1997, NIDS.

37 These tasks can include 'deployments for reconnaissance to obtain an accurate understanding of the situation, preparing to support the International Police Task...to ensure law and order and to monitor police activities...and to deter the outbreak of violence and criminal activity' (SFOR Speaker Maj. Riley at NATO/SFOR, Transcript Press Briefing, 28 August 1997, NIDS).

38 SFOR speaker Maj. White, SFOR LANDCENT Transcript, 11 February 1997, NIDS.

39 The same scenario of harassment against visitors to graveyards in the area of another and similar reactions by peacekeepers were frequently experienced by UNPROFOR. It occurred also to Spanish UNPROFOR troops when our research project visited the Mostar area at All Saints Day, November 1994.

40 RFE/RL *Bosnia Report*, Vol. 1, No. 22, 7 January 1998 (Radio Free Europe/Radio Liberty).

41 Transcript: Joint Press Conference, 20 November 1997, NATO Integrated Data Service (NIDS).

42 *Peacekeeper's Handbook*, 1984, p. 25.

43 See Heiberg, Marianne, *Peacekeepers and Local Population: Some Comments on UNIFIL*, in Rikhye and Sjelsbæk, ibid.

44 See UN reference paper, March 1994 on 'The United Nations and the Situation in the Former Yugoslavia'.

45 UN Document UNSCR 743 (1992), Lt. Gen. Ensio Siilasvuo, 'In the Service of Peace in the Middle East 1967–1979', Hurst & Company, London, 1992.

46 See Chapters 7 and 12.

47 See remarks by John Kornblum, US Ambassador to Germany, about the role of the OSCE in preventing conflict and promoting peaceful change in his interview: "The OSCE...substantially contributed to the loosening up and the ultimate demise of the Soviet system" (Kornblum, John, US Ambassador to Germany and former Assistant Secretary of State for European and Canadian Affairs, Interview with Jacqui S. Porth, in: *US Foreign Policy Agenda*, USIA Electronic Journals, Vol. 1, No. 19, December 1996).

48 Described for instance as Second Generation Peacekeeping, Wider Peacekeeping, Multifunctional Peacekeeping, Implementation of Comprehensive Settlements, or Peace Implementation or Peace Building.

49 Boutros-Ghali, B., *Supplement to an Agenda for Peace*, Position Paper, An Agenda for Peace, 2nd Edition, UN, New York, 1995, p. 14.

50 See Chapter 6.

51 Capham, Andrew and Henry, Meg, 'Peacekeeping and Human Rights in Africa and Europe' in Henkin, Alice H. (ed.), *Honouring Human Rights and Keeping the Peace, Recommendations for the United Nations*, The Aspen Institute Justice and Society Program, Washington, 1995, p. 140.

52 *US plans open-ended deployment*, United Press International (via ClariNet), 18 March 1998.

53 Some experts having been involved in the economic and political implementation work in Bosnia draw parallels to the long period of democratic and civil reconstruction after the Second World War. It took ten years until Western Germany was granted sovereignty in the Paris Treaties. (Reconciliation with Poland took about 25 years under Chancellor Willy Brandt recognizing the post-war Polish borders.) See: O'Callaghan, Garry and Schiller, Thomas, 'Developing a Legislative Economic Structure for Bosnia and Herzegovina–The Political Economy of the Quick Start Package' in *Revue des Affaires Européen*, no. 4/97, Gent, December 1997.

54 Huntington, Samuel P., *Clash of Civilizations and the Remaking of World Order*, Simon and Schuster, New York, 1996.

55 UN SRSG Kai Eide to the NATO Council, 11 June 1997 (NIDS).

Participants at DANORP UN Commanders' Workshops 1995/1996

Military background

Brig. Gen. *Gerard Bastiaans* (NL), 11th Air Mobile Brigade; former Chief UNMO UNPROFOR.

Brig. Gen. *Andrew Cumming* (UK), IFOR HQ; former Commander of UK Forces in BH.

Col. *James Daniels* (UK), Lessons Learned Team MoD/UK; former MA to Gen. Michael Rose, UNPROFOR BH HQ.

Brig. Gen. *Juha Engström* (Fin), Finnish Armed Forces; former Force Commander UNPREDEP.

Sven Frederiksen (DK), Police Inspector Glostrup Police; former Commissioner CivPol UNPROFOR.

Lt. Gen. *Günther Greindl* (A), Austrian Chancellor's Office, Austrian Armed Forces, Vienna, Austria.

Maj. Gen. *Jussi Hautamaki* (Fin).

Maj. Gen. *Ove H.-G. Hoff* (DK), COS Plans and Policy, HQ Chief of Defence, Denmark.

Col. *Howard Kuenning* (USA), US Army; former Chief of Staff FYROM.

Gen. *Bertrand de Lapresle* (F), former Force Commander UNPROFOR.

Maj. *Henrik Lettius* (S), Swedish Armed Forces International Centre (SWEDINT), Sweden.

Col. *Allan Mallinson* (UK), Ministry of Defence, Directorate of Land Warfare.

Col. *Jan Dirk van Merveldt* (UK), Chief Public Information British Forces in Germany; former UNPROFOR.

Lt. Col. *Vagn Ove M. Nielsen* (DK), former EU monitor and UNMO sector commander UNPROFOR.

Brig. Gen. *Bo Pellnäs* (S), former Chief UNMO UNPROFOR; former Military Adviser to ICFY.

Col. *Benôit Puga* (F), Military Assistant to Lt. Gen. de Lapresle.

Brig. Gen. *Pierre Peeters* (B), Chief Military Negotiation Team UNPF.

Col. *Heikki Purola* (Fin), former Dep. Military Adviser to the UN Secretary-General; former UNPROFOR Senior Military Desk Officer.

Vice-Adm. *Leonhard Revang* (N), Chief of Staff, Norwegian Defence Command.
Brig. Gen. *Andrew Ridgway* (UK), Director Operational Capability MoD/UK; former UNPROFOR FC BH South West.
Brig. Gen. *Gunnar Ridderstad* (S), Commander Life Grenadier Regiment, Territorial Commander and Chief of Garrison; former UNPROFOR FC BH North East.
Brig. Gen. *Finn Sœrmark-Thomsen* (DK), Commander HQ/Northpol Brig./IFOR; former Force Commander FYROM.
Col. AF *L. Simonsen* (DK), Danish Armed Forces, Vedbæk, Denmark.
Odemis Süleiman (Turkey), WEU Planing Cell Brussels, Belgium.
Brig. Gen. *Trygve Tellefsen* (N), Commander of Akers Fortress, Oslo; former Force Commander FYROM.
Dr *Michael Williams* (UK), former Press Speaker UNPROFOR.
Lt. Gen. *Lars-Erik Wahlgren* (S), former Force Commander UNPROFOR.
Cdr. *Pizzabioca* (I), Lessons Learned Unit of the UN DPKO.

Diplomatic or civil background

Rune Bergström (S), Lessons Learned Unit, UN DPKO, New York.
Ambassador *Istvan Gyarmarti* (H), Personal Representative of the Chairman in Office of the OSCE for former Yugoslavia, Head of the Hungarian OSCE Delegation.
Jan Egeland (N), State Secretary for Foreign Affairs.
Ambassador *Kai Eide* (N), former Deputy Co-chairman, International Conference on the former Yugoslavia (ICFY).
Thierry Germond (F), International Committee of the Red Cross (ICRC), Geneva, Switzerland.
Gerard Fischer (S), Director Civil Affairs UN Transitional Administration in Eastern Slavonia; former Head Civil Affairs UNPROFOR.
Anders Kjølberg (N), Norwegian Defence Research Institute.
Astrid Nøklebye Heiberg (N), President of the Norwegian Red Cross.
Michel Rocard (F), MEP; former French Prime Minister.
Peter Schmitz (D), Desk Officer responsible for UNPROFOR/UNPF in the UN DPKO, New York.
Thorvald Stoltenberg (N), Norwegian Ambassador to Denmark; former Co-chairman ICFY.
Dr *Susan Woodward* (USA), Brookings Institution; former Head Analysis and Assessment Unit UNPROFOR.

Bibliography

Books

Army Field Manual, *Wider Peacekeeping*, Fourth Draft, Ministry of Defence: London, 1994.

Bahr, Egon and Lutz, Dieter S. (eds.), *Unsere Gemeinsame Zukunft – Die Europäische Sicherheitsgemeinschaft (ESG)*, Nomos: Baden-Baden, 1994/95.

Berdal, Mats, *Whither UN Peacekeeping*, Adelphi Paper 281, October 1993.

Bildt, Carl, *Uppdrag Fred*, Norstedts Förlag AB: Stockholm 1997.

Boutros-Ghali, Boutros, *An Agenda for Peace, Preventive Diplomacy, Peacemaking and Peacekeeping*, United Nations: New York, 1992.

Boutros-Ghali, Boutros, *An Agenda for Peace*, 2nd edition, United Nations: New York, 1995.

Boutros-Ghali, Boutros, 'Supplement to an Agenda for Peace', *An Agenda for Peace, 2nd edition*, United Nations: New York, 1995, p. 14.

Boutros-Ghali, Boutros, *Confronting the New Challenges, Report on the Work of the Organization*, United Nations: New York, 1995.

Cahill, Kevin M., *Preventive Diplomacy: Stopping Wars before they Start*, Basic Books: New York, 1996.

Carnegie Commission on Preventing Deadly Conflict, *Preventing Deadly Conflict: Final Report*, Carnegie Corporation: Washington DC, 1997.

Dean, Jonathan, *Ending Europe's Wars, The Continuing Search for Peace and Security*, The Twentieth Century Fund Press: New York, 1994.

Durch, William (ed.), *The Evolution of UN Peacekeeping, Case Studies and Comparative Analyses*, St. Martin's Press: New York, 1993.

Evans, Gareth, *Co-operation for Peace, The Global Agenda for the 1990s and Beyond*, Allen & Unwin: St. Leonards, 1993.

Fermann, Gunnar, *Bibliography on International Peacekeeping*, Martinus Nyjhoff Publishers: Dordrecht/Boston/London, 1992.

Findlay, Trevor, *Cambodia, the Legacy and Lessons of UNTAC*, SIPRI Research Report No. 9, Oxford University Press: London, 1995.

Forndran, Erhard and Pohlmann, Hartmut (eds), *Europäische Sicherheit nach dem Ende des Warschauer Paktes*, Nomos Verlag: Baden-Baden, 1993.

Graham, James R. (ed.), *Non-Combat roles for the US Military in the Post-Cold War Era*, National Defence University Press: Washington DC, 1993.

Heintze, Hans-Joachim (ed.), *Selbstbestimmungsrecht der Völker – Herausforderung der Staatenwelt*, Dietz Verlag: Bonn, 1997.

Henkin, Alice H. (ed.), *Honouring Human Rights and Keeping the Peace, Recommendations for the United Nations*, The Aspen Institute Justice and Society Program, Washington, 1995.

Honig, Jan Willem and Both, Norbert, *Srebrenica: Record of a War Crime*, Penguin Books: London, 1996.

Huntington, Samuel P., *Kampf der Kulturen: die Neugestaltung der Weltpolitik im 21*, Jahrhundert: München, 1996.

Huntington, Samuel P., *Clash of Civilizations and the Remaking of World Order*, Simon and Schuster: New York, 1996.

IISS, *The Military Balance 1994-1995*, Brassey's: London, 1994.

IISS, *The Military Balance 1997/1998*, Oxford University Press: London, 1997.

International Peace Academy, *Peacekeeper's Handbook*, Pergamon Press: New York, 1984.

Jaberg, Sabine, *Systeme kollektiver Sicherheit in und für Europa in Theorie, Praxis und Entwurf. Ein Systemwissenschaftlicher Versuch*, Baden-Baden, 1998 (*Demokratie, Sicherheit, Frieden*, Nr. 112).

Koch, Ernst (ed.), *Die Blauhelme im Einsatz für den Frieden*, Report Verlag: Frankfurt/Bonn, 1991.

Kühne, Winrich (ed.), *Blauhelme in einer turbulenten Welt*, Nomos: Baden-Baden, 1993.

Leurdijk, Dick A., *The United Nations and NATO in former Yugoslavia*, Netherlands Atlantic Commission and Netherlands Institute of International Relations Clingendael: The Hague, 1994.

Lucas, Michael R. (ed.), *The CSCE in the 1990s: Constructing European Security and Co-operation*, Nomos Verlag: Baden-Baden, 1993.

Marten, Jens and Könitzer, Burkhard (eds), *UN-Williges Deutschland, der WEED Report zur deutschen UNO-Politik*, Dietz: Bonn, 1997.

Matthies, Volker (ed.), *Der gelungene Frieden, Beispiele und Bedingungen erfolgreicher friedlicher Konfliktbearbeitung*, Dietz: Bonn, 1997.

Murray, Wolfe (ed.), *IFOR on IFOR, NATO Peacekeepers in Bosnia-Herzegovina*, Connect: Edinburgh, 1996.

Nordic UN Tactical Manual – Volume I and II, Gummerus Kirjapaino Oy: Jyväskylä, 1992.

Office of the High Representative (ed.), *Bosnia and Herzegovina, Essential Texts*, Sarajevo, 1995.

Our Global Neighbourhood, The Report of the Commission on Global Governance, Oxford University Press: New York, 1995.

Owen, David, *Balkan Odyssee* (German edition), Carl Hanser Verlag: München/Wien, 1996.

Owen, David, *Balkan Odyssey*, Victor Gollancz: London, 1995.

Pellnäs, Bo, *De hundra dagarna, På gränsvakt i Serbien*, ScandBook AB: Falun, 1996.

Rikhye, Indar Jit, *Military Adviser to the Secretary-General, UN Peacekeeping and the Congo Crisis*, St. Martin's Press: New York 1993.

Rossanet, Bertrand de, *Peacekeeping and Peacemaking in Yugoslavia*, Kluwer Law International: The Hague, 1996.

Silber, Laura and Little, Allan, *The Death of Yugoslavia*, Penguin Books, BBC Books: London, 1995.

Skjelsbaek, Kjell and Rikhye, Indar Jit (eds), *The United Nations and Peacekeeping*, MacMillan, 1990.

Simma, Bruno a/o. (ed.), *The Charter of the United Nations, A Commentary*, Oxford University Press: Oxford, 1994.

Stoltenberg, Thorvald and Eide, Kai, *De tusen dagene, fredsmeklere på Balkan*, Gyldendal Norsk Forlag: Oslo, 1996.

The Blue Helmets, 2nd edition, United Nations: New York, 1990.

The United Nations and Cambodia 1991–1995, Department of Public Information, United Nations: New York, 1995.

Woodward, Susan, *Balkan Tragedy, Chaos and Dissolution after the Cold War*, The Brookings Institution: Washington DC, 1995.

Documents and documentations

'Agreement between the Republic of Bosnia and Herzegovina and the North Atlantic Treaty Organization (NATO) Concerning Status of NATO and its Personnel', Appendix B to Annex 1-A, in: *Proximity Peace Talks Wright-Patterson Airforce Base*, Dayton, Ohio: November 1–21, 1995.

'General Framework Agreement in Bosnia and Herzegovina, Federation Agreement', *Proximity Peace Talks Wright-Patterson Airforce Base*, Dayton, Ohio: November 1–21, 1995.

'Letter of 21 November 1995 by Momcilo Krajisnik, President of the Republika Srpska, to Sergio Silvio Balanzini, Acting Secretary-General of NATO', in: OHR, *Bosnia and Herzegovina, Essential Texts*, ibid., p. 37.

'UN Peacekeeping: Lessons learned in Managing Recent Missions', *Report to Congressional Requesters*, US General Accounting Office: Washington DC, December 1993.

Beredskap for fred. Om Norges framtidige militære FN-engagement, St. meld. nr. 14 (1992–93), Stortinget: Oslo, 18 December 1992.

Final Communiqué, Ministerial Meeting of the North Atlantic Council, Oslo, 4 June 1992.

Final Communiqué, Ministerial Meeting of the North Atlantic Council, NATO HQ, Brussels, 17 December 1992.

FM 100-23 Peace Operations, Version 6, 19 January 1994, HQ Dept. of the Army, W.D.C.

Human Rights Situation and Reports of Special Rapporteurs and Representatives, Statements, 3 October 1995, by the President of the UNSC, the UN High Commissioner on Human Rights, Ayala Lasso, and SRSG Akashi, UN General Assembly, 3 November 1995, pp. 4–18.

International Peacekeeping and Enforcement, Hearing, US Congress, Senate Committee on Armed Services, Subcommittee on Coalition, Defence and Reinforcing Forces: July 14, 1993.

Ministerial Meeting of the North Atlantic Cooperation Council, Athens, Greece, 11 June 1993, *Report to the Ministers by the NACC Ad Hoc Group on Cooperation in Peacekeeping*, Press Communiqué M-NACC- 1(93)40.

NATO/NACC/PfP Unclassified: *Seminar on Public Relations Aspects of Peacekeeping*, 10–11 April 1997.

NATO's role in peacekeeping in the former Yugoslavia, NATO Fact Sheet No. 4, March 1997.

PfP Unclassified Bi-MNC, *Directive for NATO Doctrine for Peace Support Operations*, 11 December 1995.

Report of the Secretary-General, 14 June 1993, UN Document S/25939.

The UN in former Yugoslavia, Reference Paper Revision 4, UN Department of Public Information: New York, 30 April 1995.

United Nations Documents: UN Security Council, UN General Assembly, Reports by the Secretary of NATO to the United Nations Security Council on IFOR Operations.

US Congress Document: *International Peacekeeping and Enforcement*, Statement by US Undersecretary of Defense Frank Wiesner, Hearing before the Subcommittee on Coalition Defense and Reinforcing Forces, Committee of Armed Services, US Senate: July 14, 1993.

US Congress Document: Statement by Hon. John P. White, Deputy Secretary of Defence before the House National Security Committee Hearing on Bosnia, September 25, 1996.

Articles in journals

Biermann, Wolfgang, 'Möglichkeiten und Grenzen internationaler Organisationen (UNO und OSZE)', in Pax Christi, Dt. Sektion (ed.),

Ultima Ratio? – Schriftenreihe Probleme des Friedens, KOMZI Verlag (Germany), 1996, pp. 129–141.

Biermann, Wolfgang, 'Old UN Peacekeeping Principles and New Conflicts: Some Ideas to Reduce the Troubles of Post-Cold War Peace Missions', in *European Security*, Vol 4, No. 1 (Spring 1995), pp. 39-55.

Berdal, Mats R., 'Fateful Encounter: The US and UN Peacekeeping', in *Survival*, Vol. 36, No. 1/1994.

Chopra, Jarat and Mackinley, John, 'Second Generation Multinational Operations', in *The Washington Quarterly*, Vol. 15, No. 3, Summer 1992.

Nystuen, Gro, 'The Constitution of Bosnia and Herzegovina – State versus Entities', in *Revue des Affaires Européennes*, No. 4/97, Gent: December 1997.

Kornblum, John, Interview with Jacqui S. Porth, in *US Foreign Policy Agenda*, USIA Electronic Journals, Vol. 1, No. 19, December 1996.

O'Callaghan, Gary and Schiller, Thomas, 'Developing a Legislative Economic Structure for Bosnia and Herzegovina – The Political Economy of the Quick Start Package', in *Revue des Affairs Européennes*, No. 4/97, Gent: December 1997.

Rüdiger, Michael, 'Den Frieden in Bosnien erhalten', *IFDT, Information für die Truppe*, No. 1, January 1997, p. 15.

Journals, information services and online services

BASIC, British American Security Information Council, Washington, London.

Chronologie des SFOR-Einsatzes unter besonderer Berücksichtigung des deutschen Kontingents (edited by the German MoD, http://www.bundeswehr.de/sicherheitspolitik/sfor-einsatz/sforchron.htm).

European Security, published by Frank Cass, London.

Foreign Affairs, New York.

Foreign Report, Jane's Information Group, Coulsdon.

Hamburger Beiträge zur Friedensforschung und Sicherheitspolitik, published by the Institut für Friedensforschung und Sicherheitspolitik, Hamburg.

HSFK Reports, Hessische Stiftung für Friedens- und Konfliktforschung (HSFK), Frankfurt.

Internationale Politik, Europa Archiv, Bonn.

National Geographic, ed. by the National Geographic Society, Washington DC.

NATO/SFOR Transcripts: Joint Press Conference, NATO Integrated Data Service (NIDS) (e-mail service).

NOD and Conversion, International Research Newsletter, COPRI, Copenhagen.

RFE/RL BOSNIA REPORT, Radio Free Europe/Radio Liberty, Prague, Czech Republic (e-mail service).

RFE/RL NewsLine, A daily report of developments in eastern and south-eastern Europe, Russia, the Caucasus and Central Asia prepared by the staff of Radio Free Europe/Radio Liberty (e-mail service).

S+F, Vierteljahresschrift für Frieden und Sicherheit, Nomos: Baden-Baden.

SHAPE and SFOR News, Supreme Headquarters Allied Powers Europe, SHAPE, Belgium.

SWP (Reports), Stiftung Wissenschaft und Politik, Ebenhausen.

Survival, The IISS Quarterly, Oxford.

United Nations Information Centre for the Nordic Countries, Copenhagen.

US Foreign Policy Agenda, USIA Electronic Journals.

US foreign policy summary log (e-mail service).